A Concise Companion to the Victorian Novel

Edited by Francis O'Gorman

BLACKWELL PUBLISHING
350 Main Street, Malden, MA 02148-5020, USA
108 Cowley Road, Oxford OX4 1JF, UK
550 Swanston Street, Carlton South, Melbourne, Victoria 3053, Australia

First published 2005 by Blackwell Publishing Ltd

Library of Congress Cataloging-in-Publication Data

A concise companion to the Victorian novel / edited by Francis O'Gorman.
p. cm. – (Blackwell concise companions to literature and culture)
Includes bibliographical references and index.
ISBN 1-4051-0319-1 (hardcover: alk. paper) – ISBN 1-4051-0320-5 (pbk. : alk. paper)
1. English fiction – 19th century – History and criticism – Handbooks, manuals, etc. 2. Literature and society – Great Britain – History – 19th century – Handbooks, manuals, etc. I. O'Gorman, Francis. II. Title. III. Series.
PR871.C65 2005
823'.809 – dc22
2003026895

A catalogue record for this title is available from the British Library.

Set in 10 on 12.5pt Meridien
by SNP Best-set Typesetter Ltd., Hong Kong
Printed and bound in the United Kingdom
by MPG Books, Bodmin, Cornwall

The publisher's policy is to use permanent paper from mills that operate a sustainable forestry policy, and which has been manufactured from pulp processed using acid-free and elementary chlorine-free practices. Furthermore, the publisher ensures that the text paper and cover board used have met acceptable environmental accreditation standards.

For further information on
Blackwell Publishing, visit our website:
http://www.blackwellpublishing.com

A Concise Companion to the Victorian Novel

Blackwell Concise Companions to Literature and Culture
General Editor: David Bradshaw, University of Oxford

This series offers accessible, innovative approaches to major areas of literary study. Each volume provides an indispensable companion for anyone wishing to gain an authoritative understanding of a given period or movement's intellectual character and contexts.

The Restoration and Eighteenth Century	Edited by *Cynthia Wall*
The Victorian Novel	Edited by *Francis O'Gorman*
Modernism	Edited by *David Bradshaw*
Postwar American Literature and Culture	Edited by *Josephine G. Hendin*
Feminist Theory	Edited by *Mary Eagleton*

For Dr Tracy Hargreaves

Contents

Notes on Contributors ix
Acknowledgements xii
List of illustrations xiii
Chronology xiv

Introduction 1
Francis O'Gorman

1 'The sun and moon were made to give them light': Empire in the Victorian Novel 4
Cannon Schmitt

2 'Seeing is believing?': Visuality and Victorian Fiction 25
Kate Flint

3 'The boundaries of social intercourse': Class in the Victorian Novel 47
James Eli Adams

4 Legal subjects, legal objects: The Law and Victorian Fiction 71
Clare Pettitt

5 'The withering of the individual': Psychology in the Victorian Novel 91
Nicholas Dames

6 'Telling of my weekly doings': The Material Culture of the Victorian Novel 113
Mark W. Turner

7 'Farewell poetry and aerial flights': The Function of the Author and Victorian Fiction 134
Richard Salmon

8 Everywhere and nowhere: Sexuality in the Victorian Novel 156
Carolyn Dever

9 'One of the larger lost continents': Religion in the Victorian Novel 180
Michael Wheeler

10 'The difference between human beings': Biology in the Victorian Novel 202
Angelique Richardson

11 'One great confederation?': Europe in the Victorian Novel 232
John Rignall

12 'A long deep sob of that mysterious wondrous happiness that is one with pain': Emotion in the Victorian Novel 253
Francis O'Gorman

Index 271

Notes on Contributors

James Eli Adams teaches in the Department of English at Cornell University, USA. He has published numerous studies and reviews dealing with Victorian literature and culture, including *Dandies and Desert Saints: Styles of Victorian Masculinity* (1995) and *Sexualities in Victorian Britain* (1996), which he edited with Andrew Miller. From 1993 to 2000 he co-edited *Victorian Studies*, where he remains a member of the Advisory Board; he is also the General Editor of the Grolier *Encyclopedia of the Victorian Era*. He is currently writing *A History of Victorian Literature*, to be published by Blackwell.

Nicholas Dames is Assistant Professor of English and Comparative Literature at Columbia University, USA. He is the author of *Amnesiac Selves: Nostalgia, Forgetting, and British Fiction, 1810–1870* (2001), and of several articles on British and French fiction in the nineteenth century. His current project investigates the relation between novel theory and the history of novel reading.

Carolyn Dever is Associate Professor of English and Acting Director of Women's Studies at Vanderbilt University, USA. She is the author of *Death and the Mother From Dickens to Freud: Victorian Fiction and the Anxiety of Origins* (1998), *Skeptical Feminism: Activist Theory, Activist Practice* (2004), and editor, with Margaret Cohen, of *The Literary Channel: The Trans-National Invention of the Novel* (2002). Her book in progress is titled *Queer Domesticities*.

Kate Flint is Professor of English at Rutgers University, USA, having previously taught for 15 years at Oxford University. She has published extensively on Victorian, modernist, and contemporary fiction, painting, and cultural history. Her books include *The Victorians and the Visual Imagination* (2000) and *The Woman Reader, 1837–1914* (1993), both of which won the British Academy's Rose Mary Crawshay prize. She has edited a number of works by Dickens and Virginia Woolf, among other authors. Her forthcoming book, *The Transatlantic Indian 1785–1930* looks at the interaction, both actual and imaginative, between the British and Native Americans in the nineteenth century.

Francis O'Gorman is Senior Lecturer in Victorian Literature at the University of Leeds, UK and a Fellow of the Royal Historical Society. His books include *John Ruskin* (1999), *Late Ruskin: New Contexts* (2001), and *Blackwell's Guide to the Victorian Novel* (2002) as well as *Ruskin and Gender* (edited with Dinah Birch, 2002) and *The Victorians and the Eighteenth Century: Reassessing the Tradition* (edited with Katherine Turner, 2004). His *Victorian Poetry: An Annotated Anthology* appeared in 2004 and he is currently writing about Victorian poetry and immortal life.

Clare Pettitt is Lecturer and Director of Studies in English Literature at Newnham College, Cambridge, UK. Her book, *Patent Inventions: Intellectual Property and the Victorian Novel,* was published by Oxford University Press in 2004.

Angelique Richardson is Senior Lecturer in Victorian Culture at the University of Exeter, UK. She has published widely on nineteenth-century culture and science and is currently working on a study of Hardy and the unconscious. She is the author of *Love and Eugenics in the Late Nineteenth Century: Rational Reproduction and the New Woman* (2003), editor of *Women Who Did: Stories by Men and Women, 1890–1914* (2002), and co-editor of *The New Woman in Fiction and in Fact:* Fin-de-Siècle *Feminisms* (2001). She is also on the editorial board of *Critical Quarterly*.

John Rignall is Reader in the Department of English and Comparative Literary Studies at the University of Warwick, UK. He is the author of *Realist Fiction and the Strolling Spectator* (1992) and numerous articles on nineteenth-century fiction; he has edited *George Eliot and Europe* (1997), and is the General Editor of *The Oxford Reader's Companion to George Eliot* (2000).

Richard Salmon is Senior Lecturer in the School of English, University of Leeds, UK. He is the author of *Henry James and the Culture of Publicity* (1997), *William Makepeace Thackeray* (2003), and various articles on Victorian fiction, periodicals, and cultural history. He is currently writing a book on the 'disenchantment of the author' in Victorian literary culture.

Cannon Schmitt, Associate Professor of English at Wayne State University, USA, and editor of the journal *Criticism*, is author of *Alien Nation: Nineteenth-Century Gothic Fictions and English Nationality* (1997) as well as essays in *Victorian Literature and Culture*, *ELH*, *Genre*, and elsewhere. At present he is at work on a book-length project titled *Savage Mnemonics: South America, Victorian Science, and the Reinvention of the Human*.

Mark W. Turner is lecturer in English at King's College, University of London, UK. He is the author of *Trollope and the Magazines* (1999) and *Backward Glances: Cruising the Queer Streets of New York and London* (2003), and the co-editor with Caroline Levine of *From Author to Text: Rereading George Eliot's* Romola (1998). He also co-edits the interdisciplinary journal *Media History*. Current research projects include a study of time, memory, and serial narratives in the nineteenth century.

Michael Wheeler is an independent scholar and lecturer, currently writing *The Old Enemies: Catholic and Protestant in Nineteenth-Century English Culture* for Cambridge University Press. He is Visiting Professor of English at the Universities of Southampton and Surrey Roehampton, and Honorary Professor of Lancaster University's Ruskin Programme. Formerly he was Director of Chawton House Library and Professor of English Literature at the University of Southampton, and before that Professor of English Literature and founding Director of the Ruskin Programme and Ruskin Collection Project at Lancaster, leading the campaign to build the Ruskin Library.

Acknowledgements

Thanks to friends who have been encouraging during the completion of this book, particularly Professor Dinah Birch, Professor David Fairer, Dr Juliet John, Dr Gail Marshall, Dr Clare Palmer, and Dr Helen Small. Gratitude also to my parents, John and Joyce O'Gorman, and my brother Chris O'Gorman; to Emma Bennett from Blackwell publishing too. Many thanks to Dr Clare Pettitt and Dr Cristiano Ristuccia for their hospitality in Rome, and to Dr Mark Batty and Dr John McLeod for good cheer in Leeds. I'm especially grateful for the friendship and generosity of the dedicatee.

Francis O'Gorman
La festa del Redentore, 2003
The School of English, University of Leeds

List of Illustrations

Figure 1 'Am I Not a Man and a Brother?' *Punch*, **6** (1844) 217

Figure 2 Photograph of Galton's Anthropocentric Laboratory at the International Health Exhibition, South Kensington Museum (1884–5) 221

Figure 3 Advertisement calling for people to be measured at Galton's National International Health Exhibition of 1884 222

Figure 4 Illustration from the 1885 reprinting of Charles Kingsley, *The Water-Babies: A Fairy Tale for a Land-Baby*, with 100 illustrations by Linley Sambourne 224

Chronology

1830
Death of **George IV**; accession of **William IV**; Wellington's Tories oppose electoral **reform**; Tory government falls; **Whig administration** commences, sympathetic to reform though not united; opening of **Liverpool and Manchester railway**; **Charles X** of France refuses to accept election results that have returned a majority liberal opposition, precipitating riots and eventually his **abdication**; replaced by Louis Philippe, the 'citizen king'; various European **revolutions** follow (Belgium, Italy, Poland).

1831
Reform crisis continues.

1832
Grey's Whigs succeed in passing the **Great Reform Act**, increasing the electorate to around 700,000 men, abolishing rotten boroughs and increasing the representation of cities.

1833
John Keble preaches the 'Assize Sermon' in St Mary's, the University Church at Oxford, inaugurating the **Oxford Movement**; **Factory Act** prohibits children under 9 from working in textile mills and restricts those between 9 and 13 from working more than 8 hours a day; end of the institution of **slavery** in British colonies.

1834
Poor Law Amendment Act ('New Poor Law') shifts responsibility for poor relief to unions of parishes administered by boards of guardians; it insists that all able-bodied poor could receive relief only in workhouses; **Tolpuddle Martyrs**: six agricultural labourers from Tolpuddle, Dorset, are sentenced to 7 years' transportation for unlawfully joining a trade union; the national outcry leads to the men being pardoned 2 years later.

1835
Henry Fox Talbot begins to experiment with paper repeatedly coated with salt and silver nitrate to improve the earliest **photographic techniques**.

1836
First train in London – between London Bridge and Greenwich.

1837
Death of William IV; accession of **Victoria** (–1901).

1838
Anti Corn-Law League founded. The Corn Laws – which fixed the price of corn and impeded free trade – have become symbolic of aristocratic privilege and maladministration. Brunel's ***Great Western*** crosses the Atlantic, the largest wooden ship then afloat; **'The People's Charter'** issued (foundational document of Chartism), which calls for universal adult male suffrage; secret ballot; abolition of property qualifications for MPs; payment of MPs; equal electoral districts; annual parliaments.

1839
Abortive **Chartist riots**; Fox Talbot and Daguerre announce rival processes for taking **photographs**.

1840
Penny post introduced by Roland Hill, the first pre-paid postal service in the modern world; **marriage** of Victoria and Albert; international **Anti-Slavery Convention** held in London; difficulties for women delegates attending lead Lucretia Mott and Elizabeth Cady Stanton to formulate the idea for a women's rights convention in the USA, a major initial step in the **women's rights movement**.

1841
First **paperbacks** published by Tauchnitz Verlag, Germany.

1842
Chartist riots after the rejection of the Chartist petition, containing some 3 million signatures (not all authentic); Chartism proving immensely important in forming members of the working class into a **political organization**; **Mudie's Lending Library** opened, the self-appointed guardian of bourgeois family values.

1843
Wordsworth becomes **Poet Laureate** on the death of Southey.

1844
Factory Act further shortens the working day for children and increases the amount of mandatory schooling; makes women textile workers into protected persons, giving them additional rights in law; the **electrical telegraph** is used to announce the birth of Victoria's second son, Alfred Ernest.

1845
John Henry Newman converts to Roman Catholicism, a blow to the Oxford Movement; **Irish 'Great Famine'** (1845–51) caused by potato blight and inept government attempts at relief; 1 million people die.

1846
Ragged School Union founded to provide education to the extremely poor and potentially criminal children; a later ragged school teacher was Dr Barnardo; **repeal of the Corn Laws**, a major advance for the free traders; **railway boom** underway.

1847
There are now 4,000 miles of **telegraph lines** in Britain, owned by the Electrical Telegraph Co.; **10 Hours Factory Act** establishes the much-desired 10½-hour day; James Young Simpson announces the success of **chloroform** as an anaesthetic.

1848
European revolutions in favour of liberal reform; election in France of **Louis Napoleon** Bonaparte as president of the republic; failure of the second **Chartist Petition**; serious **cholera** outbreak; formation of the **Pre-Raphaelite Brotherhood**.

1849
Siege of Rome and the subsequent restoration of Pius IX; **Disraeli** becomes Conservative leader.

1850
Tennyson becomes **Poet Laureate** on the death of Wordsworth; **North London Collegiate School** (for girls) founded by educational pioneer Frances Mary Buss; Pius IX restores Roman Catholic **ecclesiastical hierarchy** in England; **Public Libraries Act** permits cities and towns to provide a library service funded by local taxes if they wish.

1851
Great Exhibition opens in London; Louis Napoleon's *coup d'état* restores the **Empire**; ratified by a plebiscite the following year (he becomes Napoleon III); **invasion anxieties** in England.

1853
Turkey declares war on Russia to commence the **Crimean War** (–1856); Britain, anxious to avoid a Russian presence in the Mediterranean, joins forces in due course with France, the Ottoman empire and Sardinia to attack Russia.

1854
The Times (established 1785) now selling 50,000 copies a day; **Working Men's College** London founded; disastrous **charge of the Light Brigade** at Balaclava; Queen and Prince Albert open the **Crystal Palace** containing material from the Great Exhibition; it is later moved to Sydenham.

1855
Abolition of the remaining **newspaper duty**, which has impeded growth; papers such as the *Liverpool Daily Post*, *Manchester Guardian* and the *Daily Telegraph* are able to come into existence; Scottish missionary and explorer **David Livingstone** discovers **Victoria Falls** as part of the extensive exploration of **Africa**, then largely unknown in Britain; formation of the **Langham Place Group** of feminists urging change in marriage law.

1857
Indian Uprising ('Indian Mutiny'), the most serious threat to date to British rule in India. The Uprising (1857–8) leads to the replacement

of the rule of the English East India Company by the British government direct, and reform of military and civil services. **Matrimonial Causes Act** allows women limited access to divorce; right of access to children extended and women are able under certain circumstances to repossess their property after separation or following the husband's desertion.

1858
Darwin and Wallace present joint paper on evolution; **Jewish Disabilities Act** allows Jews to take their seats in both Houses of Parliament without having to swear a Christian oath; abolition of the **property qualification** for MPs allows working-class candidates for Parliament.

1859
J. S. Mill, *On Liberty*; Charles Darwin, *The Origin of Species*; Mrs Beeton's *Book of Household Management*.

1860
T. H. Huxley v. Bishop Wilberforce debate in the Oxford Museum widely viewed as a victory for **evolutionary science**; Garibaldi takes Naples leading to **unification of Italy**; Bradlaugh founds the secularist/atheist ***National Reformer***.

1861
Beginning of the **American Civil War** (to 1865); **death of Prince Albert** and Victoria's withdrawal into mourning; William Morris and others form **interior design company** (Morris, Marshall, Faulkner & Co.), a key moment in the Arts and Crafts Movement; **Criminal Law Consolidation Act** reduces the large number of capital crimes to four: murder, high treason, arson in a royal dockyard, piracy.

1862
London Exposition, showcasing many international developments in science and technology.

1864
First of the **Contagious Diseases Acts**, controversial efforts to control prostitution more effectively; Louis Pasteur invents '**pasteurization**', a breakthrough in food safety; Geneva Convention establishes **Red Cross**.

1865
Abolition of **slavery** in the USA at the end of the Civil War; Governor Edward **Eyre** viciously suppresses a slave revolt led by Paul Bogle prompting both outcry in England and support from leading intellectuals (Carlyle, Dickens, Kingsley, Ruskin, Tennyson).

1866
Second **Contagious Diseases Act**; first petition to Parliament for **female suffrage**; first functional underwater **telegraph** cable laid between North America and Europe.

1867
Second Reform Act raises electorate to around 2 million; Marx, *Das Kapital* (vol. 1); Nobel invents **dynamite**.

1868
Trades Union Congress formed in Manchester; Society of Missionaries for Africa founded; W. E. Gladstone begins first term of office as Liberal prime minister (1868–74, 1880–5, 1886, 1892–4).

1869
Girton College Cambridge for women founded; **Suez Canal** opened; Third **Contagious Diseases Act**; margarine invented; Arnold, *Culture and Anarchy*; J. S. Mill, *Subjection of Women*.

1870
William Forster's **Education Act** creates school boards to examine the provision of elementary education across the newly created school districts (*c.*2,500); **women** are allowed to serve on the school boards, an important step in recognizing women's ability in public administration; **Married Women's Property Act** allows women to keep earnings, property acquired after marriage and open a separate savings account.

1871
Religious tests abolished at Durham, Cambridge and Oxford; **FA Cup** established (Wanderers beat Royal Engineers 1–0 in the first final [1872]).

1872
Girls' Public Day School Trust established for independent girls' schools.

1873
Population of the UK at **26 million**.

1874
Women's Trade Union League formed; first **Impressionist Exhibition** in Paris.

1875
Public Health Act requires a Medical Officer and a sanitary inspector for each district and gives councils powers to build sewers, drains and public toilets; **Third Republic** proclaimed in France.

1876
Alexander Graham Bell patents the **telephone**; **Cruelty to Animals Act** provides for protection for all vertebrate animals, requiring licensing of vivisection and inspection of facilities.

1877
Queen Victoria crowned **Empress of India**; Edison perfects the **phonograph** (early sound recording device); **Grosvenor Gallery** opened in London (centre of Aesthetic Movement art); William Morris helps found the **Society for the Protection of Ancient Buildings**; first **public telephone**; frozen **meat** first shipped across the Atlantic; first All-England Lawn Tennis championship at **Wimbledon**.

1878
Paris Exhibition (**Exposition Universelle**) of arts, science and technology; *English Men of Letters* series begun by John Morley; **Second Afghan War** (1878–9); **Lady Margaret Hall** founded as a college for women in Oxford.

1879
Somerville Hall founded as a college for women in Oxford; defeat of the British Army at **Battle of Isandhlwana** (South Africa); **Rorke's Drift** (some 150 British soldiers defend remote outpost against 4,000 Zulu warriors, a celebrated incident of British Army history); **Battle of Ulundi** (Zulu army defeated by Britain to bring an end to the war widely seen as caused by Sir Bartle Frere).

1880
First **Anglo-Boer** War (1880–1); Owens College Manchester granted

a Royal Charter as the **Victoria University** (later Manchester University); **Elementary Education Act** (Mundella's Act) extends the provisions of 1876 Act about compulsory school attendance for children aged 5 to 10 years; **Greenwich Mean Time** adopted officially by British Parliament; now 30,000 telephones in use around the world.

1881
Pretoria convention recognizes independence of **Transvaal** and **Orange Free State**.

1882
Recognition of British protectorate over **Egypt**; commercial **domestic lighting** used for the first time (Central Station, New York); Leslie Stephen begins to edit the ***Dictionary of National Biography***; **Phoenix Park Murders** (Lord Frederick Cavendish, British secretary for Ireland, and Thomas Henry Burke, his undersecretary, are stabbed to death by Fenian splinter group in Dublin); Society for Psychical Research founded by group of Cambridge scholars to examine 'allegedly paranormal phenomena in a scientific and unbiased way'.

1883
Women's Cooperative Guild founded.

1884
Third Reform Act, extending franchise to most adult males; Murray begins ***Oxford English Dictionary*** (to 1928); **Fabian Society** formed (socialist society committed to gradual rather than revolutionary social reform, named after Roman general Quintus Fabius from his strategy of delaying battle until the right moment); **machine gun** invented; **petrol engine** invented.

1885
Motor car invented; first **electric tramway** at Blackpool; death of General Gordon at Khartoum.

1886
Repeal of **Contagious Diseases Acts**; Gladstone's first Irish Home Rule Bill (fails).

1887
Queen Victoria's **golden jubilee**.

1888
Kodak **box camera** invented; Dunlop patents pneumatic **tyre**; County Councils Act establishes **County Councils** (system of voting **enfranchises unmarried women**); **match girls' strike** at Bryant & May's match factory against use of fatal red phosphorus, long hours and poor pay (prominent early instance of organized industrial action).

1889
London Dock Strike (part of a wave of strikes following the match girls involving new role for unions); **Board of Education** established; 35,000 unique **telegraphic addresses** are now registered with British Post Office.

1890
Tennyson makes **wax cylinder recordings**; Frazer's ***The Golden Bough*** (–1915) begins.

1891
The great **Trans-Siberian Railway** begins; **International Copyright law**.

1892
Coal miner, unionist and journalist Kier Hardie becomes first **Independent Labour MP**; last major outbreak of **cholera** in Europe (Hamburg); first automatic **telephone exchange**.

1893
Ford builds his first car; **diesel engine** patented; second Irish Home Rule Bill (fails).

1894
Armenian massacres, a great liberal cause in the UK.

1895
Marconi sucessfully transmits a 'dot-dot-dot' radio signal (Morse code for 'S') – the beginning of **radio communication**; the Cinématographe, based on Edison's experimental Kinetograph, is used by Louis and Auguste Lumière in Paris (the beginning of **moving images**); Oscar Wilde imprisoned for **homosexual offences**.

1896
First modern **Olympic Games** (Athens); Wilhelm Conrad Röntgen (1845–1923), experimenting on cathode rays in December 1895, is amazed to see the bones in his own hand; in January 1896, he announces publicly the discovery of **X-rays**; Lord Northcliffe founds ***Daily Mail*** (founds *Daily Mirror* in 1903); **Alfred Austin** is, to the disappointment of many, appointed Poet Laureate.

1897
Queen Victoria's **diamond jubilee**; **Workmen's Compensation Act** insists employers compensate injured workmen and dependants if killed; gold discovered in the **Klondike** (Seattle, USA).

1898
M. and Mme Curie discover **radium**; Zeppelin builds **airship**.

1899
Second Anglo-Boer War (–1902); **International Women's Congress**, London; **aspirin** invented; first **international radio transmission**.

1900
Formation of **Labour Representation Committee** (predecessor of the Labour Party); 'black body' radiation explained by Max Planck (a step towards **quantum theory**).

1901
Death of **Queen Victoria**, accession of Edward VII; population of Great Britain **32 million**.

Introduction

Francis O'Gorman

History leaves its mark on writing, and it is part of the historical critic's task to reconstruct as far as possible the conditions both of a text's creation and its consumption. The meaning and significance of writing can only begin to be understood in relation to its cultural environment (where 'cultural' signifies the fullest complexity of human society). To read historically does not mean denying that a text can speak to the present, that it cannot enter a form of meaningful dialogue of difference and similarity with the contemporary moment. But texts can only be said to speak as themselves *at all* if the nature of their relationship with and their intervention into their own times is comprehended as fully as historical distance permits.

Recognizing historical difference is a prerequisite for beginning to interpret the texts of the past. Judging history from the perspective of the current moment is a peril that warps critical authority. 'Presentism', the readiness to find the past lacking because it fails to fulfil the criteria of the present, compromises historical criticism. The most critically enabling assumption about the past – its events, personalities, texts – is that it was always more complicated than it now appears; the most rewarding first question to ask is always whether our view of history is being distorted by inappropriate assumptions from our own time.

To read a text historically is not to confine it to the showcases of a museum, nor is it to fix its meaning as some single, inflexible truth. Literary texts are works of the imagination, and the imagination opens up possibilities rather than closing them down. Reading the Victorian novel requires knowledge of the culture from which it emerged. Yet if history is essential to reading, a literary work of any merit is always more than its context. The novels of the kind discussed in this study are far from interpretively exhausted by an archival investigation of their cultural environments: the critical essays included here do not determine interpretations but endeavor to identify the terms within which interpretation can begin.

The task of the historicist reader of the Victorian novel – for whom this collection is intended – is to try to understand the historical parameters within which the nineteenth-century literary imagination played. But those parameters are always beyond full description. The historicist project to recuperate the coordinates of the past is predicated on an acceptance of permanent incompletion. Yet it remains an essential critical business.

This study includes discussion of contextual domains that, in the current critical environment, are well recognized as central to the reading of Victorian fiction. Class, sexuality, empire, biological science, psychology, material culture, and religion, for instance, would be conspicuous in their absence from a volume of this kind. But it also explores contextual areas newly rising to prominence in contemporary Victorian literary studies – visuality, Europe, law, authorship – and one, the affectivity of literary fiction, that is infrequently treated with the seriousness it deserves. There are many significant omissions – politics being the most obvious, and music, economics, commerce, business, medicine, landscape, the city, the idea of Englishness, the ancient classical world, and popular culture being a tiny number of the others. There is also a (modern) emphasis on identity politics – class, gender, cultural identity – and on science and technology. The *aesthetic* context is almost entirely missing except in the bravura consideration of the novel's relation to the visual arts in chapter 2 and in the deft survey of legal arguments about the aesthetic object in chapter 4. Victorian fiction's place in the history of the novel as genre, its relation to philosophical debates about the aesthetic, its relation to the development of Victorian poetry, are but three aspects of the novel's aesthetic history which are regrettable causalities of space here.

As biblical criticism suggested the interpretive consequences of recognizing the historical nature of scriptural texts in the nineteenth century, many unexceptional Victorian Christians came to realize the extraordinary and often destabilizing affects of reading texts while possessing knowledge of the culture that produced them. Contextual interpretation in contemporary literary studies disturbs no bedrock of national religious faith, but it is an inheritor of that disturbing, surprising, and challenging reading practice nonetheless. The texts considered in this book belong neither to the ancient world nor to the canons of sacred scripture – but their interpretation is unquestionably and dramatically influenced when the marks that history left on them are, to the best extent, acknowledged and explored. It is in this spirit of sympathetic but searching historicism that this book's investigation of some of the most arresting imaginative creations of Victorian Britain is offered to its readers.

Chapter 1

'The sun and moon were made to give them light': Empire in the Victorian Novel

Cannon Schmitt

The following famous passage appears early in the first chapter of Charles Dickens's *Dombey and Son* (1846–8):

> The earth was made for Dombey and Son to trade in, and the sun and moon were made to give them light. Rivers and seas were formed to float their ships; rainbows gave them promise of fair weather; stars and planets circled in their orbits, to preserve inviolate a system of which they were the centre. Common abbreviations took new meanings in his [Dombey's] eyes, and had sole reference to them. A. D. had no concern with anno Domini, but stood for anno Dombei – and Son. (p. 2)

A concise rendering of Paul Dombey Sr.'s sense of himself and his importance, this passage appears to epitomize the imperial attitude. Dombey runs a trading firm based in London. As a consequence, that great metropolis constitutes the center around which all else revolves. Other parts of the globe are significant only insofar as they relate to Dombey and his pursuits. Not even mentioned by name, they are represented by and assimilated into a natural world (earth, rivers, seas, rainbows) made expressly for Dombey's use. The diction, cadences, and sentiment of the passage are Biblical, reminiscent in particular of the first chapter of the Book of Genesis: 'And God said unto them, Be fruitful and multiply, and replenish the earth, and subdue it: and have dominion over the fish of the sea, and over the fowl of the air, and over every living thing that moveth upon the earth' (Genesis 1: 28). A Victorian Adam, Dombey assumes centrality and dominion as a birthright. Not merely the earth and the stars but the past, present, and future take their meaning from him: the final sentence effects a momentous renomination of the current era as 'anno Dombei – and Son'.

One account of the relation between empire and the Victorian novel might put this passage in evidence to argue that Dickens and other novelists functioned as apologists for empire. According to this account, their fictions reflected imperialist assumptions and aspirations, including most crucially an anglocentric world view and a sense of obvious, perhaps divinely sanctioned British superiority. With that superiority came, in turn, the implication of a right or obligation to seize other lands, subdue other peoples, replace outmoded customs and pernicious superstitions with British laws, mores, and religion – in short, to rule the globe. Moreover, because of the far-reaching influence of the Victorian novel as an instrument of instruction as well as entertainment, texts such as *Dombey and Son* might be understood not simply to have reflected but in fact to have disseminated and naturalized the correctness, desirability, and inevitability of British imperial rule. The earth was made for the British to govern, Dickens and other novelists seem to say, and the sun and moon were made to give them light; history signifies nothing but a prelude to their rule, futurity nothing but its triumphant, infinite extension.

A host of difficulties, however, beset this familiar version of the interimplication of narrative fiction and imperial expansion in the nineteenth century – difficulties that can be shadowed forth by way of another look at the passage above. To begin with, Dombey and Son is neither a political nor a military entity but a business: the novel's original title reads *Dealings with the Firm of Dombey and Son: Wholesale, Retail and for Exportation*. Trade, although an essential component of the British Empire from its inception, cannot be conflated with imperialism as such without eliding distinctions of historical, ideological, and practical significance. If the vision of the world conveyed in the passage can fairly be labeled anything other than megalomaniacal, that vision is more nearly mercantilist than imperialist: 'The earth was made for Dombey and Son to trade in' – not necessarily to govern, occupy, or convert. Dombey's subordination of all things and relationships to the interests of business implicates empire, but a series of negotiations is required before it will be possible to suggest in what ways and with what consequences.

More important still, neither the narrator nor the author of *Dombey and Son* can easily be understood to support Dombey's cynosural sense of himself and his firm. As evidenced by the pervasively ironic tone, the narratorial stance is one of critique. 'Stars and planets circled in their orbits, to preserve inviolate a system of which they [Dombey and Son] were the centre': the claim need not be refuted directly; it refutes itself by virtue of its absurd hyperbole. The deployment of Biblical language reinforces rather than undermines such irony, for it invites readers to condemn the outrage of Dombey's arrogation of the Adamic compact. The patriarchal pretensions of Dombey's merchant house, neatly encapsulated in the name 'Dombey and Son' itself, are rendered at once monstrous and comic by way of contrast to those other founding fathers and sons, the patriarchs of the Book of Genesis. By the end of the passage, what was at first merely outrageous becomes blasphemous. The final substitution, which reads A. D. as an abbreviation not for anno Domini but rather for 'anno Dombei – and Son', places Dombey in the position not of a latter-day Adam but of the Christian God. The passage may offer up a judgment on empire, but any account of that judgment must attend closely to the ways in which it seems more nearly to condemn than to endorse the scope of imperial ambitions.

A moment of apparent clarity on closer inspection yields complexities and ambiguities: such a sequence exemplifies the difficulty of discussing empire in the Victorian novel, and most especially the difficulty – the impossibility, I want to argue – of settling on a single answer to the question of what the former had to do or might still have to do with the latter. Perhaps the only accurate general pronouncement that may be made in this context is that neither the novel, nor empire, nor their interimplication can be reduced to merely one thing. In *On the Genealogy of Morals* (1887), Friedrich Nietzsche avers: 'only that which has no history is definable' (p. 80). Since both the novel and the British Empire came into being long before Queen Victoria's 1837 accession to the throne, and since both underwent extensive alteration during the 64 years of her reign, neither is likely to be brought to book by way of static and straightforward definition.

Taking Nietzsche's dictum seriously, we might begin by attending to the history of the first of our two undefinables, the novel. The word in one sense means 'new' or 'the new thing' and so is peculiarly appropriate as a name for the most recent of major literary genres. Whereas the epic, for instance, can be traced back several thousand years, the European novelistic tradition is a matter of merely a few centuries.

Two of the most popular candidates for the probably dubious title of 'first novel in English' were published around the turn of the seventeenth century: Aphra Behn's *Oroonoko* appeared in 1688, Daniel Defoe's *Robinson Crusoe* in 1719. In his influential account of *The Rise of the Novel* (1957), Ian Watt contends that the birth of the novel at this time coincided with the birth of a new economic system, capitalism, as well as a new understanding of the place of individuals in society – or, more precisely, a new understanding of humans as 'individuals'. On this view, the typical protagonists of early novels are best thought as autonomous agents driven chiefly by pecuniary desires, and their appearance in a new literary form tailored to representing their activities marks the advent of modern economic and social organization. As Watt writes of Robinson Crusoe himself: 'his travels, like his freedom from social ties, are merely somewhat extreme cases of tendencies that are normal in modern society as a whole, since, by making the pursuit of gain a primary motive, economic individualism has much increased the mobility of the individual' (p. 67).

Nancy Armstrong, Lennard J. Davis, Michael McKeon, and many others have revisited and revised Watt's story of the origins of the English novel. That story remains useful, however, in part for what it acknowledges but does not address directly: the novel's ties to imperialism. For Crusoe's travels, which Watt reads as a metaphor for increased social mobility under capitalism, in their specificity trace a line that connects Britain to Africa and South America by way of the slave trade and British colonization of the New World. Behn's novel features the same set of geographical, political, and economic connections: *Oroonoko* tells of the enslavement of its eponymous central character in West Africa and his transportation to a plantation in the British (later Dutch) South American colony of Suriname. Dating the beginnings of the British novelistic tradition back to *Robinson Crusoe* and *Oroonoko* allows us to see that Britain's mercantile and colonial relations with non-European parts of the globe were just as indispensable to the foundations of the genre as capitalism and individualism.

Further, because *Oroonoko* and *Robinson Crusoe* interrogate as well as naturalize the role of Britons in making use of other people and places as avenues to wealth and individuation, we can note in addition that the English-language novel from the outset fits Mikhail Bakhtin's account of the novel as such. In 'Discourse in the Novel' (1934–5; English translation 1981), Bakhtin asserts that '[d]iversity of voices and heteroglossia enter the novel and organize themselves within it into a structured artistic system. This constitutes the distinguishing feature of the novel as a genre' (*Dialogic Imagination*: p. 300). According to Bakhtin, the novel provides a locus for the social conflict inherent in language. The story the novel tells can never be one story – can never be 'monologic', as Bakhtin styles it – since the very stuff of novelistic discourse consists of a welter of differing ideologies and points of view. If, for example, *Robinson Crusoe* in some sense endorses its title character's usurpation of the island on which he finds himself shipwrecked, it also and at the same time casts doubt on the legitimacy of that action. Thus the passage from *Dombey and Son* with which I began becomes legible as an exemplary novelistic moment insofar as the same words that convey a vision of London at the center of the world satirize it too.

This view of the novel and the novel's representation of imperialism in particular comports well with the emerging critical consensus about empire. Catherine Hall best expresses that consensus when she writes in *Civilizing Subjects* (2002): 'It is not possible to make sense of empire either theoretically or empirically through a binary lens' (p. 16). In one way, of course, imperialism always involves binarism or dualism insofar as it names a relationship of unequal power between one country and another (or others) whose land and resources have been seized and whose sovereignty has been abrogated. The same may be said of colonialism, a form of imperialism in which members of the colonizing country inhabit in large numbers the territory seized, in the process typically displacing or exterminating indigenous peoples. (It may be useful to note that, although technically distinct, the terms 'imperialism' and 'colonialism' are often used interchangeably – as will be my practice throughout this chapter.) In both abstract and concrete ways, the British Empire functioned dualistically: it featured structures of governance by which Britons ruled colonized peoples, systems of economic exchange that sought to exploit resources abroad for enrichment at home, and a military apparatus that brought force to bear in spectacular as well as quotidian ways. But an analysis that goes no further is inadequate to the task of coming to terms with empire, for beneath such dualisms imperialism can be characterized by a remarkable heterogeneity. Addressing the British experience, Bernard Porter points out in *The Lion's Share* that '[t]here was no single language covering the whole of empire, no one religion, no one code of laws. In the forms of government the disparities between colonies were immense. . . . There was no kind of overall logic' (pp. 1–2).

The absence of an 'overall logic' was in part the result of the long and varied history of Britain's imperial activity, which may be said to have begun during the second half of the sixteenth century. It was at that time that Queen Elizabeth I and, later, James I encouraged 'plantations' – the settling of English and Scottish people in Ireland on land forcibly taken from the native Irish. It was also Elizabeth I who, in 1600, chartered the British East India Company, a trading concern that was eventually – by the middle of the nineteenth century – to rule over much of the area occupied by present-day India, Pakistan, Bangladesh, and Sri Lanka. The seventeenth century witnessed the beginnings of large-scale British settlement in North America and parts of Caribbean, settlement that increased in scope and pace over the course of the eighteenth century. The loss of the American colonies late in that century (1776–83) marked the end of the so-called First Empire, but enormous territorial gains elsewhere, especially in India, initiated the Second. During the Victorian era, the British occupied Australia (claim beginning in 1770) and New Zealand (claimed 1840), seized parts of China (including Hong Kong in 1841), and expanded their holdings in Africa and Southeast Asia (annexing Burma, for instance, in 1886). Expansionist activity reached a crescendo with the 'scramble for Africa' in the 1880s and 1890s, a race among European powers to establish territorial rights to those parts of the continent as yet unclaimed.

Coming into contact with and subduing vastly different societies at different times in those societies' history as well as in their own, the British shaped imperial and colonial policy in an *ad hoc* manner, producing an empire united in name but varied in fact. Precisely because of such variety, however, much of the impetus behind representations of empire in the novel and elsewhere had to do with establishing and shoring up stark differences between colonizer and colonized that, although fundamentally untenable, were nevertheless often an essential component of the rationale for conquest. To quote Hall once again, this time from the introduction to her collection *Cultures of Empire* (2000): 'The work of orientalist discourse, whether in museums, Colonial Offices, the academy or popular fiction, was to secure the binaries between West and East. This could be done only by constant discursive work, fixing and refixing the boundaries between Western rationality and oriental irrationality, Western industry and oriental laziness, Western self-control and the oriental lack of it' (p. 14). Hall is writing about Western representations of the East, but her claims may be widened to include imperialist discourse more generally, which sought in manifold ways to maintain distinctions between Europe and other places, Europeans and other peoples. Several pioneering accounts of the culture of imperialism emphasize this view, including Edward Said's *Orientalism* (1978), the seminal study whose argument Hall's comments summarize. Said draws attention both to the systematic nature of writing on empire and to its function in constructing an 'otherness' that the inhabitants of Europe understood as unlike themselves in nearly every way. In the words of Frantz Fanon, among the first thinkers rigorously to interrogate the place of culture in colonial societies: 'The colonial world is a Manichean world. It is not enough for the settler to delimit physically, that is to say with the help of the army and the police force, the place of the native. As if to show the totalitarian character of colonial exploitation the settler paints the native as a sort of quintessence of evil' (*The Wretched of the Earth,* 1963: 41).

Acutely aware of the differential of power between colonizers and colonized, Fanon also recognizes the imperative for colonizers to supplement the use of force with ideas by distinguishing themselves absolutely from those they rule. Subsequent analyses, while continuing to acknowledge that differential and that imperative, contend that imperial Manicheism constitutes a place to start rather than a place to come to rest. Said himself, in *Culture and Imperialism* (1993), takes his earlier work to task for too dualistic a view of empire: if nineteenth- and twentieth-century Europeans could be said to have been orientalists to the degree that they imagined a monolithic East, Said suggests, then in *Orientalism* he might be said to have given way to 'Occidentalism', minimizing historical and geographical variations among the various European imperial powers. Sara Suleri makes a different but equally trenchant argument for the need to move away from dualistic thinking when she observes that 'alteritism represses the detail of cultural facticity by citing otherness as a universal trope, thereby suggesting that the discursive site of alterity is nothing other than the familiar and unresolved confrontation between the historical and the allegorical' (*The Rhetoric of English India,* 1992: 13). To emphasize the opposition of 'self' and 'other' in studying the literature and culture of imperialism is tantamount to repeating the divisive work of imperialist discourse itself – and, in so doing, to risk losing the particulars of both colonizers and colonized. For Said and Suleri, the analysis of the relation between imperialism and a cultural artifact such as the novel, while striving to hold constantly in view the ineluctable framework of unequal relations of power between the parties involved, should take the shape not of 'alteritism' but of something that could be called 'particularism'.

To begin to see what such particularism might look like in the case of attention to Victorian fiction, recall that both the early novels to which I make reference above achieve their distinctive form by deploying the conventions of a recognizable genre of non-fiction: the travel narrative. In *Oroonoko* and *Robinson Crusoe*, first-person narrators purport to tell of their experiences abroad, away from the English land of their birth. In this, too, these novels can be considered representative, for the novel as a genre tends to incorporate other genres into itself, borrowing from forms of writing like the newspaper, the letter, and the diary. Such an encyclopedic or parasitic tendency might be described as figuratively imperialist as well. Said proposes as much when he writes in *Culture and Imperialism*: 'Without empire . . . there is no European novel as we know it, and indeed if we study the impulses giving rise to it, we shall see the far from accidental convergence between the patterns of narrative authority constitutive of the novel on the one hand, and, on the other, a complex ideological configuration underlying the tendency to imperialism' (pp. 69–70). I will have more to say below about novelistic 'patterns of narrative authority'; for the moment the interesting thing here is the opportunity to add specificity to the case about the close ties between the novel and empire. The novel, this new thing, needed to tell a new story, and novelists met that need in part by writing about new worlds, by throwing in their lot with travelers and explorers. Drawing on and developing the work of writers such as Behn and Defoe, many Victorian novelists craft fictions about Britons in foreign lands that were actual or prospective parts of the empire. Their novels belong in the context of – to borrow the title of a book by Bernard Cohn – *Colonialism and Its Forms of Knowledge* (1996), for they share characteristics of some of the earliest and most enduring of those forms: not only the travel narrative but also the ethnographic report, the map or chart, and the collection.

Consider what is arguably the Victorian novel (or novella, given its relatively short length) most frequently discussed in terms of empire: Joseph Conrad's *Heart of Darkness* (1902). Marlow, the principal narrator, delivers his story to a group of Englishmen on the deck of a yacht waiting the turn of the tide in the Thames River. Recounting his time as the captain of a steamer on another great river, the Congo, Marlow marks what he has to say as a traveler's tale brought back from a strange place. Its interest is in large part exoticist, and nothing it details could be more exotic than Africa. 'We were wanderers on a prehistoric earth', Marlow reports, 'on an earth that wore the aspect of an unknown planet. . . . We could not understand, because we were too far and could not remember, because we were travelling in the night of first ages, of those ages that are gone, leaving hardly a sign – and no memories' (p. 62). The 'we' of the statement, a motley assortment of Europeans working for the Belgian King Leopold's colonial enterprise in central Africa, find themselves unable to comprehend the location of that enterprise because it is not a place in space so much as a place in time: 'prehistoric', 'the night of the first ages', the dark (mysterious, savage, ineffable) childhood of the human race.

Modeling his account on the familiar form of the travel narrative, Marlow employs a familiar trope of imperialist discourse as well. Johannes Fabian, writing about anthropology in *Time and the Other*, has called this trope the 'denial of coevalness' (p. 31); Anne McClintock, writing in *Imperial Leather* about the Victorian novel, names it 'anachronistic space' (p. 30). Both formulations convey the curious way in which certain European representations of non-European peoples and places transform geographical distinctions into temporal and ideological ones. It is as if the distances separating London or Paris from Cape Town, Beijing, or Buenos Aires could be measured in years or millennia as well as in miles. Europe, presumed to be at the geographical center of the world, also stands at its temporal 'center' – or, rather, at its temporal leading edge: its vital, modern present. *Heart of Darkness* and other texts that construct Africa (and Asia and Latin America, too) as an area of barbaric archaism provide a ready-made rationale for colonization in the name of modernization. Despite the fact that Marlow makes scathingly critical remarks about Belgian colonialism, anatomizing its cruelties and hypocrisies, his depiction of the African continent as a vast anachronism may be said to constitute participation in and even endorsement of empire.

Working through *Heart of Darkness* with an eye toward its implications for imperialism, then, demands as much attention to how Marlow describes the site of European depredation as to what he says about that depredation. This is to say, more broadly, that it is not enough to think about empire in the Victorian novel in terms of content alone. Matters of form are of equal significance. To recall the issue of narrative authority as well as that of colonialism and its forms of knowledge: the perceived value of a map or an ethnographic report often inheres as much in how and by whom it has been drawn up as in what it depicts. So while it is interesting that *Heart of Darkness* opens with the words of an unnamed frame narrator who rehearses the most clichéd sentiments in favor of expansionist activities and the civilizing mission, these sentiments can hardly stand as sufficient evidence of the novella's or Conrad's view of empire. They are complicated and undermined by Marlow's words and the words and actions of other characters – not least those of Kurtz, whose initial enthusiasm for the spread of Western 'light' to the 'darkness' of Africa is rendered questionable when viewed in connection with his final murderous directive, scrawled on the last page of an unfinished report drafted for the 'International Society for the Suppression of Savage Customs': 'Exterminate all the brutes!' (pp. 83, 84). *Heart of Darkness* depicts Africa as savage or barbaric and so implicitly in need of an infusion of European modernity, but it also represents European colonialists in Africa as themselves savages or barbarians, all too ready to believe in the concept of barbarism and to commit atrocities in the name of combating it.

Conradian complications of this sort reach an apogee in the (still slightly post-Victorian) *Nostromo* (1904), a novel that chronicles how the apparent backwardness and great mineral wealth of the fictional Latin American republic of Costaguana summon adventurers from Great Britain as well as from the United States. Backing a successful war of secession in a silver-rich coastal province called Sulaco, those outside powers help give birth to a new, efficient, and thoroughly up-to-date nation-state. Such a plot may seem to constitute an allegory about the ability of the West to bring geographical anachronisms back to the future, a praise-song for Euro–American interventionism. Before reaching such a conclusion, however, it is necessary to note that the bulk of the praise is dispensed by Captain Mitchell, the most garrulous and impercipient of the novel's several narrators. Like the Dombey-centric vision of the world quoted at the outset, Mitchell's fatuous celebration of Sulaco's new-found prosperity satirizes itself. And like the easy reasonableness that characterizes the frame narrator's comments at the beginning of *Heart of Darkness*, the air of common sense about that celebration becomes insupportable in view of the rest of the novel. As Benita Parry concludes about *Nostromo* in *Conrad and Imperialism* (1983): 'Against the mystification of the profit motive and the idealism of economic activities . . . the fiction's discourse mobilises a relentless attack, and the illegitimate joining of utilitarianism with idealism is condensed in the key phrase "material interests"' (p. 115).

No British or U.S. troops occupy Costaguana; no foreign rulers are installed to govern the new nation of Sulaco; no land is seized for the purposes of settling immigrants. Nonetheless, it is fair to speak of *Nostromo* as a text about a certain kind of imperialism. John Gallagher and Ronald Robinson (1953) term it 'the imperialism of free trade',

D. C. M. Platt (1977) calls it 'business imperialism': a subtle attenuation of local self-determination involving external control over loans, monopolization of infrastructural development, and application of political pressure in the service of economic gain – or, in Conrad's phrase, 'material interests'. In their monumental *British Imperialism* (1993), historians P. J. Cain and A. G. Hopkins demonstrate that informal imperialism was a major aspect of Britain's expansionist activity in the eighteenth, nineteenth, and early twentieth centuries. 'The distinguishing feature of imperialism', they write, 'is not that it takes a specific economic, cultural or political form, but that it involves an incursion, or an attempted incursion, into the sovereignty of another state' (p. 46). Anticipating such later theorizations of empire, Conrad in *Nostromo* implies that nations need not literally be incorporated into the British Empire to be considered in some sense a part of it.

Conrad also shrewdly rewrites a familiar element of the fantasy and the actuality of imperial adventure by focusing his plot on a silver mine. Britons traveled to far-flung regions pursuing mineral wealth from at least the time of Sir Walter Raleigh's 1595 and 1617 expeditions in search of El Dorado, the fabled city of gold. As Sir Richard Francis Burton's *Explorations of the Highlands of Brazil; with a Full Account of the Gold and Diamond Mines* (1869) and countless other travel narratives like it show, the appetite for gems and precious metals – as well as for writing about them – continued unabated throughout the nineteenth century. By that time, armchair travelers could easily be armchair prospectors: private investment in mining concessions all over the world but especially in South America reached into the millions of pounds from the 1820s on. The Victorians had no need to leave home to stake a claim; they could participate in the extraction of riches from the earth by proxy, as readers and investors.

Novels from Robert Louis Stevenson's *Treasure Island* (1881–3) to H. Rider Haggard's *King Solomon's Mines* (1886) and G. A. Henty's *The Treasure of the Incas* (1903) regularly traded on the narrative possibilities afforded by such riches. Moreover, those 'riches' were imagined more broadly than as simple economic returns – as *She* (1887), another Haggard novel, shows. *She* plays on the trope of anachronistic space by depicting Africa as a mausoleum on a continental scale. Introduced by a fictional editor whose frame narration provides verisimilitude as well as homiletic commentary on the adventures inside the frame, *She* is primarily narrated by Horace Ludwig Holly, whose conclusions about Africa as 'full of the relics of long dead and forgotten civilizations' echo archaeological truisms of the time (ch. 5: 62). Buried treasure, although neither gold nor diamonds, those relics attest to a majestic African past and thus, by way of contrast, to a degenerate African present. The African 'savages' found in the pages of this novel are not, as they are for Conrad's Marlow, remainders from a primitive era that have survived into the nineteenth century. Rather, they are throwbacks – people who have returned to the primitive after once having reached some 'higher', more 'civilized' stage. But the Englishman Holly, too, is a throwback or atavism, a 'monster' whose simian visage and frame confirm the 'monkey theory', the contention that humans evolved from earlier forms of life (ch. 1: 8). *She*, in evoking a savage Africa, manages to raise the question of the savagery of Great Britain as well – and even of imperialism. Holly encounters a country that is in some sense already part of an empire: that of the She of the title, a 2000-year-old Egyptian priestess who has ruled over the Africans among whom she finds herself while patiently awaiting the arrival of the reincarnation of her former lover in the form of Holly's traveling companion and charge, Leo. The inevitable comparison to the British Empire invited by the scenario of dark-skinned 'natives' governed by a White Queen is made still more pointed when She announces to a horrified Leo and Holly her plans for worldwide domination. Although those plans never come to pass, their failure with the death of She leaves Leo and Holly themselves relics, shells of broken manhood.

It is no accident that *She* and the other novels discussed so far deal largely with male Britons. They borrow from the adventure tale as much as from the travel narrative, and for much of the nineteenth century most adventure fiction was self-consciously boys' fiction – a claim not so much about its readership as its characteristic protagonists and concerns. Part of the tangled skein of Victorian masculinity, which included games and sports and which fostered a competitiveness mythologized as the English sense of 'fair play', such fiction imagined the empire as a playing field writ large. Like other spaces allegorizing national manhood, empire presented challenges to be overcome and complexities to be mastered. Walter Hartright, a character in Wilkie Collins' *The Woman in White* (1860), well expresses this sense of untamed and unexplored places as male testing grounds when he writes of a voyage in Central America: 'In the waters of a new life I had tempered my nature afresh. In the stern school of extremity and danger my will had learnt to be strong, my heart to be resolute, my mind to rely on itself. I had gone out to fly from my own future. I came back to face it, as a man should' (p. 427). Countless novels by Henty, John Buchan, R. M. Ballantyne, and others represent non-European parts of the world in these terms: as places of maturation or regeneration where boys can discover – or, in cases like Hartright's, where incomplete or failed men can rediscover – their adult masculinity.

Those novels also represent other parts of the world as sources of pleasure, portraying imperialism as if it were, again like a sport or a game, difficult but fun. Thus was empire enlisted in the service of boyhood and boyhood tied closely to imperialism. Rudyard Kipling's *Kim* (1901) is particularly clear about the nature of the connections between the two. An Irish orphan growing up in British-held India, Kim finds boundless possibilities in empire. This is nearly always the case in Victorian fiction: with few exceptions, that fiction figures the space of empire as Britain's outside, free from the strictures of life at home. As *Kim* demonstrates, however, the relation between inside and outside, home and away is always an intimate one. Kim revels in an earnest and demanding play, requiring fluency in multiple dialects, costumes, and sets of mores. Ethnographer and spymaster Colonel Creighton recognizes his expert negotiation of the variegated cultural, religious, and linguistic landscape of India as precisely suited to the needs of British intelligence. By way of Creighton's fatherly intervention, which provides a formal counterpart to Kim's informal education in the ways of empire, Kim and his expertise are almost seamlessly integrated into British expansionism in the form of Britain's competition with Russia for control of Central Asia – a competition referred to, fittingly, as 'the Great Game'.

Whether empire provides a fictional space for securing manhood, as in *Kim*, or for problematizing it, as in *She*, it always stands in relation to Britain as an elsewhere, an other scene. When Hartright writes 'I had gone out to fly from my own future. I came back to face it, as a man should', he assumes that what one flies from or returns to face is home, Britain. Even in this instance, the distinction is temporal as well as spatial: 'home' is where the 'future' lies; empire or abroad is connected with the past, with childhood – the childhood of humanity and the childhood of the Briton. But the permeability of the two spaces disallows understanding them as if they were utterly distinct from one another, or as if the traffic between them proceeded in one direction only. To do so would be to subscribe to another dualism that scholars in several disciplines have recently exploded. When discussing imperialism, it is necessary to speak not of a 'center' that makes history and a 'periphery' that merely endures it but rather of a mutual constitution of colonizing and colonized society. Robert J. C. Young (1995) and

Homi Bhabha (1994), albeit in quite different work, both demonstrate one aspect of that mutual constitution by exploring the discourse of 'hybridity' in the imperial context. Mary Louise Pratt, in *Imperial Eyes* (1992), provides a way to think about influence moving in both directions when she invokes the term 'transculturation' – the process by which subordinated or colonized groups make use of materials from the metropole or colonizing power, but also the process by which the colonizing power comes to be influenced or shaped by those it has colonized (p. 6).

Victorian novels often register the latter kind of transculturation: even when set in domestic space, the presence of empire insistently marks them. In Stevenson's *The Strange Case of Dr Jekyll and Mr Hyde* (1886), for example, the transformation of the patrician, humanitarian Jekyll into the sensual, selfish, and apelike Hyde reveals anachronism within the boundaries of Great Britain, the home, even the self. Whereas Conrad's Marlow and Haggard's Holly assert the archaism of a distant land, Stevenson's characterization of a London physician's descent into a simian monstrosity draws on the denial of coevalness to locate atavism at the heart of the imperial power. The empire bites back – or, rather, imperialist discourse does, in that Stevenson brings one of its dehumanizing tropes to bear on the imperialists themselves. But this novel also features another, more literal, and more typical instance of transculturation. When, in the first chapter, a character named Enfield recounts how he witnessed Hyde trample a young girl, he describes Hyde as a 'Juggernaut': a massive force that blindly destroys whatever it finds in its path. According to the *OED*, the word derives from a name for the Hindu god Krishna, and specifically for 'the uncouth idol of this deity at Puri in Orissa, annually dragged in procession on an enormous car, under the wheels of which many devotees are said to have formerly thrown themselves to be crushed'. In Enfield's casual use of 'Juggernaut', *The Strange Case of Dr Jekyll and Mr Hyde* reveals the deep, abiding presence of empire in the English language itself.

Addressing that presence in his 'Introductory remarks' to *Hobson-Jobson*, an omnibus 'Anglo-Indian glossary' first published in 1886, Henry Yule writes: 'Words of Indian origin have been insinuating themselves into English ever since the end of the reign of Elizabeth and the beginning of that of King James, when such terms as *calico*, *chintz*, and *gingham* had already effected a lodgment in English warehouses and shops, and were lying in wait for entrance into English literature' (Yule and Burnett, p. 466). '[I]nsinuating themselves' and 'lying in wait', the words in question seem oddly threatening – even as they and the types of cloth they name are also desirable, welcomed first into 'English warehouses and shops' and then into 'English literature'. Drawing together imperialism, trade, and language, Yule conveys the widespread influence of empire and the unsettled disposition of the English toward its products, which were seen as alluring but dangerous. A number of novels register that doubleness or contradiction, from Oscar Wilde's *The Picture of Dorian Gray* (1891) to Richard Marsh's *The Beetle* (1897), but few make it as sustained an object of concern as Collins' *The Moonstone* (1868). Centered on an Indian diamond looted by a British Army officer during the Siege of Seringapatam, a historic battle for British control of India, *The Moonstone* moots the question of the effects of empire at home. As Franklin Blake exclaims about a country estate: 'When I came here from London with that horrible Diamond . . . I don't believe there was a happier household in England than this. Look at the household now! Scattered, disunited – the very air of the place poisoned with mystery and suspicion!' (First Period, ch. 23: 188). A synecdoche for all imperial commodities, the Moonstone's overwhelming beauty is matched only by the overwhelming disturbance of English domestic life to which it gives rise.

The diamond in *The Moonstone* reflects the function of empire in the production of wealth. The confident references made in that novel to 'the' Indian or oriental character provide a reminder that empire was also a locus for the production of knowledge – ethnographic knowledge in particular. Kurtz's report on 'savage customs', Creighton's series of 'monographs on strange Asiatic cults' (ch. 10: 223), Holly's observations on the ways of the Amahagger tribe over which She rules: all attest, in the pages of fiction, to the extra-fictional role of the imperial encounter in the development of anthropology. Of all the products of that discipline in its Victorian infancy, perhaps none was more momentous than that of 'race'. Previous to the nineteenth century, conceptualizations of the differences among various humans from various parts of the world tended to view those differences as subject to change. Although Europeans during the Enlightenment, for example, ranked themselves at the top of a hierarchy of peoples, the qualities that they believed placed them there could be learned, acquired. The nineteenth-century sense of 'race', by contrast, anchored perceived differences in biology and, hence, understood them as permanent. Further, one interpretation of the implications of Darwinian biology (a misinterpretation, even though sometimes endorsed by Darwin himself) used evolutionary theory to provide scientific support for the denial of coevalness: different races, on this view, represented different stages on an evolutionary time-line to 'modern' European humanity.

In *Daniel Deronda* (1876), George Eliot at once relies on and refuses the biological account of racial difference. As in *Middlemarch* (1871–2) before it, Eliot in *Daniel Deronda* explores the fate of a remarkable woman in a society that neither educates women fully nor allows them to practice professions. Registering a protest against such limitations, the novel focuses on one of the few consequential choices women were allowed, that of whom to marry. Like courtship in so many Victorian novels, Gwendolen Harleth's choice of a mate is emplotted as a crisis of selection. I use the term 'selection' deliberately: insofar as that language evokes Darwinism, for which natural selection serves as the principal mechanism of evolution, it recognizes a link between the courtship plot and the novel's other plot, that involving Deronda and his Jewishness. From the perspective of her own choice of mates, Gwendolen figures the vicissitudes of Victorian womanhood. From the perspective of Deronda's choice, however, she figures the novel's investment in race as biology. For Deronda, to decide between Gwendolen and Mirah Cohen is also to decide between his Englishness and his Jewishness. *Daniel Deronda* connects race to biology by way of heterosexual romance and sexual reproduction. The novel's seventh book, tellingly titled 'The Mother and the Son', confirms that series of connections by relying on Deronda's first meeting with his mother to establish his Jewishness with certainty.

Deronda's meetings with a mystic named Mordecai, however, reveal another, countervailing version of race in *Daniel Deronda*. Divorced from sexual reproduction, it imagines a figurative reproduction through the male line, and it connects that reproduction not only to race but also, through race, to nation and empire. Dying of a wasting disease but convinced he has discovered the person who will take up his lifelong dream of founding 'a new Judaea' (ch. 41: 459), Mordecai explains to Deronda: 'You will be my life: it will be planted afresh; it will grow. You shall take the inheritance; it has been gathering for ages. The generations are crowding on my narrow life as a bridge: what has been and what is to be are meeting there; and the bridge is breaking. But I have found you' (ch. 40: 428). 'But I have found you': the language of romance conveys the homosocial reproduction of the next generation, the transmission of the legacy of what Mordecai elsewhere calls the Jewish 'race' from man to man.

Moreover, as Mordecai spells out, that transmission entails a nationalist and indeed an imperialist project:

> I cherish nothing for the Jewish nation, I seek nothing for them, but the good which promises good to all nations. . . . How long is it? – only two centuries since a vessel carried over the ocean the beginning of the great North American nation. The people grew like meeting waters – they were various in habit and sect – there came a time, a century ago, when they needed a polity, and there were heroes of peace among them. What had they to form a polity with but memories of Europe, corrected by the vision of a better? Let our wise and wealthy show themselves heroes. (ch. 41: 458)

Explicitly analogous to the British settlement of North America, the Jewish polity Mordecai hopes for is to be built on land outside Europe, occupied by others. *Daniel Deronda* in some measure rewrites race as an elective affinity and nationality as the offspring of male homosocial romance, but it can do so only by envisioning a return to origins and national greatness contingent on the seizure and colonization of territory.

Daniel Deronda's valorization of this version of national belonging invites reconsideration of a novel in which an expansionist, corporate entity forged between men receives less enthusiastic treatment: *Dombey and Son*. As I argued, Dombey mistakenly conflates personal relations with business transactions. 'Dombey and Son' itself, the name of Dombey's firm and of his family, in effect incorporates that family, defining it as exclusively male and subordinating it to commercial purposes. Dombey's assumption that '[t]he earth was made for Dombey and Son to trade in' betrays not only a megalomaniacal view of the earth but also an entirely economic view of the family. His travails – his son's death, his daughter Florence's alienation from him, his sham second marriage, even the eventual collapse of his firm – dramatize the catastrophe that results from his whole-hearted embrace of that view. But the novel does not rest with critique. Putting to rights what it portrays as an inverted relation between family and business, *Dombey and Son* concludes not simply with the dissolution of a capitalist enterprise that subordinates the familial to itself but with the formation of a new enterprise subservient to the family. As Mr. Toots reports on the novel's penultimate page, 'from his daughter, after all, another Dombey and Son will ascend . . . triumphant' (ch. 63: 733).

Springing from a daughter who incarnates domestic virtues rather than from a father who scorns them, the second iteration of Dombey and Son, readers are given to understand, will place love and family first, economic gain second. The novel registers the difference in manifold ways, but perhaps never more clearly than in a sentence in one of the final chapters that closely echoes the passage from the first chapter with which I began: '[T]he voices in the waves are always whispering to Florence, in their ceaseless murmuring, of love – of love, eternal and illimitable, not bounded by the confines of this world, or by the end of time, but ranging still, beyond the sea, beyond the sky, to the invisible country far away!' (ch. 57: 679). As in that initial passage, in this sentence a Dombey and a Briton seems to stand at the center of not only the world but also the universe. Waves whisper to Florence, and what they whisper of is, like Dombey's vision of his importance, 'not bounded by the confines of this world, or by the end of time'. The crucial change, however, is that not 'trade' but 'love' constitutes the center around which all else revolves – love 'eternal and illimitable': the love Florence bears for Walter Gay, her husband, and most especially the love she bears for her brother Paul, who, now dead, resides in that 'invisible country far away'.

But commerce and imperialism are not far to seek. The waves that whisper to Florence float a merchant ship carrying her and her beloved Walter from Great Britain to China (ch. 56: 657). Walter's success at Canton, a Chinese port opened to British trade by force of arms in 1841, at the conclusion of the First Opium War, provides the stability that emboldens him to propose marriage to Florence, the experience that leads to his appointment to 'a post of great trust and confidence at home', and some of the funds that underwrite the rise of that second 'Dombey and Son' from the ashes of the first (ch. 63: 733). Dickens's novel offers up the illimitable reach of love in place of the deleterious fantasy of the illimitable reach of money and power, but it also attests that such love is itself enabled by British adventurism abroad. The 'invisible country far away', which in *Dombey and Son* names the site of an afterlife, might serve as a fitting description of empire in the Victorian novel: invisible or only partially seen but ubiquitous, far away but never beyond reach.

References and Further Reading

Adams, James Eli (1995) *Dandies and Desert Saints: Styles of Victorian Masculinity*. Ithaca and London: Cornell University Press.

Armstrong, Nancy (1987) *Desire and Domestic Fiction: A Political History of the Novel*. New York: Oxford University Press.

Bakhtin, Mikhail M. (1934–5; 1981) Discourse in the novel. In Caryl Emerson and Michael Holquist (trans. and eds.) *The Dialogic Imagination*, pp. 259–422. Austin: University of Texas Press.

Barrell, John (1991) *The Infection of Thomas De Quincey: A Psychopathology of Imperialism*. New Haven and London: Yale University Press.

Baucom, Ian (1999) *Out of Place: Englishness, Empire and the Locations of Identity*. Princeton: Princeton University Press.

Behdad, Ali (1994) *Belated Travelers: Orientalism in the Age of Colonial Dissolution*. Durham: Duke University Press.

Behn, Aphra (1688; 1994) *Oroonoko*. Oxford and New York: Oxford University Press.

Bhabha, Homi (1994) *The Location of Culture*. London: Routledge.

Bivona, Daniel (1990) *Desire and Contradiction: Imperial Visions and Domestic Debates in Victorian Literature*. Manchester: Manchester University Press.

Bongie, Chris (1991) *Exotic Memories: Literature, Colonialism, and the Fin de Siècle*. Stanford: Stanford University Press.

Brantlinger, Patrick (1988) *Rule of Darkness: British Literature and Imperialism, 1830–1914*. Ithaca: Cornell University Press.

Bristow, Joseph (1991) *Empire Boys: Adventures in a Man's World*. London: HarperCollins.

Burton, Antoinette (ed.) (2001) *Politics and Empire in Victorian Britain: A Reader*. New York: Palgrave.

Burton, Sir Richard Francis (1869; 1968) *Explorations of the Highlands of Brazil; with a Full Account of the Gold and Diamond Mines*. New York: Greenwood.

Cain, P. J. and Hopkins, A. G. (1993) *British Imperialism: Innovation and Expansion 1688–1914*. London and New York: Longman.

Collins, Wilkie (1868; 1986) *The Moonstone*. Harmondsworth: Penguin.

——(1860; 1974) *The Woman in White*. Harmondsworth: Penguin.

Cohn, Bernard S. (1996) *Colonialism and its Forms of Knowledge: The British in India*. Princeton: Princeton University Press.

Conrad, Joseph (1902; 1995) *Heart of Darkness*. Harmondsworth: Penguin.

——(1904; 1983) *Nostromo: A Tale of the Seaboard*. Harmondsworth: Penguin.

David, Deirdre (1996) *Rule Britannia: Women, Empire, and Victorian Writing*. Ithaca: Cornell University Press.

Davis, Lennard J. (1997) *Factual Fictions: The Origins of the English Novel*. Philadelphia: University of Pennsylvania Press.

Dawson, Graham (1994) *Soldier Heroes: British Adventure, Empire, and the Imagining of Masculinities*. London: Routledge.

Defoe, Daniel (1719; 1998) *Robinson Crusoe*. Oxford and New York: Oxford University Press.

Dickens, Charles (1846–8; 1999) *Dombey and Son*. Oxford and New York: Oxford University Press.

Eliot, George (1876; 1998) *Daniel Deronda*. Oxford and New York: Oxford University Press.

——(1872; 1998) *Middlemarch*. Oxford and New York: Oxford University Press.

Fabian, Johannes (1983) *Time and the Other: How Anthropology Makes its Object*. New York: Columbia University Press.

Fanon, Frantz (1963) *The Wretched of the Earth*. Trans. Constance Farrington. New York: Grove.

Gallagher, John and Robinson, Ronald (1953) The imperialism of free trade. *Economic History Review*, **6**: 1–15.

Gikandi, Simon (1996) *Maps of Englishness: Writing Identity in the Culture of Colonialism*. New York: Columbia University Press.

Gilroy, Paul (1993) *The Black Atlantic: Modernity and Double Consciousness*. Cambridge, MA: Harvard University Press.

Green, Martin Burgess (1979) *Dreams of Adventure, Deeds of Empire*. New York: Basic Books.

Haggard, H. Rider (1886; 1989) *King Solomon's Mines*. Oxford and New York: Oxford University Press.

——(1887; 1991) *She*. Oxford and New York: Oxford University Press.

Hall, Catherine (2002) *Civilizing Subjects: Metropole and Colony in the English Imagination 1830–1867*. Chicago and London: University of Chicago Press.

——(2000) Introduction: Thinking the postcolonial, thinking the empire. In C. Hall (ed.) *Cultures of Empire: Colonizers in Britain and the Empire in the Nineteenth and Twentieth Centuries*, pp. 1–33). New York: Routledge.

Hardt, Michael and Negri, Antonio (2000) *Empire*. Cambridge, MA and London: Harvard University Press.

Henry, Nancy (2002) *George Eliot and Empire*. Cambridge: Cambridge University Press.

Herbert, Christopher (1991) *Culture and Anomie: Ethnographic Imagination in the Nineteenth Century*. Chicago: University of Chicago Press.

Henty, G. A. (1903; 2002) *The Treasure of the Incas*. Althouse.

Hobsbawm, Eric (1989) *The Age of Empire 1875–1914*. New York: Vintage.

JanMohamed, Abdul R. (1983) *Manichean Aesthetics: The Politics of Literature in Colonial Africa*. Amherst: University of Massachusetts Press.

Kipling, Rudyard (1901; 1987) *Kim*. Harmondsworth: Penguin.

Lane, Chrisopher (1995) *The Ruling Passion: British Colonial Allegory and the Paradox of Homosexual Desire*. Durham, NC: Duke University Press.

Marsh, Richard (1897; 1984) *The Beetle*. In Graham Greene and Sir Hugh Greene (eds.) *Victorian Villainies*, pp. 441–715. New York: Viking.

McClintock, Anne (1995) *Imperial Leather: Race, Gender, and Sexuality in the Colonial Contest*. New York and London: Routledge.

McKeon, Michael (1988) *The Origins of the English Novel, 1600–1740*. Baltimore and London: Johns Hopkins University Press.

Milligan, Barry (1995) *Pleasures and Pains: Opium and the Orient in Nineteenth-Century British Culture*. Charlottesville: University Press of Virginia.

Nietzsche, Friedrich (1887; 1989) *On the Genealogy of Morals*. Trans. Walter Kaufmann and R. J. Hollingdale. New York: Vintage.

Parry, Benita (1983) *Conrad and Imperialism: Ideological Boundaries and Visionary Frontiers*. London: Macmillan.

Perera, Suvendrini (1991) *Reaches of Empire: The English Novel from Edgeworth to Dickens*. New York: Columbia University Press.

Platt, D. C. M. (ed.) (1977) *Business Imperialism, 1840–1930: An Inquiry Based on British Experience in Latin America*. Oxford: Clarendon Press.

Porter, Bernard (1975) *The Lion's Share: A Short History of British Imperialism, 1850–1995*. London and New York: Longman.

Pratt, Mary Louise (1992) *Imperial Eyes: Travel Writing and Transculturation*. London and New York: Routledge.

Said, Edward (1993) *Culture and Imperialism*. New York: Vintage.

——(1978) *Orientalism*. London: Routledge.

Schmitt, Cannon (1997) *Alien Nation: Nineteenth-Century Gothic Fictions and English Nationality*. Philadelphia: University of Pennsylvania Press.

Spivak, Gayatri Chakravorty (1999) *A Critique of Postcolonial Reason: Toward a History of the Vanishing Present*. Cambridge, MA: Harvard University Press.

Stevenson, Robert Louis (1886; 1979) *The Strange Case of Dr. Jekyll and Mr. Hyde and Other Stories*. Harmondsworth: Penguin.

Street, Brian (1975) *The Savage in Literature: Representations of 'Primitive' Society in English Fiction 1858–1920*. London and Boston: Routledge and Kegan Paul.

Strobel, Margaret (1991) *European Women and the Second British Empire*. Bloomington and Indianapolis: Indiana University Press.

——(1881–3; 1999) *Treasure Island*. Harmondsworth: Penguin.

Suleri, Sara (1992) *The Rhetoric of English India*. Chicago and London: University of Chicago Press.

Viswanathan, Gauri (1989) *Masks of Conquest: Literary Study and British Rule in India*. New York: Columbia University Press.

Watt, Ian (1957) *The Rise of the Novel: Studies in Defoe, Richardson, and Fielding*. Berkeley and Los Angeles: University of California Press.

Wilde, Oscar (1891; 1981) *The Picture of Dorian Gray*. Oxford and New York: Oxford University Press.

Young, Robert J. C. (1995) *Colonial Desire: Hybridity in Theory, Culture, and Race*. London and New York: Routledge.

Yule, Henry and Burnell, A. C. (1902; 1996) *Hobson–Jobson: The Anglo-Indian Dictionary*. Ware: Wordsworth.

Chapter 2

'Seeing is believing?': Visuality and Victorian Fiction

Kate Flint

Early in Thomas Hardy's novel, *Desperate Remedies* (1871), the heroine, Cytherea, watches her architect father at work, supervising the construction of the upper part of a church spire. Her 'idling eyes' caught sight of these men at work, and she watched this 'curious and striking' picture from the room in Hocbridge Town Hall, where she was sitting. 'It was an illuminated miniature, framed in by the dark margin of the window, the keen-eyed shadiness of which emphasized by contrast the softness of the objects enclosed'. Hardy explores the effects of perspective and point of view as he shows how distance enhances yet further this sense of fragility: these humans 'appeared little larger than pigeons, and made their tiny movements with a soft, spirit-like silentness'. Yet since unlike pigeons, the workmen are not winged, they need to be sharply alert to their environment, not, like Cytherea's father, losing themselves in the inward form of mental vision that is reflection. A moment later, he reels off into the air, and topples downwards. But it is not the sight of his fatal precipitation that burns itself into the young woman's memory so much as the moments that follow. She faints, and comes to consciousness as she is being carried into her own house, at which instant

> her eyes caught sight of the south-western sky, and, without heeding, saw white sunlight shining in shaft-like lines from a rift in a slaty cloud. Emotions will attach themselves to scenes that are simultaneous – however foreign in essence these scenes may be – as chemical waters

> will crystallise on twigs and wires. Ever after that time any mental agony brought less vividly to Cytherea's mind the scene from the Town Hall windows than sunlight streaming in shaft-like lines (Hardy 1991: 14–15).

This brief passage encapsulates much that is telling about the place of the visual in Victorian fiction. It vividly depicts a precisely delineated scene, itself neatly framed. Yet it also is informed by a concern with the psychology of seeing, and the recognition that the perceptual element which makes the strongest impression on the mind may not be the most obvious one, but may, rather, be oblique, suggestive, evocative. To see, in other words, is to be aware of what is out there – what strikes the eye – but also, as Victorian novels continually demonstrate, it is a highly individualized and subjective activity. Moreover, individuals do not merely use their capacity for visualization in relation to the material, tangible world, but this facility is a central component in the activity of the memory and the imagination, and hence is crucial to the practices of both reading and writing. 'I don't invent it – really do not – *but see it,* and write it down', Dickens is reported to have said (Forster 1928: 720). To consider visuality in relation to fiction is to address much more than the physical attributes of *what* is represented, or the question of how the world summoned up through language relates to artistic practices of the time, or to the modes of gazing, glancing, and observing employed by the novel's characters. It is to explore a whole range of issues of representation and perception, and to ask – in the words of an article by the polymath George Lewes, whose own work on physiology, psychology, and philosophy touched on many of these themes, whether 'seeing is believing' (Lewes 1860).

Pictorial realization, Martin Meisel has argued, was the dominant cultural idiom of the Victorian period, whether in fiction, drama, or in painting itself, 'and realization is central to the persistent pressure toward writing a concrete particularity with inward signification, the materiality of things with moral and emotional force, historical fact with figural truth, the mimetic with the ideal' (Meisel 1983: 36). A reader, or a spectator at the theater, or a visitor to an art gallery was, in other words, brought to understand their contemporary world (and to envisage other periods, and other places) in terms of images. George Eliot, writing of the German social historian Riehl in 1856, opened her review by inviting one to note 'the images that are habitually associated with abstract or collective terms – what may be called the picture-writing of the mind' (Eliot 1990: 107), and this, too, points to the widespread tendency to give, and to want to give, concrete, substantial form to that which might otherwise remain too nebulous or challenging to grasp. 'Vigorous and effective minds', wrote Lewes a decade later, in 1865, 'habitually deal with concrete images' (Lewes 1898: 33), whereas Thomas Hardy, in 1886, speculated that novel writing, 'having reached the analytical stage it must transcend it by going still further in the same direction. Why not by rendering as visible essences, spectres, &c. the abstract thoughts of the analytic school?' (Hardy 1984: 183). In turn, these cultural habits were related to the growing proliferation of imagery and display in society more generally. Whether one thinks of the developments which made printing cheaper and the production and distribution of images much easier, or the growth in museums, galleries, and art and industrial exhibitions, or the expansion of consumer culture, where the potential customer's eyes were being enticed by advertisements and by window displays, Victorians were continually being invited to look, to engage in active interpretation of what they saw – and even to price it. Henry James, in *The Awkward Age* (1899) – a novel which dispassionately considers the topic of female adolescence – draws a direct parallel between the social visibility of the attractive young girl, and the blatant touting of other wares in the urban marketplace. The narrative voice remarks that

> beauty, in London . . . staring glaring obvious knock-down beauty, as plain as a poster on a wall, an advertisement of soap or whiskey . . . fetches such a price in the market that the absence of it, for a woman with a girl to marry, inspires endless terrors and constitutes for the wretched pair – to speak of mother and daughter alone – a sort of social bankruptcy. London doesn't love the latent or the lurking . . . It wants cash over the counter and letters ten feet high. (James 1899: 25)

If James, here, was writing about forms of the visible which set out to be eye-catching and public, the period also witnessed the popularity of many optical devices, from the kaleidoscope and zooscope to the magic lantern, which brought new visual technologies into the home – technologies which frequently sought to bring out the latent and the lurking. These abilities help establish the context for Jonathan Crary's useful and influential distinction between 'visibility' – that is, the theory and practice of representation which is modeled on physiological processes of looking – and 'visuality', which encompasses the theory and practice of imaging that which could not have been seen, or which could not have been seen so easily or so accurately without developments in technology (Crary 1990: 129). While my own use of the term 'visuality' encompasses the workings of the mind as well as of the machine, this must not detract from the fact that microscopes were popular educational aids, and like the discovery of the X-ray in 1895, or powerful telescopes, or photo-imaging tools, provided evidence that much more could in fact be made visible than was apparent to the naked eye – what Walter Benjamin, referring to what the camera can capture but the eye cannot see, famously termed the 'optical unconscious' (Benjamin 1972: 9). Nothing, indeed, was as important to the visual capturing and dissemination of the world as the development and commercialization of photography. By the late 1830s, the invention of the daguerreotype and photograph had made it possible to capture the evanescent forms of the visible world and make them permanent: something which, as we shall see, was to have profound implications for the terms in which representation was discussed. Whatever the reality of photography – the point of view of the person behind the camera, the potential for aesthetic manipulation in the darkroom – it appeared to offer a new standard in verifiable fidelity, and offered apparently accurate images of scenes and individuals never viewed at first hand by its consumers. As Nancy Armstrong has argued in *Fiction in the Age of Photography* (1991), this ready supply of visual material made it easy, too, for readers to 'see' according to stereotypes of gender, class, race, and so on.

The abundance of imagery, however, was not the only factor influencing Victorian fiction's drive toward accurate and detailed descriptions of environment, interior, and physical appearance. Victorian epistemology encouraged the accumulation and interrogation of detailed material evidence; and the growing emphasis on gathering and analyzing the specifics of ordinary, everyday life in history and in the developing discipline of sociology – and on linking these specifics to patterns of cause and effect – is inseparable from the visual information offered to the reader of fiction. Yet at the same time, the variability of each recording eye was being increasingly noted. James Krasner, in *The Entangled Eye*, invites one to compare 'certain landscapes described by post-Darwinian authors with those of mid-nineteenth-century novelists' – Hardy is his most persuasive example, although fiction writers as diverse in voice as James and Gissing might serve as well. Krasner maintains that in earlier writing,

> the reader sees farther and better through the narrative eye than does the figure in the landscape actually perceiving the scene. Even when the perceiving figure is the narrator, the narrative eye still gives the reader more visual information than the narrator claims to possess. In post-Darwinian portrayals, on the other hand, the reader's eye and the perceiving figure's eye tend to share the same perceptual experience. The reader, therefore, seems to be trapped in the landscape, operating by its rules, and unable to escape the limitations of physical sight. (Krasner 1992: 9)

There are some problems with this generalization – for example, the author, like the scientist, frequently provides an understanding of the temporal forces (of both long and short duration) which hold together a landscape, and which involve the employment of a historical, inwardly generated form of visualization. Nonetheless, Krasner's argument about an increasingly subjectivized vision coming to inform the fictional recording of visible detail is a fair one. In what follows, however, the emphasis will not fall sustainedly on the ways in which novelists make particular places and people vividly visible in the reader's imagination – the kind of scene painting, with a strong emphasis on decipherable narrative, that led Henry James to remark in 1884 that 'the analogy between the art of the painter and the art of the novelist is, so far as I am able to see, complete . . . as the picture is reality, so the novel is history' (James 1987: 378). Rather, my preoccupation will be with the increasing tendency of the Victorian novel – like many contemporary scientists, philosophers, psychologists, and indeed painters themselves – to defamiliarize the practice of looking, making us query both what and how we see, and preventing us from taking the visual for granted.

First, however, we should note how the book itself partook in the increased culture of consumerism, and the degree to which its own appearance was a part of this. From lavishly gilded, elaborately tooled covers to the yellow-backed popular fiction sold at railway bookstalls, books were designed to appeal to the eye in an increasingly competitive marketplace. Most conspicuously, cheaper printing techniques allowed for the illustration of novels. Illustrations could function in a whole range of ways. At their most anodyne, they did little more than break up pages of print, offering pleasant, but unmemorable impressions of social status, setting, and physical appearance: even John Millais's respectful illustrations to four of Anthony Trollope's novels (*Framley Parsonage*, 1860–1; *Orley Farm*, 1861–2; *The Small House at*

Allington, 1862–4, and *Phineas Finn*, 1867–9) add little other than social elegance. Much more interpretive were the illustrations which accompanied the part publications of both Dickens's and Thackeray's novels, which frequently amplified a storyline, or gave pointers as to the dominant metaphorical and thematic strands in the text. While George Cruikshank's brooding, introspective interpretations of the London criminal life of *Oliver Twist* (1837–8) play up the sinister aspects of that novel, they were too dark for Dickens's own taste, and he subsequently turned to a number of other graphic artists, including George Cattermole, Marcus Stone, Luke Fildes and, above all, Hablôt Knight Browne, better known as 'Phiz'. Exaggerating physical characteristics of the mentally and physically grotesque on the one hand, and oversweetening the sentimental on the other, Phiz's illustrations amplify textual characterization. More interesting, by far, are the other types of commentary which the engraved plates contain: the toy train, with carriages thrown on their sides, on the floor of the Toodles' family home (Chapter 38), which hints at the physical and financial risks inherent in the railway business; or the Roman pose – set against a background of murderous classical women – struck by Edith Dombey in the illustration to Chapter 54. Graphic art can point forwards in prophetic fashion, too. In *The Old Curiosity Shop* (1840–1), the eye is led downwards into the grave-like pit of a well in Chapter 55 by the pointing hand of the old sexton, and the rope of the bucket which descends into darkness. Although he is ostensibly giving Nell a tour of an old church, the fact that she is delineated far more ethereally than the skull-featured old man, and is bathed in a pale sunlight, which contrasts with the shadows in which he stands, heavily (and accurately) suggests that he is not just pointing at her mortality, but that she is, like her – and the reader's – gaze, inexorably drawn toward it. Thackeray illustrated his two early novels, *Vanity Fair* (1848) and *Pendennis* (1850) himself, and both intra-textual illustrations and the pictorial capitals at the beginning of chapters not only provide visual glosses of the various forms of social pretension, ambition, and romantic idealism that the novels portray, but in their deliberate exaggeration, underscores the mode of satire that he uses.

Illustrations do not just direct readers' attention toward content and approach, or even toward the prevalent atmosphere of a novel: their careful positioning can influence the very pace of one's reading, ensuring that one pause briefly – even if not, necessarily, long enough – to analyze all potential aspects of the accompanying image. Moreover, visual amplification of a text does not have to be mimetically illustrative. It may be playful, as with the ever-decreasing font sizes that describe the mouse's tapering tale/tail in *Alice in Wonderland*, or the moment in Charles Reade's *It is Never Too Late to Mend* (1856), when (rather in the mode of Laurence Sterne's *Tristram Shandy*), we read the inscription to their mother engraved on a tombstone together with the brothers George and William Fielding (Reade 1856: I. 44). Later, in Australia, George and his friend Tom Robinson look up at night and see the Southern Cross above them, represented as five stars on a black rectangle (Reade 1856: II. 293). Less conspicuous are the careful bits of typesetting which are designed to give significance to empty space – and such devices are particularly vulnerable to textual reprintings, if, indeed, they ever make it past an author's visual conceptualizing. In *Our Mutual Friend* (1864–5), after the line which concludes Bradley Headstone's vicious attack on Eugene Wrayburn, Dickens wrote in the manuscript 'Printer. A white line here', although, as Joel Brattin has noted, the fact that the line happened to fall at the bottom of a page in the proofs means that they never appeared in the original published text (Brattin 1985: 159). On yet other occasions, the disruption of print conventions seems deliberately to provoke questions of authenticity, verification, and falsification, both as they function thematically within a novel, and, yet more significantly, in relation to the whole practice of writing imaginative fiction. No one could mistake the outrageous fantasy of Rider Haggard's *She* (1887) for genuine travel writing or anthropology, yet the careful 'facsimiles' of the 'Sherd of Amenartas' reproduced at the front of the book, together with the gothic script of a couplet from the same sherd that appears on the title page, is part of the apparatus through which the author encourages the reader to suspend disbelief. To see, in such instances, is very far from being credulous. Even before readers are invited to interpret the possible nuances and ambiguities of the words on the page, they are implicitly cautioned against relying on visible material evidence.

When direct references to painting are made within fiction, the reader is quite explicitly being invited to think about practices of looking. In Geraldine Jewsbury's *The Half-Sisters* (1848), the genealogical relationship that has been explicit throughout the text becomes revealed to the two major protagonists when Bianca recognizes a portrait of their mutual father hanging over her half-sister Alice's mantelpiece. Jewsbury's novel has foregrounded issues of display throughout, from the questions of propriety surrounding a woman whose stage career means that she is an object of the public's gaze, to the respectable appearance which the middle-class woman is expected to maintain at all costs. In prompting literal recognition, the invitation to recognize a range of parallels which exist between these ostensibly different women's lifestyles is intensified, bringing out the fact that both, by virtue of their gender, submit to highly scrutinized performance. Women's visibility – and we have already seen James bringing this out in a deliberately crude way – is a recurrent theme in Victorian fiction, and the theme is underscored by a repeated employment of painted likenesses. The codes which are thus invoked may be broad ones which associate youth with beauty, as when, in *Felix Holt* (1866), Mr. Jermyn looks at the portrait of the 'brilliant smiling young woman' which hangs above the fireplace, and contrasts it with the appearance of his former lover 'withered and frosted by many winters, and with lips and eyes from which the smile had departed' (Eliot 1980: 334), or they may draw on more specific associations with particular genres of painting. When Robert Audley and his friend George Talboys come upon the portrait which is being executed of Lady Audley – about whom they and the reader are growing increasingly suspicious – Mary Braddon (1862) expects her reader to find the style over-sensuous, and hence something which reflects badly on the subject. 'No one but a pre-Raphaelite' would have painted in this way, sexualizing Lady Audley's representation through a 'lurid' complexion, a 'crimson dress, the sunshine on the face, the red gold gleaming in the yellow hair, the ripe scarlet of the pouting lips, the glowing colours of each accessory of the minutely-painted background' (Braddon 1987: 71). These are aesthetically marked features that serve to damn her in the mind of the imagined morally conventional spectator/reader.

In *Villette* (1853), Charlotte Brontë makes deliberate play on this tendency to collapse woman as representation, and woman as living being, when she sets up an encounter in an art gallery between the outwardly demure, inwardly feisty Lucy Snowe and the Catholic upholder of rigid stereotypes of correct female behavior, Paul Emanuel. The latter praises what seems to Lucy the 'flat, dead, pale and formal' emblems of 'La vie d'une femme' (representations of a prim young girl emerging from church; a bride kneeling in prayer; a young mother 'hanging disconsolate over a clayey and puffy baby with a face like an unwholesome full moon' (Brontë 1900: 238), and a widow in deep mourning), while the former prefers looking at – if not admiring – a voluptuous 'Cleopatra', Brontë avoids turning the incident into an over-schematized clash of cultures and genders by guaranteeing that the ensuing bantering over the subject-matter of the paintings is an oblique, almost perverse form of flirtation. Looking and talking about paintings, that is to say, may readily be a substitute for something else. Similarly, in relation to *Jane Eyre* (1847), Peter Bellis has argued that Jane, in opening her portfolio for Rochester's gaze, 'deflects and tames' it, 'substituting her pictures for herself as its object' (Bellis 1987: 642). But another, and ultimately more important form of substitution is in operation here. By having Jane bring out water colors of a stormy sea with a disappearing boat and the glimpse of a drowned corpse; a mysterious female form rising into the dusk with streaming hair, dark wild eyes, and a star on her forehead; and an iceberg set against the northern lights, with another strangely lit womanly head rising in the foreground, Brontë not only suggests her protagonist's strong, original imagination – for these works seem more prefigurations of symbolist art than anything on view at the Royal Academy of the 1840s – but hints that the unconscious can figure itself in imagery which, like dreams, give up their meanings obliquely. These works are not representations of Jane's outward life, as sketches of the landscape around Lowood might be: they are revelatory of her inner life.

This indirect assertion of the importance of that inward vision, which constitutes one form of the creative imagination, points to another feature of Victorian fiction's employment of deliberate, self-conscious references to the visual environment, the way in which the artist comes to function as a surrogate figure for the author, or for issues concerning authorship. When in *Little Dorrit* the languorous and cynical Henry Gowan talks about how he views his paintings as commodities – 'What I do in my trade, I do to sell. What all we fellows do, we do to sell. If we didn't want to sell it for the most we can get for it, we shouldn't do it' (Dickens 1994: 403) – he is a jaded projection of Dickens's anxieties about the demands which the marketplace puts on the writer, and about the author's ownership of his work. In *Olive* (1850), Dinah Craik – who had herself studied at Government School of Design, Somerset House, in 1843 – centers the figure of the woman artist, but it is crucial that she is portrayed as having a twisted spine, and as having an 'almost masculine power of mind', as if artistic abilities are a departure from a norm which is signaled through somatic means. Moreover, the narrator does not contradict the view of a senior male painter that 'there were bounds that she could not pass; but as far as in her lay, she sought to lift herself above her sex's weakness and want of perseverance' (Craik 1996: 127). The heroine of Ella Hepworth Dixon's *The Story of a Modern Woman* (1894), studying painting, and trying to make a living by writing, finds that both spheres expect the work of women artists to conform to a well-established set of conventions. Interestingly, however, in *The Romance of a Shop* (1888), Amy Levy's main women characters express few of these anxieties in running their very commercialized photographic studio after their father's death, whatever the responses of their more traditionally minded relatives and acquaintances, who, in turn, are viewed with 'three pairs of searching and intensely modern young eyes' (Levy 1993: 64). Their familiarity with cameras and studio props, with printing frames and developing chemicals, and even their willingness to undertake such commissions as photographing a corpse on her death bed are simultaneously signs of their modernity and courageous efforts at establishing financial independence. Significantly, although the story ends with two of the sisters married (and one dead from consumption), this is not the end of their profession. For Lucy, who marries an illustrator, 'the photography . . . has not been crowded out by domestic duties . . . [she] has succumbed to the modern practice of specializing, and only the other day carried off a medal for photographs of young children from an industrial exhibition' (Levy 1993: 195). Public display of art is no longer envisaged as a woman's means to an end, as it was for Helen Graham in Anne Brontë's *The Tenant of Wildfell Hall* (1848).

Yet when considering the relationship between visuality and the novel, a number of other elements in *The Romance of a Shop* stand out which go far beyond the fascination of the subject matter. Just as Lucy and her sister Gertrude are used to framing their subjects, placing them in an effective light, and bringing out their personalities, so is Levy alert to the ways in which people speculate about what they look at – gazing at the street or the flat opposite from a window, say; to the effects of atmosphere on the appearance of the material world ('A dun–coloured haze, thin and transparent, hung in the air, softening the long perspective of the street' (Levy 1993: 164); to the ways in which states of mind may be expressed through an unconscious pose; to the ways in which visually provoked introspection of one era echoes that of a former time. As Gertrude's eye 'fell on her own reflection she remembered Lucy Snowe's words – "I saw myself in the glass, in my mourning dress, a faded, hollow-eyed vision. Yet I thought little of the wan spectacle . . . I still felt life at life's sources"' (Levy 1993: 188–9). Most interestingly of all, however, is the occasion when the metaphorical language of this short novel overlaps with its broader theme. When Gertrude first encounters Lord Watergate (who is eventually to become her husband), she has just been photographing his late wife's body:

> For one brief but vivid moment, her eyes encountered the glance of two miserable grey eyes, looking out with a sort of dazed wonder from a pale and sunken face. The broad forehead, projecting over the eyes; the fine, but rough-hewn features; the brown hair and beard; the tall, stooping, sinewy figure: these together formed a picture which imprinted itself as by a flash on Gertrude's overwrought consciousness, and was destined not to fade for many days to come. (Levy 1993: 93)

The mind as a photographic plate: this was one of the many figures used by Victorian theorists of mind to describe the operations of the memory. But such a simile was relatively rare within Victorian fiction. To be sure, photographs themselves make their appearance, to signify modernity, say – as when Pip, in *Great Expectations* (1861) tells us that he never saw any likeness of his parents, 'for their days were long before the days of photographs' (Dickens 1996: 3). But there are curiously few direct sustained references to this new technology of imaging in fiction until the last quarter of Victoria's reign. Robert Dingley has explored some of the reasons for this, arguing that

> realistic fiction seeks to identify and define its own superior epistemology *by contrast,* to distance its own purchase on truth from that of mechanical reproduction. And that implicit distinction, between the camera's external, and the novel's inward, grasp of reality invites (and seems designed to invite) the reader's warm endorsement of the latter . . . The mistrust of photography, then, might plausibly be presented as part of Victorian fiction's larger, and vocal, resistance to the dehumanizing effects of technological and other forms of regulation, which it courageously defies, both in the values it upholds and in the modes of knowledge it exemplifies. (Dingley 2001: 49)

But he wants to go beyond this, understandably acknowledging that Victorian fiction is not exactly resistant to displaying forms of self-discipline and self-regulation, and to providing paradigms of cause and effect in the realm of behavior. It is, indeed, this emphasis on narrative sequence that most tellingly severs the operations of a novel from that of a photograph, which promises to freeze an instant of time. Fiction's kind of surveillance, as Dingley puts it, 'is crucially premised on its capacity to operate teleologically – to establish narrative progressions over time. The photograph, conversely, can only function instantaneously – photographic technology, indeed, seeks from the first to reduce the time taken to register an image – so its mode of control is necessarily restricted to the taxonomic' (Dingley 2001: 50).

By contrast, many mid-Victorian paintings deliberately sought to expand their temporal presence, encoding references to the past of their protagonists or items which pointed proleptically at the future: a drive toward narrativization which, while in part an acknowledgment of the growing cultural dominance of the novel, increasingly infuriated artists and art critics for the primacy which it seemed to grant the written word, rather than the formal and painterly qualities of a visual work of art. Moreover, as Jennifer Green-Lewis has pointed out in her important book about Victorian photography and culture, photographs were often presented and received as 'apparently authorless texts, independently capable of describing and classifying human beings and human behavior' (Green-Lewis 1996: 4). Such ostensible denial of an attributable point of view cuts across both third and first person practices of employing a didactic, or intimate, or informative, or speculative narrative voice.

Yet as Green-Lewis also puts it,

> Because realism's own relation to truth (or lying) is so well illustrated by the workings of photography, photography became useful as the metaphorical substance in which wider representational topics with both ethical and practical imperatives could be argued. What realism ought to do and what it was actually capable of were topics for which photography was able to provide confirmation. (Green-Lewis 1996: 20)

Richard Altick has noted how the daguerreotype and photograph soon became 'a permanent part of the [literary] critical vocabulary, reviewers using the words as nouns, adjectives and verbs to signify fidelity to the eye's report' (Altick 1991: 337–8). The *Spectator*, for example, remarked, not altogether flatteringly, about *Little Dorrit* that

> So crowded is the canvas which Mr Dickens has stretched and so casual the connection that gives to his composition whatever unity it has, that a daguerreotype of Fleet Street at noon-day would be the aptest symbol to be found for it; though the daguerreotype would have the advantage in accuracy of representation. (*Spectator*, 26 September 1853: 924)

When George Eliot, in the *Natural History of German Life* review, commended Dickens's ability to capture the world's externals with 'the delicate accuracy of a sun picture' (Eliot 1963: 271), she, also, intended to draw attention to the daguerreotype's limitations as well as its power. For her major complaint against Dickens – and, as it might be, of the new medium – is that he fails to render internal traits with the same care for detail. As she expressed it in the early part of her career, 'truthfulness' in literature or art involved not just physical replication, but acknowledging ordinariness, rather than exceptionalism, at the level of human existence and shared emotions. This was the reason that, in *Adam Bede*, she praised Dutch genre paintings for their faithful representation of a monotonous homely existence, demanding that art always remind one of 'common, coarse people, who have no picturesque sentimental wretchedness', and that there are always artists 'ready to give the loving pains of a life to the faithful representing of common things' (Eliot 1985: 224). One might argue that such representations are as likely to stimulate a stock response as the conventionally prettified, only the important thing is that in Eliot's terms this is a *moral* response, an acknowledgment not just of the folly of judging by external appearances, but of attending to the inner qualities of individuals, and of recognizing the human obligation to extend sympathy toward them. As she was to ventriloquize through Will Ladislaw in *Middlemarch* (1871–2), in a phrase which recognizes the intertwining of perception, imagination, and emotional feeling: '"The true seeing is within"' (Eliot 1977: 133).

This oscillation between inner and outer vision, between recording the visible details of a crowded material world, and giving a sense of the complex interior lives of perceiving experiential subjects – a refusal to be satisfied with the representation of surfaces – characterized British realism of the mid and late nineteenth century. The oscillation could be found, too, in the dialog between a desire for objective recording of facts – rather as the camera lens might provide – and the recognition that all records are both the product of a point of view (both literal and figurative) and of the variables attendant on the medium that captures and records them. As George Levine has astutely summarized it, uncertainty was an intrinsic part of nineteenth-century realism, which should not be regarded as 'a solidly self-satisfied vision based in a misguided objectivity and faith in representation, but a highly self-conscious attempt to explore or create a new reality. Its massive self-confidence implied a radical doubt, its strategies of truth-telling, a profound self-consciousness' (Levine 1981: 19–20). Numerous fictional scenes rely on the uncertainty of visual evidence, and on the dangers of inferring too much from what one sees. In Hardy's *A Pair of Blue Eyes* (1872–3), Elfride observes the young man in whom she's interested, Stephen Smith, in silhouette:

> On the blind was a shadow from somebody close inside it – a person in profile. The profile was unmistakably that of Stephen . . . Then another shadow appeared . . . This was the shadow of a woman. She turned her back towards Stephen: he lifted and held out what now proved to be a shawl or mantle – placed it carefully – *so* carefully – round the lady; disappeared; re-appeared in her front – fastened the mantle. Did he then kiss her? Surely not. Yet the motion *might* have been a kiss. Then both shadows swelled to colossal dimensions – grew distorted – vanished. (Hardy 1965: 42–3)

It later turns out that Stephen is meeting his mother, whom, since she is of a lower class, he has hesitated to introduce to Elfride's family: the distorted spectacle thus serves not just as a reminder about not jumping to conclusions about the evidence which appears to be in front of one's eyes, but it functions metaphorically, suggesting that ideologically forged assumptions can stand in the way of a fair interpretation of human relations.

As well as demonstrating the unreliability of *what* one sees, Hardy continually emphasizes how both spectatorial positioning and personal bias inflects vision. In *The Mayor of Casterbridge* (1886), he offers two perspectives of the same view, the second gradually altering as the traveler nears the town.

> To birds of the more soaring kind Casterbridge must have appeared on this fine evening as a mosaic- work of subdued reds, browns, greys, and crystals, held together by a rectangular frame of deep green. To the level eye of humanity it stood as an indistinct mass behind a dense stockade of limes and chestnuts, set in the midst of miles of rotund down and concave field. The mass became gradually dissected by the vision into towers, gables, chimneys, and casements, the highest glazings shining bleared and bloodshot with the coppery fire they caught from the belt of sunlit cloud in the west. (Hardy 1997: 27–8)

Whatever the point of origin of each line of sight, however, Hardy envisages the scene in terms of formal composition, with shapes and colors balancing one another, the abstract arrangement here regarded as being of equal value to the representational. It is no coincidence that at the time Hardy wrote the novel, he was envisaging the craft of the novelist as being like 'looking at a carpet', when 'by following one colour a certain pattern is suggested, by following another colour, another' (Hardy 1928: 198). Elsewhere, he borrows from the terminology of modern art to reinforce his point about the partiality of point of view. For example, near the beginning of *The Woodlanders* (1887), Marty South's luxurious hair is observed by the covetous, professional eye of Barber Percombe:

> In her present beholder's mind the scene formed by the girlish spar-maker composed itself into an impression-picture of extremest type, wherein the girl's hair alone, as the focus of observation, was depicted with intensity and distinctness, while her face, shoulders, hands, and figure in general were a blurred mass of unimportant detail lost in haze and obscurity. (Hardy 2000: 11)

This combination of clarity and diffusion provides an analogy to the aestheticization of modern consciousness which Walter Pater puts forward in the Conclusion to *The Renaissance* (1873), when, writing of the 'impressions of the individual mind', he explains how each of these impressions is so momentary that it has already departed by the time we have recognized it, and that such transience lies at the heart not just of perception, but of existence:

> all that is actual in it being a single moment, gone while we try to apprehend it, of which it may ever more truly be said that it has ceased to be than that it is. To such a tremulous wisp constantly re-forming itself on the stream, to a single sharp impression, with a sense in it, a relic more or less fleeting, of such moments gone by, what is real in our life fines itself down. It is with this movement, with the passage and dissolution of impressions, images, sensations, that analysis leaves off – that continual vanishing away, that strange, perpetual, weaving and unweaving of ourselves. (Pater 1986: 218–19)

The idea that a novelist should try to catch and hold this flow of impressions lies behind Henry James's conception of the atmosphere of the mind – the mind that will both capture experience and transmute it into imaginative writing – as 'an immense sensibility, a kind of huge spider-web of the finest silken threads suspended in the chamber of consciousness, and catching every air-borne particle in its tissue' (James 1987: 194).

But, as we have already seen, less figurative apparatuses for capturing the moment existed. Hardy, for one, would have resisted drawing too close a parallel between his verbal art and photography – writing during the time that he was composing *The Mayor of Casterbridge* that although his process involved a Ruskinian 'going to Nature', the result was 'no mere photograph, but purely the product of the writer's own mind' (Hardy 1984: 158). Nonetheless the technique had a peculiarly privileged position in relation to the real. As Roland Barthes poignantly put it in *Camera Lucida*, 'from a real body, which was there, proceed radiations which ultimately touch me, who am here; the duration of the transmission is insignificant; the photograph of the missing being, as Sontag says, will touch me like the delayed rays of a star' (Barthes 1981: 80–1). Yet this apparent guarantee that the photograph represented the real could also mislead the gullible, and novelists were ready to exploit this claim to truth-status, adding another twist to the theme of vision's unreliability. Writing with Hawthorne, Hardy, and James particularly in mind, Green-Lewis claims that

> The camera, its products, and its agents provided a potent source not just, as one might anticipate, for self-proclaimed realists in whose work photography could be celebrated as the apotheosis of objectivity but also for the writer of romance and melodrama, whose representations of photography range from uncontrollable magic to harmful science to failed bourgeois realism. Such representations reveal far less about their authors' attitudes toward photography than they do about anxieties regarding their own status as writers of romance in an age of realism. (Green-Lewis 1996: 67)

When, in other words, is it permissible to manipulate, to exaggerate, to fake? Deliberate photographic deception is invariably equated with deplorable behavior. In *Desperate Remedies*, which owes a good deal to the sensation genre, the villain's unmasking depends on Elfride working out that the photographic portrait that Manston was claiming was of his wife must in fact be of another woman. For a while, in Hardy's *A Laodicean* (1881), Paula Power believes in the veracity of a photograph she is shown of her suitor Somerset, which apparently shows him with 'the distorted features and wild attitude of a man advanced in intoxication' (Hardy 1991: 319). In the latter case, the reader is hardly likely to be duped by the fakery, but in the earlier novel, our own credulity is temporarily exploited and then, as with much melodrama, part of the pleasure lies in recognizing the perils of suspending disbelief.

Such suspension is a necessary part of the ghost story, too. Marjorie Garber has drawn a neat parallel between ghosts and the photograph, acknowledging that both are 'original copies' of forever-gone people or events (Garber 1987: 16). Ghosts and hallucinations provide one of the most obvious examples of how Victorian fiction explores and plays upon the idea of the instability of the eye. Sometimes, as with the ghosts of Christmas Past and Christmas Future in *A Christmas Carol*, these apparitions are turned to didactic ends, but increasingly, the presence of ghosts signifies an indeterminacy in interpretation. In Rudyard Kipling's short story 'The Phantom Rickshaw', for example, the reader is left with the option that the phantom is caused by physiological disturbances – or that Western belief systems simply cannot come up with adequate ways of articulating the effects of Indian culture and climate on non-natives. Henry James's 'The Turn of the Screw' leaves it entirely open as to whether Peter Quint and Miss Jessel are actual *revenants*, or the productions of a fantasizing mind of a neurotic governess. In this genre, modern technologies of image reproduction are invoked, and their supposed fidelity called into question – or rather, the credulity of fictional characters is brought into dialog with the reader's own capacity to draw meaning out of an event – or to be unable to do so. Hardy, again, in 'An Imaginative Woman' (1894), tells of a bored married woman who falls in love with the photograph of a poet, who commits suicide shortly after the occasion on which they nearly met in person. Nine months later, she dies giving birth: a couple of years later, her husband compares with horror a photograph he finds in her belongings with his offspring's face: 'By a known but inexplicable trick of Nature there were undoubtedly strong traces of resemblance to the man Ella had never seen; the dreamy and peculiar expression of the poet's face sat, as the transmitted idea, upon the child's . . .' (Hardy 1979: 330). He rejects his own son. Here, it would seem as though the woman has been as 'impressionable' as a piece of chemically treated paper, but *how* this maternal impressioning has worked remains a mystery. Similarly, we are given no explanation as to what was actually visible when, in Kipling's 'At the End of the Passage' (1891), Spurslow emerges pale from the bathroom where he'd just hammered to pieces the film – or even the Kodak camera itself – on which he'd taken photographs of a dead man's eyes, claiming – but neither the other characters nor the reader can quite believe him – that he'd found no image on their eyeballs. Nor is any explanation offered in Charlotte Mew's 'Mark Stafford's Wife' (1904) as to why, when the narrator develops the photographic plate which was taken of Kate the day that she ran off with her lover – only to fall to her death the same evening – the image showed 'the semblance of another face; twisting round, immediately behind her, close over her shoulder; not at first to me a thing human or recognizable, but gradually growing hideously distinct, monstrously familiar – the face of her husband – of Mark himself!' (Mew 1981: 193). Mark had been away from home at the time. In part, all of these examples employ the supernatural to suggest the irrational power of the emotions. But it is significant that these examples are drawn from the short story. This genre, increasingly popular at the end of the century, frequently depended on the imagistic, rather than a narrative worked through in full causative mode. Something occurring on the borders of vision, ambiguously situated within and outside the imagination, was ideally suited to exploit the genre's technical interest in open-endedness.

The *fin de siècle* further challenged the idea of the stability of the visual – and hence the dominance of the realist mode, however nuanced – in a number of other ways. Oscar Wilde's *The Picture of Dorian Gray* (1890) is a work dominated by the power of the senses – smell, touch, sound, and taste, as well as sight. But their unreliability, and hence the unreliability of the material world itself, is underscored by the novel's dominant representation, the painting of Dorian. Notoriously, this canvas *doppelgänger* ages and decays while its subject never loses his golden youthful beauty, however heinous his debaucheries and crimes. The picture's true existence, as an unchanging encapsulation of potential, can only be restored through stabbing – at the cost of the life of the instantly withered and wrinkled Dorian, recognizable only through his external trappings. While an extraordinarily powerful fable about the dangers of separating art and life – among other things – Wilde's novel is not unique, but takes its place in a whole series of 'magic picture' works, which, as Kerry Powell has pointed out, had 'swelled to the proportions of a deluge' by the late 1880s (Powell 1983: 151).

What would it mean to 'believe what one saw' in these pictures? At one's most credulous, one reads them as supernatural objects: a curious twist in the Victorian period's fascination with the material object, and indeed with consumerism: their animism is dependent on the transference of agency from the human world to the world of things. One can project onto them a desire to believe that even inanimate matter is affected by human morality and choices: in an increasingly secular society, possessions take over the position of divine arbiter. But there is a difference in a mass-produced item of furniture behaving in such a manner, and a picture taking on a life of its own – or of its subject – since a painting is conventionally understood as the product not just of human agency, but of an individual's imaginative, aesthetic, and emotional drives. In a way, these magic paintings have run away with the hypothesis of the early Ruskin that each work of art betrays the moral condition of the person who created it – only now, the agency has shifted from representer to represented. More than this, however, these pictures may be seen as stand-ins for another form of creativity: that of fiction. They can be interpreted as covertly expressing the wish that a novel may not be an inert form, but that it has the capacity to transform itself autonomously. Such pictures contain the germ of a desire to abnegate authorial responsibility after a certain point. Once the outlines of character and the design of the plot have been laid down, the interpretive responsibility for a work of fiction belongs to the reader. Novels, that is to say, become surfaces onto which readers will project their own desires, irrespective of the author's original intentions.

This imaging of an abstract issue has, moreover, a wider application. Theodore Adorno commented in *Minima Moralia* that 'the objective tendency of the Enlightenment, to wipe out the power of images over man, is not matched by any subjective progress on the part of enlightened thinking towards freedom from images' (Adorno 1978: 140). Throughout the Victorian period, fiction encouraged its readers to think *through* images. But it also encouraged readers to think, critically and skeptically, about the category of the visual itself. Its deployment of tropes of painting, design, and photography was frequently intended to make its audience aware of the problematics of looking, and to be highly cautious when it came to believing automatically in the fidelity of what it saw.

References and Further Reading

Adorno, Theodore (1978) *Minima Moralia.* New York: Verso.

Altick, Richard D. (1991) *The Presence of the Present: Topics of the Day in the Victorian Novel.* Columbus: Ohio State University Press.

Anderson, Patricia (1991) *The Printed Image and the Transformation of Popular Culture 1790–1860.* Oxford: Clarendon.

Andres, Sophia (1996) Gendered incongruities in George Eliot's Pre-Raphaelite paintings'. *Journal of Pre-Raphaelite Studies,* **5**: 45–60.

Armstrong, Nancy (1991) *Fiction in the Age of Photography: The Legacy of British Realism.* Cambridge, MA: Harvard University Press.

Austin, Linda (1987) Painterly perspective and authority in Victorian writings. *Mosaic,* **22**: 71–80.

Barthes, Roland (1981) *Camera Lucida. Reflections on Photography.* Translated by Richard Howard. New York: Farrar, Straus and Giroux.

Bellis, Peter J. (1987) In the window-seat: Vision and power in *Jane Eyre*. *English Literary History*, **54**: 639–42.

Benjamin, Walter (1972) A short history of photography. *Screen*, **13**: 5–26.

Braddon, Mary (1987) *Lady Audley's Secret*. Oxford: Oxford University Press.

Brattin, Joel (1985) Dickens' creation of Bradley headstone. *Dickens Studies Annual*, **14**: 147–65.

Brontë, Charlotte (1900) *Villette*. New York and London: Harper and Brothers.

Brown, Monika (1990) Dutch painters and British novel-readers: *Adam Bede* in the context of Victorian cultural literacy. *Victorians Institute Journal*, **18**: 113–32.

Bullen, J. B. (1986) *The Expressive Eye: Fiction and Perception in the Work of Thomas Hardy*. Oxford: Clarendon.

Byerly, Alison (1997) *Realism, Representation, and the Arts in Nineteenth-Century Literature*. Cambridge: Cambridge University Press.

Christ, Carol, and Jordan, John (eds.) (1995) *Victorian Literature and the Victorian Visual Imagination*. Berkeley: University of California Press.

Craik, Dinah (1996). *Olive*. Oxford: Oxford University Press.

Crary, Jonathan (1990) *Techniques of the Observer: On Vision and Modernity in the Nineteenth Century*. Cambridge, MA: MIT Press.

Denisoff, Dennis (1999) Lady in green with novel: the gendered economics of the visual arts and mid-Victorian women's writing. In Nicola Diane Thompson (ed.) *Victorian Women Writers and the Woman Question*, pp. 151–69. Cambridge: Cambridge University Press.

Dickens, Charles (1994) *Little Dorrit*. Harmondsworth: Penguin.

——(1996) *Great Expectations*. Harmondsworth: Penguin.

Dingley, Robert (2001) The unreliable camera: Photography as evidence in mid-Victorian fiction. *Victorian Review*, **27**: 42–55.

Eliot, George (1963) *Essays of George Eliot*. Edited by Thomas Pinney. New York: New York University Press.

——(1977) *Middlemarch*. New York: W. W. Norton.

——(1980) *Felix Holt, The Radical*. Oxford: Clarendon Press.

——(1985) *Adam Bede*. Harmondsworth: Penguin.

——(1990) *Selected Essays, Poems and Other Writings*. Edited by A. S. Byatt and Nicholas Warren. Harmondsworth: Penguin.

Flaxman, Rhoda L. (1987) *Victorian Word-Painting and Narrative: Toward the Blending of Genres*. Ann Arbor: University of Michigan Press.

Flint, Kate (2000) *The Victorians and the Visual Imagination*. Cambridge: Cambridge University Press.

Forster, J. (1928) *Life of Dickens*. Edited and Annotated with an Introduction by J. W. T. Ley. London: Cecil Palmer.

Garber, Marjorie (1987) *Shakespeare's Ghost Writers*. New York: Methuen.

Goldman, Paul (1996) *Victorian Illustration: The Pre-Raphaelites, the Idyllic School and the High Victorians*. Aldershot: Scolar.

Green-Lewis, Jennifer (1996) *Framing the Victorians: Photography and the Culture of Realism*. Ithaca: Cornell University Press.

Grundy, Jane (1979) *Hardy and the Sister Arts*. New York: Barnes and Noble.

Hall, N. John (1980) *Trollope and His Illustrators*. London: Macmillan.

Hardy, Thomas (1965) *A Pair of Blue Eyes*. London: Macmillan.

——(1979) *The Distracted Preacher and Other Tales*. Harmondsworth: Penguin.

——(1984) *The Life and Work of Thomas Hardy*. Edited by Michael Millgate. London and Basingstoke: Macmillan.

——(1991) *A Laodicean*. Oxford and New York: Oxford University Press.

——(1991) *Desperate Remedies*. Harmondsworth: Penguin.

——(1997) *The Mayor of Casterbridge*. Harmondsworth: Penguin.

——(2000) *The Woodlanders*. Oxford: Oxford University Press.

Hardy, Thomas and Florence Hardy (1928, vol. I; 1930, vol. II) *Life of Thomas Hardy*, 2 vols. London: Macmillan.

Harvey, John R. (1971) *Victorian Novelists and Their Illustrators*. New York: New York University Press.

Heady, Emily Walker (2002) The negative's capability: Real images and the allegory of the unseen in Dickens's Christmas books. *Dickens Studies Annual*, **31**: 1–21.

Hinton, James (1871) Seeing with the eyes shut (1862), reprinted in *Thoughts on Health, and Some of its Conditions*. London: Smith, Elder.

Ivins, William Mills Jr. (1953) *Prints and Visual Communication*. London: Routledge.

Jackson, Arlene (1984) Photography as style and metaphor in the art of Thomas Hardy. *Thomas Hardy Annual* 2, ed. Norman Page. London: Macmillan.

James, Henry (1899) *The Awkward Age*. New York. Scribner.

——(1987) The art of fiction. In *The Critical Muse: Selected Literary Criticism*. Harmondsworth: Penguin.

Krasner, James (1992) *The Entangled Eye*. New York: Oxford University Press.

Lettis, Richard (1985) Dickens and art. *Dickens Studies Annual*, **14**: 93–146.

Levy, Amy (1993) *The Complete Novels and Selected Writings of Amy Levy 1861–1889*. Edited by Melvyn New. Gainesville: University Press of Florida.

Levine, George (1981) *The Realistic Imagination*. Chicago: University of Chicago Press.

Lewes, G. H. (1860) Seeing is believing. *Blackwood's Edinburgh Magazine*, **88**: 381–95.

——(1898) *The Principles of Success in Literature*. Ed. T. Sharper Knowlson. London: Walter Scott.

Meisel, Martin (1983) *Realizations: Narrative, Pictorial, and Theatrical Arts in Nineteenth-Century England*. Princeton: Princeton University Press.

Mew, Charlotte (1981) *Collected Poems and Prose*. Edited by Val Warner. Manchester: Carcanet.

Miller, Andrew H. (1995) *Novels Behind Glass: Commodity Culture and Victorian Narrative*. Cambridge: Cambridge University Press.

Nadel, Ira Bruce (1977) Wonderful deception: Art and the artist in *Little Dorrit*. *Criticism: A Quarterly for Literature and the Arts*, **19**: 17–33.

Pater, Walter (1986) *Walter Pater: Three Major Texts* (The Renaissance, Appreciations *and* Imaginary Portraits). New York and London: New York University Press.

Powell, Kerry (1983) Tom, Dick, and Dorian Gray: Magic-picture mania in late Victorian fiction. *Philological Quarterly*, **62**: 147–70.

Ray, Gordon N. (1976) *The Illustrator and the Book in England from 1790 to 1914*. Oxford: Oxford University Press.

Reade, Charles (1856) *'It is never too late to Mend': A Matter of Fact Romance*, 2 vols. London: Bentley.

Roston, Murray (1996) *Victorian Contexts: Literature and the Visual Arts*. New York: New York University Press.

Smith, Lindsay (1995) *Victorian Photography, Painting and Poetry: The Enigma of Visibility in Ruskin, Morris and the Pre-Raphaelites*. Cambridge: Cambridge University Press.

Spiegel, Alan (1976) *Fiction and the Camera Eye: Visual Consciousness in Film and the Modern Novel*. Charlottesville: University Press of Virginia.

Steig, Michael (1978) *Dickens and 'Phiz'*. Bloomington: Indiana University Press.

Wakeman, Geoffrey (1973) *Victorian Book Illustration: The Technical Revolution*. Detroit. Gale Research.

Witemeyer, Hugh (1979) *George Eliot and the Visual Arts*. New Haven: Yale University Press.

Chapter 3

'The boundaries of social intercourse': Class in the Victorian Novel

James Eli Adams

> Old provincial society had its share of this subtle movement: had not only its striking downfalls, its brilliant young professional dandies who ended by living up an entry with a drab and six children for their establishment, but also those less marked vicissitudes which are constantly shifting the boundaries of social intercourse, and begetting new consciousness of interdependence. Some slipped a little downward, some got higher footing: people denied aspirates, gained wealth, and fastidious gentlemen stood for boroughs . . . (*Middlemarch* ch. 11: 97)

In the middle of the night, in the middle of the high road, the hero of Wilkie Collins's *The Woman in White* (1860) is startled by a touch on his shoulder, and turns to find 'the figure of a solitary Woman':

> There was nothing wild, nothing immodest in her manner: it was quiet and self-controlled, a little melancholy and a little touched by suspicion; not exactly the manner of a lady, and, at the same time, not the manner of a woman in the humblest ranks of life. (Epoch I, ch. 4: 24)

It is bewildering, because contrary to all social norms, to encounter a solitary woman thus. To make sense of the situation, Walter Hartright needs to place her within the social order, which entails trying to read her 'manner' as a sign of her social standing. He seems to feel secure in his command of that language, and trusts that his audience likewise will understand what 'a lady' and 'a woman in the humblest ranks' might be expected to look like. In this presumption Hartright is not at all eccentric; his response is echoed in countless Victorian novels, which suggest how powerfully social life is structured by the hierarchy of class – so much so that Victorians could hardly make sense of the world without it. Yet the encounter also marks a crisis, inasmuch as the figure eludes secure placement. The woman remains a mystery, Hartright remains unsettled, and we are plunged into a plot in which class identity becomes most pressing when it seems least secure, when the people one meets elude or confuse the distinctions of class.

The Woman in White thus encapsulates a dynamic writ large in the Victorian novel. The language and experience of social class become especially insistent themes in the novel in conjunction with new forms of social mobility in nineteenth-century Britain, but such mobility in turn frequently generates crises of understanding because it strains existing categories. Hence the sort of confusion we observe in Dickens's *Great Expectations* (1860–1), as Pip is bewildered by his own rapid social ascent. 'I was a blacksmith's boy but yesterday; I am – what shall I say I am – to-day?' (ch. 30: 248). Here Hartright's scrutiny is turned inward, and generates what we have since come to call an identity crisis. Such crises are not something new to the nineteenth century – Oedipus had an even worse time of it – but Dickens's novel suggests that the experience will become newly pervasive in a world that affords such transformations as Pip undergoes.

Beginning in the latter half of the eighteenth century, the development of steam power in Britain gave rise to a newly dynamic industrial economy, in which forms of mechanized production transformed not only the rhythms of daily life but also the very sense of human possibility. The impacts on social order were profound and paradoxical. On the one hand, the new economy offered unrivalled potential for the accumulation (and loss) of capital, and hence for social mobility. As never before in history, 'rags to riches' could seem something more than a fairy-tale transformation gained by plunder or a king's favor. At the same time, however, the rise of industrial capitalism led individuals to see themselves locked into economic conflict with those who occupied different roles in the dynamics of production. In the preindustrial economic order, social hierarchy was presumed to be harmonized by reciprocal bonds of moral obligation. Under capitalism, those bonds seemed increasingly subsumed by contractual arrangements and economic transactions, within which every individual competed to maximize his own self-interest. 'We call it a Society', wrote

Thomas Carlyle in 1843, 'and go about professing openly the totalest separation, isolation. Our life is not a mutual helpfulness; but rather, cloaked under due laws-of-war, named "fair competition" and so forth, it is a mutual hostility' (p. 148). As 'cash payment', in Carlyle's rendering, became the foundation of human relations, individuals discovered forms of collective affiliation through shared economic interests; factory workers, for example, came to see themselves as members of a group inherently at odds with their employer. With this development, a new form of social awareness came into being: the modern experience of social class.

The experience of class in nineteenth-century Britain would have an impact around the world, particularly through its analysis in the writings of Karl Marx. Yet whereas Marx understood class conflict in purely economic terms, more recent scholarship has tended to study class as the elaboration of an entire way of life (Hall et al. 2000: 13–20). Class in this view entails a complex mediation between economic and social orders, which depends on recognition across a wide social spectrum – a form of social exchange that the novel was especially well equipped to represent. As it requires recognition from others, social class frequently becomes entangled with status hierarchies that seem arcane or downright arbitrary – but nonetheless powerful. 'It is indisputable that while you cannot possibly be genteel and bake', remarks a bemused Herbert Pocket in *Great Expectations*, 'you may be as genteel as never was and brew' (ch. 22: 180). Class affiliation is further complicated by the inertial force of ancestry, which acts as a brake on social mobility (both upward and downward). The individual who realized a new level of income or economic activity rarely escaped the suspicions attached to the *parvenu* or *arriviste*, whose social standing hovered uneasily between established classes (the proliferation of such terms in the nineteenth century in itself suggests the conservative dynamics of class). As a rule, secure class membership tended to be reserved for those born into the relevant milieu; the triumphs of the upwardly mobile could only be fully enjoyed by their children, or more remote descendants. (Hence frequent snide remarks in Victorian novels about characters who wouldn't know their own grandparents.) Conversely, families that had descended economically might cling to an ever-more distant affiliation with a higher class. Dickens in particular savors the mingled pathos and snobbery of this predicament, offering a gallery of portraits of wounded gentility who sustain their self-worth by dwelling in the past. Ancestry might also subtly divide individuals within the same economic groups: does a university tutor of aristocratic descent, for example, belong to the same class as a colleague whose father was a grocer?

Given such complications, one can sympathize with the outsider baffled by the intricacies of Victorian social hierarchy: 'Gracious', exclaims the young American heroine of Henry James's *Portrait of a Lady* (1881), 'how many classes have they? About fifty, I suppose' (ch. 6: 110). But these subtleties typically were articulated within the framework of a broadly tripartite pyramid, which persisted from an older discourse (Adam Smith in *The Wealth of Nations* referred to three 'interests' or 'orders' in society, see Briggs 1983: 11). At the (very narrow) top, the upper class comprised primarily the aristocracy and landed gentry, whose income derived principally from the ownership of land. Over the course of the century, it increasingly accommodated families who had amassed large fortunes in industry and commerce – one of many developments that complicated class boundaries. Then came the broad middle class, comprising those engaged in either the professions or 'trade', which might include anything from banking to manufacturing to retail exchange, so long as it entailed the ownership of capital or stock, and extending down into a borderland of office workers, many of whom made little more than well-trained craftsmen, but who clung to a place in the upper half of George Gissing's memorable division of society into 'those who do, and those who do not, wear collars' (Keating 1971: 30). At the broad base of the pyramid, much the largest in population, were 'the working classes', whose property inhered almost entirely in their labor power. This group encompassed highly skilled artisans – the 'labor aristocracy', such as watchmakers, tool makers, and iron workers – lesser skilled or unskilled laborers, of whom agricultural workers formed the largest category, domestic servants, and finally a variable but large number of the desperately poor (often, but not always, unemployed) referred to variously as 'paupers' or (later in the century) 'the residuum'. As many commentators note, the distinction between 'working class' and 'poor' is especially unstable: given low wages and erratic employment, nearly all members of the working class at times lived in poverty.

Of course the boundaries in such schemes always are blurred. Quite apart from the subtle but momentous gradations within the large strata – as between 'squires' and 'farmers', for example – the division even between working class and middle class could be elusive: 'trade', for example, was a term that might well blur distinctions between highly skilled artisans, who owned their own tools and perhaps even workshops, and 'manufacturers' (indeed, at the beginning of the century that term actually referred to those who worked with their hands). But the large structures of class offered a framework within which historical individuals experienced, and novelists attempted to represent, far more complex and highly individuated forms of experience and identity. One of the special appeals of the novel was precisely the intricacy with which it drew 'the boundaries of social intercourse', in Eliot's phrase, and evoked a sharply particularized social psychology, often through resistance to large categories. The novel seemed a discourse uniquely suited to capture the textures of social interaction, aspiration, conflict, and anxiety, within which social hierarchy could seem both a barrier and a stimulus to new awareness, including (again in Eliot's terms) 'new consciousness of interdependence' connecting disparate individuals and groups. The novel achieved this primarily through focus on private life, on forms of experience ostensibly insulated from the world of economic and political conflict. Victorian domesticity was proverbially a refuge from the rough and tumble of a newly volatile economy, but the ideal was itself a marker of material success – it required income sufficient to exempt a woman from paid labor – and at the same time could not seal off a host of social anxieties. Indeed, domestic life was the realm in which the most anxious of classes, the middle, made their most energetic claims to status.

Not only were they vulnerable to economic upheaval, but middle-class ideals of self-determination also energized a more subtle web of social anxieties that figure centrally in the Victorian novel. With enhanced geographical mobility and the declining importance (however gradual) of kinship and patronage, social exchange of all kinds increasingly brought one into contact with strangers, with whom one had to negotiate an appropriate, mutual recognition of social standing. In a world where personal or family history no longer offered a ready guide to social identity, the interpretation of strangers had to rely more on palpable social signs: dress, speech, behavior, place of residence, style of living. Thus the emblematic social importance that so many novels locate in outwardly trivial distinctions: whether one used wax or tallow candles, for example, or wore satin rather than silk dresses. Much of the elaborate etiquette we think of as distinctively Victorian – rituals of introduction, calling cards, the chaperoning of unmarried women, intricate decorums of dress – is at root a strategy for dealing with social mobility. Etiquette, that is, affirms one's own claims to social recognition while at the same time sustaining a social distance that allows one confidently to 'place' new acquaintances (Davidoff 1973). Like any system of signs, however, the markers of social class generated challenges – and occasionally crises – of interpretation. Most radically, those signs could be used to deceive, to fabricate social identities at odds with personal character and history – a possibility that agitates a wide range of Victorian novels, from narratives of financial scandal to the vogue of 'sensation fiction' of the 1860s, in which narratives of blackmail and exposure figure prominently. In the most searching explorations of this theme, the very boundary of public and private begins to dissolve, and we find ourselves on the threshold of what cultural critics a century later will call 'the performing self'.

As it represents these social codes and the forms of desire bound up with them, the novel is an extraordinarily rich guide to Victorian culture. But of course the novel is not a transparent medium. Its representations are shaped by narrative structure and convention, which are themselves powerfully responsive to class consciousness. Most obviously, the novel gives a prominence to upper-class and middle-class life out of all proportion to actual population – but in line with collective wealth. In 1867, upper-class households, those earning more than 1000 pounds per year, amounted to less than 1/2 of one percent of the population. Only another one and a half percent earned a securely middle-class income of between 300 and 1000 pounds per year. A further 24 percent hovered on the fringes of the middle class, with incomes of between 75 and 300 pounds. This left nearly 75 percent of the population, most of whom lived by manual labor, with incomes of 73 pounds or less. On aggregate, however, the most affluent 2 percent of households received 37 percent of national income – as much as the entire working class, which made up three-quarters of the population (Perkin 1985: 420).

These statistics alone suggest the bias of the novel toward representation of more affluent modes of life. Within those representations, novelists devote much energy to discriminating between aristocratic and middle-class value systems, which frequently are embodied in an emblematic juxtaposition of female characters. This pattern is rehearsed in a number of familiar novels: Estella and Biddy in *Great Expectations*, Rosamond Vincy and Mary Garth in *Middlemarch* (1871–2), Lizzie Eustace and Lucy Morris in *The Eustace Diamonds* (1873), but perhaps most memorably in *Jane Eyre* (1847). In Brontë's novel, an aristocratic order that locates value in wealth and kinship finds its expression in Blanche Ingram: beautiful, elegant, theatrical, and disdainful of all outside her sphere, she incarnates aristocratic luxury and display in her very body, which is doubled in the more overt, and explicitly erotic, pathology of Bertha Rochester. In Jane, by contrast – 'poor, disconnected, and plain' – Blanche's ornamental being is countered by an ideal of inner worth, of moral character located in earnestness, independence, and self-discipline (emblematically, Blanche delights in paying charades, whereas Jane has never heard of the activity). The aristocrat and the madwoman thus become foils to a fundamentally middle-class ethos – which of course ultimately is embraced by Rochester as well. This contrast incorporates a momentous social and cultural history. From the first half of the eighteenth century, writers had associated the growing economic power of the 'middling' ranks with a new moral authority, which reflected the enduring force of puritanism in English life. Over against an aristocracy grown idle, profligate, and dissolute, so it was increasingly argued (the reigns of the Georges offered ample cautionary tales), those who earned their living through trade had proven themselves energetic, earnest, resourceful, and disciplined (both economically and sexually). Here were virtues that drew on an ideal of individual character and self-determination rather than inherited rank and connections of kinship or patronage.

The fabled ethos of 'Victorianism' thus began to take shape well before the Queen came to the throne, and was developed with special force within the novel, where we see that ethos reflected not only in plot conventions, but in the structures of novelistic character. 'Realistic' character, as contrasted with techniques derived from melodrama or romance, becomes associated above all with a sense of interiority or psychic depth, which is the sign of strongly individuated and autonomous powers of action and reflection, directed by an independent consciousness that struggles against social determination. Such autonomy, as Regenia Gagnier and other scholars have pointed out, was much less readily accessible to the working classes. The middle-class virtues of modesty and self-restraint also resonate powerfully with the basic skepticism of novelistic realism. From the time of *Don Quixote* novelists have insisted on their fidelity to a reality that has power to resist or thwart fantasy, and have denigrated other literary forms, such as fairy tale or romance, that encourage dreaming and wish-fulfillment. Given this emphasis, fantasies like those of Rosamond Vincy in *Middlemarch* – 'Here was Mr. Lydgate . . . possessing connections which offered vistas of that middle-class heaven, rank' (ch. 12: 118) – typically are doomed to disappointment. But the chastening of fantasy also affirms a particular ordering of society: Rosamond's 'dreamland' is a yearning for aristocratic life that is not only beyond her means but morally shallow, a dream of indolent luxury, which is set against the clear-sighted, energetic self-reliance of her cousin, Mary Garth. This might seem a fundamentally conservative stance, which would have the middle classes affirm their moral pre-eminence by renouncing the desire to be anything else. The criticism strikes home equally, however, at the complacency of the aristocracy, which in a number of novels is emblematically humbled by figures of disciplined desire. Thus Jane Eyre, for example, famously attempts to repress her desire for Rochester because, as she tells herself, 'He is not of your order', yet she ultimately overcomes that barrier. Her social ascent confirms a moral triumph: through her self-denial, Jane surpasses and ultimately displaces her ostensible rival, the aristocratic Blanche Ingram, who is a creature of unreflective appetite.

As both *Middlemarch* and *Jane Eyre* suggest, the growing cultural authority of the middle class did not extinguish the allure of aristocratic social forms. Indeed, the influence of film and television adaptations of Victorian fiction, with their eye for country houses, opulent interiors, and elegantly idle characters, may lull us into thinking of the novel as a primarily aristocratic form. In fact, however, aristocratic life has a relatively marginal (albeit vivid) place in the Victorian novel, and figures most prominently in works that aim to capture a broad spectrum of social life – whether in the smaller and more tightly woven communities of provincial towns (Gaskell's *Wives and Daughters* (1864–6), Eliot's *Felix Holt* (1866), Trollope's *Barchester Towers* (1857)) or in self-consciously panoramic treatments with primarily urban settings (Thackeray's *Vanity Fair* (1847–8), Dickens's *Bleak House* (1852–3), Trollope's *The Way We Live Now* (1875)). Within such novels, both the narrative point of view and the protagonists themselves typically incarnate distinctly middle-class perspectives. The aristocracy and landed gentry frequently embody forms of tradition and continuity set against (for better or worse) the currents of social change. Landed property in particular often figures as an ideal of stability within a more volatile world of capital and credit, an association that, when combined with the enduring cachet of aristocratic styles of life, may explain why so may successful manufacturers left 'trade' behind and turned their profits to the purchase of country estates. Yet novels also register an inexorable shift of power toward a newer order – as in Dickens's *Bleak House*, where the aging Sir Leicester Dedlock – the surname speaks volumes – ultimately yields to the rising ironmaster and newly elected M.P. Rouncewell, who is the son of Sir Leicester's housekeeper. In the six Palliser novels of Trollope (1864–80), which center on

parliamentary intrigue and the extended circle of the wryly titled Duke of Omnium, the action focuses on rising young men of more humble backgrounds: Phineas Finn, Frank Greystoke, and others. Even the suave, paternalistic aristocrats of Disraeli's 'young England' trilogy (1844–7) operate within an explicit apology for continued aristocratic predominance in Parliament, which registers the pressure of growing resentment from below. In every case, the aristocratic world retains a fundamental exoticism; it is presented from the vantage of outsiders, whether as an object of eager emulation or as a foil to the moral striving that ostensibly characterizes less affluent modes of life. This remains true even toward the end of the century, in novels such as James's *Portrait of a Lady* or Oscar Wilde's *The Picture of Dorian Gray* (1891), where aristocratic glamour is bound up less with politics than with the pursuit of artistic culture: traditions of aristocratic connoisseurship are recast through the lens of aestheticism, and wealth becomes the basis for cultivating a life of epicurean pleasures.

Most often, the aristocracy and landed gentry figure in the Victorian novel as an insular, self-absorbed world, frequently decaying from its own inanition, even as it decries the bourgeois energy that threatens to displace it. Again Dickens's Sir Leicester is characteristic, though his wife, Lady Dedlock, experiences more fully the potentially suffocating confinement of affluence – a pattern that is enacted with special vividness in George Eliot's later heroines such as Mrs. Transome in *Felix Holt*, Dorothea Brooke in *Middlemarch*, and Gwendolen Harleth in *Daniel Deronda* (1876), for all of whom life becomes, in the terms of *Felix Holt*, 'a well-cushioned despair' (ch. 49: 592). This emphasis hearkens back to the earliest appeals to class interest in Britain, which divided the world into two classes, the productive and unproductive, although the contrast becomes more complex over the course of the period – perhaps reflecting a gradually more assured sense of middle-class ascendancy. Dickens's career is especially telling in this regard: his early novels, such as *Nicholas Nickleby* (1838–9), are full of conventional aristocratic predators drawn from stage melodrama, but from the 1850s these figures give way to the more complex representations of upper-class 'grey men', as they have been called: deracinated, aimless idlers such as James Harthouse in *Hard Times* (1854), Charles Darnay in *A Tale of Two Cities* (1859), Eugene Wrayburn in *Our Mutual Friend* (1864–5). These figures associate social privilege with waste and squandered possibility, which can be redeemed only through self-sacrifice and earnest devotion – qualities typically realized through submission to romantic love for a woman who realizes those virtues.

The pattern broadly parallels the juxtaposition of aristocratic and middle-class women, as a contrast between elegant, self-absorbed display and a realm of inner being – in particular, a capacity for earnest, selfless devotion – associated with domestic womanhood.

As such humblings of aristocratic manhood (actual or aspiring) echo in novels as diverse as *Jane Eyre, Middlemarch,* Braddon's *Lady Audley's Secret* (1862), and (sardonically) Hardy's *Tess of the D'Urbervilles* (1891), they point to a contest over the most potent of status markers for men, the idea of the gentleman. As a marker of elite social status, the norm was traditionally associated principally with inherited rank, but also with a host of virtues derived ultimately from a martial ethos: independence, courage, fidelity, and above all, honor. The gentleman, so this ethos implied, was free from concern for the grubby particulars of self-interest that characterized 'trade', a traditional object of aristocratic disdain. Novelists had great fun with this taboo – Thackeray in *Vanity Fair* sketches bullying schoolboys 'who rightly considered that the selling of goods at retail is a shameful and infamous practice, meriting the contempt and scorn of all gentlemen' (ch. 5: 48) – but the prejudice was deeply engrained in upper-class circles. Thomas Arnold, for example, the famous 'reforming' headmaster of Rugby School, excluded any 'retail trader' from 'the circle of gentlemen' (Honey 1977: 33). The snobbish Mrs. Gibson in Gaskell's *Wives and Daughters* similarly chides her stepdaughter for dancing with the sons of merchants: 'if you go on this way, you will have to shake hands over the counter tomorrow morning with some of your partners of tonight' (ch. 26: 324). Over against such attitudes, the rising economic and political influence attached to mercantile and industrial wealth (as distinct from ownership of land) naturally led to efforts to wrest the idea of the gentleman from its traditional associations, to make it more emphatically a moral ideal. 'When I use the term, gentleman', announces Twemlow on the final page of Dickens's *Our Mutual Friend,* 'I use it in the sense in which the degree may be attained by any man' (Book 4, ch. 17: 891). *Vanity Fair,* for example, despite its cynicism is centrally preoccupied with the nature of the gentleman: in a world where the aristocracy offers little but corruption, two sons of mercantile wealth – George Osborne and William Dobbin – embody competing versions of the ideal, in which the more dashing but ultimately shallow and heartless aristocratic version is shown up by the outwardly unprepossessing but selfless integrity and devotion of the new.

Of course as it demanded something beyond mere wealth for social recognition, the idea of the gentleman might also be a means of resisting mobility. A more overt challenge to traditional norms of inherited rank was embodied in another model of masculine identity: the self-made man. A host of Victorian conduct and inspirational literature – most famously, Samuel Smiles's best-selling *Self-Help* (1859) – celebrated the possibilities for social advancement and self-determination that awaited those with sufficient talent, initiative, and self-discipline. The self-made man was an apotheosis of the bourgeois ethos, the very quintessence of the power of self-determination, and as such a recurrent feature of the Victorian novel, perhaps most strikingly in Dinah Craik's best-selling *John Halifax, Gentleman* (1856). As the admiring narrator puts it, Halifax 'was indebted to no forefathers for a family history . . . the chronicle commenced with himself, and was his own making' (ch. 1: 11). Yet this fantasy of perfect autonomy – of owing nothing to anything but one's own powers – naturally aroused skepticism and suspicion. Hardy's *Jude the Obscure* (1895) is only the most memorable of a host of novels evoking the persistent social prejudice that hobbled working-class aspirations. More often, novelists were engaged by the ease with which ambition shaded into self-mystifying ruthlessness. In *Hard Times*, for example, the banker Josiah Bounderby thumbs his nose at the established order by insisting that he was 'brought up in the gutter' – but this proud defiance conceals the existence of a loving and eminently respectable mother, whose presence compromises Bounderby's dream of immaculate self-conception.

Elsewhere in the novel fictions of self-fashioning devolve into more far-reaching and destructive webs of fraud. This emphasis responds in part to actual financial scandals, such as the spectacular collapse of George Hudson 'the railway king' in 1849. Almost invariably, however, specifically financial deception is enveloped in more diffuse anxieties aroused by social encounters with strangers. 'Have no antecedents, no established character, no cultivation, no ideas, no manners. Have shares' – so the narrator of Dickens's *Our Mutual Friend* remarks of the Lammles, shadowy acquaintances of the tellingly named Veneerings (Book I, ch. 10: 60–1). One response to this anxiety was the increasingly elaborate articulation of class markers in the period: from etiquette to styles of dress to public school education to modes of speech to vigilant enforcement of 'respectability' among the lower middle and working classes. But reliance on such signs brought with it the prospect captured by the Veneerings: that social identity might itself become wholly externalized, a mode of performance that concealed, or even replaced, some more essential self. A host of major novels – *Vanity Fair*, Dickens's *Little Dorrit* (1855–7), *Lady Audley's Secret, Our Mutual Friend,*

Middlemarch, The Way We Live Now – chart the social rise and fall of brilliantly resourceful performers, whose careers remind us that the term 'credit' (from Latin *credere*, to believe) links financial commitment to a more encompassing faith in appearances.

Such virtuoso performance tends to be especially unsettling in female characters, largely because it seems to ally social mobility with seduction, perhaps even prostitution. For women, virtually the sole avenue to social ascent came through marriage. Whereas men could lay claim to middle-class standing through independent action, women remained 'relative creatures', who derived their status principally from their relation to men. 'We don't ask what a woman does – we ask whom she belongs to', remarks Mr. Wakem in George Eliot's *The Mill on the Floss* (1860) (Book 6, ch. 8: 542–3). The consequent obstacles to self-determination among middle-class women – compounded by the constraints of the domestic ideal – help to explain the remarkable prominence of the governess in Victorian fiction. Employment as a governess was one of the very few forms of independent economic agency available to middle-class women, but for that reason it defined a precarious, even paradoxical social position. A governess needed to possess sufficient social standing to avoid compromising the respectability of the family that employed her to watch over its children, yet the very fact of being paid for her services challenged the ideal of middle-class womanhood as a place outside the realm of exchange. The figure thus brought into focus the stresses besetting middle-class women who wished to shape a life outside of domesticity; it also captured anxieties such aspirations might arouse in the society at large. As an independent, unmarried, but nominally middle-class woman living within another family's household, the governess was readily associated with various forms of hidden design – which typically devolved into some form of sexual threat, inasmuch as marriage remained a woman's most secure route to social advance. This is the thread that links Thackeray's Becky Sharp to the title character of *Lady Audley's Secret* (the liminal social standing of the governess made her an especially apt figure of mystery and danger in sensation fiction). Alongside such figures of spectacular transgression we encounter many governesses of more modest ambitions: Brontë's Jane Eyre and Lucy Snowe (in *Vilette* (1853)), Clare Kirkpatrick in *Wives and Daughters*, Lucy Morris in *The Eustace Diamonds*, to name only a few.

The predicament of the governess also throws into sharp relief the fear of social decline that shadows so much Victorian fiction. Though a single woman of middle-class background but no independent income was especially vulnerable to loss of status, virtually the whole of the middle class was exposed to economic volatility that could cost them income or employment, and thus their social position. (For the poor, the more immediate fear was less social stigma than starvation.) Though the consequent falls could be precipitous – witness the bankruptcies of Sedley in *Vanity Fair*, Dombey in Dickens's *Dombey and Son* (1847–8), Melmotte in *The Way We Live Now* – the fear of decline seems to have been especially gnawing in that expanding section of society that came to be known as the lower middle class. (The term was 'now fashionable', noted a review of Eliot's *Silas Marner* (1861), see Young 1999: 84.) This group comprised the very large group of office workers and retail employees, but also more humble forms of literature and journalism (the latter of which Gissing famously chronicled in *New Grub Street* (1891)). The 'shabby genteel', as this class was known, had its special laureate in Dickens, who was himself famously an offspring of this milieu (his father was a fitfully employed government clerk, memorialized in the figure of Micawber in *David Copperfield* (1849–50)). Dickens's novels find a rich mixture of comedy and pathos in the economic struggles of those clinging to the skirts of respectability, such as the Wilfers in *Our Mutual Friend* or the Pockets in *Great Expectations*. But the anguish associated with social decline as something akin to contamination may be most hauntingly evoked in chapter 34 of *Oliver Twist* (1837–8), where Oliver, dozing in the security of the Maylies' drawing-room, catches a terrifying glimpse of Fagin looking in at the window, as if incarnating the specter of poverty from which Oliver has been rescued.

The lower middle class was at the same time a threshold for the upwardly mobile, but as such it was frequently a butt of comedy. From the late 1830s, Thackeray and Dickens joined with *Fraser's Magazine*, *Punch*, and other periodicals in caricaturing 'the gent', a callow, awkward young man whose ill-fitting clothing and over-eager manners shabbily mimicked those of the more affluent classes he aspired to join: 'Chick' Smallweed in *Bleak House* epitomizes the type. Frequently feminized and 'little', the gent embodies a kind of social impotence – which makes his prominence rather perplexing. Arlene Young has argued, however, that the figure was not only a displacement of middle-class anxieties about appearing vulgar, but also the embodiment of an expanding class that threatened to dilute middle-class distinction. Not until the 1880s does the lower middle class start to come into its own as an object of more serious representation, which reflects not only its continued expansion, but also a newly prominent influx of single women into its ranks, particularly as office workers. As these workers came to occupy expanding suburbs, they were recognized as a significant sociological development in their own right, famously memorialized in Mr. Pooter, the protagonist of the Grossmiths' *Diary of a Nobody* (1892).

Representations of the working class in the Victorian novel tend to be riven by ambivalence. Seen as they are through predominantly middle-class eyes, to a remarkable extent the poor come into sustained focus in the novel in conjunction with social problems: poverty, unemployment, squalid housing, factory conditions, child labor, political unrest. In such contexts, novelistic and humanitarian engagements are closely intertwined. Gaskell's *Mary Barton* (1848), for example, is keen to illuminate the sufferings of unemployed industrial workers, particularly as that understanding might help to explain the labor unrest that unsettled many of her middle-class readers. At the same time, however, the poor remained a class apart – worthy of sympathy, but rarely objects of close acquaintance, and when considered *en masse*, often the source of a mingled revulsion and fear. One byproduct of the moralizing of social mobility – the insistence that virtue would be rewarded – was a widespread sense that poverty was somehow deserved. As Bulwer put it in 1833, 'In other countries poverty is a misfortune; with us it is a crime' (p. 34). The consequent shame often attached to lower-class standing is vividly anatomized in *Great Expectations*, where Estella so readily persuades the young Pip that he is 'coarse and common': 'Her contempt was so strong, that it became contagious, and I caught it' (ch. 8: 60). Relationships between the poor and more affluent classes (beyond mere economic transactions) were notoriously uncommon, and almost always associated with moral laxity and danger. One realm for such relations was the sporting world of pugilism, horse-trading, and gambling, where confident young gentlemen like Fred Vincy in *Middlemarch* typically find themselves victimized by working-class sharps. A parallel realm was the '*demi-monde*', where affluent men typically mingled with women of lower rank and social daring, who made their living catering to male pleasures, as barmaids, dancers, models, actresses, or prostitutes (the categories often blurred).

The increasing segregation of Victorian society along class lines, often noted by contemporary commentators, is registered most obviously in sharply differentiated patterns of speech. Novelists typically render the speech of securely middle-class characters in standard, 'unmarked' English, against which both aristocratic drawls and a host of working-class idioms seem departures from the norm, which usually are conveyed with some degree of phonetic spelling. The power of this distinction is especially potent in Dickens's novels, where certain working-class characters destined for social ascent – most notably, Oliver Twist and Pip – are set apart from their peers by an uncanny habit of speaking linguistically unmarked English. In his earliest groping toward literacy, Pip's phonetic spelling captures a recognizably working-class pronunciation, most notably in the use of aspirated and unaspirated 'h' – 'MI DEER JO i OPE U R KRWITE WELL i OPE i SHAL SON B HABELL 4 2 TEEDGE U JO . . .' – but he never speaks thus. When his stepfather Joe Gargery commends him, 'what a scholar you are! An't you?' Pip responds, 'I should like to be' (ch. 7: 45). Apparently a speech as heavily marked as Joe's would have seemed an insuperable barrier to Pip's 'great expectations' – or at least to the credulity of Dickens's audience. Joe's presence also reminds us that such distinctions derive primarily from vast differences in education, which are a recurrent point of class division and social aspiration in the novel. Joe is a blacksmith who has never learned to read, and who is reluctant to try to learn, because his wife 'would not be over partial to my being a scholar, for fear as I might rise. Like a sort of rebel, don't you see?' (ch. 7: 47). The comedy softens a pointed reality: the association of education with social ascent – or revolt – often created generational frictions within the working-class family, as in Hardy's *Tess of the D'Urbervilles*, where the heroine 'spoke two languages; the dialect at home, more or less; ordinary English abroad and to persons of quality' (ch. 3: 58). At the same time, Joe's remark speaks to pointed fears of working-class education among conservative elements in the affluent classes. State-sponsored education was not widely available until the 1870s, owing not only to sectarian conflict – many believed the most weighty task of educators was the inculcation of religious faith – but to a good deal of resistance grounded in the time-honored recognition that knowledge is power.

The fear of popular education was but one facet of resistance to large-scale social mobility among the poor. Whereas middle-class hymns to work typically held out the promise of increased affluence and corresponding status (early political economy figured investment itself as 'abstinence' that would be repaid by deferred gratification), working-class labor continued to figure primarily as its own reward, a peremptory obligation to fulfill the 'place' or 'station' into which the laborer had been born. (This strain often blends with middle-class appeals to traditions of artisanal pride as a constraint of working-class social ambitions; the protagonists of Kingsley's *Alton Locke* (1850) and Eliot's *Felix Holt*, for example, both renounce such ambition as a form of class betrayal.) Appeals to providential social design ebbed over the course of the century, but they remained a vigorous thread in conservative thinking – as in Cathy Rigby's famous review of *Jane Eyre* in the *Quarterly Review* of 1848:

> There is throughout it a murmuring against the comforts of the rich and the privations of the poor, which, as far as each individual is concerned, is a murmuring against God's appointment . . . We do not hesitate to say that the tone of mind and thought which has overthrown authority and violated every code human and divide abroad, and fostered Chartism and rebellion at home, is the same which has also written *Jane Eyre*. (Brontë 1999: 591)

Rigby's comments anticipate Joe Gargery's, inasmuch as they associate 'rising' with uprising: they capture a deep and widespread fear of working-class violence. This is a persistent thread in Victorian social history, but it is most acute at two different junctures in that history, in the 1830s and 1840s, and then in the 1880s, each of which marks a distinctive development in the history of the novel. The fear of civil insurrection (as Rigby's comments suggest) has its most obvious symbol in the French Revolution of 1789, which continued to reverberate in revolutions on the continent in 1830 and 1848, as well as in political agitation closer to home. (Civil uprising had seemed a very real possibility on the eve of the Reform Bill in 1832, after the House of Lords twice threw out reform measures passed by the Commons.) These tremors can be felt in historical fiction of the period, not only Dickens's *A Tale of Two Cities* and *Barnaby Rudge* (1841) – the latter recounting the Gordon Riots of 1780 – but a host of lesser known works by the likes of William Ainsworth, which also suggest the haunting force of mob violence in the Victorian imaginary. From very early in the century, however, long-standing demands for greater representation among the disenfranchised (the vast majority of the male population, even after the First Reform Bill was enacted) converged with newer causes: protests brought about by the increasing mechanization of labor. As workers suffered widespread unemployment, both through the decline of older forms of labour (such as handloom weaving) and the newly volatile business cycles of an industrial economy, they increasingly looked to trades unions and strikes in order to press their grievances. These twin currents led to popular association of industrial labor with Chartism, a predominantly working-class political movement devoted to a six-point charter, which included such radical notions as universal male suffrage and a secret ballot. As Chartism came to national prominence from the late 1830s, its recourse to mass rallies profoundly unsettled the propertied classes, in whose imaginations it often became conflated with trades unions: both seemed working-class conspiracies bent on the destruction of British society.

All of these anxieties converged in the industrial novel, which in many ways might just as aptly be called the insurrection novel. Every major example of the form (Disraeli's *Sybil* (1844), Gaskell's *Mary Barton* and *North and South* (1855), Kingsley's *Alton Locke*, Dickens's *Hard Times*, Eliot's *Felix Holt*) features a riot or related act of violence incited by unscrupulous agitators exploiting working-class discontent. Yet this violence is combined, tellingly, with expressions of deep sympathy for the predicament of the working class. Typically, this tension is managed by focusing on an isolated protagonist – Felix Holt, Alton Locke, Stephen Blackpool in *Hard Times* – who is estranged from both his masters and his fellow workers, and who must struggle to express his sense of injustice without allowing frustration to boil over into violence. In these conflicts, the primary vehicle of persuasion is the display of self-mastery: when a protagonist resists the temptation to violence, he claims from middle-class characters (and readers) an enhanced dignity and moral regard. But this framing of the conflict entails that its resolution avoids any fundamental change in the political or social order. Instead, as in the Victorian novel generally, politics is resolved into personal relationships, forms of individual moral understanding and sympathy. Thus *Mary Barton*, for example, culminates in a reconciliation of the aggrieved manufacturer with the desperate workman who has murdered his son; the clash of economic interests is submerged in an appeal to a common human heart.

The industrial novel may be the sub-genre most commonly associated with the working class, but it represents a relatively small segment of the laboring population, and its vogue is of relatively short duration (from the late 1830s through the late 1850s) primarily because it is so bound up with the historical conjunction of industrial unrest and Chartist agitation. (*Felix Holt*, the last major example of the form (1866), resonates with anxieties surrounding the extension of the working-class franchise effected in the Second Reform Bill of 1867.) By contrast, as Peter Keating reminds us, the urban working class generally, as distinct from industrial laborers of the burgeoning northern towns, had a far more varied and durable place in the Victorian novel, where they are associated above all with London. Dickens's novels are the central reference point here: though their imaginative center tends to be the lower middle classes rather than the working poor, the range and vividness of his depiction of London life powerfully shaped popular conceptions of the poor. With the dramatic growth of population over the course of the century, urban geography had never been so segregated along class lines. Increasingly large areas of London were given over to slums into which no 'respectable' persons would willingly travel. Reviewers analyzing the spectacular success of *The Pickwick Papers* (1836–7) often pointed to this social isolation, and commended the novel for representing the rich and poor in social harmony. (When in *Oliver Twist* Dickens attacked the New Poor Law, he was widely criticized for diluting his comedy with politics.) Dickens's career also encapsulates a gradual shift in representation of the urban poor, from the largely comic or picturesque treatment of the early part of the period to an increasingly somber mode of vision which associated urban poverty with a range of acute social problems. *Oliver Twist* and 'the Newgate novel' of course offered frequent examples of brutal criminality. Yet a character like Bill Sykes in *Oliver Twist* – thief, drunkard, sexual profligate, murderer – is hardly offered as representative of a larger group; he is memorable in his very singularity, as an object of fear and loathing even to his criminal colleagues. A more pointedly sociological imagination of the poor begins to enter the novel in the 1840s, as the sheer remoteness of their world from comfortable Victorian life made them the objects of 'urban investigation', a quasi-anthropological mode of study most influentially represented by Henry Mayhew's *London Labour and the London Poor* (1861–2) and Charles Booth's *Life and Labour of the People of London* (1889–1902). We see the impact of such study most often in the casual encounters of Victorian novels, as when Mrs. Pardiggle in chapter 8 of *Bleak House* ventures into the hovel of an unemployed bricklayer – who, tellingly, is never named, but who offers a savagely eloquent account of his situation: 'Yes, it is dirty – it's nat'rally dirty, and it's nat'rally onwholesome, and we've had five dirty and onwholesome children, as is all dead infants, and so much the better for them, and for us besides . . .' (ch. 8: 158).

In the 1880s, largely through the popular success of Walter Besant's *All Sorts and Conditions of Men* (1882), the poverty of the East End of London became a lightning rod of concern akin to that generated by industrial labor 40 years earlier. A new, more complex attention to the poor, in which humanitarian sympathy jostles with more detached description influenced by French naturalism, homes in on the sheer degradation of poverty – a feature especially prominent in the novels of George Gissing and in Arthur Morrison's *A Child of the Jago* (1896). These capture a tenacious effort among the poor to distinguish between the 'rough' and the 'respectable', yet they trade in a durable association of poverty with license and brutality. We glimpse this in the industrial novels, where the protagonist is individualized by a moral and social *chiaroscuro*, singled out from the crowd but nonetheless shadowed by its anger and appetite. These associations come into the foreground in novels of slum life, which in obvious ways are closely bound up with contemporary typologies of deviance exploited in criminology and eugenics. Throughout the Victorian novel, however, descriptions of the poor also betray an element of prurient fascination, as if they allowed novelists to imagine forms of psychological extremity that could not be accommodated by middle-class settings. Undoubtedly life in London slums gave rise to a good deal of casual brutality, as Mayhew and others recorded. But there seems to be a large element of fantasy in the representation of transgression along class lines. Simply from the evidence of divorce actions, for example, which were avidly reported in the popular press, we know that middle-class domesticity could be riven by a host of betrayals, from sexual infidelity to harrowing rage and physical violence. Yet Victorian fiction very rarely represents such upheaval in a middle-class household. It is typically displaced instead onto working-class characters, like the bricklayer in *Bleak House*, who readily claims responsibility for his wife's black eye. In effect, middle-class violence becomes an oxymoron, since middle-class status is so powerfully associated with self-restraint. When Melmotte in *The Way We Live Now* strikes his daughter, he explodes his pretensions to gentility, and the elaborate cultivation of social acceptance that would enhance the status of his mysterious wealth.

The women thus victimized by male aggression often serve as testaments to a deeply cherished Victorian faith in the power of an essential and uncorrupted femininity, which takes a special pathos from the simple dignity and fortitude with which a character might endure such ordeals. Yet in the novel poor women, like their male counterparts, also frequently embody a failure of middle-class discipline that reinforces stark boundaries of respectability. As male violence or drunkenness exiles a character from bourgeois standing, so, too – and even more irrevocably – does illicit female sexuality. The stigma attached to 'fallen' sexuality does not obviate pointed appeals to the reader's sympathy, as in Gaskell's *Ruth* (1853), for example, or even in *Oliver Twist*, where Nancy's prostitution is so disturbing that Dickens cannot quite bring himself to name it. Yet such figures also reaffirm the moral ascendancy of the middle classes. Tellingly, figures like Ruth or Hetty Sorrel in Eliot's *Adam Bede* (1859), both of whom bear an illegitimate child, seem punished as much for their social aspirations as for their sexual laxity. They are captivated by dreams of a more affluent life personified by their seducers – who are almost invariably wealthy – but romance cannot withstand the pressures of class difference, which licenses the man to ignore the sexual restraint that would distinguish true courtship.

Such depictions thus buttress a typology of class, while at the same time allowing novelists to represent in marginalized bodies forms of wayward desire that cannot be accommodated within representations of middle-class womanhood. Working-class women were in this regard closely akin to women in the socially liminal world of the stage and artistic bohemia, as well as what Leonore Davidoff calls the 'twilight social world' of the 'demi-monde' (p. 34). All represented a relatively public femininity, typically outside the shelter of domesticity, and thus to middle-class imaginations readily suggesting various forms of heterodoxy, including sexual availability. For this reason, the forms of theatricality that arouse suspicion in Victorian novels are more troubling when incarnated in a female character; the actress is more unsettling than the actor, an icon more readily aligned with a social mobility defiant of moral (especially sexual) norms. As such, the actress or female artist becomes a character of increasing prominence in later Victorian novels, such as *Daniel Deronda*, Hardy's *Hand of Ethelberta* (1876), Meredith's *Diana of the Crossways* (1885), and Du Maurier's bestseller, *Trilby* (1896).

Though accounts of factory labor may be the most vivid emblem of Victorian working-class experience, factory workers were decidedly less numerous than domestic servants and agricultural laborers, two groups which tended to have distinctive functions within the novel. Within middle-class families, servants were essential not merely for labor, but as a badge of social rank: as Eric Hobsbawm points out, 'the safest way of distinguishing oneself from the labourers was to employ labour oneself' (Robbins 1993: 15). Hence the pervasiveness of servants in the novel (even the shabbiest of shabby genteel families often have at least one servant to maintain their tenuous claims to respectability). As signs of the master's own economic standing, servants are often faceless presences in the novel – a status epitomized in upper-class homes, which were designed to minimize incidental contact between the family and servants; and where, when such contact did take place, custom dictated servants avert their faces so as not to disrupt the family's privacy. At the same time, when servants do acquire a name and a sense of distinct identity within a novel, they often function as special confidantes to those they serve. The wildly popular Sam Weller in *The Pickwick Papers*, for example, epitomizes in his relations with Mr. Pickwick an understanding and insight derived from the peculiar combination of physical proximity and social distance. Their relationship also embodies a paternalist sense of quasi-familial obligation very different from the wage-relations enforced by contract.

Agricultural workers, for much of the century the single largest occupational group in England, likewise hark back to an earlier social order, and thereby frequently serve more as picturesque backdrop than as individuated characters. Indeed, they are oftentimes dehumanized into barely sentient labor, summed up as the eponymous 'Hodge'. By the same token, however, as agricultural workers seemed especially distant from the increasingly mechanized rhythms of modern life – including the demand for greater political representation – they could suggestively register the incursions of modernity on the vestiges of a traditional social order. Thus in Chapter 56 of *Middlemarch* a 'party in smock-frocks' harassing railway surveyors places the novel's action in a larger history. Only with the novels of Hardy, however, do the lives of agricultural laborers become the focal point of novelistic action, perhaps most memorably in *Tess of the D'Urbervilles* – a novel excruciatingly conscious that it is recording a vanishing way of life. Once again the novel sustained its popularity by conjuring up a world remote from that of its predominantly middle-class readership: in this regard, the countryside is unexpectedly akin to the urban slum.

Whatever the setting, however, Victorian novels represent a world in which social class seems interwoven with virtually every facet of experience. Class so powerfully structures character and conflict in the novel that it is difficult to represent forms of desire, and thus structures of conflict and resolution, outside its reach. The pressure of class may thus suggest how very difficult it is to maintain our familiar image of Victorian culture as a world of sharply demarcated 'separate spheres' of public and private life. It may also suggest one facet of the enduring, manifold bearing of the Victorian novel on our own times.

References and Further Reading

Armstrong, Nancy (1987) *Desire and Domestic Fiction: A Political History of the Novel*. New York: Oxford University Press.
Besant, Walter (1997) *All Sorts and Conditions of Men*. Oxford and New York: Oxford University Press.
Booth, Charles (1902) *Life and Labour of the People in London*, 7 vols. London and New York: Macmillan.
Braddon, Mary Elizabeth (1998) *Lady Audley's Secret*. Harmondsworth: Penguin.
Brantlinger, Patrick (1977) *The Spirit of Reform: British Literature and Politics, 1832–1867*. Cambridge, MA: Harvard University Press.
Briggs, Asa (1983) The language of 'class' in early nineteenth-century Britain. In R. S. Neale (ed.) *History and Class: Essential Readings in Theory and Interpretation* (pp. 2–29). Oxford: Blackwell.
Brontë, Charlotte (1999) *Jane Eyre*. Peterborough, CA: Broadview.
——(1980) *Villette*. Harmondsworth: Penguin.
Bulwer, Edward Lytton (1970) *England and the English*. Chicago and London: University of Chicago Press.
Carlyle, Thomas (1965) *Past and Present*. New York: New York University Press.
Collins, Wilkie (1999) *The Woman in White*. Harmondsworth: Penguin.
Craik, Dinah Mulock (1962) *John Halifax, Gentleman*. London: Dent.
Davidoff, Leonore (1973) *The Best Circles: Women and Society in Victorian England*. Totowa, NJ: Rowman & Littlefield.
Davidoff, Leonore and Catherine Hall (1987). *Family Fortunes: Men and Women of the English Middle Class, 1780–1850*. Chicago: University of Chicago Press.
Dickens, Charles (1973) *Barnaby Rudge*. Harmondsworth: Penguin.
——(1971) *Bleak House*. Harmondsworth: Penguin.
——(1985) *David Copperfield*. Harmondsworth: Penguin.
——(1970) *Dombey and Son*. Harmondsworth: Penguin.
——(1996) *Great Expectations*. Harmondsworth: Penguin.
——(1990) *Hard Times*. New York: Norton.
——(1967) *Little Dorrit*. Harmondsworth: Penguin.
——(1978) *Nicholas Nickleby*. Harmondsworth: Penguin.
——(1999) *Oliver Twist*. Oxford and New York: Oxford University Press.
——(1970) *Our Mutual Friend*. Harmondsworth: Penguin.
——(1972) *The Pickwick Papers*. Harmondsworth: Penguin.
——(2000) *A Tale of Two Cities*. Oxford and New York: Oxford University Press.
Disraeli, Isaac (1980) *Sybil, or The Two Nations*. Harmondsworth: Penguin.
Du Maurier, George (1894) *Trilby, a Novel*. New York: Harper.
Eliot, George (1985) *Adam Bede*. Harmondsworth: Penguin.
——(1995) *Daniel Deronda*. Harmondsworth: Penguin.
——(1995) *Felix Holt, The Radical*. Harmondsworth: Penguin.

——(1994) *Middlemarch*. Harmondsworth: Penguin.
——(1973) *Silas Marner*. Harmondsworth: Penguin.
——(1979) *The Mill on the Floss*. Harmondsworth: Penguin.
Gagnier, Regenia (1991) *Subjectivities: A History of Self-Representation in Britain*. New York and Oxford: Oxford University Press.
Gallagher, Catherine (1985) *The Industrial Reformation of English Fiction: Social Discourse and Narrative Form, 1832–1867*. Chicago and London: University of Chicago Press.
Gaskell, Elizabeth (1970) *Mary Barton*. Harmondsworth: Penguin.
——(1970) *North and South*. Harmondsworth: Penguin.
——(2001) *Ruth*. London: Dent.
——(1969) *Wives and Daughters*. Harmondsworth: Penguin.
Gilmour, Robin (1981) *The Idea of the Gentleman in the Victorian Novel*. London: George Allen and Unwin.
Gissing, George (1968) *New Grub Street*. Harmondsworth: Penguin.
Grossmith, George and Weedon (1991) *Diary of a Nobody*. Wolfeboro Falls, NH: Alan Sutton.
Hall, Catherine, McClelland, Keith, and Rendall, Jane (2000) *Defining the Victorian Nation: Class, Race, Gender, and the Reform Act of 1867*. Cambridge: Cambridge University Press.
Hardy, Thomas (1975) *The Hand of Ethelberta*. London: Macmillan.
——(1998) *Jude the Obscure*. Harmondsworth: Penguin.
——(1978) *Tess of the D'Urbervilles*. Harmondsworth: Penguin.
Honey, J. R. de' S (1977) *Tom Brown's Universe: The Development of the Victorian Public School*. London: Millington.
James, Henry (1881) *Portrait of a Lady*. Harmondsworth: Penguin.
Jones, Gareth Stedman (1983) *The Languages of Class: Studies in English Working-Class History*. Cambridge: Cambridge University Press.
Joyce, Patrick (1996) *Democratic Subjects: The Self and the Social in Nineteenth-Century Britain*. Cambridge: Cambridge University Press.
Keating, P. J. (1971) *The Working Classes in Victorian Fiction*. London: Routledge Kegan Paul.
Kingsley, Charles (1983) *Alton Locke*. Oxford and New York: Oxford University Press.
Mayhew, Henry (1968) *London Labour and the London Poor*, 4 vols. New York: Dover.
Meredith, George (1897) *Diana of the Crossways*. New York: Scribners.
Morrison, Arthur (1896) *A Child of the Jago*. Chicago: Stone.
Neale, R. S. (ed.) (1983) *History and Class: Essential Readings in Theory and Interpretation*. Oxford: Blackwell.
Perkin, Harold (1985) *The Origins of Modern English Society*. London: ARK.
Phillips, K. C. (1984) *Language and Class in Victorian Britain*. Oxford: Blackwell.
Robbins, Bruce (1993) *The Servant's Hand. English Literature from Below*. Durham and London: Duke University Press.

Smiles, Samuel (1859) *Self-Help: With Illustrations of Character and Conduct*. London: John Murray.

Thackeray, William Makepeace (1998) *Vanity Fair*. Harmondsworth: Penguin.

Thompson, F. M. L. (1988) *The Rise of Respectable Society: A Social History of Britain, 1830–1900*. Cambridge, MA: Harvard University Press.

Trollope, Anthony (1980) *Barchester Towers*. Oxford and New York: Oxford University Press.

——(1969) *The Eustace Diamonds*. Harmondsworth: Penguin.

——(1982) *The Way We Live Now*. Oxford and New York: Oxford University Press.

Wilde, Oscar (1988) *The Picture of Dorian Gray*. New York: Norton.

Young, Arlene (1999) *Culture, Class, and Gender in the Victorian Novel: Gentleman, Gents, and Working Women*. New York: St. Martin's.

Chapter 4

Legal subjects, legal objects: The Law and Victorian Fiction

Clare Pettitt

In *Pendennis* (1848–50), Thackeray, who had himself spent a brief and miserable time reading for the bar, reminds us that Victorian novelists and Victorian lawyers could not always be easily distinguished from one another. In this semi-autobiographical novel he muses that, despite their unhygienic dilapidation, the Inns of Court were necessarily imbued with romantic associations for the mid-nineteenth-century novelist:

> [B]ut the man of letters can't but love the place which has been inhabited by so many of his brethren, or peopled by their creations as real to us at this day as the authors whose children they were – and Sir Roger de Coverley walking in the Temple Garden, and discoursing with Mr. Spectator about the beauties in hoops and patches who are sauntering over the grass, is just as lively a figure to me as old Samuel Johnson rolling through the fog with the Scotch gentleman at his heels on their way to Dr. Goldsmith's chambers in Brick Court; or Harry Fielding, with inked ruffles and a wet towel round his head, dashing off articles at midnight for the Covent Garden Journal, while the printer's boy is asleep in the passage (*Pendennis*, ch. 29: 367).

The eighteenth-century English novel had a peculiarly intimate relation with the Inner Temple. The migration from law to letters, and the literary moonlighting of lawyers such as Fielding, suggest that, in the eighteenth and early nineteenth centuries, the older profession was being used to fund and legitimize a career in the newer, emergent world of literary work. By the mid-nineteenth century, the 'profession' of letters may even have seemed more promising than that of the law. W. J. Reader records that there was a glut of attorneys between 1841 and 1851, and that '[s]hocking stories were told of young barristers slowly starving to death, from want of employment, in their chambers in the Temple' (1966: 154). As literacy extended and technological advances created both more and more affordable publications as well as a growing appetite for literary entertainment, new opportunities for the professional writer were opening up. By 1847, G. H. Lewes felt able to declare in an article in *Fraser's*, '[l]iterature has become a profession. It is a means of subsistence almost as certain as the bar or the church' 1847: 285). As Janice Carlisle (1981) has aptly shown, the Victorian novelist, like the judge or bishop, was intensely conscious of his or her own role as making both moral and political interventions in the public life of the period. In attempting to establish literature as a 'profession', its practitioners often aspired to the status of the cleric or the lawyer, thereby sometimes giving the impression of bearing a rivalrous relation to the other, older professions. In fact rivalry is not entirely sufficient as a description of the relationship between the law and letters in Victorian Britain, despite the fact that it is frequently used as a model by contemporary theorists of the subject. For a start, the professions were too intertwined to support such a simple paradigm of influence. In John Sutherland's sample of 676 Victorian novelists (1995), one in six was, at some time, a lawyer. Certainly, many of the most influential male novelists of the period had experience of the law. Charles Dickens, for example, was a law office clerk from 1827 to 1828, and then worked as a shorthand reporter at Doctors Commons, before becoming a parliamentary reporter in 1831. Although he never practiced law, Wilkie Collins was a law student at Lincoln's Inn and was called to the bar in 1851, the same year in which he first met Dickens. Obviously the female novelists were not lawyers, although many of them were knowledgeable about the law. George Eliot's private library, for example, contained many legal textbooks and she discussed the complexities of the law at length with barrister Frederic Harrison when she was devising the plot for *Felix Holt: The Radical* in 1866.

Sutherland's conclusion that 'there is probably an affinity between the mentalities of jurisprudence and Victorian fiction, shaped as both were by the study of individual cases and the canons of justice' seems at once intriguing and insufficient (1995: 163). After all, it could equally be argued that there is 'probably' an affinity between the practice of nineteenth-century science and literature – shaped as both were by developing positivist ideas of evidence and inference. Surely any such simple 'affinity' between the practice of Victorian law and letters was vested only in their shared use of language as the primary professional tool? Ian Watt long ago drew the parallel between the eighteenth-century novel and the practice of law, 'the novel's mode of imitating reality may therefore be equally well summarized in terms of the procedures of . . . the jury in a court of law' (1957: 31). But if we try to look beyond loose comparisons, and to inquire further into the relationship between the novel and the law, we rapidly find ourselves grappling with some of the knottiest problems available to literary critics today. One of the more subtle writers on the law and literature, Kieran Dolin, has written of 'the complex strands which connect the novel and the law during the nineteenth and early twentieth centuries' (1999: 2). But what exactly *are* these 'complex strands'? How much did the law affect the fiction of the nineteenth century? And precisely how did it come to affect it? How far can we describe the law and literature as 'sharing a culture' and how far must we resist the forgiving haze of the *zeitgeist*, and attempt to assert the vital differences between the two practices?

Law and Literature: An Emergent Field

Since the publication of James Boyd White's *The Legal Imagination* in 1973, the field of 'law and literature' has been expanding its acreage every year. In North America, particularly, for some 30 years now, a law and literature movement has been active within the law schools themselves. Richard Posner, one of its most vocal apologists, posits a 'new model . . . [which] in general seeks to promote compassion and empathy by enlarging the imagination of lawyers and judges' (1988: viii). Growing out of the American liberal arts tradition, in Posner's model, literature is approached as an instrumental tool with which to adjust students morally and to make better people of them. Ian Ward, too, insists that '[t]he educative ambition of law and literature . . . is both a credible and a creditable one. Moreover, it is one which teachers of law should not seek to dispute, if they do indeed cherish the ambition of educating lawyers to be more than simply lawyers' (1995: 27). In support of this thesis, Ward paraphrases Nancy Cook, who remarks that '[t]he art of teaching . . . has always lain in analogy and metaphor' (1995: 24). The problem with this approach for the literary scholar is the somewhat cavalier use of 'literature' as an 'analogy' – as if it were a reflection of the more 'real' discourse of law. While it may be a good pedagogic strategy to turn to *Bleak House* (1852–3) or *The Woman in White* (1859–60) to engage students' interest in the development of contemporary laws of inheritance or property, such a practice does little to illuminate or understand the literary text. And the implied hierarchy, in which the literary text becomes instrumental to acquiring the seemingly truer and more substantial body of legal knowledge, skews the actual cultural relation between, for example, Dickens's *Bleak House* and its relationship with a very specific moment in mid-Victorian legal and public culture.

But the study of literature in law schools is not my primary concern here. The body of work that is most relevant to this discussion was generated not so much by the publication of White's textbook, *The Legal Imagination*, as by another important publication at about the same time. The appearance of Foucault's *Discipline and Punish: The Birth of the Prison* in 1975 was to have a far-reaching effect on the discipline of English studies. Kieran Dolin describes its 'ground-breaking argument about the extent to which disciplinary techniques associated with the criminal law have ramified throughout modern society' (1999: 7). Discourse theory gave literary scholars a route back to history that promised to interact with the literary text, rather than sideline it. Contemporary developments in the law no longer formed merely a kind of semi-detached 'historical context' to the Victorian novel, they were the living stuff of which literature was made. Since the early 1980s, Foucauldian readings of varying levels of sophistication have been appearing about the Victorian novel. For example, Catherine Belsey (1980), Jeremy Tambling (1995), and D. A. Miller (1988) have each usefully re-read Dickens as complicit in a 'disciplinary' project. But the 'ramification' of criminal law reforms throughout society still raises difficult questions about transmission and influence, and the problem with Foucauldian theory as specifically applied to literary texts is that it can threaten to 'flatten' them into documents which are not formally distinguishable from Parliamentary Acts, newspaper articles, or – finally – laundry lists. This is not to deny that much Foucauldian analysis of the Victorian novel has been extremely fruitful, it is merely to sound the caution that this cannot – or indeed must not – be the only or 'correct' way to read Victorian fiction: by illuminating certain elements of the literary text, it obscures others. The use by some critics of a Foucauldian hermeneutic which tends to the totalitarian does not allow the literary text itself to answer back, and the result can be a mechanical rehearsal of the ways in which the Victorian novel is complicit in the construction of a middle-class disciplinary culture in the nineteenth century. I have argued elsewhere that the Victorian novel is rarely doing anything so straightforward (see Pettitt 2004). Such a reading would necessitate a monolithic model of 'culture' in which everything is constantly tending to the same outcome. But the problem with history is its fecundity, and the way in which so many different cultures, narratives, and counter-narratives play against one another at any given moment. Indeed, recent work by post-colonial scholars has highlighted this point by showing how the picture is complicated if applied to the colonial experience. See, for example, Upamanyu Pablo Mukherjee's *Crime and Empire* (2003).

The post-Foucauldian interdisciplinary study of law and literature has attracted many literary scholars; some, such as Mary Poovey, Alexander Welsh and Andrew H. Miller, are literary critics or historians interested in the interface between social and cultural history and literature, and others are ex-professional lawyers, such as Kieran Dolin and Jan-Melissa Schramm. It would be impossible to give a comprehensive survey here of the many interventions in this field in the last 20 years. (For useful studies of the genesis and subsequent development of the 'law and literature movement', see the first two chapters of Kieran Dolin, *Fiction and the Law* (1999) and Chapter 1, 'Law and Literature: A Continuing Debate' in Ian Ward, *Law and Literature: Possibilities and Perspectives* (1995), pp. 3–27). It is striking, however, that while Welsh, Poovey, and Miller write about the ways in which certain ideas seem to reappear in various different categories of Victorian discussion, the studies by ex-lawyers tend to posit the relationship between the law and literature as a much more direct, deliberate and fundamentally rivalrous one. 'How is it that the canons of legal evidence come *to govern* the practice of fictional storytelling?' asks Dolin, speaking of 'fiction's claim *to rival* the law as an authoritative interpreter of reality' (1999: 2, 193, italic added). At the end of her fascinating book, Jan-Melissa Schramm writes that, 'I conclude that the rise of the third-person realist novel is simultaneously in imitation of, and in reaction against, the increasing prominence of defence counsel. Their *competition* with authors for the most truthful representation of the "real" ensured that testimony remained a focal point for the expression and attempted resolution of many of the era's most persistent epistemological anxieties' (2000: 23, italic added). This model of rivalry and mastery needs further examination. Why should the novel have rivaled the law as representative of 'reality'? Was not the nature of reality itself under severe interrogation throughout the period from many different directions?

Kiernan Dolin suggests some qualitative difference between the law and the novel when he concedes that '[t]he novel represents itself as an intervention in the public sphere, more particularly as a supplement to the law, going where it cannot go, but performing a similar function' (1999: 1). A 'supplement' acknowledges that the two genres are not precisely equal, although the suggestion that literature 'performs a similar function' is problematic. The law *represents*, after all, a very much more direct form of social control than literary writing does. Similarly, Schramm declares that '[a]s with legal discourse, the history of the realist genre is also the history of the construction of credible testimonies' (2000: 66). But the argument of her book shifts from this loose model of 'analogy' toward a more determined view of the novel as primarily a form of response to – in particular – the Prisoners' Counsel Act of 1836 which allowed full legal representation for alleged felons. In this argument the novel seems less analogous to than consequent upon the legal development, a position which is called into question if we are prepared to disagree with Kiernan Dolin's proposition that the Victorian law and the Victorian novel 'performed a similar function'. Literary writing is not simply 'functional' in the way this suggests. Some of the preoccupations and complexities we find in the Victorian novel may, indeed, be read as 'analogous to' similar debates in other epistemological systems in the period, but the challenge is to delineate the precise anatomy of the connection which the 'analogy' indicates but fails fully to describe.

The Law and the Aesthetic Moment

This line of argument leads, in Ian Ward's words, to 'the whole area of historicity and hermeneutics, which lies at the very core of critical theory' and is also an 'extremely contentious one in contemporary legal writings' (1995: 4). In literary criticism, this has always been a contentious area and there are signs that the discipline's return to history over the last 20 years or so may now be – perhaps predictably – leading to the re-galvanizing of a debate about the status of the aesthetic. What demands more scrupulous attention than it has hitherto been given by literary scholars is the process by which the aesthetic has been historically – and indeed legally – constructed. Even (perhaps especially) theorists who claim to reject the 'aesthetic' as a bourgeois construct are only half-heartedly historicizing and are failing to consider alternative ways in which the aesthetic has been or could be constructed to answer historically different needs. Too often a simple dichotomous opposition is assumed between the historico-political and the aesthetic. The challenge is to understand the ways in which the aesthetic is both contingent on historical and political determinants, but also capable of transforming them by a synergistic process.

As Isobel Armstrong has recently suggested, the model of the 'aesthetic' which emerges from the work of Derrida and de Man, among others, is an 'archaic, individualist theory of art we associate historically with the nineteenth century. But this obsolete, subject-based bourgeois account of the aesthetic is universalized as *the* aesthetic' (2000: 54, italic original). This 'subject-based aesthetic' was largely the creation of the Romantic writers of the late eighteenth century, already in flight from the specter of mass publishing. I suggest that, despite already showing signs of obsolescence in the early Victorian period, it was underwritten and perpetuated by the changes in intellectual property law in the nineteenth century. The debate around the reform of intellectual property law at this time is an important one as it shows the tenacity of literary writers such as Dickens in protecting such an obsolescent idea against the arguments of the free-trade anti-monopolists who wanted to abolish both copyright and patent protection. Although theoretically there is no opposition between free-trade policy and patent or copyright law, this was not the opinion of many MPs and lobbyists at the time. Macaulay, for example, anathematized copyright as 'monopoly' in his famous 1841 parliamentary speech (1853: 292). Talfourd's Copyright Bill, first introduced in 1837, fell repeatedly before it was finally passed in 1842. The question of who should be allowed to hold intellectual property was fundamental to an emerging democracy, and was crucial to writers and inventors who were campaigning for professional status. The powerful rhetoric used in defense of the protective law was not economic, but moral. The author was represented as the lonely artist in his garret producing works of immense social value. The pro-copyright lobby deployed all the referents of Romantic inspiration: the solitariness of the artist, the unconscious nature or 'trance' of the creative act, and the bodily suffering and martyrdom entailed by it. The poem published in Dickens's *Household Words* which suggested that in order to be a successful author, 'a man should live in a garret aloof, And have few friends, and be poorly clad' was characteristic of this popular rhetorical construction in the mid-century (Anon 1850: 49). It presents a striking contrast with

Dickens as author, who could hardly be described as aloof, working hard but cheerfully to meet his copy deadlines, surrounded by friends, a dandified dresser and a great party and theatre-goer.

The law, of course, was extending rapidly in many directions in the Victorian period, with a concentration of reform activity in the middle third of the century. I am concerned here with a particular aspect of property law, but there is also much to be said about commercial law, especially the emerging law of contract in the period, the Limited Liability Act (1855) and the Bankruptcy and Insolvency Act (1861). Electoral law was changing throughout the Victorian period, as was criminal law, starting with the Metropolitan Police Act of 1829. The notorious Poor Law Amendment Act (1834) was followed by a succession of legislative reforms intended to alleviate the working and living conditions of the poor, such as the Public Health Acts (1848/75) and the Factory Acts, of which there was at least one every decade between 1830 and 1870. The Catholic Emancipation Act (1829), the new laws on lunacy, and laws affecting women, including the Matrimonial Causes Act (1857); the Married Women's Property Acts (1870/82) and the Deceased Wife's Sister Bill and the Criminal Law Amendment Act (1885): all bear witness to an increasing public intervention in private lives. This busy legislative activity is indicative of the many political debates that found their way into other forms of writing too.

As I have already argued, any attempt to nail down the exact relationship between the Victorian law and Victorian fiction is perilous. Nevertheless, examining the changing law of intellectual property in the nineteenth century as a context for Victorian fiction offers one partial, and rewardingly complex, point of entry for a discussion that must necessarily be brief. By considering the novelists' encounters with this debate, and the evidence of some of the novels themselves, we can begin to make out a small part of the synergistic and often contradictory relationship between the law and the novel.

Intellectual Property Law at Mid-Century

Of the raft of reforms in the period that created the law as we still recognize it today, the amendments to the laws governing intellectual property directly affected the status and earnings of novelists. They also helped to embed the idea of the original author firmly in the culture. These laws were changed in response to new ideas about authorship and ownership. The copyright and patent acts of the mid-century were fundamental to the legal construction of the 'individual private subject' – in Althusser's terms they constituted agents of the 'interpellation of the subject'. It is, I believe, because of our continued investment in these laws that we continue to invoke an 'obsolete' individualist theory of authorship into the twenty-first century, despite the resounding challenge to such a construction represented by the new dimension of cyberspace. The model of the solitary individual artist can still blind us to the radical possibilities of acknowledging the social production of art and aesthetic forms.

The law did not make itself. Victorian writers such as Dickens, Collins, Thackeray, Hardy, Talfourd, and Carlyle, among others, self-consciously struggled to achieve professional status for literary writing and saw the law as one of the means to effect this end. Some of them wrote petitions to Parliament and lobbied their powerful political friends. But while they were all fighting to enshrine the romantic image of the solitary subject as artist in the law, their work bears witness to the immense pressure that was driving this conservative reflex. As we are all highly conscious, the speed of technological advance at mid-century was unprecedented. It was in the 1840s and 1850s that the inventions of the late eighteenth and early nineteenth centuries began radically to change patterns of production and distribution, and patterns of consumption. Steam presses and new methods of paper manufacture, steel engraving, and improved communications which speeded up distribution, meant that creative work could reach more consumers than ever before. To understand the stubborn endurance of a late eighteenth-century model of the aesthetic, it is necessary to feel the strangeness behind this truism of Victorian history, and to envision the bewildering impact of these technologies on all types of artistic productions, including the novel. This strangeness posed problems for the writers and artists who were trying to establish and enforce their right to ownership of their work. First, facility of copying meant that unlicensed imitation and piracy were ever more common. Second, the automation of the productive processes meant that it became increasingly difficult to discern the 'subject-based' origin of the work. Not only were far more people involved in the 'creation' of the work, but also the distance between producer and consumer was increasing all the time. Perhaps more than any other period preceding it, the middle of the nineteenth century offered the opportunity of embracing this radical change in the symbolic location of the artist.

Intellectual property law could have evolved in very different directions. Indeed, throughout the nineteenth century there was a vociferous lobby that argued for the total abolition of copyright and patent protection for individuals. In fact, free-trade, anti-monopolist arguments were never to win out in any debate over intellectual property in the nineteenth century. The response of the most influential of the artists was to cling to traditional romantic ideas of originality in order to buoy up the campaign for enhanced copyright protection at home and abroad. Charles Dickens, famously a ferocious champion of copyright, was influential in the powerful literary lobby that helped to push the Patent Amendment Bill through Parliament in 1852. The Copyright Act of 1842 definitively shifted copyright protection from the publisher to the author. The Patent Act of 1852 – despite pressure to abolish patents altogether from many inside the engineering profession, including Isambard Kingdom Brunel – constructed the inventor along the same lines as the original and single author. In both Patent and Copyright Acts the law came to embody the opinions of the literary lobby and consequently helped to perpetuate this model of individual creativity. The legal ideal of intellectual property – of property corporally identified with the artist who 'enters into his labors' – clashed with the pragmatic reality of intellectual property rights. Copyrights and patents were always more flexible than the rhetoric of the Parliamentary Acts suggested. They could be leased, sold outright, or split half and half with publishers or manufacturers. In fact, the vast majority of jobbing writers in the nineteenth century were too poor to gamble on the possibility of a long-term return on their copyrights, and were obliged to sell off all their rights to the publishers immediately. Most inventors labored under the same necessities. The publisher George Routledge confirmed that it was only '[m]en like Lord Lytton and Dickens, and others, [who] did keep their own copyrights; but they did not keep them at first; they sold them and then repurchased them' (*Royal Commission on Copyright*: 246).

Dickens was always aware of the fundamental discrepancy between the written law and the lived practice. His narrator exclaims in *Pickwick Papers* (1836–7), '[t]he body! It is the lawyer's term for the restless whirling mass of cares and anxieties, affections, hopes, and griefs, that make up the living man' (ch. 45: 735–6). The 'lawyer's term' is laconic – solid, corporeal and static – but the 'reality' is evanescent and mobile, a 'whirling mass' of contradictions. And so it was with intellectual property law, which set up the 'body' of the artist's property as static and solid in a way that hardly reflected the frenzied state of the modernizing marketplace. Dickens's perception of the reification of the human in and by the law is everywhere apparent in his writing: Pip, for example, is fascinated and repelled by the 'two ghastly casts on the shelf' in Jaggers's chambers (*Great Expectations*, book 2, ch. 17: 282). Dickens's own relationship with the law in his work is similarly double. It is not only rivalrous, as Dolin and Schramm have both suggested, nor is it only satiric, as Forster remembers: 'of the Pickwickian sense which so often takes the place of common sense in our legislature, he omitted no opportunity of declaring his contempt at every part of his life' (1911, I: 58). It is both these things, but it is also a curiously fetishized relationship, as if Dickens nurses a kind of nostalgia for the solidity and stability of 'the lawyer's term' by which his property would be bound to him, 'locked fast in a kind of mortmain for ever' as Burke put it, with a somewhat awkward mixed metaphor (1968: 120). Yet Dickens also recognizes the death-dealing power of the 'lawyer's term', which was particularly literal at a time when capital crimes were still punished with execution. Symbolically too, the law represents the kind of codification and taxonomy which seemed to Dickens to foreclose on the possibilities of human experience. If Dickens fetishizes the law, he also recognizes the closure and aporia of the fetish. It is perhaps no accident that property is so often associated with death in *Bleak House*. Dickens sees the process by which the law reifies the human as indicative of a kind of deathliness, but this is not to say that he does not simultaneously recognize the power of the law, as is testified by his strenuous exertions to encourage its reform.

There is, after all, a conflict at the heart of the liberal ideology of property, and it is a conflict that many of Dickens's novels address. To maintain a sense of freedom and autonomy, a subject must be at liberty to sell his/her property, but property is necessarily identified with the person, so that alienation breaks the link between the property and the person. The breakage threatens to transform 'freedom' into 'estrangement'. Victorian novelists tried to hold on to the ideal of the bond between the person and the property for their work, while also needing the flexibility, and ultimately, the freedom of contract that allowed them not merely to own, but also to sell and disperse, their books. This conflict between a retentive and a dispersed model of property in ideas reappears again and again in disguised ways in Victorian fiction.

So, even while they publicly campaigned to maintain an ideal of the romantic originator, the mid-Victorian novelists were experimenting through their work with alternative models of creativity and asking the difficult question of how far it was ever actually possible to own a creative act. Ironically, even while they were using analogies of land ownership to defend their intellectual property rights, their novels were dramatizing the transformation from a land-owning elitist model of property to a more democratic, communal, and fundamentally more mobile version of cultural patrimony. In its self-conscious creation of an imaginary, the Victorian novel not only reflects social relationships as they are conventionally articulated through the institutions of the law, education, and so on, but also posits new ways of structuring and thinking about such relationships. The imaginary space of the realist novel does not substitute so much as revolve around and amplify any given account of the social contract. If we are prepared to follow these arguments which take place by proxy in the work, it appears that the ascendancy of the bourgeois 'subject' is considerably less clear than much recent criticism would have us believe. It is true that the law reforms of the nineteenth century did, on the whole, shift toward a model of possessive individualism, but it does not follow that Victorian fiction either obediently imitated the law, or competed with it to achieve the same result. In fact Victorian novels interrogate just such 'individualism' in all sorts of ways. Their deliberate formal experiments were just as radical as the changing nature of production and dissemination which necessarily affected their form. For example, Dickens may have been hoping to reach the greatest possible number of readers by writing *Bleak House* as a serial, but he did not have to write it as two separate narratives. The serial form imposed a structure on him but the double narrative was his decision. It is important to make such distinctions between the form that the writers were given to work with, and the deliberate choices they made which reveal their active and deliberate participation in the debate about originality and the ownership of art. Many other novels of the nineteenth century also ask awkward questions about the possibility of establishing originality. Some examples might be George Eliot's *Felix Holt* (1866) and *Middlemarch* (1871–2); Dickens's *Great Expectations* (1860–1) and Thomas Hardy's *The Well-Beloved* (1898). All ask fundamental questions about the social production of the individual, and all articulate, with varying degrees of obliquity, the worries attendant on repetition and copying.

So, while at mid-century Dickens is deeply engaged with contemporary debate about intellectual property, both for inventors and for writers, this does not make for a simple 'mapping' of the issues into his novels. Of course, in *Little Dorrit* (1855–7) Daniel Doyce, Pancks, and Henry Gowan are clearly related to the debate over patent law and intellectual property more generally, which had flared up after the Great Exhibition of 1851. But even an earlier novel, such as *Bleak House*, is engaged in some kind of conversation with the same problems about the proper limits of the novelist's property in his work. The double narrative of that novel imaginatively enacts Dickens's own difficulty in finding a model of ownership for his writing. Esther's intense and embodied personal identity is pitted against the other dispersed, disembodied and apparently sourceless narration. Dickens's deep possessiveness and self-identification with everything he produced, exacerbated by his own bitter experience of piracy and unauthorized copying, competes in *Bleak House* with both his genuine generosity and need to be instrumental in his writing, and his lurking suspicion that all creativity is, ultimately, unownable. The double-text of *Bleak House* raises complicated questions about the origin of art, and the ownership of the art object, none of which is visible in the reform of the copyright law for which Dickens had congratulated his friend Talfourd for 'securing to [authors] and their descendants a permanent interest in the copyright of their works' (*Pickwick Papers*, Dedication: 39). Frederic Jameson has described literature as 'a symbolic meditation on the destiny of community' (1981: 70). Dickens was quick to insist on the privacy of his work as his personal property but the work itself represents just such a meditation on the destiny of community, and furthermore it could be argued that it had its own instrumental effect on creating that community.

The novel perhaps more than any other genre in the Victorian period was perceived both as the property of the public and the author. The increase in serial publication of novels as the century progressed contributed to this perception, as the reading public were encouraged to engage in the experience of assembling the 'story' themselves, part by part. Part issue made it impossible to ignore the temporality and topicality which exposes the notion of the autotelic art object – the art object that has an end or purpose in itself – and makes fiction a particularly problematic genre in relation to the copyright debate. Its conspicuous state of incompletion as each number appeared exposed traditional arguments about the perfection of artistic form. Its dissemination to a demographically wide readership, its implied investment in new print technologies, its frequent juxtaposition to journalistic discussion, and its capacity to react fast to public debate, make the serial an eloquently modern and interactive form of writing in the nineteenth century.

Trevor Ross (1992) has argued that the copyright debate actively created the public domain in the mid-eighteenth century, and that, until then, there was no sense of a national literature belonging to the people. I would argue that, while Ross's claim is an important one, the historical fluctuations between the two 'terms' of the copyright law were more nuanced than this account suggests, and that the two ideas – that of a culture belonging to the people, and that of knowledge as privately owned – were both in play at once, and that the Victorian novelist wanted to subscribe to both. The challenge for writers working in the high Victorian period was to find a workable balance between them.

Private and Public: Wilkie Collins's *The Law and the Lady*

The debate over intellectual property mimics that much wider negotiation in the period between 'private' and 'public', which, as Jürgen Habermas and others have shown, were terms which depended on one another for their currency. Habermas contends that '[t]he positive meaning of "private" emerged precisely in reference to the concept of free power of control over property that functioned in capitalist fashion' (1989: 74). For the nineteenth-century writer or inventor, private property was necessarily staked on an open marketplace and retaining a 'free power of control' could prove difficult in such a competitive and unregulated environment. For example, any writer's identity could be falsely assumed, as Hardy's was in 1882 when some indifferent poems appeared under his name in a periodical.

Dickens's friend and collaborator, Wilkie Collins, was fascinated by the possibilities of such imposture and impersonation. He was also interested in the extent to which the construction of a personal, private identity was staked on legal codification, and much of his fiction reflects this interest in the conflict between the private and the public – and the seepage between the two. The plot of *Man and Wife* (1870), for example, centers around the lack of legal control that married women had over their property. In *The Law and the Lady* (1875), Collins seems to be deliberately taking on the question of how far the law constitutes and constructs the categories of social existence.

The Law and the Lady begins with Old Testament law. The Anglican marriage service ends with the example of Sarah, the dutiful and obedient wife of Abraham. The legal process of the marriage of Valeria

Brinton and Eustace Woodville is further insisted on by two facsimile reproductions representing their signatures on the marriage register. Valeria's ominous 'mistake' in signing her 'married instead of [her] maiden name' prepares the reader for complications to come (ch. 1: 8). For this is a novel which asks bold questions about the sufficiency of the law as the repository of 'truth'. The lacunae that open up in the legal narrative of the trial, a narrative which is – plainly – embedded in the novel's text, culminate in the ignominious image of the dust heap at the back of the house at Gleninch. From this heap of detritus, the 'fragments of written paper, all stuck together in a little lump' (ch. 45: 380) are disinterred and are reconstructed to supply the confession of suicide which vindicates Eustace Macallan from any responsibility for his wife's death. Like the legal plot of Dickens's *Bleak House*, which ends with the case of *Jarndyce* vs. *Jarndyce* collapsing into a giant dumping of scrap paper – 'great bundles of paper began to be carried out – bundles in bags, bundles too large to be got into any bags, immense masses of papers . . . which the bearers staggered under, and threw down . . . anyhow, on the Hall pavement' (ch. 65: 922) – the legal plot of Collins's novel ends with 'fragments of written paper'. Although these are reconstituted into the legible document that vindicates him, Eustace and his wife choose to leave the document in its envelope unopened, and the 'Not Proven' verdict unchallenged. In a scene that recalls the final stage of Dickens's *Little Dorrit,* in which Arthur Clennam and Amy Dorrit choose to burn the legal document which proves that Clennam's family have appropriated Amy's fortune, Collins, like Dickens, suggests that the public law has not always the power to resolve private griefs and injustices.

In *The Law and the Lady,* Valeria decides to take up her husband's case to prove his innocence, and she writes to tell him that '[w]hat the Law has failed to do for you, your Wife must do for you' (ch. 14: 116). The novel acts out this leeching of power from the public to the private sphere with the added radical charge that the power devolves on a woman. In the 1870s and 1880s, there was growing concern about the extension of the law into all areas of private life. Collins here seems to be suggesting that it is only private, individual relationships which can establish true identity – and that to rely on a public settlement is downright dangerous. 'The greatest lawyers are mortal men; the greatest lawyers have made mistakes before now. You can't deny that' (ch. 12: 107). The conflict between public and private versions of the 'truth' in the novel, and the couple's decision to leave the fragments from the dustheap undisturbed, suggest a deeply layered private sphere which does not conform to the categories of the law. Collins may have based some of the legal detail in the novel on J. H. Burton's *Narratives from Criminal Trials in Scotland* (1852) of which he owned a copy. For a novel which is so concerned with the precise mechanisms of the Scottish law, *The Law and the Lady* seems oddly anxious to establish the nullity of legal procedure. Rivalry between the novel's 'personal' truth and the legal 'public' truth might offer one reading of this internal contradiction, but I would prefer a reading that suggests that Collins's novel contrives to be both 'inside' and 'outside' the law, and thus able to pose awkward questions of legal definitions while never entirely renouncing them.

Dickens and Collins are both horrified and fascinated by the reach of the law into private lives, by its constitutive power, and by its hegemonic hold. While both novelists wanted to establish literary writing as a profession, they were also skeptical of the kind of professionalism that circumvented accountability or responsibility. '"It's not personal; it's professional: only professional"', Wemmick assures Pip about the lawyer, Jaggers's, offputting manner in *Great Expectations* (book 2, ch. 5: 196). Such professional detachment is criticized by both Dickens and Collins. In *The Woman in White*, the Chancery Lane solicitor, Vincent Gilmore, remarks that '"[i]t is the great beauty of the Law that it can dispute any human statement, made under any circumstances, and reduced to any form"'('The Story Continued by Vincent Gilmore', section 1: 154–5). And Dickens's professionally disinterested lawyer Tulkinghorn in *Bleak House* 'is indifferent to everything but his calling. His calling is the acquisition of secrets, and the holding possession of such power as they give him, with no sharer or opponent in it' (ch. 36: 567). Tulkinghorn's dead collection of secrets represents power without responsibility and Dickens rejects the complacent professionalism which sanctions such a withdrawal from personal accountability. Tulkinghorn also wants to 'hold possession . . . with no sharer' while Dickens is seeking a way, in this novel, to possess and to share. Indeed, the profession which seems to offer the author a more workable model is the other young and emergent one of medicine. Alan Woodcourt treads a delicate path between professional disinterestedness and human involvement for which he is rewarded at the end of the novel.

Bruce Robbins, discussing Dickens's ambivalence about the growth of an impersonal state, has argued that 'professions, as in *Bleak House*, might belong both to the problem and to the solution' (1998: 157). Dickens certainly seems to suggest that an engaged and accountable professionalism is crucial for literary writers who need to balance their private ownership of their literary property, with its publication and instrumentality. But the law does not offer a sufficient model of professionalism for the Victorian novelist, struggling as he/she was with the conflict between professional withdrawal and writerly involvement. As I have argued elsewhere (see Pettitt 2004: ch. 5), women novelists in this period were also struggling, albeit in slightly different ways, with the conflict between privacy and public accountability.

I would, therefore, challenge any simple reading of fiction as 'supplementary' or 'rivalrous' to the law – suggesting instead that much Victorian fiction seeks to resituate the law in a wider cultural debate. The Victorian novel is able to maintain a position both 'inside' and 'outside' of the law. Fiction bears a far more complex relationship to the law, and indeed, to other public discourses, than has yet been fully investigated, and there is plenty of work still to be done. Critics such as Andrew H. Miller and Mary Poovey have set an example in suggesting ways in which literary texts partake of a cultural history, without being entirely determined by it. Future work could examine not only the law, but also other fields such as educational policy or economics. Bruce Robbins's work on professionalization seems to offer an excellent starting point for further research into the complex and shifting divisions and connections between private and public spheres which constituted 'subjectivity' in the nineteenth century. There is more work, too, to be done on 'commodity culture' in the period. Marxist theories of commodification seem to me to demand more thorough historicization, so that it becomes possible to unravel the specific ways in which material culture and literary culture play upon one another at particular points in this period. In addition, Isobel Armstrong, among others, has started the work of de-aestheticizing aesthetics. An enormous amount of work remains to be done in investigating the ways in which different notions of the aesthetic were simultaneously available to different groups in the nineteenth century.

The emerging field of law and literature, then, suggests diverse directions. Growing out of Foucauldian theory in the 1980s, it now offers us the opportunity to develop beyond a simple disciplinary model of nineteenth-century culture, and to restore the agency of the literary text. Such a move would help us to understand more of the multivocality of Victorian culture, and would allow the novel to restore some of those many voices to us. Literature does not merely imitate the dominant culture, but also suggests the dependence of dominance on dissent. In *Bleak House*, Dickens dramatized the difficulties of owning a voice in the new technological age of the mid-nineteenth century. It was precisely because of such difficulties that the copyright law was amended in such a way as to prioritize the claim of the author. The law did not 'solve' the difficulty, but it responded to it. The difficulty continued nevertheless.

References and Further Reading

Allen, Christopher (1997) *The Law of Evidence in Victorian England*. Cambridge: Cambridge University Press.

Anon. (1850) The flight of the goddess. *Household Words*, 13 April.

Armstrong, Isobel (2000) *The Radical Aesthetic*. Oxford: Blackwell.

Baird, John D. (1977) Divorce and matrimonial causes: An aspect of *Hard Times*. *Victorian Studies*, **20**: 401–12.

Barrell, John (1992) *The Birth of Pandora and the Division of Knowledge*. Basingstoke: Macmillan.

Belsey, Catherine (1980) *Critical Practice*. London: Methuen.

Bender, John (1987) *Imagining the Penitentiary: Fiction and the Architecture of Mind in Eighteenth-Century England*. Chicago: University of Chicago Press.

Burke, Edmund (1968) *Reflections on the Revolution in France*, ed., Conor Cruise O'Brien. Harmondsworth: Penguin.

Carlisle, Janice (1981) *The Sense of an Audience: Dickens, Thackeray and George Eliot at Mid-Century*. Athens: University of Georgia Press.

Collins, Philip (1962) *Dickens and Crime*. Basingstoke: Macmillan.

Collins, Wilkie (1992) *The Law and the Lady*. Oxford and New York: Oxford University Press.

Cook, Nancy (1988) Shakespeare comes to the law school classroom. *Denver University Law Review*, **68**: 577–88.

Cover, Robert (1993) *Narrative, Violence, and the Law: The Essays of Robert Cover*, ed. Martha Minow *et al.* Ann Arbor: University of Michigan Press.

Decicco, Lynne Marie (1996) *Women and Lawyers in the Mid-Nineteenth Century Novel: Uneasy Alliances and Narrative Misrepresentation*. Lewiston: Mellen.

Dickens, Charles (1985) *Bleak House*. Harmondsworth: Penguin.

——(1986) *The Posthumous Papers of the Pickwick Club*. Harmondsworth: Penguin.

——(1993) *Great Expectations*. Oxford and New York: Oxford University Press.

Dolin, Kieran (1999) *Fiction and the Law: Legal Discourse in Victorian and Modernist Literature*. Cambridge: Cambridge University Press.

Foucault, Michel (1977) *Discipline and Punish: The Birth of the Prison*, trans. Alan Sheridan. London: Allen Lane.

Grigsby, Ann (1996) Charles Reade's *Hard Cash*: Lunacy reform through sensationalism. *Dickens Studies Annual*, **25**: 141–58.

Gullette, Margaret-Morganroth (1990) The puzzling case of the deceased wife's sister: Nineteenth-century England deals with a second-chance plot. *Representations*, **31**: 142–66.

Forster, John (1911) *The Life of Charles Dickens*. London: Chapman and Hall, 2 vols.

Habermas, Jürgen (1989) *The Structural Transformation of the Public Sphere: An Inquiry into a Category of Bourgeois Society*, 1962, trans. Thomas Burger. Cambridge, MA: MIT Press.

Jameson, Frederic (1981) *The Political Unconscious: Narrative as a Socially Symbolic Act*. Ithaca: Cornell University Press.

Kornstein, Daniel (1994) *Kill All the Lawyers? Shakespeare's Legal Appeal*. Princeton: Princeton University Press.

Lewes, G. H. (1847) The condition of authors in England, Germany, and France. *Fraser's Magazine*, March: 285–95.

Macaulay, Thomas Babington (1853) Literary copyright' [February 5 1841]. *Speeches, Parliamentary and Miscellaneous*, **I**: 285–300.

Miller, Andrew H. (1994) Subjectivity Ltd: The discourse of liability in the Joint Stock Companies Act of 1856 and Gaskell's *Cranford*. *English Literary History*, **61**: 139–57.

Miller, D. A. (1988) *The Novel and the Police*. Berkeley and London: University of California Press.

Mukherjee, Upamanyu Pablo (2003) *Crime and Empire*. Oxford: Oxford University Press.

Pettit, Alexander (1990) Sympathetic criminality in the mid-Victorian novel. *Dickens Studies Annual*, **19**: 281–300.

Pettitt, Clare (2004) *Patent Inventions: Intellectual Property and the Victorian Novel*. Oxford: Oxford University Press.

Poovey, Mary (1988) *Uneven Developments: The Ideological Work of Gender in Mid-Victorian England*. Chicago: University of Chicago Press.

Posner, Richard A. (1988) *Law and Literature*. Revised and Enlarged Edition. Cambridge, MA and London: Harvard University Press.

Reader, W. J. (1966) *Professional Men: The Rise of the Professional Classes in Nineteenth-Century England*. London: Weidenfeld and Nicolson.

Robbins, Bruce (1998) Telescopic philanthropy: Professionalism and responsibility in *Bleak House*. In Jeremy Tambling (ed.) *New Casebooks. Bleak House, Charles Dickens*, pp. 139–62. Basingstoke: Macmillan.

Rockwood, Bruce L. (ed.) (1998) *Law and Literature Perspectives*. New York: Peter Lang.

Ross, Trevor (1992) Copyright and the invention of tradition. *Eighteenth-CenturyStudies*, **26**: 1–27.

Schmidgen, Wolfram (2002) *Eighteenth-Century Fiction and the Law of Property*. Cambridge: Cambridge University Press.

Schramm, Jan-Melissa (2000) *Testimony and Advocacy in Victorian Law, Literature, and Theology*. Cambridge: Cambridge University Press.

Sutherland, John (1995) The Victorian novelists: Who were they? In *Victorian Fiction: Writers, Publishers, Readers*. Basingstoke: Macmillan.

Tambling, Jeremy (1995) *Dickens, Violence and the Modern State: Dreams of the Scaffold*. Basingstoke: Macmillan.

Thackeray, William Makepeace (1994) *The History of Pendennis*. Oxford and New York: Oxford University Press.

Thomas, Ronald R. (1999) *Detective Fiction and the Rise of Forensic Science*. Cambridge and New York: Cambridge University Press.

Ward, Ian (1995) *Law and Literature: Possibilities and Perspectives*. Cambridge: Cambridge University Press.

Watt, Ian (1957) *The Rise of the Novel*. London: Chatto and Windus.

Weisberg, Richard (1984) *The Failure of the Word: The Protagonist as Lawyer in Modern Fiction*. New Haven: Yale University Press.

Welsh, Alexander (1992) *Strong Representations: Narrative and Circumstantial Evidence in England*. Baltimore: Johns Hopkins University Press.

White, James Boyd (1973) *The Legal Imagination: Studies in the Nature of Legal Thought and Expression*. Boston: Little, Brown.

Wiener, Martin J. (1990) *Reconstructing the Criminal: Culture, Law, and Policy in England 1830–1914*. Cambridge: Cambridge University Press.

Ziolkowski, Theodore (1997) *The Mirror of Justice: Literary Reflections of Legal Crises*. Princeton: Princeton University Press.

Zomchick, John P. (1993) *Family and the Law in Eighteenth-Century Fiction: The Public Conscience and the Private Sphere*. Cambridge: Cambridge University Press.

Chapter 5

'The withering of the individual': Psychology in the Victorian Novel

Nicholas Dames

That the terms 'psychology' and 'novel' are first explicitly allied in the nineteenth century should come as no surprise, given that the Victorian era saw the gradual codification and institutionalization of both psychology and the novel alike. That their initial combination, however, occurs in the context of a wittily self-ironizing slur by George Eliot, one of the Victorian era's leading practitioners of what came to be called 'psychological novels', is a less predictable fact. Reviewing Charles Kingsley's 1855 *Westward Ho!* in the pages of the *Westminster Review*, Eliot refers, with mock disdain, to '"psychological" novels (very excellent things in their way), where life seems made up of talking and journalizing, and men are judged almost entirely on "carpet consideration"' (1855: 88). To these supposedly tepid and decorous fictions, Eliot contrasts Kingsley's historical romance, with its vivid adventures and straightforward characterizations. What begins as a partially comic designation for English domestic fiction, however – stressing its talkiness, its indoor stillness, its feminization of masculine energy – will eventually metamorphose into a generic description of great weight and dignity, one which Eliot's own novels will be taken to exemplify. Late nineteenth-century historians of the novel, draining Eliot's term of its irony, were fond of distinguishing a strand of Victorian fiction properly called 'psychological', and continually asserted that in psychological fiction the era's narrative writers found their true calling. One such critic, Wilbur Cross, defined this fictional style in his 1899 summary *The Development of the English Novel* as stressing 'an inner sequence of thought and feeling, which is brought into harmony with an ethical formula and accounted for in an analysis of motive' (1899: 287); alongside Eliot, Cross adduced the work of Elizabeth Gaskell and George Meredith as key instances of this technique. Indeed, by the start of the twentieth century one could assert with no great risk that the 'psychological novel' was the most important and sophisticated of Victorian novel styles, possibly even a definition of Victorian fiction *tout court* – as if all Victorian novels were, by default, 'psychological', concerned with the workings of consciousness and motive, analyzing an inner life richer than any mere plot could describe.

The description 'psychological novel' has, in short, been a powerful one, and we still rely on it for much of our discussion of Victorian fiction. That novelists from Charlotte Brontë to Thomas Hardy worked toward the ends of psychology – that is, in the precise depiction of emotions, sensations, and moods, of a whole host of mental operations – is a truism no one would deny. But only recently have critics turned their attention to an unresolved problem in this commonplace sense of nineteenth-century fiction: what, for the Victorians, was 'psychology'? What did they understand by the term, and what specific kinds of concerns or analytic procedures did they group under it? To answer that question, one must turn to a very different set of questions and answers than those that we are used to ask under the umbrella of the 'psychological'. Restoring a properly historical understanding of nineteenth-century psychology to the novels that would eventually be read as so thoroughly 'psychological' yields a far stranger, even at times foreign, picture of the mind and its capabilities, tasks, and tendencies than that which is so habitually ascribed to Victorian novels.

Our understanding of Victorian psychology, however, has tended to encounter several obstacles. By far the most historically distorting obstacle standing between us and the Victorians in this regard is Freudian psychoanalytic theory. While the great mid-twentieth-century vogue for Freudian-informed criticism has largely passed, the vocabulary of psychoanalysis lingers as a default mode for the discussion of Victorian fiction and its characters. Terms like 'repression', 'trauma', or 'symptom' continually occur in analyses of the period's novels, usually without the recognition that such terms were not only unfamiliar to the Victorians themselves, but described phenomena for which Victorian psychological theories had very different explanations, and to which Victorian psychologists attached very different weight. In effect the task of the investigator of Victorian psychology is a kind of willed forgetting: temporarily to ignore the tremendous impact that psychoanalysis had on our definition of 'psychology' starting in the late nineteenth century, and therefore to arrive at the scattered field of theorizing that Freud's work did so much to obscure and, institutionally speaking, defeat.

'Scattered' perhaps scarcely does justice to the wild proliferations of psychology in the nineteenth century, which is the second major dilemma facing an accurate understanding of Victorian theories of mind. 'Psychology' was no single discipline and described no single set of methodological tools and assumptions. Individuals working from a range of different premises – from natural history, Lockean philosophy, chemistry, evolutionary science, medicine, and, of course, fiction and literary criticism – could claim to be 'doing' psychology, in an era in which psychology had yet to consolidate itself as a single discipline. Victorian psychology was animated above all by a series of sharp contentions about what did or did not constitute valid psychological evidence, what were useful questions to ask, what, in short, their pursuit looked like. Victorian psychologies, with no single institutional structure supporting its study and credentialing its students, could at once embrace figures as disparate as crowd-pleasing mesmerists, laboratory researchers studying the workings of the mammalian nervous system, and metaphysicians discoursing on the properties of Mind and Soul.

The resulting field was richer for its intellectual diversity. It was capacious enough to contain elements of what we would now recognize as anthropology, sociology, and philosophy; it was responsive to social and historical questions, and shifts in social structures and behaviors, in a way that contemporary psychology has largely abdicated. Part of the story of Victorian psychology, in fact, is the story of that gradual abdication: the restriction of the field to measurable, empirically verifiable results, which by the end of the nineteenth century became the dominant model for psychology as a newly minted science. That narrowing was, however, still incomplete at the end of the Victorian era, and for much of the nineteenth century to theorize mental operations could involve any number of discursive or rhetorical practices – including, for instance, novel writing. In the largest sense, the importance of psychology to a study of the novel lies in the simultaneous emergence of both as discrete forms of intellectual and artistic activity, and their mutual implication: their shared formal concerns (ways of writing, or narrating, the self), their shared imaginative powers (ways of picturing the mind), and their shared goals (a satisfyingly complete image of the mind's processes). To write novels in the Victorian period often meant to devote serious attention to advanced questions of mental functioning; thus it was that Charles Dickens avidly pursued mesmerism, that Charlotte Brontë had a deep understanding of phrenological tenets, that Wilkie Collins read up-to-date discourses on physiology, and that George Eliot, along with her partner G. H. Lewes, studied comparative anatomy in order to understand the workings of the nerves and brain. The novel, in brief, was part of the story of psychology, just as surely as psychology is part of the history of the novel form. To different degrees, both began the nineteenth century as loosely definable practices, and ended it as more rigidly codified styles of writing – but in between, the age of the 'psychological novel' remains, an age which could not envision one pursuit without the other.

The Institutions of Victorian Psychology

As *David Copperfield* opens, Dickens offers us a tableau of the young David, alone in bed, 'reading as if for life': 'Every barn in the neighbourhood, every stone in the church, and every foot of the churchyard, had some association of its own, in my mind, connected with these books, and stood for some locality made famous in them' (ch. 4: 56). Innocuous as it is to a contemporary ear, the term 'association' had not only a specific referent in nineteenth-century psychological theory, but was at the core of most Victorian theories of mind. To foreign observers, it seemed as if the primary locus of agreement among British mental philosophers was the theory of 'associationism'. In his 1870 textbook *La Psychologie Anglaise Contemporaine*, the French experimental psychologist Théodule Ribot, the preeminent continental popularizer of British scientific ideas, called associationism 'la phénomène vraiment fondamental [the truly fundamental phenomenon]' of British psychology (1870: 242). Ribot's claim was undoubtedly accurate, though odder than he himself recognized; it left British psychology in thrall to a theory that dated back to the first half of the eighteenth century, and beyond that to John Locke's 1690 *Essay Concerning Human Understanding* and its chapter 'On the Association of Ideas'. Unwittingly, Ribot depicted nineteenth-century British psychological theory – about which he could be enthusiastic – as a series of footnotes to an older, totalizing theory of mental processes.

Ribot was not wholly wrong; associationism was perhaps the closest thing Victorian psychology had to an orthodoxy. But the homage paid by Victorian theorists to this particular orthodoxy was, by mid-century, becoming more and more rote, and threatening finally to undo the work of the eighteenth- and early nineteenth-century associationists. The orthodoxy was initially, however, in full possession of the field. Most of the major figures in British psychology at the moment of Victoria's accession – James Mill, Dugald Stewart, John Abercrombie – were all relatively doctrinaire associationists. That is to say, their major works, from Stewart's *Elements of the Philosophy of the Human Mind* (1792–1827) to Mill's *Analysis of the Phenomena of the Human Mind* (1829), were subtle reworkings of the central associationist claim: that mental life consists entirely of sensory data which, via a vast series of associations with other sensations, become 'ideas', or what we might call perceptual data – in other words, that our beliefs are structured by the almost innumerable combinations of sensations, known as 'associations', that the mind spontaneously and predictably forms. The sensations, for instance, that David Copperfield absorbs – the sensory data of the view from his bedroom window – become 'beliefs' (that is, achieve their imaginary status as places from the novels he reads) through their constant association with the act of reading. Associationist theory, at least in its more formal Lockean form, assumed the famous *tabula rasa* ('blank page') of the mind: since we are given no associations at birth, they can be molded or formed by early experiences, particularly education. The importance given to the educator, the power he or she theoretically possessed, was potentially infinite. As for the 'laws' of association, they varied according to the terminological practice of the given theorist, but they tended toward a familiar triad: sensations are associated with each other, or with ideas, by contiguity (either temporal or spatial), similarity, or contrast.

Many nineteenth-century voices were raised in protest over associationism – not least that of Dickens himself, who in *Hard Times* (1854) satirized the dictatorial ambitions of teachers who believed in the passive blank slates of their pupils and sought to form, in brutal and repetitive ways, their 'associations' or mental pathways. But that Dickens could also rely on 'association' as a useful term for describing the fantasy life of his *alter ego* David is a crucial fact; it testifies to the cultural pervasiveness that the vocabulary of Lockean associationism had attained. In essence, Dickens could rely on his reader's understanding of the term, even as he personally bucked against the theory's social implications. Associationism's most entrenched antagonist, the strand of thinking known as 'faculty psychology', exemplified by Thomas Reid's 1785 *Essays on the Intellectual Powers of Man*, offered a vision of innate 'faculties' derived from Kantian metaphysics, such as memory, will, or belief, faculties that are not experimentally or empirically knowable but that can be posited through reasoning. The emphasis on fixed, God-given faculties was congenial to anti-reformist Tory thought in general, and added a political contestation to the more broadly philosophical disagreement between associationists and faculty psychologists. Faculty psychology's exponents also enjoyed institutional success: Reid's most well-known expositor and follower, Sir William Hamilton, was named Professor of Logic and Metaphysics at the University of Edinburgh in 1836, a position of wide influence and prestige. Furthermore, faculty psychology managed, just like its antagonist, to influence the course of ordinary language, and bequeathed to the British novel a term that would have a long and persistent life. 'Women are supposed to be very calm generally: but women feel just as men feel; they need exercise for their faculties and a field for their efforts as much as their brothers do', proclaims Jane Eyre in one of the more well known of her readerly addresses (ch. 12: 141). Brontë's reference here to faculty psychology, usually considered the 'conservative' alternative to associationist reformism, helps illuminate one quality of this debate: in the wider cultural arena, terms from associationism and faculty psychology circulated without necessary reference to the sociopolitical poles they were supposed to imply, and in fact each school of thought could be recruited for a wide variety of ends. If Brontë's early-feminist peroration, representing a position more familiar to associationist writers, could use the language of the ostensibly Tory faculty psychologists, those very psychologists often employed concepts from associationism – the preferred school of social radicals such as John Stuart and Harriet Taylor Mill – to buttress their own claims.

What is in fact more important than the distinctions between associationism and faculty psychology is the common ground they occupy, a ground which dictated the path of most Victorian psychologies. We might call this common ground the institutional consensus of early Victorian mental theorizing: that the key problem of mental life is how sensations, the irreducibly physical units of experience, become perceptions, the beliefs and ideas of consciousness; and that this problem is finally not solvable through any experimental investigation, but only through the ratiocination of metaphysics, whether that metaphysics traces its roots back to Lockean empiricism or Kantian transcendentalism. Put simply: the business of psychology is the problem of cognition – how we know the world – and cognition (or 'mind') is not wholly, or not at all, rooted in the pathways of the brain. Associationism tended toward a description of a master *process*, while faculty psychology tended toward a spatialized master *taxonomy* of the mind, but the differences were in many respects complementary; to speak of God-given innate faculties or associationist pathways of human origin were two different answers to an identical question. A wide range of political and philosophical beliefs could therefore comfortably fit within this consensus, and together, between them, associationism and faculty psychology seemed poised, at least by the 1830s, to settle contentedly into an amicable institutional quarrel, dividing up university chairs in philosophy and metaphysics between them, while their vocabularies filtered into general usage, making them available for novelists and critics, among others.

The consensus would not last long. The pressure on these two orthodoxies came from two distinct locations: from the experimental science known as physiology, and from a series of increasingly popular 'pseudosciences', such as physiognomy, phrenology, and mesmerism. The first directly challenged the metaphysics of psychology, returning the physical study of nerves and brain into the question. The second, while also asserting (in more surprising ways) the importance of a physical study of mind, challenged as well the institutional bases of this consensus by directly appealing to a mass public, and by making claims for clinical effectiveness, in a way that associationism or faculty psychology could never manage. Each of these two challenges to the early nineteenth-century consensus, which had a tremendous impact on Victorian fiction, will be described in more detail shortly. What it is necessary initially to grasp, however, is how each challenge exploded the institutional profile of Regency and early-Victorian psychology, and by doing so created an era of inclusiveness for psychology that remains a hallmark of the period.

Associationism and faculty psychology both, as Rick Rylance (2000) has recently noted, belonged to a philosophical discourse deriving from the major schools of eighteenth-century thought, one which had a reliable institutional profile: university chairs, long essays in the major periodicals of the early nineteenth century (the *Edinburgh Review*, the *Quarterly Review*, *Blackwood's*), and the occasional publication of large summary works such as Hamilton's posthumous 1859 *Lectures on Metaphysics and Logic*. Despite the filtering of their vocabulary into ordinary discourse, both the great scientific fact of their time, the explosion in methods of experimental research, and the great social fact of their time, the growth of a mass reading public, were unexploited by these 'mental philosophers'. They represented what might be called the higher professional reaches of nineteenth-century psychology, but as the century neared its midpoint that model of professionalization was under attack.

That attack was led, from different areas, by a newer breed of psychological theorists who produced uncomfortable hybrids of the old methods with the new. Two such figures are particularly exemplary. The first, the renowned Scottish phrenological theorist George Combe, was a legendarily marginal figure within the academic establishment of mental philosophy; he campaigned vigorously but unsuccessfully for the university chair the more traditional Hamilton won in 1836, while his *magnum opus, The Constitution of Man, Considered in Relation to External Objects* (1828), was apparently outsold only by such perennial bestsellers as the Bible, Bunyan's *Pilgrim's Progress*, and Defoe's *Robinson Crusoe* in the century's middle decades. Combe's brand of phrenology – the science of reading skull protrusions as an index to personality – was heavily inflected both by the vocabulary of revealed religion and that of faculty psychology; his work often read as if the new phrenological organs were merely up-to-date, multiplied, and more specific versions of the old faculties. Yet Combe also imported into his phrenology a version of the familiar associationist insistence on self-improvement through education: although each individual has God-given faculties with various unique strengths and weaknesses which are visible on the face and head, self-examination should ideally lead to the impulse to employ one's strengths to the fullest while recognizing, and avoiding, one's weaknesses. This odd blend of determinism, clinical investigation, reformism, and wide popularity helped unsettle familiar intellectual and social boundaries, and led to considerable dispersal: for instance, it seems likely that the young Charlotte Brontë read Combe in Yorkshire, as her early work *The Professor* (1857) contains direct, if unnamed, references to some of his phrenological 'portraits' in *The Constitution of Man*.

The second example of the new hybrid psychologies is perhaps Victorian psychology's most central figure, Alexander Bain – like Combe, also a Scotsman. Bain's early work – his seminal texts *The Senses and the Intellect* (1855) and *The Emotions and the Will* (1859), both of which would be standard psychological textbooks well into the later decades of the century – offer an attempt to marry cerebrospinal physiology to associationism. This synthesis would eventually be persuasive, even normative, for British theorists, but initially it earned him contempt from all sides: from faculty psychologists, for whom it reintroduced the error of physicalizing mind; from traditional associationists, who saw in this physicalizing a dangerous abdication of the reformist political tradition of the *tabula rasa*; and from a host of lay reviewers, who detected in Bain's physiological associationism a lurking, radical empiricism. But Bain was by no means an open radical, and unlike many of his later followers he sought acceptance in the academic establishment just as Combe had – although unlike Combe he succeeded, finally, in being accepted, and was elected to the chair in logic at the University of Aberdeen.

Two Scotsmen, Combe and Bain, one slightly outside, one partially inside, the established structures of early nineteenth-century psychology: their example, by proving the porousness of various boundaries, helped make the new, contentious arena of mid-Victorian psychology a pursuit open to a host of generalists. Indeed, if we move from officially sanctioned psychological theorists such as Hamilton to more controversial figures as Combe and Bain, we can detect a host of amateur psychological researchers and writers who come from well outside the institutions with which Combe and Bain grappled. Among them we find some key examples, particularly for the British novel. G. H. Lewes, sometime novelist, successful reviewer, and eminent London intellectual, avidly pursued an interest in physiology that resulted in a European reputation, despite his lack of formal training or academic recognition; the odd disciplinary combination that he represents – vivisectionist physiology and literary criticism – was, however, not entirely unique. Two other important critics of the period, E. S. Dallas and Frances Power Cobbe, took serious interest in psychology and physiology, marrying the two in their more literary work. Dallas's 1866 *The Gay Science*, one of the more remarkable aesthetic treatises of the period, was in part a manifesto for the application of recent psychological discoveries in literary criticism: 'it would seem', he wrote, 'that at the stage which criticism has now reached there is nothing so much wanting to it as a correct psychology' (1866, vol. 1: 42).

The permeability between psychological and fictional or literary discourses was not only a fact of genre definition. It had the added effect of opening up new questions that psychology might address. The central question of early Victorian psychology, the question of cognition – how do we know the world? – was one of great interest to realist writers, but with the breakup of the early Victorian mental philosophy consensus, new questions could now be asked, and insofar as these were both psychological and social questions, the novel took them up with vigor. For novelists interested in the burgeoning world of physiology, one such question was: what role do unconscious or automatic, instinctive processes play in our everyday behavior? As the century progressed, and accounts of the 'unconscious' proliferated, the newly revealed world of the reflexes, the body's autonomic or purely mechanical functions, and even heredity provided novelists with a range of vocabularies for actions not solely explicable by conscious motivations. For other writers of fiction, who found themselves interested in the body-reading psychologies of phrenology or physiognomy, a new question was: how can we know others, or even ourselves, through visual examination, without extensive acquaintanceship? What parts of the personality are visible and encoded in the body? Here the newer psychologies of the period provided answers to some of the mysteries of everyday social encounters that it was the novel's usual task to describe.

The Mind Made Visible

Few literary genres have been as dependent on the significance of exterior bodily features as the mainstream Victorian novel. What has only recently become apparent, however, is the degree to which that significance was a scientized one, licensed by a host of theories of mind that we today group, however unfairly or inaccurately, under the term 'pseudoscience'. Take the initial appearance of one of the period's most notorious villains, the political and financial careerist Ferdinand Lopez, in Anthony Trollope's 1876 *The Prime Minister*: 'He was nearly six feet tall, very dark, and very thin, with regular, well-cut features indicating little to the physiognomist unless it be the great gift of self-possession' (vol. 1, ch. 1: 4). The veiled, sphinx-like qualities of Lopez's face are overtly contextualized with reference to physiognomy, the science of reading facial features as an index to personality; and though it is asserted that Lopez is opaque to a physiognomical reading, Trollope's narrator proceeds to analyze his visage anyway:

> But about the mouth and chin of this man there was a something of softness, perhaps in the play of the lips, perhaps in the dimple, which in some degree lessened the feeling of hardness which was produced by the square brow and bold, unflinching eyes. They who knew him and liked him were reconciled by the lower face. The greater number who knew him and did not like him felt and resented, – even though in nine cases out of ten they might express no resentment even to themselves, – the pugnacity of his steady glance. (vol. 1, ch. 1: 5)

A common enough moment in Victorian fiction – the introductory portrait of a character – here relies on the meaningfulness of facial characteristics, their capacity to unveil the workings of a personality, while simultaneously disowning the scientific practice, physiognomy, that gave a cultural warrant to such an unveiling. The structure of the passage is by no means peculiar. It is a prevalent practice among Victorian novelists, who both employed the means and underlying assumptions of the body-reading theories of the nineteenth century while displaying a certain embarrassment about them. Whether in collusion with body-reading sciences or in competition with them – or, more likely, a combination of both – Victorian fiction could not avoid the pull of their hypotheses.

Two such sciences, physiognomy and phrenology, deserve most comment. Physiognomy was the elder of the two, dating back to the publication in the 1770s of Johann Caspar Lavater's *Physiognomische Fragmente*; English editions, starting with a translation by the radical Thomas Holcroft, began appearing in 1789. Lavaterian physiognomy was a guide to the signifying systems of the body: insofar as the inner self is expressed in quasi-linguistic fashion by facial features, the face can be considered to have a grammar (the combination of different features, such as prominent noses and large eyes) as well as a vocabulary (the meaning of certain facial expressions). The importance of Lavater rested not so much on the uniqueness of his claims – that the face might reveal the soul was, of course, an assumption with an ancient lineage – but on the systematic quality with which they could be pressed; the *Fragmente* abounded in complex diagrams discussing the various classes or types of noses, brows, and lips, and as such physiognomy looked remarkably like the taxonomical sciences of the eighteenth century, particularly Linnaean botany. In Lavater's hands physiognomy became the human analog to the revealed religion implicit in botanical taxonomies: if a complete taxonomy of flora or fauna might bring us closer to the mind of God, Lavater's analysis of human features might similarly reveal the divine intentions behind the bewildering multiplicity of national, racial, and individual faces.

The move from physiognomy, with its concentration on the mobile or soft, fleshy aspects of face and expression, to phrenology, which concentrated on the bony structures of the forehead and skull, began to take hold from 1810 to 1830, particularly in Britain. It is at this time that Franz Joseph Gall's seminal work, *On the Functions of the Brain* (1822–5), was published, and when his primary disciple and popularizer, Johann Gaspar Spurzheim, organized a series of lecture tours of

Britain. This was swiftly followed by Combe's popular work, and from the mid-1820s phrenology enjoyed a serious vogue that would last well into the 1850s, despite its continual repudiation by most corners of the scientific establishment. The transition from physiognomy to phrenology can be largely considered as part of a general early nineteenth-century transition from taxonomical science to a more rigorously empirical procedure: no longer content simply to describe and categorize the signifying features of the body, Gall and Spurzheim collaborated to produce a scientific project that would explain the root of these signifying features in the localization of brain function. The resulting theory presented itself as far more 'scientized': possessed of a unique, and often formidably obscure, vocabulary, and with claims for clinical effectiveness. At least two major British novelists, Charlotte Brontë and George Eliot, had their skulls 'read' and evaluated by trained phrenologists; in Brontë's case the clinical report has survived, insofar as it was transcribed into a letter she wrote to her publisher George Smith.

Gall and Spurzheim's theory was deceptively simple. Admit that the brain is composed of numerous smaller areas, called 'organs', each dedicated to a different function; what follows is that the more vibrant and powerful the function, the larger the organ has to be, and therefore the larger the area of the skull or brow that covers it. Simple empirical investigation – measuring skulls, and comparing those measurements with the known propensities of their possessors – could quickly establish a representative map of the head, which would be in essence a map of the brain and, therefore, of Mind itself. The phrenological map that Gall produced was composed of 27 'organs', to which Spurzheim later added eight more; this map would, with small alterations, last throughout the nineteenth century, and would reappear in Combe's work as well as in the mass-market pamphlets of the brothers O. S. and L. N. Fowler, who carried phrenology to the United States. A complete understanding of the phrenological map would, in theory, enable even laypeople to read and assess the propensities, talents, and weaknesses of others. Phrenology was at once therefore a clinical psychology – one that trained individuals with a series of diagnostic skills – and a popular pursuit. It was perhaps the most thoroughly disseminated manifestation of positivistic mental theories the nineteenth century would see.

Apparent in scattered places throughout Victorian fiction, phrenology is nowhere so visible as in Charlotte Brontë's fiction, where it is used with an unequalled obviousness, often as a supplement to the unsatisfyingly vague workings of physiognomy. The following description from *Shirley* (1849), of the austere reformist Hiram Yorke, is representative. It begins with a national physiognomy: 'His forehead was broad, not high; his face fresh and hale; the harshness of the north was seen in his features, as it was heard in his voice; every trait was thoroughly English, not a Norman line anywhere; it was an inelegant, unclassic, unaristocratic mould of visage' (ch. 4: 76). From here, however, the passage confesses the need for a more rigorous system:

> I did not find it easy to sketch Mr Yorke's person, but it is more difficult to indicate his mind . . . Mr Yorke, in the first place, was without the organ of Veneration – a great want, and which throws a man wrong on every point where veneration is required. Secondly, he was without the organ of Comparison – a deficiency which strips a man of sympathy; and, thirdly, he had too little of the organs of Benevolence and Ideality, which took the glory and softness from his nature, and for him diminished those divine qualities throughout the universe. (ch. 4: 76)

Here physiognomy stops at the level of 'person', while phrenology can access 'mind'. For most adherents the distinction was key: phrenology was less a poetic taxonomy of facial types than a totalizing account of mental processes, capable of delivering a complete, because more rigorously located in the cerebral cortex, portrait of an individual's psychology. Whereas physiognomical descriptions were capable of social repression, insofar as the vagaries of 'expression' were its subject, phrenology focused on the unalterable aspects of skull and brow, on the always-visible betrayals of one's mental makeup.

The vocabulary of phrenology, however, is rarely used with such unembarrassed confidence, since its jargon clashed too violently with more traditional methods of characterization. But physiognomy slid easily into phrenology and vice versa: both insisted on the knowability of mental traits through visual examination. And both were wedded to a series of largely unacknowledged premises, which had a serious impact on the description of character in Victorian fiction, insofar as the novel was itself dedicated to the outward signification of inner subjectivity. The first of these premises we might call the *detachability* of traits from each other: the possibility of considering mental traits in isolation from their adjacent or analogous brethren. Best symbolized by the elaborate tables of detached noses and eyes in Lavater, this tendency produced a vision of the mind as an aggregate of isolated powers, a kind of miniature society of independent actors, where some few selected traits will inevitably triumph over others.

Unlike the mechanics of psychoanalysis, where a wide variety of mental capacities can be all traced back to a small set of complexes or neuroses, Victorian body-reading sciences envisioned a barely regulated competition of powers or organs; the mind functioned not as a result of a centralized organizing power but as the more or less efficient division of mental labor among a series of discrete neural units. One result was the discourse of 'monomania': the unbalance resulting from a too-complete victory of one such trait. Monomania exerted a powerful influence over Victorian theories of insanity well after the disappearance of phrenology or physiognomy from the intellectual scene. Even outside the realm of mental illness, however, the unified self was thoroughly discredited; as Sally Shuttleworth has claimed, 'Cartesian man ceased to exist' (1996: 51).

The second general tendency of these body-reading sciences, of equal importance to the novel, was what we might call the *surfacing* of character: the ability of mental habits to express themselves visibly, without any necessary knowledge of the individual's history or background. Mental traits, particularly in phrenology, have no personal history; they are static constants, reliable and largely inborn, if susceptible to development or control. As a result, the idea of excavation – the importance of an individual's past – recedes. The phrenological psyche is not the result of a formation over time but instead of a constantly warring, or cooperating, set of propensities; and a propensity is less a 'symptom', a sign of some past deformation, than a capacity for future action. Both physiognomy and phrenology reflect, in short, a largely memory-free vision of psychic operations; unlike the absolute centrality that memory has in psychoanalytic theory, phrenology failed even to place remembrance in its mental map. Visible only to skilled initiates, free of the encumbrances of the past, a loose confederacy of psychic traits operating as independent actors: the individual envisioned by Victorian body-reading sciences was, one could say, an image of the modern, bourgeois self – exaggerated or caricatured perhaps, but all the more vivid and persuasive for the exaggerations.

In the largest sense, these sciences of psychic visibility offered solutions to one of the central epistemological problems of Victorian society: the extent to which other people, those strangers to whom an increasingly mobile and urbanized society made everyone more intimately linked, can be known without the benefit of long-term acquaintance. As social networks increased in size and complexity, and social interactions increased in rapidity, it became necessary to find answers to the inscrutability of an ever more mysterious, unmarked mass of individuals. The clarifications offered by body-reading sciences were both troubling and comforting: troubling insofar as they implied one's own vulnerability to trained sight, comforting insofar as they allowed for a reciprocal visibility. Everyday interactions could therefore be imagined – particularly in the novel – as the interplay of veiling and revealing, hiding oneself while penetrating the recesses of one's interlocutor. These solutions were, however, of limited use. By the 1860s and 1870s they were already antiquated, and their history after this time is scarcely edifying: they feed into the development of eugenics and racialized sciences that would have such a catastrophic twentieth-century career. But in the meantime a new source of unknowability in the self was being posited and explored by both the novel and psychology: the realm of the 'unconscious'.

The Hidden Self

The novel, as a form, began the nineteenth century with various skills and techniques solidly in place; among these, one of the most salient was its interest in the careful delineations of motive: the conscious or semi-conscious sources of action. No small part of the growth to dominance of the so-called 'omniscient' narrator in British fiction can be ascribed to the need to be ever more precise about the ambiguities and contortions of motive. But as the century proceeded, motive becomes more elusive and mysterious, particularly to the individual characters themselves, who often act without motive but with what we might call 'unconscious' motivation: hidden impulses of action that are less amenable to rational discussion or analysis. The trap of unconsciousness can befall even the most supposedly alert and informed of characters. George Eliot's Lydgate, from *Middlemarch* (1871–2), is himself a pathological or physiological researcher, working in his laboratory toward a knowledge of 'those minute processes which prepare human misery and joy . . . that delicate poise and transition which determine the growth of happy or unhappy consciousness' (book two, ch. 16: 194). Yet he too is capable of barely analyzable action; his pursuit of Rosamond Vincy is characterized as 'made of spontaneous beliefs and indefinable joys', a 'scarcely perceptible' web of emotions that springs from no conscious source (book 4, ch. 36: 380). One might easily say that Lydgate's actions come from something called his 'unconscious' self.

Yet it is precisely here that the historian of Victorian psychology, as well as the literary analyst, should be wary. As Alison Winter has asserted, the 'unconscious' today is a term freighted with Freudian baggage, which has 'charged this term in a way that makes it misleading when applied to the early and mid-Victorians' (1998: 10). To work back to its pre-Freudian meaning means to restore to it a certain multiplicity, for under the conceptual umbrella of the 'unconscious' was a host of different approaches. Each approach, however, sought an answer to a question that increasingly preoccupied the range of Victorian mental theories: how, and to what extent, are visible actions and behaviors governed by non-rational processes unavailable to consciousness? Four of these versions of the unconscious are particularly important for the student of Victorian fiction. The first, what the historian Edward Reed terms the 'logical unconscious', derives from mid-century revisions to associationist theory; the second, mesmerism, provided a model for an interpersonal version of the unconscious; the third, the unconscious of physiology, added new and dense accounts of reflex actions and autonomic behavior to the range of states the novel could describe; and the fourth, evolutionary or hereditary psychologies, offered behavioral explanations for the unconscious rooted in a more or less distant past which we would now recognize as genetic. Each model offered a distinct, even competing, version of what E. S. Dallas posited as the key to aesthetics and the horizon of contemporary theory: the 'hidden soul', the 'secret flow of thought which is not less energetic than the conscious flow, an absent mind which haunts us like a ghost or a dream and is an essential part of our lives' (1866, vol. 1: 199).

Studies of the unconscious begin as a solution to the intractable problem faced by associationist theory, the cognitive dilemma discussed earlier: how do sensations become perceptions or ideas? In John Stuart Mill's 1843 *Logic,* the solution was a capacity for forming 'inferences' based on sensations, which would then be used in the formation of fully conscious perceptions. The inferential capacity of the mind would, essentially, be an unconscious faculty – not a repository of dreams, memories, or repressed desire so much as the mind's hidden ability to synthesize the basic units of sensation into useable perceptual wholes. This flew in the face of the common-sense school of associationists, who believed that the sensation/perception link was finally insoluble; and it rescued associationist thought at the cost of introducing a third term that no associationist theorist had yet considered.

Later versions diverged considerably from this philosophical, even metaphysical, conception of the unconscious. But it is worthwhile keeping in mind that the initial postulate of an unconscious mental process was as a solution to the cognitive question that had so long animated, and frustrated, philosophers of mind.

The mesmeric unconscious was different in almost every respect. Like its often-allied sibling phrenology, mesmerism grew out of the work of a late-eighteenth-century pioneer – in this case, Anton Mesmer, who first postulated the presence of an invisible, magnetic fluid which bound person to person and which could, in trained hands, be manipulated and communicated in order to restore a given subject, placed in a mesmeric 'trance', to health. Although Mesmer's work was published in France as early as 1779, the British vogue did not begin until the 1830s – as the example of phrenology had already indicated, clearly a combustible decade – when the well-known John Elliotson, Professor of Medicine at University College, London, first espoused mesmerist principles and began running experiments in mesmeric therapy. Dickens himself studied Elliotson's experiments in the late 1830s and received some training in producing the mesmeric trance. A movement that had one foot in the official scientific establishment and one foot well outside it, mesmerism was yet another key battleground for the definition of a truly 'scientific' psychology, and its ability to span the realms of occultism and laboratory science makes it a particularly vivid example of the capaciousness of Victorian theories of mind. But for the British novel, mesmerism's most notable legacy is not a succession of scenes of hypnotism, trance, and séance – which are as relatively absent from the mainstream novel as scenes of phrenological assessment with calipers – so much as a master metaphor for the workings of a hidden intersubjectivity, which Alison Winter has called 'consensus' and which we might call 'atmosphere' or 'milieu'. The idea of a single current running invisibly through countless individuals, one which can yet be mastered and controlled by a powerful figure, helps make sense of the increasing power Victorian novelists gave to *environments*, such as Fagin's den in *Oliver Twist* (1837–8) or the Manchester slums of Elizabeth Gaskell's *Mary Barton* (1848). Mesmerism led in no one obvious direction for Victorian novelists, but it remained a suggestive model for thinking through the hidden mental springs of communities and social groupings, particularly the ways in which social groups form, grow, or deteriorate without explicit or conscious motivation.

If the mesmerist unconscious suggested links between individuals, the physiological unconscious made the category of 'individual' much more unstable. Insofar as nineteenth-century physiology, particularly such well-known works as G. H. Lewes's *The Physiology of Common Life* (1859), centered on the description of the processes of the nervous system, particularly the vexed role of the autonomic or 'lower' functions it carries out, the modulations of conscious personality, or what we might call 'character', were not part of its program. Here physiology worked in collaboration with the growth of 'reflex theory', inaugurated by Marshall Hall's 1837 *Memoirs of the Nervous System*, which offered a comprehensive theory of unwilled bodily actions. The important conceptual breakthrough of physiology, however, was its erasure of the line between the conscious workings of the cerebrum and the unconscious mechanisms of the spinal apparatus. This line is crossed most dramatically by William Carpenter's 1874 *Principles of Mental Physiology*, which laid out the case for a 'cerebral reflex', or the automatic workings of all mental activity. As Carpenter put it: 'Our Mental activity is, in the first instance, entirely *spontaneous* or *automatic*; being determined by our congenital nervous Organization, and by the conditions of its early development. It may be stated as a fundamental principle, that the Will can never *originate* any form of Mental activity' (1874: 25).

Carpenter's cerebral reflex was not an entirely new concept – similar ideas had been in circulation under the term 'unconscious cerebration' – but the unambiguous demotion of volition that his *Mental Physiology* announced was proof of physiology's potentially radical reorientation of the psyche. It is worthwhile stressing that the physiological unconscious was no psychoanalytic well from which repressed desire springs, but instead a vast reservoir of entirely unwilled, physicalized motor and cognitive activity. The nineteenth-century conception of the physiological unconscious, unlike our post-Freudian conception of the unconscious, is less a secret self than something alien to selfhood altogether. The consequences for the novel were profound. Physiology gave the lie to the notion – so key to realist fiction – that the individual was entirely responsible for his actions, and it demoted consciousness itself to the rank of a secondary function largely subservient to the prior workings of the nervous system. How a novelist might describe both action and thought in the wake of these discoveries became much more fraught with difficulty; 'personality' itself seemed to dissolve in the face of the spinal ganglia and its manipulations of the body.

Oddly enough, many of the precepts of the physiological unconscious had already been anticipated by the school of sensation fiction, perhaps the key sub-genre of British fiction in the second half of the nineteenth century. Descriptions of reflex actions, shock, surprise, and automatic states of action (trance, somnambulism, hallucination, intoxication) are virtually constitutive of the genre initiated by Wilkie Collins with his 1860 *The Woman in White* and followed by such publishing successes as Ellen Wood's *East Lynne* (1861) and Mary Braddon's *Lady Audley's Secret* (1862). The physiological root of the genre's name itself suggested something of the key reorientation both psychology and the novel were undergoing at this time; the familiar cognitive question, how sensation becomes perception, was turned on its head, and both psychology and fiction seemed far more interested in tracing perceptions backward to the sensations that were their 'real', physicalized origin than in tracing the coming-to-consciousness of an idea. The effect on the novel was more widespread than a popular sub-genre, however. Acute critics of the novel in the 1860s began to notice a shift away from character delineation and toward vivid plotting. E. S. Dallas termed this tendency 'the withering of the individual as an exceptional hero, and his growth as a multiplicand unit [i.e., a unit identical to a multiplicity of others]' (1866, vol. 2: 287). Dallas's term is telling: the hero is both multiple – in other words, composed now of a set of impulses and reflexes rather than a coherent core personality – but also part of a wider multiplicity, a community of similarly composed characters who, at bottom, share the pulsations and sensations of *nerves*. Here physiology helped explain the mass success of sensation fiction, a success as rapid as the movements of that other great electrical process, the telegraph: increasingly community itself, particularly reading communities, could be compared to the twitching of wires along branching paths.

The 'withering of the individual' carried out by the physiological unconscious was matched, and perhaps more profoundly extended, by the final psychological school that replaced the rational conception of motive with hidden springs of action: the evolutionary psychologists. Insofar as any one tendency in nineteenth-century mental theory can be said to have won possession of the psychological 'field', evolutionary psychology was such a victor. Theorists from a variety of different approaches had to retool their theories in the light of Darwinian evolution: Bain's later editions of his central texts were overhauled to give pride of place to a developmental theory of mind, which largely replaced his physiological emphasis, while Lewes turned increasingly to considerations of the adaptive functions of mental processes. Key texts in the movement, such as the 1855 and 1870 editions of Herbert Spencer's *The Principles of Psychology*, read the 'unconscious' as an instinctive adjustment to the environment, and replaced the temporally static dynamics of the physiological nervous system with a pervasive sense of *process*: mental operations as a continually unfolding development, not only over a single lifespan but over the lifespan of a family or a species.

The gradual transition from associationism and faculty psychology to the evolutionary psychologies of Spencer and the later work of Bain – in short, the passage in British psychology from the beginning of the nineteenth century to the 1870s and 1880s – would seem to describe a gradual declension in the power and centrality of conscious processes and the human will. It is nowhere more evidently reflected than in the mature fiction of Thomas Hardy, where human projects are continually defeated by the invasions of hereditary stains and unconscious lapses; his tragic figures, such as Tess Durbeyfield or Jude Fawley, are victims of lurking capacities and incapacities of which they are never wholly conscious. This abandonment of will is the most striking of the developments in the history of Victorian mental theories, and perhaps, in terms of its public position, its most self-destructive; with the demise of associationism, faculty psychology, phrenology, and mesmerism, what went under the name 'psychology' gradually lost its political or social voice, and increasingly receded into an ever more professionalized, but nonetheless marginalized, public silence. The way had been prepared for the entrance of psychoanalysis, a dramatically unified theory of the unconscious which restored to it some real agency. But as the collaboration between Victorian fiction and psychology came to an end, its final images were of individuals whose 'hidden souls' – either nerves, hereditary traits, or embedded habits – were masters of their conscious selves.

References and Further Reading

Brontë, Charlotte (1847) *Jane Eyre*. Ed. Q. D. Leavis. Harmondsworth: Penguin.

——(1849) *Shirley*. Eds. Andrew and Judith Hook. Harmondsworth: Penguin.

Carpenter, William (1874) *Principles of Mental Physiology*. London: Henry King.

Clarke, Edwin, and Jacyna, L. S. (1987) *Nineteenth-Century Origins of Neuroscientific Concepts*. Berkeley: University of California Press.

Cooter, Roger (1984) *The Cultural Meaning of Popular Science: Phrenology and the Organization of Consent in Nineteenth-Century Britain*. Cambridge: Cambridge University Press.

Cross, Wilbur (1899) *The Development of the English Novel*. London: Macmillan.

Dallas, E. S. (1866) *The Gay Science*. 2 vols. London: Chapman and Hall.

Dames, Nicholas (2001) *Amnesiac Selves: Nostalgia, Forgetting, and British Fiction, 1810–1870*. New York: Oxford University Press.

Dickens, Charles (1850) *The Personal History of David Copperfield*. Oxford: Oxford University Press.

Eliot, George (1855) Belles lettres. *Westminster Review*, **64**: 288–307.

——(1871–2) *Middlemarch: A Study of Provincial Life*. Ed. W. J. Harvey. Harmondsworth: Penguin.

Ellenberger, Henri (1970) *The Discovery of the Unconscious: The History and Evolution of Dynamic Psychiatry*. New York: Basic Books.

Harrington, Anne (1987) *Medicine, Mind, and the Double Brain: A Study in Nineteenth-Century Thought*. Princeton: Princeton University Press.

Hartley, Lucy (2001) *Physiognomy and the Meaning of Expression in Nineteenth-Century Culture*. Cambridge: Cambridge University Press.

Kearns, Michael (1987) *Metaphors of Mind in Fiction and Psychology*. Lexington: University Press of Kentucky.

Logan, Peter Melville (1997) *Nerves and Narratives: A Cultural History of Hysteria in Nineteenth-Century British Prose*. Berkeley: University of California Press.

Matus, Jill (2001) Trauma, memory, and railway disasters: The Dickensian connection. *Victorian Studies*, **43**: 413–36.

Otis, Laura (1994) *Organic Memory: History and the Body in the Late Nineteenth and Early Twentieth Centuries*. Lincoln: University of Nebraska Press.

Reed, Edward (1997) *From Soul to Mind: The Emergence of Psychology, from Erasmus Darwin to William James*. New Haven: Yale University Press.

Ribot, Théodule (1870) *La Psychologie Anglaise Contemporaine: école experimentale*. Paris: Ladrange.

Rylance, Rick (2000) *Victorian Psychology and British Culture, 1850–1880*. Oxford: Oxford University Press.

Small, Helen (1996) *Love's Madness: Medicine, the Novel and Female Insanity, 1800–1865*. Oxford: Oxford University Press.

Shuttleworth, Sally (1996) *Charlotte Brontë and Victorian Psychology*. Cambridge: Cambridge University Press.

Taylor, Jenny Bourne (1988) *In the Secret Theatre of Home: Wilkie Collins, Sensation Narrative, and Nineteenth-Century Psychology*. London: Routledge.

——and Shuttleworth, Sally (eds.) (1998) *Embodied Selves: An Anthology of Psychological Texts, 1830–1890*. Oxford: Clarendon Press.

Trollope, Anthony (1876) *The Prime Minister*. Ed. Jennifer Uglow. Oxford: Oxford University Press.

Tytler, Graeme (1982) *Physiognomy in the European Novel: Faces and Fortunes*. Princeton: Princeton University Press.

Vrettos, Athena (1995) *Somatic Fictions: Imagining Illness in Victorian Culture*. Stanford: Stanford University Press.

——(2000) Defining habits: Dickens and the psychology of repetition. *Victorian Studies*, **42**: 399–426.

Winter, Alison (1998) *Mesmerized: Powers of Mind in Victorian Britain*. Chicago: University of Chicago Press.

Wood, Jane (2001) *Passion and Pathology in Victorian Fiction*. Oxford: Oxford University Press.

Young, Robert (1970) *Mind, Brain, and Adaptation in the Nineteenth Century: Cerebral Localization and its Biological Context from Gall to Ferrier*. Oxford: Oxford University Press.

Chapter 6

'Telling of my weekly doings': The Material Culture of the Victorian Novel

Mark W. Turner

In the twenty-first century, we tend to read the Victorian novel in rigidly consistent ways. Largely, the breadth of Victorian fiction, and novels in particular, are published by a very small number of presses who offer their titles to us as part of a series of 'classics'. Penguin Classics, Oxford University Press's 'Oxford World's Classics', Norton, and Broadview editions, to name only the most popular editions used by students – these different series package and market Victorian fiction alongside works from other periods, in a seamless, harmonious manner with similar covers, styles, and presentation. Such relatively inexpensive paperbacks accumulate to constitute a 'library' of available texts that amount to something akin to a canon of classic English literature, broadly speaking. Works by Victorian novelists find themselves packaged up neatly to sit alongside the works of distant relations – Aphra Behn and Daniel Defoe, for example – and in their outward appearance, no consideration at all is given to the different forms in which the Victorian novel actually appeared. The Penguin Classics today suit our own reading needs rather than reflect on Victorian publishing reading habits, for perfectly understandable reasons. This is, perhaps, as it should be since one reason these novels live on today is because they speak to us, in many different ways, about the present, and the relationship between the past and present, not because they are museum pieces. Still, it is worth remembering that the object we hold in our hands and read today bears little resemblance to that produced in the nineteenth century, and that the inexpensive paperback as we understand it was an invention of the early twentieth century. In fact, the Victorian novel appeared in many forms in its day and fiction then was far less uniform in its presentation than the series of 'classics' we now read suggests.

While modes of publication varied, there was a dominant form for the book publication of Victorian novels, a uniform three volumes, the 'triple-decker' as it is often called. The three-volume novel was the standard form for novels in book form for much of the period but it was an expensive commodity, costing a hefty 31 shillings and 6 pence (31s 6d), putting it out of the financial reach of most ordinary readers. By the middle of the century, the large bulk of Victorian readers did not purchase triple-deckers at all; instead, they bought subscriptions to circulating libraries that allowed them to borrow a volume of a novel instead. A subscription to a circulating library such as Mudie's Select Library, the powerful industry leader for much of the century, cost only a guinea and allowed subscribers to take out an unlimited number of volumes during the year (although they could only take out one volume of a novel at a time). There were different subscription rates according to whether you lived in the city or country, and how many volumes you wished to borrow at any given time (Griest 1970: 38–9). In the library system, family members could borrow volumes from several novels simultaneously and pass them round. Economically, the system benefited both the publishers and, in particular, the circulating libraries, for whom the substantial financial return was consistent and guaranteed, but it also benefited average middle-class readers who otherwise could not afford to purchase expensive triple-deckers.

In addition to the dominant triple-deckers, there were many other book forms in which the novel appeared, including expensively bound Library Editions, more modestly bound collected works, and there were two- and four-volume novels as well. Furthermore, after the publication of the multi-volume novels, works were often reissued in a cheaper one-volume form (often available at railway bookstalls such as W. H. Smith). New types of printing presses, new kinds of paper, and developments in advertising and marketing – all part of a nascent mass media system – are all reasons why Victorian fiction took different forms at different periods of the century. The invention of the railways in the 1830s allowed for vastly improved systems of distribution for novels, which led to increased demand. As technology changed, so, too, did the look and form of the novel (Hamer 1987: 6–11).

However, volume form was not the only way in which the Victorian novel appeared; indeed, it may not even have been the most prominent form. While today we almost always read our contemporary fiction in either hardback or paperback, and while we almost always think of the reading process as a lone, individual activity, the Victorians frequently did not read their fiction as self-contained texts at all. On the contrary, much Victorian literature – the novel, in particular, but also non-fiction including biography, science, travel literature, even the Bible – was presented to the reading public in serial parts. That is, readers encountered their stories over extended periods of time, with enforced pauses or gaps in time between installments. Serialization of novels in the nineteenth century took a number of forms including weekly and monthly installments that were bound and sold separately (what is called part-issue serialization), and weekly and monthly installments that appeared in a wide range of magazines and newspapers. Depending on the length of the work and the frequency of serial installments, a reader might commonly read and 'live with' a novel for a year or more without ever being able to read ahead (see Hughes and Lund 1991: 1–14), and it is the dynamics and meanings produced by the serial form of the novel that I wish to focus on in this chapter.

The Novel in Parts

Although Victorian readers embraced serial forms of reading, serialization was not new to the nineteenth century and there were many precedents for reading literature in serial parts before the Victorians. Essay-led periodicals in the eighteenth century, such as *Tatler* and the *Spectator*, were important precursors, and by the end of the eighteenth century, sentimental fiction was appearing in periodicals such as the *Lady's Magazine* (Law 2000: 3–7). Yet, if serial literature was a feature of literary culture before, it was not really until the Victorians that a culture of serial reading became pervasive and, arguably, the most significant literary form for much of the century.

The move toward serial publishing became unstoppable with the publication of a single serial narrative beginning in 1836, Charles Dickens's *The Posthumous Papers of The Pickwick Club*, published under the pseudonym 'Boz'. The emergence and overwhelming impact of *Pickwick* is well documented. The young Dickens, a jobbing journalist at the time, was commissioned to produce brief narratives to accompany illustrations by Robert Seymour (and shortly thereafter, Hablôt Browne or 'Phiz', who became Dickens's most important illustrator for the next 20 years) on the comic subject of Cockney sporting life. What began as something akin to hackwork for the writer swiftly became one of the most significant publishing events of the nineteenth century, and this serialization utterly transformed the publishing industry. As Robert Patten suggests, after *Pickwick*, 'parts publication became for thirty years a chief means of democratizing and enormously expanding the Victorian book-reading and book-buying public' (Patten 1978: 45). The serial parts, issued monthly from April 1836–November 1837, contained two or three chapters in each installment, and eventually numbered a standard 32 pages. The monthly installment and part-issue had an illustrated cover (the same each month), was wrapped in advertising (that is, adverts were sewn into the binding), and each monthly part cost a shilling. With some exceptions, this became the standard form for all of Dickens's fiction published serially as part-issues, and it became a standard that many other novelists also adapted in an effort to match Dickens's success (Schlike 1999: 514–19).

While Dickens began writing the linked narratives around the idea of the Pickwick Club, he certainly did not begin *Pickwick* with any sense of an entire narrative whole. In other words, the overall shape of *Pickwick* was haphazard and unplanned, and its unparalleled reception by the reading public a wholly accidental phenomenon. Indeed, for some readers and critics, whether *Pickwick* is in fact a novel at all is a matter of some debate. Its debt to eighteenth-century novelists is clear (it is part romance, part mock-heroic, part picaresque), but the lack of cohesion and a clearly sustained single, structured vision and its origins as a series of sketches have led some readers to question what kind of fiction *Pickwick* actually is. The fact is that the final shape of *Pickwick* reflects its composition as an ongoing work in parts, and whether this fragmentation prevented it from being a novel did not overly trouble its original readers. Although capturing their imaginations with this monthly rollicking, episodic narrative was not quite instant, by the end of 1837, sales had reached a staggering 40,000. When the project began, the publishers were hoping for regular sales of about 500. Such success unsurprisingly spawned numerous imitators who pirated characters and plot lines from Dickens and invented new adventures – *The Post-Humourous Notes of the Pickwickian Club* and *Pickwick in America*, both serialized in weekly numbers in the years immediately following Dickens's publishing triumph – but none was able to match Dickens's own innovation and invention. For Dickens, part-issues were not only lucrative, but also a way for him to keep in touch with a reading public over an extended period of time.

The obvious question to ask is, *why* were the adventures of Mr. Pickwick and Sam Weller so popular? Partly this must be answered in purely artistic terms; *Pickwick* is a great comic achievement. But the serial form that Dickens used, accidentally, also enabled the work continuously to gain new readers, month to month, and consolidate those readers already purchasing shilling copies of the installments. This is for a number of reasons that help explain why serialization remained such a significant form of publication for so long. Firstly, part-issue serialization made purchasing a novel affordable. Rather than paying for a prohibitively expensive work of fiction in volume form, the reading public could pay a shilling a month, spreading the cost out over the extent of the run (19 months for Dickens), and still end up paying less for the whole than if they were to buy a triple-decker at 31s. 6d. The significance of making fiction affordable to an increasingly literature mass public cannot be underestimated. Secondly, as the serial became more popular the monthly part-issue numbers were reviewed by the press; these reviews, which occurred during the 'pause' in the story, were part of the enforced temporal break in the narrative that allowed readers to speculate about what might occur next, or to reflect on events that had already passed. Reviews offered talking points for readers, and on a regular basis, and they garnered interest which also increased sales (Patten 1978: 67). The monthly reading cycle became a kind of social event that brought readers together over a single topic – the latest number of *Pickwick* (Hughes and Lund 1991: 9–10). Furthermore, Dickens cleverly exploited the serial form so that the lives and times in the fiction in part reflected the lives of readers. Beginning with number six, Dickens began to link novel time to 'real' time; he builds the seasons into the narrative, and included such significant temporal and social markers as Christmas and Valentine's Day. This, of course, is something we now take for granted in the serials that impact on our lives – those serial television programs, soaps, and sit-coms, that are are so much a part of Anglo-American popular culture – and the ratings-winning Christmas episode (or Thanksgiving episode, or back-to-school episode, etc.) all owe some debt to Dickens in this respect.

The success of *Pickwick* ensured that Dickens continued to use serialization for virtually all of his subsequent novels, and it ensured that many other authors seeking to match his popularity would also try their hand. Clearly, serialization made sound commercial sense for publishers who could sell a novel twice: once by selling monthly shilling parts to individual readers and then again by selling expensive volumes of the novel to the circulating libraries (who might purchase thousands of copies of the most popular authors' novels). Furthermore, additional income could be generated through advertising revenue, which was guaranteed, since advertisers might buy a package of advertising space monthly or weekly throughout the entire run of a novel, particularly those written by the most popular novelists. Financially, it was a low-risk situation for publishers, and for the shrewdest popular writers – such as Dickens or his contemporary Anthony Trollope, both of whom paid close attention to their contracts and copyrights – serialization could be a tremendously lucrative mode of publication.

One result of the commodification of the novel on a large scale was that debates about the cultural value of contemporary popular fiction raged intermittently throughout the century. These debates were particularly fierce during the 1860s when the enthusiasm for so-called 'sensation novels', by writers including Wilkie Collins, Mary Braddon, and Ellen Wood, flooded the serials and magazines market with tales of murder, bigamy, madness, and deceit. For many cultural commentators, the field of popular cultural production was a debased one, in which the popular novel as a literary genre was a sign of immoral times (Wynne 2001: 4–6). But more than its propensity to produce cliff-hanging tales of suspense, the serial novel was seen by many critics as unartistic. Writing by numbers (as a study of Trollope's serial fiction is titled) was interpreted as evidence of the mechanization of art in pursuit of profit. Great literature, it was suggested, was naturally at odds with highly popular literature and simply could not be produced on regular cycles. One example of this might stand for others. When, after his death, Trollope's workman-like method of writing his novels for serialization was revealed in his *Autobiography* (1883) –250 words per quarter-hour, for three hours each morning, producing something like three triple-deckers per year – his reputation as a writer declined. Henry James detected a 'perceptibly mechanical process' in the production of Trollope's *oeuvre* and he believed that 'he sacrificed quality for quantity' (James 1948: 1). No true artist, it was felt, could produce 'great' literature like clockwork. Even leaving aside debates about what constitutes 'greatness' in a literary work, the evidence suggests the contrary. In addition to such figures as Dickens, Trollope, and Wilkie Collins, virtually all Victorian novelists of merit published their work in one serial form or other at some point during their career – George Eliot, Elizabeth Gaskell, Thackeray, Hardy, and even Henry James, to name only a few.

We need not rehearse the specifics of the argument against popular culture and the marketplace; in fact, it is probably simpler to acknowledge that the Victorian novel *was* an important part of the increasingly commercial publishing industry, that, in the words of Michael Lund and Linda K. Hughes, the serial form 'harmonized in several respects with capital ideology' (Hughes and Lund 1991: 4; see also Feltes 1986). On the one hand, there is nothing new in this since the production and dissemination of literary texts have always been linked to the marketplace; publishing has always been profit driven. While the serial form may appear to be excessively linked to commercial aims, other material forms of the novel, for example the book or volume form, are no less linked to the bottom line. Indeed, literature and commerce have always been (and no doubt will always be) odd bedfellows, and Victorian publishing is not unique in this regard. On the other hand, it is true that the competition for large numbers of newly literate readers in the nineteenth century suggests a fiercer marketplace increasingly appealing to the mass rather than to relatively small groups of readers. The nature of this shift is ongoing throughout the century rather than sudden, but certainly by the 1890s, a mass readership is in place and new kinds of publishing practices and new literary forms reflect that change. The reading public at the turn of the twentieth century was very different than when Dickens was writing *Pickwick* in the 1830s, but the success of Dickens's mode of publication is arguably the start of a process of change throughout the century that leads us ineluctably from the concept of the 'popular' to the 'mass'. The material forms the novel, which change according to technological and social shifts, help us to track that process.

Despite the ease with which we could do so, it would be an oversimplification to interpret the dominance of serialization merely as a money-spinning mode of publishing popular fiction. Although *Pickwick* was unplanned and accidental, Dickens's fiction after it was carefully organized as he kept the serial to the fore when devising its overall structure and plots. He thought about his novels *through* the serial form, we might say. Other novelists did, too. Once Trollope hit on popular success through the magazine serialization of *Framley Parsonage* in 1860, he never abandoned serialization as an organizing and creative principle for his novels (Hamer 1987: ch. 1; Turner 2000: 8–9). While Dickens favored the form devised in the initial *Pickwick* venture

– 19 monthly parts of 32 pages, with two illustrations, and the final number a double issue – he also adapted the form and tried other methods. *The Old Curiosity Shop* and *Barnaby Rudge* both appeared weekly in Dickens's own journal, *Master Humphrey's Clock* (all of which was written by Dickens), and *Oliver Twist,* nine years after it first appeared as a magazine serial in *Bentley's Miscellany* and had been issued in three volumes, was reissued in 10 monthly shilling parts. Dickens, the great innovator of serialization, continued to experiment with the form, exploring new ideas about how best to write a narrative in parts intended to be read over an extended period of time. The layered complexity of such serial works as *David Copperfield* (with its exploration of time, memory, and the self) or *Bleak House* (with its use of two narrative voices to tell the story) are linked to such exploration.

Although the monthly part-issue serial form was the one that Dickens was most comfortable with, there were many other cycles and serial rhythms overlapping in the literary marketplace. In the 1860s, magazine serialization challenged part-issue serialization significantly, since new technologies reduced the cost in producing good quality periodicals (as opposed to cheaper penny weeklies). The monthly magazine boom in the 1860s, in which a whole range of new titles was launched aiming to capture the middle-class reading market. There were magazines catering for women, men, and the family, magazines with a religious fervor or political bias, magazines that were high and low brow. It was a competitive market in which the use of serial novels to attract readers was crucial, and the launch of the shilling monthly *Cornhill Magazine,* which first appeared in January 1860, is often regarded as a watershed moment in Victorian publishing. Published by Smith, Elder and initially edited by Thackeray, *Cornhill* posed a fundamental challenge to part-issue serialization because, for the price of a shilling, readers were given installments from two novels simultaneously, in addition to all the other miscellaneous articles that made up the contents of an issue. Each issue of the *Cornhill* was 128 pages, and it included full-page illustrations by significant artists including the Pre-Raphaelite Millais. In the first issue of the *Cornhill,* the contents included the opening installments of Trollope's *Framley Parsonage* and Thackeray's *Lovel the Widower,* poetry, and articles on such topics as natural science, politics in China, and the literary figure Leigh Hunt, in addition to other material. All this, with high quality woodcut illustrations, for the price of a shilling, the same as Dickens's monthly part-issues. The *Cornhill* quickly established itself as a market leader with legendary sales figures of over 100,000 in its early heyday, although these dropped and other magazines led the market by the mid-1860s. Still, these initial sales were significantly higher – by three or four times – than Dickens's most successful part-issue runs and suggested a whole new middle-class family magazine reading market opening up in which serial fiction would play an important part. Following swiftly and hoping to emulate the triumph of the *Cornhill*, a whole spate of magazines were launched with greater or lesser pretensions: *Temple Bar*, *Belgravia*, *Good Words*, *St. Paul's Magazine*, *St. James's*, and many more.

Although it is difficult to say absolutely, it is almost certain that these fiction-led magazines – many of which heavily advertised the 'star' novelists whom they published – were as popular as they were because of the fiction they carried. Edited by Thackeray, and then by figures such as G. H. Lewes and Leslie Stephen, the *Cornhill* was initially the most high-brow of the shilling monthlies and its reputation during its first two decades as the leading monthly magazine for fiction was well earned. In addition to works by Trollope and Thackeray, Elizabeth Gaskell, George Eliot and Wilkie Collins also serialized novels in the shilling monthly in its first few years.

For us looking back at the Victorian novel, it is sometimes difficult to conceive what it might have meant to read a work of fiction over an extended period of time, without being able to read ahead. In other words, the dynamics of Victorian serial reading – whether part-issue or in magazines or newspapers – pose special challenges for us, since we have to try imagining a very different kind of reading culture, in which reading aloud from a shilling monthly in the family circle, for example, was as likely to be the scene of reading as more private, individual reading from a volume. Thinking about serialization as a primary form for the novel forces particular questions to the fore: what did readers do during the pause between installments? How did readers remember complicated, multi-plot narratives for such an extended period of time, especially if they were reading a number of installments of novels simultaneously from month to month? What did it mean to read an installment in a magazine, with other kinds of material published alongside it – did this influence the interpretation of the fiction? What was the relationship between literary text and image where serial novels were illustrated; that is, did readers think of characters through the visual images provided by illustrators? All of these questions are valid and suggestive ways of beginning to explore how meaning might be produced in the serial novel.

The Serial Novel and the Media

One way of thinking about the form of the serial novel published in magazines that touches on all these questions is to consider it as a part of the print media that circulated in the Victorian period. We tend to think of the media today as being composed of newspapers and broadcasting, but it also includes all our magazines and advertising – in fact, all the many forms of cultural production that constitute our varied forms and networks of communication. If we think about the media in these terms, as the cultural forms of communication in any given moment, then reading the serialized novel as part of the periodical print media is appropriate; indeed, it may shift our interpretation of Victorian fiction in suggestive ways, not least because of the need to consider the role of time in the media.

Time, however you think about it, is essential to what the periodical print media is. By its very definition, periodicals – all regularly issued newspapers and journal and even part-issues that appear over time – are continually on the move, across time. Thinking of the serial novel in relation to time suggests another set of questions: what is the relationship between the novel and the press? What do the different cycles of time in the Victorian print media mean at the level of reading? How does time get imagined and represented in the print media? How do understandings about time in the period impact on our own understandings of time and history? If we think about the serial novel as part of the media, time becomes a significant conceptual problem, but one that helps elucidate the links between the meaning of a text and its material form in the period.

The dynamics of periodicity – what it means to read in a weekly form, or a monthly form, and how the significant differences between those temporal forms affect interpretation – are a central concern in serial publication in the Victorian period. But what makes studying the concept of time in relation to material cultural forms so interesting is that the whole idea of 'time' was a problem for the Victorians. In the nineteenth century, time both slowed down – if we think of the conceptual challenges of geology or evolution that extended the 'history' of time from thousands to millions of years – and sped up – if we think of the development of the telegraph or the railway which radically accelerated communications across time and space. It depends on what sort of time you are talking about, which suggests that there are different 'kinds' of time. Certainly, until the late nineteenth century, time was not fixed. There were many ways of understanding time globally (in addition to nationally or regionally) which was one significant reason for the movement toward the standardization of time that became such an imperative, particularly in Europe and North America during the century. Before standardized time according to the prime meridian in Greenwich, there was no agreement within countries, let alone across countries, about what time it actually was. In fact, standard time was only adopted across Britain in 1880 and international time zones established in 1884 (Macey 1994: 575). In an 1881 pamphlet calling for the standardization of time, Sandford Fleming, a Canadian engineer and one of the first to come up with a global system for measuring time, neatly outlines the problem of time in the period:

> If we take into view the whole earth, we have at the same instant in absolute time, noon, midnight, sunrise, sunset, and all intermediate gradations of the day. The telegraph system, which is gradually spreading like a spider's web over the surface of the globe, is practically bringing this view of the sphere before all civilized communities. It leaves no interval of time between widely separated places proportionate to their distances apart. It brings points remote from one another, enjoying all the different hours of daylight and darkness, into very close contact. Under our present system of notation, confusion is developed, and all count of time is thrown into disorder. (Fleming 1881: 5)

Synchronicity is virtually impossible in a culture of competing timetables, and technological developments in media (in particular the telegraph and, later, the telephone) but also the railways exacerbated what comes to be seen as a kind of crisis in interpreting time. Global space is understood to be shrinking, bringing communities closer together than ever before, and time is speeding up, but the result of this is something like a new world order, producing 'social and commercial conditions which never previously existed in the history of the human race' (Fleming 1881: 7). According to Fleming, time confuses and disturbs, and it can even be dangerous. What is so interesting about the periodical press of which serialized novels were so much a part is the way it both registered anxieties about the shifting nature of time and participated in creating those anxieties. Each of the different temporal patterns used in Dickens's serials, then, could suggest different ways of thinking about the content of the novel – different kinds of breaks in the rhythm could mean different things to readers.

I am suggesting two things: that the periodical media provides the rhythm of everyday life for its readers, but that there is no single rhythm. The periodical press in particular moves to a number of different beats. The asynchronic world that Stanford Fleming identifies due to railways and telegraphs can equally be said to exist in the periodical press. The journalist T. P. O'Connor, in an 1889 article often cited by scholars for the way it registers the changes taking place in the New Journalism toward the end of the century, suggests precisely the overabundance of competing forms of print culture:

> We live in an age of hurry and of multitudinous newspapers. The newspaper is not read in the secrecy and silence of the closet as is the book. It is picked up at a railway station, hurried over in a railway carriage, dropped incontinently when read. To get your ideas through the hurried eyes into the whirling brains that are employed in the reading of a newspaper there must be no mistake about your meaning: to use a somewhat familiar phrase, you must strike your reader between the eyes. (O'Connor 1889: 434)

O'Connor writes of the need to seize readers' attention with a more forceful journalism than had previously been known, yet he also insists on the need for journalism to match the hurried pace of modern life with an equally hurried form of prose. What was true of the newspapers was equally true of the magazines, and in a culture of 'multitudinous' and competing titles, such abundance can come across as riotous. In her most recent book, *Print in Transition* (2001), Laurel Brake discusses precisely this perceived new phenomenon and the ways a print culture of multiple periodical rhythms led to disquiet. Brake discusses an article by Innes Shand, a mostly forgotten novelist, critic, and contributor to periodicals in the late nineteenth century, who worried that the intellectually weighty quarterly reviews were losing their privileged position in print journalism, 'in these days when everybody is living so fast, that a quarter seems much the same thing as a century' (quoted in Brake 2001: 11). She locates Shand's anxiety in the context of a periodical culture that is accelerating and multiplying:

> Shand is registering the regular, insistent, and cacophonous rhythms of the serial press: morning and evening, weekly, Sundays, monthly, and quarterly. The periodical press of the last two categories (and perhaps monthly part-issues?) also contributed emphatically to this noise and rhythm in their Magazine Day, when Paternoster Row worked flat-out to supply the retailers' orders. The regularity and public nature of these

> issue days created numerous and large communities of readers, all of whom were reading the same publication at roughly the same time all over the country. (Brake 2001: 11)

On the one hand, a particular rhythm can create what sociologists of time call 'temporal symmetry' (Zerubavel 1981: 64) – the daily cycle, the weekly cycle, the monthly cycle, etc. – with readers interacting with the media at roughly the same time. This kind of simultaneity becomes increasingly significant in a collective media culture, and can lead to a form of social bonding with a community of readers all engaged in the same activity. In other words, if time is one of the ties that bond, as sociologists such as Emile Durkheim suggests (Durkheim 1915: 10–11), and the periodical press is one of the chief ways that time is organized, then all the different periodicities – each of those segments or cycles of time – are also socially binding. During a weekly or monthly pause, readers were looking back at events that had occurred in previous installments and were projecting forward, thinking about the future of the narrative, and they were doing this together. But we also ought to acknowledge that there might equally be temporal *asymmetry*; that is, because there are competing, overlapping cycles of time that confront the reader in the different periodical cycles in the nineteenth century, the result could as easily be confusion as cohesion. Innes Shand's uncertainty about the hurried, multitudinous periodicities suggests that one could be out of sync, rather than always in sync. So while there *is* a repetition of cycles, a regularity to the press in one sense that could lead to a synchronic social experience, there is no single cycle, no single motion which somehow contains it all. Magazine Day, that much anticipated moment when the monthly magazines with all their serial installments were published all at once on a single day, was one way of organizing time – it was a ritual of media time; but, however significant a marker it was, it was only one event on the media calendar, created by the rhythm of the press and publishing industry.

Nineteenth-century Magazine Day suggests the importance of the monthly cycle in the temporal scheduling of everyday life, particularly significant because that is when the next installment of serial fiction appears in the monthly magazines, and this monthly ritual on the media calendar was certainly met with a great deal of anticipation by readers. But monthliness has to be seen alongside other temporalities: 'quarterliness' (the weighty reviews, especially important in the first half of the century); weekliness (the cheap penny weeklies with serials, and also more highbrow journals of current events); dailiness (the morning and evening newspapers, some with serials); and even 'annualness' (if we include the rhythm of almanacs, annual volumes, and the significance of Christmas books on the publishing calendar). In fact, when we begin to look at all the different ways that the periodical press divided and constructed time, we are confronted with a plethora of different meanings, of subtle differences with distinct cycles of time.

The periodical press, then, constructs the time of our lives in as much as it demarcates different kinds of time for readers. However, these artificial segments of time are meaningful and not simply arbitrary – a daily cycle has meaning to everyday lives, a weekly cycle has meaning to everyday lives, and a daily cycle means something different from a weekly cycle, etc. To put it differently, in addition to scheduling our lives, the temporalities created by the press are linked to cultural values. We value some time more than others. For example, in debates about the Sabbath and Sunday reading, which flair up from time to time in the nineteenth century – debates that question whether such material as the serial novel was appropriate for Sunday reading – we see precisely the way in which time schedules constructed by the press are linked to debates about the value of time. Is Sunday time more precious than other time? Is that the case for everyone? Can we read periodicals at all on Sundays, and if not, what kind of material ought we read? What such questions suggest is that temporalities are meaningful, but if we wanted to determine the different meanings of time more specifically, we would need to consider a whole range of cultural and social determinants, including class, gender, and location, most obviously.

The Problem with Time

Richard Terdiman, in his study of modernity and memory, *Present Past* (1993), identifies a memory crisis in the nineteenth century – a crisis in understanding time and memory that comes to define modernity. As he argues, arising out the late eighteenth-century revolutions was a sense that the 'past had somehow evaded memory, that recollection had ceased to integrate with consciousness. In this memory crisis the very coherence of time and of subjectivity seemed disarticulated' (Terdiman 1993: 4). One result of this is the nineteenth-century's obsession with the past and with the making of history, but also with memory as a way of understanding and recording the past. Thinking in broad historical terms, Terdiman suggests that there was an 'epochal rupture' in the anxiety felt by the 'disruption of organic connection with the past'. The starting and stopping, slowing down and speeding up of time in the nineteenth century challenges a notion of 'time's continuous flow' (Terdiman 1993: 5). We might be tempted to think of the periodical media's organization of time in the nineteenth century as offering numerous ways of trying to create a continuous flow – but again, I think we are left with the problem that there is no single rhythm, there is always cacophony.

If we return to a shilling monthly magazine such as the *Cornhill*, we can begin to tease out some of the implications the problem of time has for interpreting serial texts. One thing that is fascinating to note of the *Cornhill*s in the early 1860s in particular (at that moment when the shilling monthly magazine made such a bold challenge to serial part-issue form) is the amount of fiction in which anxieties related to time are imagined. There is the striking example of Trollope's work, for example. His first *Cornhill* novel was *Framley Parsonage*, but this novel is in fact the fourth novel in what eventually came to be packaged as the 'Barsetshire novels'. He relies on the memories of his readers and expects that at least some will be able to connect *Framley Parsonage* to others set in the fictional Barsetshire published previously (*The Warden*, *Barchester Towers*, and *Doctor Thorne*, none of which was serialized). In other words, there is a sequence of novels published irregularly, but which, over time, link together and can be thought of as part of a single imaginative world. The fifth novel set in Trollope's Barsetshire, *The Small House at Allington* was also serialized in the *Cornhill* (1862–4). Readers of the magazine who lived with *Framley Parsonage* for so many months would no doubt have had a different kind of reading experience of *The Small House at Allington*, and so, whether Trollope was intending this or not, there were many levels of memory and recollection involved for readers, for whom returning to Barsetshire time and again created its own kind of pattern. Furthermore, the Barsetshire novels are deeply nostalgic about the past, while also recognizing the need for incremental, ongoing change and reform. In *The Warden* (1855), the intrusion of the urban metropolitan press into local Barsetshire events creates a disturbance that rocks the foundations of the community as the new media takes on older ways and habits of being. In *Barchester Towers*, a comic medieval tournament is staged at one point, which acts as a comment on backward-looking tendencies without advocating the ruthlessly competitive ways of contemporary society. In Trollope, retrospection is an important part of the novels published in sequence.

Elizabeth Gaskell's short novel, *Cousin Phillis*, published in four parts in the *Cornhill* between 1863–4 offers a more striking example of the way the problem of time enters the discourse of the novel, through the representation of technological time threatening natural time as the railway encroaches on a rural community. The story is narrated by Paul Manning, a young man on the verge of adulthood who works as an engineer laying the railway in Lancashire. He makes contact with relatives at nearby Hope Farm, and becomes a welcome friend of the family, in particular his cousin Phillis. Eventually, Manning brings his older, more worldly colleague Edward Holdsworth to the farm, and, after an illness which keeps him there, Holdsworth woos Phillis, who hopes he will marry her. She becomes heart-broken and lapses into a fever when she learns that Holdsworth has accepted a promotion in Canada, where he eventually marries another woman. It is one of Gaskell's most gentle tales, and a supreme achievement of the short novel. Of interest here, however, is the way the emphasis on the pastoral (Phillis's life at Hope Farm) is contrasted with the inevitability of change and new ways of behaving. The laying of the railway acts as one of the chief metaphors for a new kind of technological time interrupting the established, seasonal routines of agricultural life; but it is also the means through which a new type of man, a 'restless, vehement man' (1991: 297), Edward Holdsworth, disrupts patterns and rituals of pastoral love. In addition to these thematic uses of time, Gaskell continually reminds of us the ways time regulates and shapes our lives. Paul writes home to his parents every Saturday 'telling of my weekly doings' (1991: 261), despite the fact that his life has no variety and there is nothing to tell. His life is regulated by time – 'I was at my desk by eight o'clock, home to dinner at one, back at the office by two' (1991: 261) – and after a year, he confesses that 'there is not much to tell about this first year of mine at Eltham' (1991: 262). Paul's move into maturation is in part an introduction to the cycles of clockwork.

We are further reminded of shifting time at the beginning of each serial part. The opening installment leads with a rite of passage; Paul leaves home to make his way in the world for the first time. In the second installment, Paul reads aloud from the weekly country newspaper, as his aunt mends stockings while Phillis helps. It is another kind of social ritual – reading aloud the weekly newspaper – and it is one that surely would have had reverberations for the *Cornhill* reader, who may have been reading Gaskell's story aloud (or listening to it be read aloud). Part three of the novel opens after Paul returns from a week's holiday. This installment appeared in January 1864, just after the Christmas holiday for *Cornhill* readers, and so Paul's return to his family during the pause of the serial would have taken on a particular, and readily understood, set of meanings for the reader. Furthermore, the installment ends with Paul going to stay with his relatives at Hope Farm for the Christmas holidays, echoing the readers' own experiences, and marking a significant moment in the annual calendar. Finally, the fourth installment begins just after Easter, signaling both renewal and the passing of seasons to spring. This final installment, in which Phillis falls ill, ends with an appeal to our understanding of time as Phillis hopes that soon everything 'will go back to the peace of the old days' (1991: 354). A young man's maturation; the passing of seasons and religious holidays; the reading of local print media – all of these are ways that different constructions of time enter the novel, requiring the reader to consider the encroaching of the new against the stability of the old. In the end, the old must pass and the new comes and goes – like the railway itself – and the pastoral mode is seen to be, if not quite old-fashioned, then at least a mode of living (and writing) that must confront alternative ways of being.

Published serially in any periodical, the uses of time throughout Gaskell's tale would be highlighted. However, that the narrative appears in the *Cornhill* makes it all the more poignant, because the *Cornhill* was a competitive leader in an aggressive market, but one that projected an old-world gentility. Despite being named after a street in the financial center of London, the cover of the magazine by Godfrey Sykes, much heralded at the time, is an elaborate depiction of the four seasons represented by figures engaged in plowing, sowing, reaping, and threshing. In the middle of the figures is the title of the magazine, suitably garlanded. At the top and bottom of the cover is the date: No. 1 January at the top, 1860 at the bottom. In such an image, we can begin to uncover an example of time in crisis and cultural memory at work. The title of the magazine – at which many baulked at the time, but whose use of a metropolitan location became instantly fashionable and much copied (*Belgravia, Temple Bar, St. Paul's* all appeared shortly thereafter) – locates the magazine in a street in the City. It is an urban cultural production, part of an audacious commercial venture launched by the lavish publisher George Smith, and the title signals its commercialism straightforwardly. It is a monthly magazine – part of the rhythm and ritual of Magazine Day – yet its cover hearkens back in time in at least two ways. It reminds us of a different temporal pattern – a quarterly pattern and an agricultural, seasonal, even 'natural' pattern that is largely a thing of the past in 1860. This quarterly temporality speaks both to previous modes of living *and* previous modes of publishing. The shilling monthly boom inaugurated in part by the *Cornhill* did much to eclipse the weighty quarterlies that were increasingly offbeat in the new rhythms of modernity. The quarterly temporal pattern is paid homage to by this new upstart but still genteel monthly, and the cover encodes this conflict of time. The temporal disruption is partly registered visually on every cover (a cover image which lasted well into the twentieth century, by which time it looked absolutely old-fashioned rather than reflective). More interesting perhaps is the seasonal, natural reading of time on the cover: here what is paid homage to is not just a type of periodicity (the quarterly) but also a way of life – a pre-industrial, pre-urban vision which appears natural, in tune with nature, a slower way of life, but one that really was no longer part of the here and now, the present except as nostalgia, or memory.

However, I do not wish to make this cover seem simpler than it is because to say that the seasonal past exists in memory, or as nostalgia is a complicated assertion. But what I want to point out is that the simple division between past and present that one perhaps hopes for in the workings of time and memory – that we perhaps need in order to maintain subjective stability – is in fact not separate at all. The present *is* the past here – and it is the future too, if we remember the next issue awaits us on the following Magazine Day. Terdiman suggests that 'memory . . . complicates the rationalist segmentation of chronology into "then" and "now". In memory, the time line becomes tangled and folds back in one itself. Such a complication constitutes our lives and defines our experience' (Terdiman 1993: 8). The cover to *Cornhill*, I suggest, is an example of time folding back on itself. Even here, in the first issue, the periodical stretches back in time while simultaneously projecting the future – No. 2, February, 1860. Furthermore, the serial stories in the pages of the magazine reinforce that constant tension between past, present, and future. What is fascinating to note of these early *Cornhill*s in particular is the amount of fiction in which something like this tension is imagined.

The *Cornhill*, then, is one example of the way the medium might require us to think differently about the content of serialized fiction. The importance of time and periodicity – the monthly installment of the magazine, but also the way readers would have imagined installments across time as well – is both represented and constructed by magazine and the serial narratives it published. In the *Cornhill* cover and in the thematic strands of the magazine's contents, we see such a dislodging of time taking place – natural time replaced by synthetic time (see Gitlin 1980: 236) – the quarterly schedule replaced by the monthly schedule, the railway reminding us of the shifts in the meanings of time that were, by the 1860s, already a generation old.

What a monthly magazine such as the *Cornhill* also offers its readers is plenty of time to pause, reflect, and remember, but all periodicals have built into them some notion of gap, some kind of *duration*. In a special 'Theory Issue' of the journal *Victorian Periodicals Review* in 1989, Margaret Beetham urges scholars to attend to the ways 'the formal qualities of the periodical are shaped by its particular relationship to time' (Beetham 1989: 97). To a large degree, Linda Hughes and Michael Lund, in a chapter on seriality and history in their important work, *The Victorian Serial* (1991) respond to that call when discussing the way the action of Dickens's novel *A Tale of Two Cities*, serialized in Dickens's own magazine *Household Words*, alternates between 'travel and rest, between movement and cessation' and by asserting that this pattern of 'progress and pause' was in tune with the rhythm of nineteenth-century life (Hughes and Lund 1991: 63). 'Progress' is certainly an important feature of serial narratives – progress in the sense of advancement, of 'what's next', of 'how will the story progress'. This is one of the characteristics of serial narratives that Wolfgang Iser discusses in his book *Prospecting* (1989): 'The reader is forced by the pauses imposed on him to imagine more than he could have done if his reading were continuous, and so, if the text of a serialized novel makes a different impression from the text in book form, this is principally because it introduces additional gaps, or alternatively accentuates existing gaps by means of a break until the next installment' (Iser 1989: 11–12). Iser's approach to understanding serial narratives is a useful one, but it is also instructive to shift Iser's emphasis here and see the indeterminate gaps in narratives as indeterminate gaps in media time. In other words, I think it is significant to shift the emphasis from narrative to medium.

Built into the material form of so many Victorian novels published in parts is necessarily some conceptualization of waiting. The pause is a constitutive feature of periodical-ness, of all periodicities – there must be a break in time. What is important about this break is that it is the space that allows us to communicate. The media, first and foremost, is about communication, and without the pauses in the periodical schedules of the nineteenth century, there would be much less communication. As Barbara Adam reminds us, 'meaning cannot be communicated if everybody speaks at once; it depends on people taking turns in speaking and listening, since communication is a *serial*, single-order medium' (Adam 1994: 124). In the breaks in the narratives of periodicals and in the lapses in time – over a day, over a week, over a month – is where particular forms of meaning reside. That pause is when the interaction and communication occurs, and that period of waiting and reading is the link between the past and the future.

References and Further Reading

Adam, Barbara (1994) *Time and Social Theory*. Cambridge: Polity.

Beetham, Margaret (1989) Open and closed: The periodical as a publishing genre. *Victorian Periodicals Review*, **22**(3): 96–100.

Brake, Laurel (2001) *Print in Transition, 1850–1910: Studies in Media and Book History*. Basingstoke: Palgrave.

Durkheim, Emile (1915) *The Elementary Forms of the Religious Life: A Study in Religious Sociology*, trans Joseph Ward Swain. London: Allen & Unwin.

Feltes, N. N. (1986) *Modes of Production of Victorian Novels*. Chicago: University of Chicago Press.

Fleming, Sandford (1881) *The Adoption of A Prime Meridian to be Common to All Nationals. The Establishment of Standard Meridians for the Regulation of Time. Read Before the International Geographical Congress at Venice, September, 1881*. London: Waterlow.

Gaskell, Elizabeth (1991) *Cousin Phillis and Other Tales*, ed. Angus Easson. Oxford: Oxford University Press.

Gitlin, Todd (1980) *The Whole World is Watching: Mass Media in the Making and Unmaking of the New Left*. Berkeley: University of California Press.

Griest, Guinevere L. (1970) *Mudie's Circulating Library and the Victorian Novel*. Bloomington: Indiana University Press.

Hamer, Mary (1987) *Writing by Numbers: Trollope's Serial Fiction*. Cambridge: Cambridge University Press.

Hughes, Linda K. and Lund, Michael (1991) *The Victorian Serial*. Charlottesville: University Press of Virginia.

Iser, Wolfgang (1989) *Prospecting: From Reader Response to Literary Anthropology*. Baltimore: Johns Hopkins University Press.

James, Henry (1948) The Art of Fiction, and Other Essays. Edited by Morris Roberts. New York: Oxford University Press.

Law, Graham (2000) *Serializing Fiction in the Victorian Press*. Basingstoke: Palgrave.

Macey, Samuel L. (1994) *The Encyclopaedia of Time*. New York: Garland.

O'Connor, T. P. (1889) The New Journalism. *The New Review*, **1**(5): 423–34.

Patten, Robert L. (1978) *Charles Dickens and His Publishers*. Oxford: Clarendon.

Schlike, Paul (ed.) (1999) *Oxford Reader's Companion to Dickens*. Oxford: Oxford University Press.

Terdiman, Richard (1993) *Present Past: Modernity and the Memory Crisis*. Ithaca: Cornell University Press.

Turner, Mark W. (2000) *Trollope and the Magazines: Gendered Issues in Mid-Victorian Britain*. Basingstoke: Macmillan.

Wynne, Deborah (2001) *The Sensation Novel and the Victorian Family Magazine*. Basingstoke: Palgrave.

Zerubavel, Eviatar (1981) *Hidden Rhythms: Schedules and Calendars in Social Life*. Chicago: University of Chicago Press.

Chapter 7

'Farewell poetry and aerial flights': The Function of the Author and Victorian Fiction

Richard Salmon

Arguably the most important single influence on early to mid-Victorian aspirations for the cultural status of the novelist can be located in the work of a writer who, notoriously, had little time for 'fiction'. In Thomas Carlyle's celebrated lecture series on the historical forms of heroism and hero-worship, the penultimate lecture, delivered in May 1840, focused on 'The Hero as Man of Letters', a case which he presented as *the* symptomatically modern manifestation of the heroic type. Carlyle's chosen exempla for this lecture were three eighteenth-century writers – Jean-Jacques Rousseau, Samuel Johnson, and Robert Burns – whose literary production encompassed the novel, but who were not chosen on this, or any other narrowly generic, ground. (The same could be said of Goethe, for Carlyle a more complete model of the literary hero, who is briefly considered as a possible subject for the lecture at its outset.) The category of the 'man of letters', then, designates a generically indeterminate identity for the modern (male) author, albeit one that Carlyle distinguishes from the putatively older manifestation of the 'hero as poet' (the subject of the third lecture in the series). What characterizes the modernity of the 'man of letters' is, rather, his association with the medium of writing and the technology of printing, as opposed to the 'oral' medium of earlier forms of heroism. Carlyle, at one level, celebrates the capacity of modern print culture to disseminate the divinely inspired words of the hero on a scale hitherto unknown. Yet, as this already implies, he construes the underlying substance of the heroic character as essentially unchanged: the man of letters performs the same function in modern culture as prophets and priests in a former age:

> He that can write a true Book, to persuade England, is not he the Bishop and Archbishop, the Primate of England and of All England? I many a time say, the writers of Newspapers, Pamphlets, Books, these *are* the real working effective Church of a modern country (162, emphasis original).

By placing the 'man of letters' close to the end of a series purporting to trace the historical evolution of the human capacity for heroism and hero-worship from its origins in the manifestation and apprehension of divinity itself, Carlyle clearly bestows on nineteenth-century authors of printed texts (interestingly, both newspapers and books) an exalted, transcendental genealogy. On the one hand, this gesture may be read in the context of what Paul Bénichou (1999), the historian of French Romanticism, has described as the 'consecration of the author' in late-eighteenth and early-nineteenth-century literary culture. Carlyle's notion of the heroic man of letters might, indeed, be conceived as distinctively 'Romantic' in its quasi-religious sanctification of authorship: 'In the true Literary Man', he declares, 'there is thus ever, acknowledged or not by the world, a sacredness' (p. 157). And yet, on the other hand, Carlyle's emphasis on the material technology of print culture could be said to render the hero as man of letters a characteristically 'Victorian' cultural figure, one in whom sacred and secular concerns are rudely intermingled. In fact, the positioning of this figure in the lecture series is ambiguous, for it conveys not only a sense of the unprecedented capacity for spiritual transmission contained in the medium of writing, but also, as Eloise Behnken suggests, of the simultaneous processes of rationalization and disenchantment by which this capacity is released (1978: 25–6). Although Carlyle's modern man of letters occupies the enduring (transhistorical) role of prophet or priest, he stands at a further remove from the originary source of spiritual plenitude to which such archetypal figures claim access. By harnessing the power of print culture to disseminate his gift of spiritual insight, the man of letters unavoidably participates in the very realm of degraded mechanical forms and material interests which he is called on to protest. Carlyle is acutely conscious of the ways in which material forces both facilitate and constrain the ideal vocation of the man of letters. Thus, he begins his lecture by conceding that the heroism of the man of letters is 'in various respects, a very singular phenomenon': the 'Great Soul' whose 'inspiration' is embodied in the form of 'Printed Books' is, by the same token, a producer of commodities to be 'sold and bought' in the 'marketplace' (p. 154). Indeed, by extension, it is the man of letters himself who functions as such a commodity: 'Few shapes of Heroism can be more unexpected', Carlyle notes (p. 154).

It is for these, or similar, reasons that Terry Eagleton (1996) has characterized Carlyle's elevation of the man of letters to 'heroic stature' as a 'profoundly bathetic gesture'; a 'strained' attempt to reconcile an ideal of spiritual or intellectual authority (the figure of the 'sage') with the prosaic reality of the literary market (the figure of the 'hack') (1996: 46). Eagleton is surely right to sense an anti-climactic undercurrent to the culmination of Carlyle's grand historical narrative of heroism, yet neglects to consider that this is partly its point. In the wider context of the emerging nineteenth-century understanding of the status and conditions of authorship, the significance of the Carlylean man of letters lies precisely in his uncomfortable occupation of a juncture between the ideal and the material; between the consecrated ground of the 'poet-prophet' and the disenchanted world of print culture.

The Novelist as Hero

For Victorian novelists, neither expressly excluded from, nor positively embraced by, Carlyle's definition of the 'man of letters', the prospect of aspiring to the status of literary 'hero' must clearly have been attractive, but uncertain. In a period when the cultural status of the novel remained relatively low (despite the prestige accrued through the early-nineteenth-century example of Walter Scott), Carlyle offered writers of printed books the possibility of exercising a vital role in the moral or spiritual regeneration of contemporary society, and (albeit churlishly) did not deny that such influence might be obtained by even the most commonplace form of romance. Elizabeth Gaskell testifies to the equivocal promise of Carlyle's teaching in her ironic choice of a quotation from his essay 'Biography' (1832) as an epigraph for her first novel, *Mary Barton: A Tale of Manchester Life* (1848):

> 'How knowest thou,' may the distressed Novel-wright exclaim, 'that I, here where I sit, am the Foolishest of existing mortals; that this my Long-

> ear of a fictitious Biography shall not find one and the other, into whose still longer ears it may be the means, under Providence, of instilling somewhat?' We answer, 'None knows, none can certainly know: therefore, write on, worthy Brother, even as thou canst, even as it is given thee.' (*Mary Barton*, title page)

Gaskell's irony can be read either as deprecating her own position as novelist, by accepting the limited aspirations of the genre, or (more likely) as questioning Carlyle's somewhat patronizing assumption of its inferior status. But, either way, Gaskell is invoking the Carlylean model of the heroic writer and applying it as a template for her own novelistic practice. The implication of the choice of epigraph is that even if *Mary Barton* cannot claim to occupy the most elevated spheres of moral discourse or political science (a claim which the novel itself refuses to make), its capacity of 'instilling somewhat' in its readers has been taken in all seriousness by the author. Hence, most readers of *Mary Barton* would have difficulty in describing its morally committed social realism as that of a mere 'long-ear[ed] . . . fictitious Biography'.

Similarly, throughout the century, novelists were to use the heroic potential of the writer as a normative measure by which to test and assert their moral, cultural, and artistic ambitions or, alternatively, to define opposing authorial identities, whether or not they remained in explicit dialogue with Carlyle. Although Carlyle's direct influence on debates concerning the ethical and aesthetic status of the novel is at its strongest in the early to mid-Victorian period, it is worth noting (as I suggest in further detail below) that a novel such as George Gissing's *New Grub Street* (1891), the seminal late-Victorian consideration of the condition of modern authorship, remains specifically preoccupied with the possibility, or impossibility, of novelists attaining an heroic cultural status. *New Grub Street* is, indeed, one of the last in a succession of nineteenth-century novels in which novelists are figured as heroes partly by virtue of the fact that their 'heroes' are figured as novelists. The emergence of the novelist as hero, in other words, can be attributed not only to the influence of Carlylean doctrine, but also to the contemporaneous representation of novelists (and writers in general) as fictional characters.

This phenomenon can be traced back at least as far as the 1840s and later 1830s, during which period a plethora of novels featuring writers as heroes appeared in the relatively new novelistic form of the *Bildungsroman*. Arguably, the first self-conscious exponent of this genre in the English language was Edward Bulwer-Lytton (later Lord

Lytton), whose novels *Ernest Maltravers* (1837) and its sequel *Alice; or, The Mysteries* (1838) follow the personal and intellectual development of a generically indeterminate 'author' through a narrative explicitly informed by Goethe's *Wilhelm Meister's Apprenticeship* (1795), the text commonly recognized as the founding model of the *Bildungsroman* (and, incidentally, translated by Carlyle in 1824). Though Bulwer's Ernest Maltravers also derives, in part, from the figure of the Byronic hero, and a concomitant iconography of poetic 'genius', he is carefully contrasted with a naive figure of the Romantic poet, Castruccio Cesarini. The overarching trajectory of his development moves from the sphere of the 'Ideal' to the 'Practical', from poetic self-absorption to active engagement in public affairs: a narrative pattern often seen as distinctively 'Victorian' (*Alice*: 237). Thus, while Bulwer generally refrains from specifying the concrete forms of Maltravers's writing – he is an author of printed books, including poetry, but is at no point characterized as a novelist – his literary apprenticeship gestures beyond the 'Romantic' discovery of poetic self-consciousness. Like Carlyle, however, Bulwer's hero fully subscribes to the sacerdotal function of the author, becoming an 'intense enthusiast in the priesthood he had entered' (*Ernest Maltravers*: 201), while also manifesting an ardent commitment to worldly concerns.

In this, as in other cases, the significance of Bulwer-Lytton's fiction can, perhaps, best be measured by its effects on later novelists rather than by its own testimony. In the late 1840s, the form of the literary *Bildungsroman*, now modeled partly on the example of *Ernest Maltravers*, was further refined in novels by G. H. Lewes, W. M. Thackeray, Charles Dickens, and Charles Kingsley, among others. The most important of these novels – Thackeray's *The History of Pendennis* (1848–50) and Dickens's *David Copperfield* (1849–50) – could also be said to contain the first specific fictional representations of the novelist as hero. Common to both texts is an account of the maturation of a novelist's personal and professional identity traced from its 'origins' in the experiences of early life. Echoing Bulwer, moreover, both Thackeray and Dickens present the biographical self-formation of their novelist-heroes as indicative of a broader historico-cultural shift from the 'Ideal' to the 'Practical', from the undisciplined poetic imagination of the eighteenth-century/Romantic past to the trammeled literary labor of the Victorian professional author. In the case of Thackeray's Arthur Pendennis, this narrative of literary apprenticeship can be understood, quite literally, as tracing a passage from poetic to novelistic (or, perhaps more accurately, *prosaic*) forms of authorship. Pen's earliest authorial identity is a youthful and idealistic poet of sensibility, consciously modeling himself on the personae of Lord Byron and the hero of Goethe's *Sorrows of Young Werther* (1774), but his growing experience of the material reality of modern literary commerce forces him to shed his Romantic 'illusions'. Situated in the literary-journalistic world of the 1830s and 1840s, Pen's individual transformation into a hack journalist and writer of commercially successful novels suggests a generic account of the emergence of modern literary production (as his abbreviated surname implies). Similarly, in *David Copperfield*, Dickens unfolds the process by which David's childhood propensity for imaginative story-telling (a gift associated with his reading of eighteenth-century fiction) is, first, disciplined by his mechanical labor as a parliamentary reporter and legal copy-writer, and, ultimately, channeled into his career as a supremely efficient professional novelist. Poetic imagination, this narrative suggests, is an essential, but of itself inadequate, component in the making of a successful novelist; of equal importance is the capacity for strenuous labor and moral earnestness, as manifested in professional habits of 'punctuality, order, and diligence' (ch. 42: 560). Just as Thackeray characterizes Pen's literary apprenticeship as a process by which 'Pegasus' – the mythical emblem of Imagination – is put 'in harness' (*Pendennis*, ch. 36: 450), so Dickens predicates David's triumphant ascent to literary fame on a necessary acceptance of (self-imposed) material constraints.

As with Carlyle's 'hero as man of letters', then, the figure of the hero as novelist, as embodied in the novels of Thackeray and Dickens, risks achieving a certain effect of bathos. In these mid-century narratives, the figure of the novelist is granted heroic status by virtue of his position at the center of the novels' concerns, and yet in order to achieve this position is, to varying degrees, stripped of the aura of Romantic idealism and reduced to a prosaic, even at times banal, instrument of literary production. The elevation of authorial status offered on the one hand is problematized by the disenchantment (or de-consecration) of the author enacted with the other. This apparent contradiction suggests considerable ambivalence surrounding the idea of the novelist's heroic cultural status in early to mid-Victorian fiction. Does the hero as novelist represent a necessary modernization and rationalization of the archaic role of the poet-prophet (a possible extrapolation from Carlyle's theory of the hero as man of letters), or does the discontinuity between poetic imagination and the practical exigencies of professional authorship suggest, rather, a process of cultural degradation? Should the passage from youthful 'illusion' to adult responsibility be described as a narrative of progress or of decline? Is the novelist closer to the poet or to the journalist (or even to the clerk)? These are some of the uneasy, and in some ways unanswered, questions posed in both Thackeray's and Dickens's fictional accounts of the formation of the Victorian novelist.

It is particularly worth noting here the urgency of the last of these questions. For, as *Pendennis* and, to a lesser extent, *David Copperfield* record, novelists of the early to mid-Victorian period were, indeed, often apprenticed in the less than exalted environment of contemporary journalism. Journalism, rather than poetry, can be seen as the true 'precursor' of the Victorian novel, both in terms of the formative professional experience of many novelists and the formal development of the genre. Thackeray, for example, began his literary career in the late 1830s as a regular contributor of reviews, sketches, and tales to *Fraser's Magazine*, made numerous irregular contributions to *The Times*, *The Morning Chronicle*, and other newspapers, before gravitating toward the newly founded comic magazine *Punch* in the 1840s. From a slightly earlier beginning, Dickens famously worked as a shorthand reporter for the *Mirror of Parliament*, contributed urban sketches to the *Morning* and *Evening Chronicles* and *Bell's Life in London*, and in January 1837 was appointed editor of *Bentley's Miscellany*. It was through these early experiences of journalistic contribution, moreover, that some of the characteristic forms of their mature fiction began to emerge. Not only were Thackeray's first two novels – *Catherine: A Story* (1839) and *The Luck of Barry Lyndon* (1844) – originally published as serials in *Fraser's Magazine*, but, more significantly, the novel which first gained him major critical and commercial success – *Vanity Fair* (1847–8) – began as an offshoot of *Punch*, published in separate serial numbers. Thackeray's early journalistic specialism of producing both visual and verbal 'sketches' is directly reflected in *Vanity Fair*'s original subtitle, *Pen and Pencil Sketches of English Society* – the more familiar subtitle *A Novel Without a Hero* appearing only in subsequent volume editions. Likewise, the ephemeral journalistic sketch provided Dickens with the substance and structure of his first book publication, *Sketches by Boz* (1836), and enabled him to develop the techniques of urban reportage that he used throughout his later novels. In addition, it was *Bentley's Miscellany*, under Dickens's editorship, which provided a vehicle for the successful serialization of *Oliver Twist* (1837).

It is not the purpose of this essay to offer a full consideration of the many ways in which Victorian fiction is shaped by the contexts of journalistic media, nor is it to extend an account of the journalistic affiliations of Thackeray and Dickens beyond this brief outline of its preliminary stage. My aim, here, is simply to adumbrate the extent to which the cultural status of the Victorian novelist was forged in differing sites of material and ideological production, and thus accrued conflicting interpretations and rival genealogies. At the very moment when novelists were thought capable by some of assuming the role of secular cultural prophets, the production of the novel was increasingly aligned with the condition of journalism and its more ephemeral forms of popular entertainment. One of the more striking phenomena of the Victorian serialization of fiction, it is often claimed, was its reconfiguration of the felt relationship between authors and readers into a state of apparently unmediated intimacy. Thus, journalistic modes of production and publication could be said to have enhanced, not diminished, the personal reputation of the novelist, even stimulating the very notion of authorial 'personality'. Yet, as Mary Poovey has argued, serialization also emphasized the instrumental commercial relationship between authors and readers, thus paradoxically revealing a system of abstract and impersonal economic exchange (1989: 104). Certainly, the proximity between fiction and journalism during this period was liable to be perceived as damaging to the cultural prestige of the novel, and it is hardly surprising that the mid-nineteenth century also witnessed the first sustained efforts to defend (and, in the process, define) the 'professional' status of the novelist.

Professional Labor

The most visible manifestation of contemporary anxieties around the professional status, social reputation, commercial interest, and class identity of novelists can be seen in the critical controversy which erupted half-way through the publication of Thackeray's *Pendennis* in early 1850. Thackeray's satirical portrayal of Arthur Pendennis's growth from naive poetic sensibility to cynically pragmatic journalist and novelist was viewed by some critics as a scurrilous attack on the moral integrity and social standing of the literary profession – an affront to 'The Dignity of Literature', as the controversy came to be known. Writing in response to his critics, Thackeray himself noted that *Pendennis* was charged with 'condescending to caricature . . . literary fellow-labourers' and so 'fostering a baneful prejudice' against them (Thackeray 1913: 629). The source of this critical discomfort is not difficult to identify, for in *Pendennis*, as I suggested in the previous section, the 'heroic' narrative status of the novelist/man of letters is used primarily to demonstrate the delusive nature of prevailing myths of Romantic literary heroism. Indeed, Thackeray persistently deflates his hero's claim to heroic stature, most explicitly in the final sentence of the novel, which defines Pen not as a 'hero . . . but only a man and a brother', an allusion to the contemporary anti-slavery slogan that ironically reminds us of the enslaved condition of the modern writer which the novel has sought to exhibit (*Pendennis*, ch. 75: 977).

It is the representation of literary production as a form of oppressed or alienated labor which seems, especially, to have provoked critical hostility to *Pendennis*. Revealing the prosaic, material constraints on the imagination of the modern 'professional writer', the novel implies his diminution in status to a 'literary hack' (the figurative antithesis of the winged horse 'Pegasus'). In Chapter 36, for example, the narrator reflects that:

> A literary man has often to work for his bread against time, or against his will, or in spite of his health, or of his indolence, or of his repugnance to the subject on which he is called to exert himself, just like any other daily toiler. When you want to make money by Pegasus (as he must, perhaps, who has no other saleable property), farewell poetry and aerial flights: Pegasus only rises now like Mr. Green's balloon, at periods advertised beforehand, and when the spectator's money has been paid. Pegasus trots in harness, over the stony pavement, and pulls a cart or a cab behind him. Often Pegasus does his work with panting sides and trembling knees, and not seldom gets a cut of the whip from his driver. (*Pendennis*, ch. 36: 450)

What seems most striking in this statement is Thackeray's willingness to conceive of the work of writing in merely the same terms as any other form of social labor, even to the extent of propounding a quasi-Marxian analysis of the conversion of commodified literary labor into capital. For the writer 'who has no other saleable property' but his capacity to write (utilizing the imaginative resource of 'Pegasus') is truly in the same position as any other 'daily toiler' forced to alienate his labor in exchange for wages. Moreover, while, of course, the exploitation of 'genius' at the hands of avaricious, slave-driving publishers or book-sellers is a familiar theme of eighteenth and early nineteenth-century literary polemics, Thackeray's narrator's point is that '[t]here is no reason' why authors '*should* be exempt from labour, or illness, or decay, any more than any of the other creatures of God's world' (my emphasis; *Pendennis*: 450). His aim is not to foster 'pity' for the oppressed condition of the literary proletariat (this is no radical statement in a Marxian spirit), but to debunk 'the doctrine which some poetical sympathizers are inclined to put forward, viz., that men of letters, and what is called genius, are to be exempt from the prose duties of this daily, bread-wanting, tax-paying life, and are not to be made to work and pay like their neighbours' (*Pendennis*: 450). Thus, the narrator refuses to succor the Romantic discourse of martyred genius, in which the figure of the literary hack serves as a purely negative exemplar. While it may be questionable to assume that the satirical voice of the narrator represents Thackeray's view in its entirety, it is clear, nevertheless, that *Pendennis* conveys a deeply unsentimental and demystified perception of the nature of the literary 'profession'.

Thackeray's most prominent critic in the 'Dignity of Literature' controversy was John Forster, the close associate, and later biographer, of Charles Dickens, and it has often been inferred that Dickens himself was critical of the representation of 'literary fellow-labourers' in *Pendennis*. Despite, or perhaps because of, its formal and thematic similarity to Thackeray's novel, Dickens's contemporaneous *David Copperfield* is customarily viewed as a diametrically opposed statement on the cultural 'dignity' of the literary profession, an uncomplicated affirmation (or mystification, depending on one's point of view) of the heroic potential of the novelist. Yet, in *David Copperfield*, writing too is strongly identified as a determinate form of social labor, not entirely incommensurate with other types of work. Dickens would, at one level, have endorsed Thackeray's proposition that writers are not to be 'exempt from the prose duties of this daily, bread-wanting, tax-paying life', and, indeed, precisely the same point is made in David Copperfield's attribution of the 'source' of his 'success' as a novelist:

> I have never believed it possible that any natural or improved ability can claim immunity from the companionship of the steady, plain, hard-working qualities, and hope to gain its end. There is no such thing as such fulfilment on this earth. Some happy talent, and some fortunate opportunity, may form the two sides of the ladder on which some men mount, but the rounds of that ladder must be made of stuff to stand wear and tear; and there is no substitute for thorough-going, ardent, and sincere earnestness. Never to put one hand to anything, on which I could throw my whole self; and never to affect depreciation of my work, whatever it was; I find, now, to have been my golden rules. (ch. 42: 560)

For David, however, the insistence that the author must also become a type of *worker* serves a very different logic of individual and social narrative development than is the case in *Pendennis*. Whereas Thackeray satirically reduces Pen's work as a literary hack to the abstract form of alienated labor, a reduction ambiguously corresponding to his descent in social status from leisured gentleman to disreputable bohemian, Dickens employs the trope of literary labor as a vehicle for conveying David's aspiration to professional autonomy, a status which, for him, represents intellectual growth and social ascent, as his metaphor of climbing the 'ladder' of success reveals. To this extent, *David Copperfield* could, indeed, be said to offer a coded critique of *Pendennis*, one that seeks to associate the 'steady, plain, hard-working qualities' of the professional writer with the contemporary bourgeois ideology of 'self-help', rather than with the socially degraded ('proletarian') experience of commodified labor.

This helps to explain the peculiar rhetorical strategy by which some mid-nineteenth-century novelists, otherwise committed to the elevated cultural status of the literary profession, sought an affiliation with the common 'necessity' of labor while simultaneously claiming to transcend it. In an advertisement for a cheap collected edition of his novels published in 1847, for example, Bulwer-Lytton addressed its putatively working-class readership in the following terms:

> May these works, then, thus cheaply equipped for a wider and more popular mission than they have hitherto fulfilled, find favour in those hours when the shop is closed, when the flocks are penned, and the loom has released its prisoners; – may they be read by those who, like myself, are workmen (Quoted in Sutherland 1976: 33).

Here, Bulwer proudly (or is it humbly?) avows a shared identity with other 'workmen', yet, in the same gesture, tacitly assumes a distinction between those forms of labor which merely imprison or alienate the self and the 'labor' of the novelist, which, by association with the worker's 'hours' of leisure, promises to restore its freedom. Although the aristocratic Bulwer-Lytton may not have espoused David Copperfield's aspirational doctrine of self-help, his use of the rhetoric of literary labor similarly enhances the moral vocation of the novelist while anxiously preserving distinctions of class status. This is the dual ideological imperative which underlies contemporary efforts to define the work of writing as a form of *professional labor*, a perceptibly ambiguous identity for authors which both Dickens and Bulwer were instrumental in seeking to establish during the 1840s and 1850s. Not long after completing *David Copperfield*, for example, in May 1851, Dickens published a proposal for forming 'a Society of Authors and Artists by profession', to be known as 'The Guild of Literature and Art', in which he outlined the need for professional autonomy and solidarity among authors in order to lessen the dependence of 'distressed and divided followers' on aristocratic patronage, chiefly administered (as he saw it) by the existing Royal Literary Fund (Dickens 1983: 328). Authorship, Dickens urged, should be recognized as a fully fledged professional occupation, whose practitioners adhere to accepted standards of professional conduct, including the 'duties of prudence and foresight', and are, in return, entitled to receive material benefits adapted to 'the ordinary habits and necessary comforts of gentlemen' (Dickens 1983: 326). For his part, Bulwer allocated land from his Knebworth estate for the erection of cottages to house authors in need of financial support from their fellow professionals (apparently oblivious to the ironic resemblance to traditional aristocratic patronage), as well as writing the pastiche comedy of manners, *Not so Bad as We Seem* (1851), a play designed to mark the foundation of the Guild of Literature and Art and to subsidize its activities, in which the Thackerayan figure of the literary hack is firmly relegated to an outmoded eighteenth-century past.

Thus, the emerging discourse of literary professionalism, marked by such efforts, sought to provide an adequate definition of the author's class identity, one which reconciled the desire for dignified professional autonomy with the need to produce alienable commodities for the market by combining the functions of capital and labor in the same figure. Equally, however, professionalization may be seen as an attempt to define authorship (and, especially, the authorship of novels) in gendered terms, more specifically as an occupation appropriate to the status of 'gentleman', as Dickens's proposal for the Guild of Literature and Art reveals. It is worth pointing out that neither the Royal Literary Fund nor the Guild of Literature and Art, nor even the later 'Society of Authors' (established by Walter Besant in 1883), offered full membership to female authors in their original constitutions. Given the particularly high percentage of women among the total number of Victorian novelists, according to most scholarly estimates, it is not surprising, then, that professionalization has been viewed as an unacknowledged strategy of 'masculinization', aimed at enhancing the cultural prestige of the novel by diminishing its reputation as a suitably 'feminine' genre, a prevalent assumption of the late-eighteenth and early-nineteenth centuries. For the sociologist Gaye Tuchman, for instance, the ethos of literary professionalism is one of the ideological mechanisms by which women writers were dislodged from their culturally dominant position in the field of novel-writing in the mid to late Victorian period (1989: 9–11). The incipient effects of this strategy can, perhaps, already be witnessed in Dickens's fictional account of David Copperfield's triumphant ascent of the ladder of professional success, a process which depends crucially on his occupation of, and displacement of others from, the traditionally female site of domestic labor. Poovey has argued that the persistent alignment of domestic and authorial space in *David Copperfield* serves to establish their common identity as sites of non-alienated work, seemingly exempt from the social estrangement and degradation of industrial labor, as represented by David's childhood experience of working in the bottling factory (Poovey 1989: 122–5). If, on the one hand, David's domestic authorship would appear to problematize normative codes of masculinity (his identity is often playfully feminized), on the other, it is characterized by an exertion of patriarchal order in the home. The iconic domestic scene in which David's wife Dora is depicted holding the pens of the famous author asserts a crudely hierarchical division of gendered literary labor, all the more egregious since Dickens makes Dora expressly desire her subservient role (see Chapter 44, 'Our Housekeeping'). In an embarrassingly literal sense, therefore, *David Copperfield* shows how the formation of the male professional novelist's authorial identity requires the expropriation of domestic space from women and the marginalization of female labor in the home.

Unsurprisingly, a rather different account of the relationship between authorial identity and the domestic sphere emerges in contemporary auto/biographical writings by, and about, female novelists. Whereas Dickens presents the male writer's withdrawal into domestic space as crucial to the construction of his recognized authorial identity, enforcing a separation of private and public spheres which the successful novelist moves fluidly between, a more common scenario in Victorian representations of female authorship displays a radical schism between these competing spheres. A well-known example of this scenario may be extracted from Elizabeth Gaskell's *The Life of Charlotte Brontë* (1857), in which Gaskell contrasts Brontë's supposed self-division with the unified subjectivity of male authors:

> Henceforward Charlotte Brontë's existence becomes divided into two parallel currents – her life as Currer Bell, the author; her life as Char-

> lotte Brontë, the woman. There were separate duties belonging to each character – not opposing each other; not impossible, but difficult to be reconciled. When a man becomes an author, it is probably merely a change of employment to him. He takes a portion of that time which has hitherto been devoted to some other study or pursuit; he gives up something of the legal or medical profession, in which he has hitherto endeavoured to serve others, or relinquishes part of the trade or business by which he has been striving to gain a livelihood; and another merchant or lawyer, or doctor, steps into his vacant place, and probably does as well as he. But no other can take up the quiet, regular duties of the daughter, the wife, or the mother, as well as she whom God has appointed to fill that particular place: a woman's principal work in life is hardly left to her own choice; nor can she drop the domestic charges devolving on her as an individual, for the exercise of the most splendid talents that were ever bestowed. (Vol. 2 ch. 2: 258–9)

The significance of this passage does not derive from the validity of its claim to represent a particular biographical truth concerning Charlotte Brontë, but, rather, the testimony which it provides to the differential effects of the development of literary professionalism on the culturally mediated experience of male and female authors. Gaskell's point is that whereas men are encouraged to view the occupation of authorship as a means of 'employment' potentially interchangeable with other bourgeois professions, in the case of women authorship cannot be exchanged for any existing occupation because what precedes becoming an author is deemed absolutely inalienable from the self. Similarly, the female author cannot exchange public and private sites of professional employment given that the private space of literary labor is already inhabited by the 'domestic charges' for which she is held uniquely responsible. Hence, Gaskell's supposition that the over-determination of the domestic sphere gives rise to the two 'parallel currents' of Brontë's divided self, to a schism between 'author' and 'woman'. Writing much later in the century, in her posthumously published *Autobiography* (1899), the novelist and critic Margaret Oliphant testified to a similar experience of conflicting roles in the domestic sphere, manifested in her inability to establish a clear spatial demarcation between the work of writing and the responsibilities of motherhood. For most of her career, Oliphant records:

> . . . I have never been shut up in a separate room, or hedged off with any observances. My study, all the study I have ever attained to, is the little second drawing-room of my house, with a wide opening into the

> other drawing-room where all the (feminine) life of the house goes on; and I don't think I have ever had two hours undisturbed . . . during my whole literary life. (p. 30)

Literary life and family life are, thus, literally impossible to compartmentalize in the interconnected zones of Oliphant's domestic space: one 'opening into' the other, to the detriment, she believed, of her professional reputation.

Technology and Fine Art

In the later Victorian period, the contradictory strands of the ideology of professional labor emerging from both the Carlyean consecration of the hero as man of letters and the mid-century debate on the 'Dignity of Literature' (and perhaps definitively embodied in the fictive figure of David Copperfield), become increasingly apparent to contemporary writers of fiction. At one extreme, the logic of professionalization could be said to culminate in the apprehension of literary production as a purely mechanical process, subject to the rationalization of work methods, the incorporation of new forms of communication technology, and the extension of property relations between authors and texts. The figure of the 'literary machine', used to invoke both progressive and dystopian scenarios of modernity in writings of the 1880s and 1890s, provides a graphic example of this tendency. At the other extreme, professionalization leads to a reinvigorated late-Romantic cult of the author as hero, yet focused now on his transcendental aesthetic (rather than moral or political) vocation. Late-nineteenth-century Anglo-American aestheticism has been described by Jonathan Freedman, for example, as a development of the claim to professional competence in the supposedly autonomous domain of aesthetic experience (1990: 52–8). In this variant of professional ideology, however, the rationalization of literary production is commonly effaced, thus detaching the ethos of disciplined labor from the aura of professional status. From both sides of the equation, in other words, the Dickensian synthesis of labor and professionalism comes under mounting pressure.

One of the most notorious examples of the former strand of professionalism is provided by the career of Anthony Trollope, or, rather, by Trollope's autobiographical retrospective of his career, written during the mid- to late 1870s and published posthumously in 1883.

In some ways, the consummation of mid-century debates on the professional status of authorship, Trollope's *An Autobiography* also prefigures late Victorian fascination with the mechanization (or de-humanization) of literary production. While Trollope's fanatical insistence on the equation between disciplined labor and professional success clearly echoes the aspirational bourgeois narrative of *David Copperfield*, he also sets out to demystify the aura of monopolistic professionalism, taking Thackeray as his acknowledged master. Thus, Trollope combines the anti-heroic and anti-Romantic rhetoric of the latter with the strenuous work ethic of the former. The industry of the novelist is compared with the manufacture of shoes (in neither case can the worker afford to rely on the vagaries of 'inspiration'), yet also with the assiduous clerk who rises to enjoy the pastimes of a country gentleman. Most notoriously of all, Trollope describes the material labor of literary production, not with the dignified generality of David Copperfield, but the quantifiable detail of a clerical ledger:

> When I have commenced a new book, I have always prepared a diary, divided into weeks, and carried on for the period which I have allowed myself for the completion of the work. In this I have entered, day by day, the number of pages I have written, so that if at any time I have slipped into idleness for a day or two, the record of that idleness has been there, staring me in the face, and demanding of me increased labour, so that the deficiency might be supplied. According to the circumstances of the time, – whether my other business might be then heavy or light, or whether the book which I was writing was or was not wanted with speed, – I have allotted myself so many pages a week. The average number has been about 40. It has been placed as low as 20, and has risen to 112. And as a page is an ambiguous term, my page has been made to contain 250 words; and as words, if not watched, will have a tendency to straggle, I have had every word counted as I went. (ch. 7: 118–9)

Based neither on the figure of the oppressed hack nor of the autonomous professional, the model of authorship conceived here suggests a willed internalization of the demands of industrial commodity production, such that the author becomes simultaneously a stern taskmaster and exploitable labor. In extraordinary metaphors, the materials of writing itself are personified as recalcitrant or lax workers ('straggling' and 'ambiguous'), whom the author subdues to the mechanical factory discipline of his 'self-imposed laws' (p. 118). Fittingly enough, *An Autobiography* 'concludes' with a list of Trollope's books, their dates of publication, and the sums of money received from their sale to publishers: a final act of accounting that presents a certain quantity of novels as the end product of a given quantity of pages and words.

In framing this autobiographical narrative, Trollope explicitly disclaims any attempt to write a Rousseauvian 'confessional' history of the private self, and instead presents his career as a novelist in the depersonalized form of a literary manual, a text offering qualified advice and the wisdom of experience to 'aspirant' professional writers. In this respect, the form of *An Autobiography* bears witness to the burgeoning literary professionalism of the 1880s as much as its content: published in the same year as the establishment of The Society of Authors, an organization preoccupied with the dissemination of professional advice on matters relating to 'literary property', copyright legislation, relations between authors and publishers, and the appropriate use of literary agents, it may be seen as one of numerous 'practical' guides to authorship which appeared during the decade. One of the most popular of these books, Percy Russell's *The Literary Manual or, A Complete Guide to Authorship* (1886), reveals with particular clarity the rationalization and technologization of literary production which they served to foster. Like Trollope, though lacking an ostensible ethical imperative, Russell claims to demystify the archaic notion of 'divine afflatus' which still defines the received image of authorial creativity, promising his readers 'practical suggestions for acquiring the readiest means, for obtaining the kind of *working* information that is marketable in a Literary sense, and necessarily involves useful hints on the kind of books that should be read with the view of producing the greatest possible Literary effects with the minimum expenditure of time' (Russell 1886: 7). This openly utilitarian advice to aspiring authors is cast under the rubric of what Russell terms 'Literary Technics' or 'Literary Technology', a body of seemingly esoteric professional knowledge into which readers are initiated. Thus, here, the promise of demystification is itself a profoundly mystifying gesture, used to generate the aura around 'technical' proficiency which it claims to dispel. Although Russell's reduction of the authorial function to a series of mechanical procedures for assimilating and deploying 'Literary effects' to maximum commercial advantage may seem like a bizarre caricature of the extension of professional ideology, for some critical observers of the period it appears to have accurately reflected the prevailing cultural tendency.

Henry James, for example, characterized Trollope's novel production as a 'perceptibly mechanical process' in an essay which represents one of the earliest critical responses to *An Autobiography* (James 1962: 89), and, in the following year, he famously challenged Walter Besant's account of 'The Art of Fiction' (originally delivered as a lecture to the Royal Institution in April 1884) on similar grounds in his essay of the same title. While James welcomed Besant's elevation of the novel to high cultural status – his insistence 'upon the fact that fiction is one of the *fine* arts, deserving in its turn of all the honours and emoluments that have hitherto been reserved for the successful profession of music, poetry, painting, architecture' (1962: 26) – he rejected the possibility of its reduction to a codified discipline whose 'laws . . . may be laid down and taught with as much precision and exactness as the laws of harmony, perspective, and proportion' (1962: 30). James's essay on 'The Art of Fiction', in other words, views Besant (the founder of The Society of Authors, it will be recalled) as far too mechanistic in his attempt to prescribe uniform professional standards for the writing of fiction, yet it also rejects the unself-conscious amateurism associated with the existing tradition of the English novel, and so proceeds to develop an alternative account of literary professionalism based on the novel's new cultural status as 'one of the *fine* arts'. The essay's well-known exposition of the 'liberty' of the novelist's artistic consciousness and the 'organic' continuity of the novel emerges in direct response to Besant's reified categories of 'experience', 'character', and 'story', and is implicitly designed to suggest the value of what the novelist 'can never learn in any manual' (1962: 33).

Arguably, though, the most memorable contemporary critique of the mechanistic 'technological' development of professional authorship, inscribed in the literary manuals of the 1880s and 1890s, is to be found in George Gissing's bitterly satirical novel, *New Grub Street* (1891). It is in this text that the characteristic late-nineteenth-century bifurcation of the professional author into 'high' artistic consciousness or 'low' commodity producer is most starkly depicted. Through the schematically opposed careers of Edwin Reardon – a novelist committed to the status of fiction as 'fine art' – and Jasper Milvain – a journalist cynically aware of the 'practical' requirements of modern literary commerce – Gissing effectively demonstrates the impossibility of reconciling the two versions of authorial identity that were bound together in the mid-century figure of David Copperfield. On one side of the novel's antinomy, Milvain carries the Trollopian demystification of Romantic 'inspiration' a stage further, stripping all transcendental residues from modern print culture:

> People have got that ancient prejudice so firmly rooted in their heads – that one mustn't write save at the dictation of the Holy Spirit . . . There's no question of the divine afflatus; that belongs to another sphere of life. We talk of literature as a trade, not of Homer, Dante, and Shakespeare. If I could only get that into poor Reardon's head. He thinks me a gross beast, often enough. What the devil – I mean what on earth is there in typography to make everything it deals with sacred? (ch. 1: 43)

Here, then, Carlyle's belief that '[i]n the true Literary Man there is thus ever, acknowledged or not by the world, a sacredness' is finally consigned to irrelevance, if not altogether contradicted. While Milvain does not, in fact, deny the existence of the 'true Literary Man', the very elevation of his 'sphere' reinforces the mundanity of literary trade: contrary to Carlyle, therefore, the 'author-god' (to use Roland Barthes' suggestive term) becomes a type of *deus absconditus*, absent from the realm of mere typography. From the other side of the divide, Reardon (as a putative 'realist' novelist) also questions the validity of the transcendental view of authorship, but is unable to embrace the full materialist logic of Milvain's cynical conclusions. Reardon may be read as an author who tries and fails to follow the advice of contemporary literary manuals by adopting rationalized methods of production, but through his failure exposes the crass philistinism of commercialized professional ideology. Whereas Trollope, for instance, urges the aspiring novelist to submit his imagination to the 'trammels' of routine physical labor, adopting as his motto the phrase '*Mens sana in corpore sano!*' ('A healthy mind in a healthy body!', 120–1), Reardon's experience of a similar self-imposed discipline reveals a fatal maladjustment of mind and body. Unlike Trollope, he concludes that the mental labor of the artist cannot be modeled on that of the clerk, whose work may be pursued irrespective of 'mood and feeling' and, for the same quantity of time and labor, retains its value as a commodity. This leads Reardon (in a somewhat backhanded compliment) to envy the labor of the clerk, but also to believe that to 'make a trade of an art' is 'the unpardonable sin' (p. 81).

Gissing's satire is likewise targeted at those contemporary forms of professional ideology which adjust the production of art to the conditions of trade, and thus willingly embrace the commercialization of (professional) literary-aesthetic values. Central to his representation of this process is the image of the 'literary machine', which constitutes the dominant emblem of literary production in the world of *New Grub Street*. While Reardon, I have suggested, fails in his attempt to become a Trollopian 'novel-machine', modeled on the advice of the literary manuals, one of the novel's most iconic moments is a scene in which Marian Yule – another oppressed literary laborer – spots an advertisement in a newspaper for an actual 'Literary Machine', and gratefully assumes the invention of 'some automaton to supply the place of such poor creatures as herself, to turn out books and articles'. Unfortunately, for Marian, this machine is merely a device 'for holding volumes conveniently, that the work of literary manufacture might be physically lightened' (products of this description were, indeed, advertised as 'literary machines' in periodicals of the 1890s), but the satirical point has been made (p. 138). The 'Literary Machine' which Marian wishes to have been invented is, of course, an emblem of what she herself has perforce become, though remaining, like Reardon, ill-adapted to her function. Failure to adjust to the 'machinery' of modern literary production becomes, in this light, a residual protest against the processes of rationalization and commodification which Gissing presents as the dominant pressures of late-Victorian culture.

New Grub Street is often read either as an early-modernist attack on the debasement of 'mass culture' or as a late-Romantic defense of the integrity of the embattled 'artist', both historical positions amounting to a similar polemical stance. In this essay, I have focused on the latter perspective, approaching Gissing's novel as the continuation of a long-standing Victorian debate on the disenchantment of the author in modern literary culture. Like James, Gissing could be said to exemplify a reinvigorated late nineteenth-century discourse on the 'consecration' of the artistic vocation, albeit one which is now aestheticized, secularized, and ironized (in *New Grub Street*, the death-scenes of Reardon and Biffen, replete with Keatsian and Chattertonian allusions, are particularly visible examples of the persistence of this Romantic mythology of the artist). Yet the elevation of the novelist to the status of autonomous artist, I have argued, is, at least in part, a *negation* of the 'technological' development of literary professionalism during the same period: a reaction against a perceived mechanization of literary production which is, thus, largely defined by the process which it seeks to renounce. To this extent, novelists such as Gissing and James participate in the same dialectic as their predecessors Thackeray, Dickens, and Trollope, each of whom sought to define the place and the function of the author in a period for which (as Carlyle wrote of the eighteenth century) 'The "age of miracles" had been, or perhaps had not been; but it was not any longer' (1966: 171). In other words, whether or not these writers individually paid credence to the possibility of restoring the 'miraculous' power of their vocation, as Carlyle had instructed, all assume that the age of the professional novelist is no longer an 'age of miracles', but one in which authorship has become a sentence of prosaic labor.

References and Further Reading

Barthes, Roland (1977) The death of the author. In Stephen Heath, Trans. *Image Music Text*, pp. 142–8. London: Fontana.

Behnken, Eloise M. (1978) *Thomas Carlyle: 'Calvinist without the Theology'*. Columbia and London: University of Missouri Press.

Bénichou, Paul (1999) *The Consecration of the Writer, 1750–1830*. Trans. Mark K. Jensen. Lincoln and London: University of Nebraska Press (original work published 1973).

Bonham-Carter, Victor (1978) *Authors by Profession (Vol. 1)*. London: The Society of Authors.

Carlyle, Thomas (1966) *On Heroes, Hero-Worship and the Heroic in History*. Ed. Carl Niemeyer. Lincoln and London: University of Nebraska Press.

Cronin, Mark (1999) Henry Gowan, William Makepeace Thackeray, and 'The Dignity of Literature' controversy. *Dickens Quarterly*, **16**(2): 104–15.

Cross, Nigel (1985) *The Common Writer: Life in Nineteenth-Century Grub Street*. Cambridge: Cambridge University Press.

Dickens, Charles (1983) The Guild of Literature and Art. In *Miscellaneous Papers*. Volume 1, pp. 324–9. Millwood, NY: Kraus Reprint.

——(1996) *David Copperfield*. Ed. Jeremy Tambling. Harmondsworth: Penguin.

Dowling, Andrew (2001) *Manliness and the Male Novelist in Victorian Literature*. Aldershot: Ashgate.

Eagleton, Terry (1996) *The Function of Criticism: From The Spectator to Post-Structuralism*. London and New York: Verso.

Erickson, Lee (1996) *The Economy of Literary Form: English Literature and the Industrialization of Publishing, 1800–1850*. Baltimore and London: John Hopkins University Press.

Feltes, N. N. (1986) *Modes of Production of Victorian Novels*. Chicago and London: University of Chicago Press.

Foucault, Michel (1986) What is an Author? In Paul Rabinow (ed.) *The Foucault Reader*, pp. 101–20. Harmondsworth: Penguin.

Freedman, Jonathan (1990) *Professions of Taste: Henry James, British Aestheticism, and Commodity Culture*. Stanford, CA: Stanford University Press.

Gaskell, Elizabeth (1987) *Mary Barton*. Ed. Edgar Wright. Oxford and New York: Oxford University Press.

——(1997) *The Life of Charlotte Brontë*. Ed. Elisabeth Jay. Harmondsworth: Penguin.

Gissing, George (1968) *New Grub Street*. Ed. Bernard Bergonzi. Harmondsworth: Penguin.

Howes, Craig (1986) *Pendennis* and the controversy on the 'Dignity of Literature'. *Nineteenth-Century Literature*, **41**(3): 269–98.

James, Henry (1962) *The House of Fiction: Essays on the Novel by Henry James*. Ed. Leon Edel. London: Mercury.

Keating, Peter (1991). *The Haunted Study: A Social History of the English Novel 1875–1914*. London: Fontana.

Lytton, The Right Hon. Lord (1873) *Alice; or, The Mysteries*. London: Routledge.

——(1837) *Ernest Maltravers*. London: Routledge.

Oliphant, Margaret (1990) *The Autobiography of Margaret Oliphant*. Ed. Elisabeth Jay. Oxford and New York: Oxford University Press.

Poovey, Mary (1989) *Uneven Developments: The Ideological Work of Gender in Mid-Victorian England*. London: Virago Press.

Russell, Percy (1886) *The Literary Manual or, A Complete Guide to Authorship*. London: London Literary Society.

Ruth, Jennifer (1999) Mental capital, industrial time, and the professional in *David Copperfield*. *Novel: A Forum on Fiction*, **32**(3): 303–30.

Shillingsburg, Peter L. (1992) *Pegasus in Harness: Victorian Publishing and W. M. Thackeray*. Charlottesville and London: University Press of Virginia.

Siskin, Clifford (1998) *The Work of Writing: Literature and Social Change in Britain, 1700–1830*. Baltimore and London: John Hopkins University Press.

Small, Helen (2004) The debt to society: Dickens, Fielding, and the genealogy of independence. In Francis O'Gorman and Katherine Turner (eds.) *The Victorians and the Eighteenth Century: Reassessing the Tradition*. Aldershot and Burlington, VT: Ashgate.

Sutherland, J. A. (1976) *Victorian Novelists and Publishers*. London: The Athlone Press.

Thackeray, William Makepeace (1913) 'The Dignity of Literature'. In *Ballads and Miscellanies. The Complete Works of William Makepeace Thackeray*. Vol. XIII, pp. 629–33. London: Murray.

——(1994) *The History of Pendennis*. Ed. John Sutherland. Oxford and New York: Oxford University Press.

Trollope, Anthony (1980) *An Autobiography*. Eds. Michael Sadleir and Frederick Page. Oxford and New York: Oxford University Press.

Tuchman, Gaye with Nina E. Fortin (1989). *Edging Women Out: Victorian Novelists, Publishers, and Social Change*. London: Routledge.

Chapter 8

Everywhere and nowhere: Sexuality in Victorian Fiction

Carolyn Dever

> They were standing in the narrow pathway of the gate leading from the bridge into the gardens of the Great House, and the shadow of the thick-spreading laurels was around them. But the moonlight still pierced brightly through the little avenue, and she, as she looked up to him, could see the form of his face and the loving softness of his eye. 'Because –', said he; and then he stooped over her and pressed her closely, while she put up her lips to his, standing on tip-toe that she might reach to his face. 'Oh, my love!' she said. 'My love! my love!' (Trollope, *The Small House at Allington*, p. 98)

At this dramatic moment in Anthony Trollope's 1864 novel *The Small House at Allington*, the heroine Lily Dale presses her lips to those of her fiancé, Adolphus Crosbie. What Lily doesn't know – but the reader does – is that Crosbie's intentions are not what they appear. Sure enough, shortly after this moonlight kiss, Crosbie jilts Lily for the glamorous but frosty Lady Alexandrina de Courcy.

For Lily, the kiss represents her initiation into sexual, rather than simply romantic, desire. And from here there is no turning back: from this point forward, Lily considers herself married to Crosbie, bound to him morally if not legally. Crosbie, on the other hand, is overwhelmed by Lily's love and repelled by the thought of middle-class marriage. The double standard kicks in. To Lily's mind, she has 'married' Crosbie because she has expressed her arousal to him; indeed, it is she who kisses him. She now possesses the sexual knowledge of a married woman. Crosbie, bound by no such constraints on sexual knowledge, moves on to another woman.

The kiss is also a turning point for sexual narratives in Victorian fiction. Lily and Crosbie do not wind up married to one another. By derailing the marriage plot at the exact moment of Lily's erotic self-expression, Trollope exposes an open secret of Victorian literary representation: lust is a key component of the marriage plot for virtuous young ladies as well as for bachelors. Andrew Miller and James Eli Adams describe the famous sexual prudery with which its descendants credited Victorian culture, beginning with Freud in the early twentieth century:

> [T]he Victorians were notorious as the great enemies of sexuality; indeed, in Freud's representative account, sexuality seems to be whatever it was that the middle-class Victorian mind attempted to hide, evade, repress, deny. So prominent was this agonistic construction of Victorian culture that soon after the very adjective 'Victorian' came into widespread usage it tended to be sexualized, as a virtual synonym for 'repressive'. (1996: 1–2)

Victorian novels offer a paradox. The marriage plot is the dominant form of literary fiction in this period, and it is a plot concerned both with the expression of sexual desire and with its limitation within comfortable, familiar social boundaries. In the medium of the marriage plot, direct expressions of sexual desire such as Lily Dale's are the exception to the rule: the genre more often displaces sexuality into conventions of romance and domesticity. Sexuality, therefore, emerges primarily in disguised and coded terms, and by means of displacement rather than express representation. John Kucich, in a study of repression in the Victorian novel, describes 'the nineteenth-century cultural decision to value silenced or negated feeling over affirmed feeling, and the corresponding cultural prohibitions placed on display, disclosure, confession, assertion' (1987: 3). Kucich argues that Victorian culture worked to silence rather than to express conflicted emotional concepts, and sexuality in particular. Thus to read Victorian novels for their sexual content is to read them, by necessity, between the lines, not for what they say but for what they show; not for what they represent but for those significant silences that speak volumes.

Sexuality in the Victorian novel is at once everywhere and nowhere. Figured in virgins with hearts of stone and whores with hearts of gold; in rakish bachelors, squirrelly adolescents, and wily widows, eroticism saturates the world of Victorian fiction. Yet it does so in terms that remain strangely invisible. Novels of this period are dominated by the marriage plot, and the marriage plot is itself a site for the expression of sexual possibilities ranging from the conventionally heterosexual to the polymorphously perverse. Even as it grounds the representation of sexuality in Victorian fiction, however, the marriage plot can serve a strategy of containment: because it institutionalizes heterosexual marriage as the only logical outcome, as inevitable, climactic, and conclusive, the marriage plot can lure our attention away from the many other forms of sexuality that circulate in Victorian fictional texts.

This chapter places the marriage plot in context among a number of competing and often complementary modes of desire functioning in the Victorian novel, reading heterosexual marriage not as an inevitability but as one choice among others. I argue that Victorian novels map trajectories of desire in multiple and often unexpected ways: courtship and marriage for some characters contrasts with an investment in chastity for others, which is in turn displaced into an investment in career, money, or social status for others. Novelists construct heterosexual marriage as a formal device that frames a still wider array of sexual possibilities. By reading Victorian novels in terms of the genuinely polymorphous range of sexualities they present, we gain insight into the complexity of erotic expression in Victorian Britain. We also gain insight to the ways in which Victorian novels themselves contribute to their culture's imagination of sexual possibilities.

Theories of Sexuality in Victorian Britain

Discourses of literature and culture in the Victorian period are suffused with questions about and images of human sexuality. Steven Marcus links the development of the novel in nineteenth-century Britain to the development of other cultural industries, including the vigorous trade in visual and written pornography. 'In addition', Marcus writes, 'the scientific spirit of the age found major expression in advances in the biological sciences and in medicine; and this, coupled with the strong social and reforming temper of the times, made for a situation in which considerable public discussion of sexual matters took place' (1966: 2). To consider just one example of the robust pornographic literature of the time, the 1881 novel *Sins of the Cities of the Plain, or the Recollections of a Mary-Ann,* locates homosexual activity on a continuum of sexual pleasures detached from judgments of virtue and vice. The novel's narrator enjoys a diverse range of erotic possibilities available for the asking, both in London and in the English countryside; as the narrator traces his erotic development from childhood to maturity, following the classic form of the *Bildungsroman*, he reports that his favorite sexual escapades involve men. The novel includes a boyhood chapter set in the dormitory of a distinguished public school and an encounter with the main players in the case of Boulton and Park, arrested for public transvestitism in 1870, and later charged with felony sodomy. *Sins of the Cities of the Plain* concludes with three brief, nonpornographic, informational essays, 'The Same Old Story – Arses Preferred to Cunts', 'A Short Essay on Sodomy, Etc.', and 'Tribadism'. These essays offer a historical context for both male and female homosexual desire.

Sins of the Cities of the Plain also offers a parody of the literary marketplace: each time the narrator provides his patron with a few more pages of the novel's manuscript, he is rewarded with sex. The novel suggests an equation of textuality and sexuality that reflects Michel Foucault's theory of Victorian culture. According to Foucault, the modern concepts of 'sex' and 'sexuality' are relics of the Victorian period, and signs of shifting relations of power rather than transparent truths of bodily fact. Indeed, Foucault reads Victorian and post-Victorian sexuality as having very little to do with the body; sex, he contends, comes into its modern incarnation as a phenomenon of discourse, having more to do with language, with writing and speech, than with physical bodies. In the Victorian period, however, the endless proliferation of discourses about sex ran into a roadblock: the cultural prohibition of those very discourses, as Kucich suggested. Thus, Foucault argues, sexuality came into being as the ultimate open secret. He writes: 'What is peculiar to modern societies, in fact, is not that they consigned sex to a shadow existence, but that they dedicated themselves to speaking of it *ad infinitum*, while exploiting it as *the* secret' (1990: 35, emphasis original).

Sex, Foucault argues, emerged in post-Enlightenment Europe as a problem requiring vigilant social control. Even as Victorian industries of pornography and prostitution flourished, institutions ranging from criminal justice to medicine, from political economy to education and even to literature, emerged to regulate sexual expression in the name of moral authority. Writing of these burgeoning sexual discourses, Foucault describes:

> all those social controls, cropping up at the end of the [nineteenth] century, which screened the sexuality of couples, parents and children, dangerous and endangered adolescents – undertaking to protect, sepa-

> rate, and forewarn, signaling perils everywhere, awakening people's attention, calling for diagnoses, piling up reports, organizing therapies. These sites radiated discourses aimed at sex, intensifying people's awareness of it as a constant danger, and this in turn created a further incentive to talk about it. (1990: 30–1)

Sex, in other words, seemed like such a danger that the entire range of modern, socially authoritative discourses – medicine, the law, religion, the press, and literature – organized themselves to contain it. Of course there is an irony at the heart of what Foucault called the 'repressive hypothesis': these discourses, mobilized for the conscription of sexuality, put that which they seek to conceal on public display. Foucault writes:

> All these negative elements – defenses, censorships, denials – which the repressive hypothesis groups together in one great central mechanism destined to say no, are doubtless only component parts that have a local and tactical role to play in a transformation into discourse, a technology of power, and a will to knowledge that are far from being reducible to the former. (1990: 12)

The Victorian novel, with its obsessive investment in the marriage plot, is a form of the 'will to knowledge' Foucault describes. Victorian fiction participated in the expression of sexuality as '*the* secret' at the center of cultural modernity.

Sex achieves such extraordinary importance, Foucault contends, because it is a discourse of power. To seek knowledge about sex is to seek knowledge about power. Sexuality offers access to power writ small – 'the life of the body' – and power writ large – 'the life of the species' (1990: 146). Viewed as a matrix of power, the meaning of 'sex' in Victorian Britain varied enormously based on each individual's class, gender, and racial identity; in other words, on his or her position in the cultural hierarchy. Like Foucault, Gayle Rubin views capitalism as the system of power that operates through the vigilant regulation of sex: it requires the association of maleness with activity and femaleness with passivity, and attempts to present these associations as the natural order of things. Rubin describes this form of social construction as the 'sex/gender system': 'the set of arrangements by which a society transforms biological sexuality into products of human activity, and in which these transformed sexual needs are satisfied' (1975: 159). Rubin argues that 'biological sexuality' underpins many aspects of culture. Sexuality serves as an organizing system not only for people's bodies but also for economic systems, which have something at stake in understanding certain bodies – bodies of a particular gender, for example, or a particular race, or a particular class – as functioning in highly specified ways given their context in the larger social system. Though the meaning of individual bodies, and the meaning of 'sex', as well, is culturally constructed, bodies are read as having their own 'natural' meaning, needs, and urges that precede, and which exist outside of, culture. 'Sex is sex', Rubin writes, 'but what counts as sex is equally culturally determined and obtained. Every society also has a sex/gender system – a set of arrangements the biological raw material of human sex and procreation is shaped by human, social intervention and satisfied in a conventional manner, no matter how bizarre some of the conventions may be' (1975: 165).

In Rubin's mind as in Foucault's, the concept of 'sex' reveals more about a culture's general anxieties, desires, and frustrations than about the disposition of physical bodies in relation to one another; what Rubin calls the 'biological raw material of human sex and procreation'. In this view, sex is a symptom of culture: what is considered 'conventional' in one place and time is 'bizarre' in another. Significantly, then, Victorian novels not only reflected but also helped to shape their culture's perception of sexual conventions: literature helped to determine 'what counts as sex'. In this context, those popular novels that follow the template of the courtship plot – a young man and a young woman meet, explore their attractions to each other, and eventually make their way to the altar – worked to consolidate marriage as equal to sexual virtue.

In this kind of marriage plot, so familiar as to seem 'natural', not only sexuality but also gender operates in specific ways. 'At its most general level', writes Rubin, 'the social organization of sex rests upon gender, obligatory heterosexuality, and the constraint of female sexuality'. Following the argument of Claude Lévi-Strauss, Rubin suggests that marriage is a form of gift exchange in which women work to cement patriarchal bonds between men. Thus kinship systems, and the capitalist patriarchy that emerges from kinship systems, require – and invent – a certain kind of femininity. Women are limited to the passive role of an object gifted. Constrained to the private domain, they are barred from intervention in the economic sphere. In the burgeoning empire of Victorian Britain, 'femininity' was a category of race as well as gender; the feminine ideal was predicated on the assumption of whiteness. Anne McClintock argues that the circulation of female sexuality works not only to consolidate gender hierarchies but those of race as well. She describes 'three of the governing themes of Western imperialism: the transmission of white, male power through control of colonized women; the emergence of a new global order of cultural knowledge; and the imperial command of commodity capital' (1995: 1–3). Arguing that imperialism is a white, patriarchal system that subsists through the subjection of women of color, McClintock, like Foucault and Rubin, suggests that this form of power protects certain forms of knowledge and particular access to money.

The Victorian domestic ideal of white, middle-class femininity was a cultural myth, an ideology. Louis Althusser argues that 'Ideology represents the imaginary relationship of individuals to their real conditions of existence' (1971: 153). The virtuous, asexual Victorian woman is an imaginary figure serving ideological ends: she provides a frame of reference that allowed Victorian subjects to interpret their experience. Yet as Althusser points out ideologies may be mythical but they can have a powerfully tangible influence. This one is no exception. Feminine 'delicacy' was frequently cited as a truth rather than an interpretation; as a natural fact justifying some people as true and good, and others as false, fallen, and vicious; and as a fact that entitled some men and women – and not others – to resources such as education, wealth, and social prestige.

As Mary Poovey has pointed out, for example, Victorian medical men interpreted the female reproductive cycle as 'natural' justification for the ideology of separate spheres, the middle-class ideal in which women ruled at home and men in the world (1988: 36–7). This ideal was attached to a concept of femininity that linked women's sexuality to one of two alternatives: virtue, embodied in middle-class marriage; or vice, embodied in everything else. To borrow a phrase from Sherlock Holmes, however, the Victorian medical community was here theorizing in advance of its evidence, ignoring many other aspects of female personhood, sexuality, and embodiment in favor of an egregiously narrow interpretation of women's social options. Poovey argues persuasively that the 'separate spheres' ideology is always already unconvincing. Its crudeness, its blatant instabilities, reveal it to be not a reflection of Victorian culture, but rather an attempt to *shape* Victorian culture in the image of, and for the benefit of, a very particular bourgeois norm. 'The rhetorical separation of the spheres and the image of domesticated, feminized morality', Poovey writes, 'were crucial to the consolidation of bourgeois power because linking morality to a figure (rhetorically) immune to the self-interest and competition integral to economic success preserved virtue without inhibiting productivity' (1988: 10). In other words, this paradigm of constrained female sexuality works silently for the benefit of capitalism: feminine goodness signifies an abstract ideal of virtue which appears to be 'natural', and thus outside the marketplace.

> In promoting a distinction between kinds of labor (paid versus unpaid, mandatory versus voluntary, productive versus reproductive, alienated versus self-fulfilling), the segregation of the domestic ideal created the illusion of an alternative to competition; this alternative, moreover, was the prize that inspired hard work, for a prosperous family was the goal represented as desirable and available to every man. Locating difference between men and women also helped to set limits to the groups that actually had access to liberalism's promise of universal economic opportunities. (Poovey 1988: 10)

Poovey points out that the domestic ideal of feminine virtue also secured a reciprocal model of masculine virtue embedded firmly in the marketplace; to stereotype the stereotype itself, it was as if women never left the home while men never entered it. The task of the bourgeois male is to labor in the public sphere in order to protect and maintain the unpaid female labor taking place in that particular private sphere – the home – for which he is responsible. Poovey also suggests that the segregation of labor based on gender identity works to protect a limited labor pool: the association of virtuous femininity with unpaid, private work means that fewer workers – males alone rather than males and females together – will compete for available jobs. Thus the figure that critics have dubbed, borrowing the term from Coventry Patmore, the 'Angel in the House' came into being simultaneously with the hard-charging capitalistic male. Together the two constitute dominant sexual ideals of femininity and masculinity in Victorian Britain. As Foucault and Rubin would observe, however, their idealization has less to do with sexuality *per se* than with sex as a means of organizing the distribution of labor in a market economy.

Female Sexuality in Victorian Fiction

As I will argue, Victorian novels concern themselves almost obsessively with this sex/gender system, but not simply as a means of bolstering its rigid self-assertion. To be sure, novelists engage the terms virgin and whore, domestic woman and ambitious man. But novels are works of the imagination rather than social documentation. Thus they reserve the privilege of *questioning* culture rather than describing it; even in realist fictions, their responsibility is to the conundrum, not to the solution. Thus the engagement with dominant terms of gender and sexuality in Victorian novels is by definition unruly: novelists test the very foundational ideas of cultural identity, and by so doing they expose the cracks, the illogics, the limitations that ideologies strive to conceal and contain. From the 'Angel in the House' to Hardy's Tess Durbeyfield, whose baby and marriage follow in the wrong order, representations of female sexuality in Victorian fiction contend with ideals of middle-class, wifely, maternal, domestic femininity. But as the example of the 'fallen' Tess suggests, Victorian novelists frequently invoke the feminine domestic ideal – but as the backdrop from which they then depart. In this section, I argue that Victorian novelists demonstrate great ambivalence toward the 'Angel in the House': identifying her as a site of the symbolic and material power associated with feminine moral virtue, they locate alternative modes of power in figures who subvert her ideal.

For example, Walter Hartright, protagonist of Wilkie Collins's popular sensation novel *The Woman in White*, encounters a mysterious woman on a moonlit road from Hampstead to London late one night. Beautiful and oddly stirring, the woman is unaccompanied on a public thoroughfare in the middle of the night, and as she approaches him, Walter registers the peculiarity of her situation: 'What sort of woman she was, and how she came to be out alone in the high-road, an hour after midnight, I altogether failed to guess' (First Epoch, ch. 4: 24). Hinting at sexual availability, the woman is also, however, clad in bridal white from head to toe; she is an angel paradoxically wandering in the dark. Thus offering a fusion of the iconographies of whore and virgin, this woman is soon revealed as Anne Catherick, escaped mental patient.

Anne's status is further mystified the very next day when Walter takes himself off to a new job as drawing-master to a rich young lady – and realizes that this young and proper lady, Laura Fairlie, is somehow, mysteriously, identical to Anne Catherick. Public woman, private lady; two women, certainly strangers, suggesting the hint of vice even at the heart of virtue.

Victorian novelists had frequent recourse to the strategy Collins uses here. By polarizing female identity into two neat categories – virgin and whore, angel and demon, victim and queen – novelists associate goodness with asexuality; badness with hypersexuality. The obvious goodness, chastity, and innocence of Laura Fairlie provides a foil for Laura's double, Anne, just as the wild animal Bertha Mason Rochester, also a wanderer in the night, offers a foil for her cool rival, Jane Eyre. In less obviously eroticized terms, the domestic ineptitude of David Copperfield's first wife, Dora, makes the competence of her successor Agnes emerge all the more vividly. The foils proliferate: Becky Sharp versus Amelia Sedley of Thackeray's *Vanity Fair*, Catherine versus her daughter Cathy of Emily Brontë's *Wuthering Heights*; the evil lurking in lovely Lucy, Lady Audley in Braddon's sensational *Lady Audley's Secret*; and Mina Harker versus the vampiric Lucy in Stoker's *Dracula*. Such contrasts – bad woman, good woman – help to make tangible the abstractions 'virtue' and 'vice'.

Yet, as Nina Auerbach (1982), Eric Trudgill (1976), and other critics suggest, even as Victorian novelists such as Collins and the Brontës put this representational strategy to use, they subvert it in the next breath. For Jane Eyre, too, becomes a night-wanderer, and she, too, becomes Mrs. Rochester, just as Dora and Agnes share the name Mrs. Copperfield, wives of David. Similarly, Anne and Laura, who resemble one another closely enough that they might be twins, find themselves embroiled in a conspiracy that treats them not as opposites but as identical. And of course the novel reveals later, after the mysterious death of one of them – Anne, though buried in a gravestone marked with Laura's name – that they are half-sisters. Anne is the product of Mr. Fairlie's encounter with a servant shortly before Mr. Fairlie married Laura's mother.

To complicate matters still further, Laura has a second foil in Marian Halcombe, a half-sister on the maternal side. Walter encounters Marian first from behind:

> I looked from the table to the window farthest from me, and saw a lady standing at it, with her back turned towards me. The instant my eyes rested on her, I was struck by the rare beauty of her form, and by the unaffected grace of her attitude. Her figure was tall, yet not too tall; comely and well-developed, yet not fat; her head sat on her shoulders with an easy, pliant firmness; her waist, perfection in the eyes of a man, for it occupied its natural place, it filled out its natural circle, it was visibly and delightfully undeformed by stays . . . The easy elegance of every movement of her limbs and body as soon as she began to advance from the far end of the room, set me in a flutter of expectation to see her face clearly. She left the window – and I said to myself, The lady is dark. She moved forward a few steps – and I said to myself, The lady is

> young. She approached nearer – and I said to myself (with a sense of surprise which words fail me to express), The lady is ugly! (First Epoch, ch. 6: 34)

Marian's natural, and to Walter extremely sexy, body provides a shocking contrast to her dark, hirsute, revolting face. Matched with what we soon learn is her sharp intelligence, Marian emerges as half man and half woman: feminine form and heart, masculine head and mind. She looks nothing like her half-sister Laura; she is as dark as Laura is blonde, as intelligent as Laura is retiring. If Laura and her *doppelgänger* Anne are sisters and foils of one sort, Laura and Marian are sisters and foils of another. The contrast reveals the burgeoning possibilities for the representation of Victorian female sexuality hidden even in the apparently conventional either–or, good–bad assignment of roles between two women. In its representation of Marian Halcombe as a woman split between the desirable and the revolting, *The Woman in White* also locates the spinster as a figure of erotic possibility for Victorian fiction. The spinster, like her counterpart the widow, wields a strange form of sexual power in Victorian novels. Because she is outside the marriage market identified by Rubin, she confounds the categories of sexual identity that Rubin's sex/gender system secures.

Marian, for example, lives with Walter and Laura after their marriage, and it is even she who proposes to Laura on Walter's behalf. Immensely protective of Laura both physically and psychologically, Marian emerges as a kind of friend to Walter as together they work to support Laura in her weakened, vulnerable state. A certain ambiguity characterizes Marian's gender identification in *The Woman in White*: ' "Can you look at Miss Halcombe" ', asks Count Fosco, ' "and not see that she has the foresight and the resolution of a man?" ' (Second Epoch, ch. 9: 324). Marian is not only ambiguously gendered; her sexuality is also open to interpretation. Riding shotgun to Walter, Marian resembles Walter in the sense that she too directs her desires toward Laura. The novel ratifies Marian's same-sex desire, and indeed constructs it as a virtue, by situating it in a half-sibling relationship, and a heterosexual, albeit three-way, domestic 'marriage'. Thus the social and narrative convention of marriage remains on the surface undisturbed even as it undergoes a substantial challenge from the ambiguous figure of Marian Halcombe.

As this example suggests, familiar roles such as 'spinster' and 'widow' conceal a multitude of 'sins' for women in Victorian novels. These possibilities concern power as well as sexuality, and indeed, the two seem inextricable. The (putative) widow Signora Neroni of Trollope's *Barchester Towers*, for example, rules the world from an invalid's couch. The very theatricality with which the Signora performs her bodily weakness serves as the means of thrusting forth her sexual body, suggestively recumbent, into Barchester's circuit of social exchange. Miss Betsy Trotwood, of Dickens's *David Copperfield*, wields a deterministic power over her nephew's life from the first, deploying financial and psychological power that would be unavailable to her had she been circumscribed by the role of 'wife'. The widow Lizzie Eustace, of Trollope's *Eustace Diamonds*, reveals her insidious power less by means of her physical form than by action:

> Her feet and hands might have been taken as models by a sculptor. Her figure was lithe, and soft, and slim, and slender. If it had a fault it was this, – that it had in it too much of movement. There were some who said that she was almost snake-like in her rapid bendings and the almost too easy gestures of her body; for she was much given to action, and to the expression of her thought by the motion of her limbs. She might certainly have made her way as an actress, had fortune called upon her to earn her bread in that fashion (Ch. 2: 16–17)

Associated both with a snake and an actress, the young Lady Eustace gives the impression that her femininity is a put-on, a performance.

In contrast to these women who resist the sex/gender system, Miss Tox, in *Dombey and Son*, constructs her spinsterhood differently: she wants to be part of the system of heterosexual marriage. Setting her sights on Mr. Dombey in the earliest moments of his widowerhood, Miss Tox, unlike Marian Halcombe, Miss Betsy Trotwood, and Signora Neroni, offers herself as a woman in want of a man. Miss Havisham, of *Great Expectations*, takes a commanding and theatrical potency from her embodiment of the role of a woman left at the altar. Similarly, Lily Dale of Trollope's *Small House* takes her jilting as a form of identity: married and not married, at once virgin and sexually initiated. As it does for Miss Havisham, Lily's spinsterhood becomes her sexual role, chastity her sexual act; she participates in the sexual economy through her resistance to its most ingrained conventions, literary and otherwise. Lily and Miss Havisham alike construct for themselves a twilight world: as women who are not married, but not *not* married, they neatly thwart yet another form of female identity constructed as an either/or proposition. Their choice carves out a role for women outside conventions of heterosexual marriage.

By breaking the frame of social convention, these unmarried female characters also break the frame of narrative convention, taking the Victorian marriage plot in new directions that seem quite ambivalent about marriage. I have suggested that female sexuality in Victorian fiction is constructed and deconstructed through several key tropes: the virgin/whore opposition, which collapses into indeterminacy even while establishing a binary opposition; and the powerful single woman, a spinster or widow whose awareness of her cultural capital, and whose resistance or failure to become conscripted in the marriage plot, poses a challenge to the sex/gender system of 'patriarchal' power. Literary critics have associated the complexity of female sexual representation with the rise of the female novelist in Victorian Britain. Sandra M. Gilbert and Susan Gubar write of the relationship of male sexuality and male authorship: 'Male sexuality . . . is not just analogically but actually the essence of literary power. The poet's pen is in some sense (even more than figuratively) a penis' (2000: 4). Competing with the phallic power of the pen, women writers seek alternative strategies for the representation of female sexual selves, writing differently about the generative pleasures and powers of writing:

> [A] woman writer must examine, assimilate, and transcend the extreme images of 'angel' and 'monster' which male authors have generated for her. Before we women can write, declared Virginia Woolf, we must 'kill' the 'angel in the house'. In other words, women must kill the aesthetic ideal through which they themselves have been 'killed' into art. And similarly, all women writers must kill the angel's necessary opposite and double, the 'monster' in the house, whose Medusa-face also kills female creativity. (2000: 17)

Given this argument for authorship itself as a concept saturated with implications of gender, sexuality, and power, the representation of the virtuous domestic woman in Victorian fiction is an ambivalent proposition for male and female authors alike. Bram Stoker's *Dracula* (1897), which has not one but two lovely young female protagonists, succeeds in containing neither. Lucy Westenra, beautiful and sweet, is appealing to, and herself desires, not one man but many: 'Why can't they let a girl marry three men', she writes to her friend Mina, 'or as many as want her, and save all this trouble?' (Ch. 5: 81). Lucy is a girl who cannot say no. And it is Lucy who bids the vampire enter her bedroom; she falls as Count Dracula's first English victim. Her subsequent infection, her vampiric wanderings in the night, her death, and then her additional, undead wanderings in the night, produce the need for her exorcism. Dr. Seward reports from the scene:

> The Thing in the coffin writhed; and a hideous, blood-curdling screech came from the opened red lips. The body shook and quivered and twisted in wild contortions; the sharp white teeth champed together till the lips were cut, and the mouth was smeared with a crimson foam. But Arthur never faltered. He looked like a figure of Thor as his untrembling arm rose and fell, driving deeper and deeper the mercy-bearing stake, whilst the blood from the pierced heart welled and spurted up around it. (Ch. 16: 277)

Lucy's penetration by the 'mercy-bearing stake' helps her achieve in death what she failed to achieve in life: 'There, in the coffin lay no longer the foul Thing that we had so dreaded and grown to hate that the work of her destruction was yielded as a privilege to the one best entitled to it, but Lucy as we had seen her in life, with her face of unequalled sweetness and purity . . . . One and all we felt that the holy calm that lay like sunshine over the wasted face and form was only an earthly token and symbol of the calm that was to reign forever' (Ch. 16: 278).

Lucy's friends then close the crypt on her, literally and figuratively consigning her to an eternity of passivity enforced by the phallus. Her living counterpart, Mina Murray Harker, is another story, however. Far less obviously a candidate for 'Angel of the House', Mina affiliates herself with the modish, and sexually suggestive, figure of the New Woman; conversant with stenography, the typewriter, and the train timetables of Western and Eastern Europe alike, she does a great deal to keep both plot and narrative moving. Mina, the Professor exclaims, possesses a '"man's brain – a brain that a man should have were he much gifted – and [a] woman's heart"' (Ch. 18: 302). Just as it was for Marian Halcombe, Mina's masculinized, cerebral qualities seem to offer a recipe for success, or at least for survival; just as *The Woman in White* ends with Marian in a loving family circle, dandling a child, her nephew, on her knee, *Dracula* concludes with a portrait of Mina and her baby, surrounded by a circle of faithful men.

Such positive endings for powerful women – women who buck the cultural ideal of passive, enforced domesticity – suggest that Victorian novels work to complicate as much as to consolidate their culture's ideologies. Similarly Thackeray's narrator, at the end of *Vanity Fair*, bids farewell to his Amelia Sedley Osborne Dobbin in none too flattering terms. Making manifest the fact that his representation of Amelia as Angel is satirical, Thackeray emphasizes not the figure's desirability but her more insidiously threatening qualities: 'Farewell, dear Amelia. – Grow green again, tender little parasite, round the rugged old oak to which you cling!' (Ch. 67: 792). And at the end of *Middlemarch*, Eliot's narrator reports a typically antipathetic conversation between the doctor Lydgate and his wife Rosamond: 'He once called her a basil plant; and when she asked for an explanation, said that basil was a plant which had flourished wonderfully on a murdered man's brains' (Finale: 893). Parasites, basil plants, and Angels in the House. Novelists of Victorian Britain were as invested in deconstructing the ideal of domestic feminine sexuality as they were in constructing it.

Male Sexuality in Victorian Fiction

It is a curious fact that in a genre so dominated by the marriage plot, there is a dearth of normative male heterosexuality in Victorian fiction. Yet given the extraordinary range of female sexualities in the Victorian novel, perhaps the accompanying dismantling of male sexuality should seem less surprising. In Lord Arthur of Stoker's *Dracula* driving his mercy-bearing stake again and again through the undead heart of his beloved Lucy, the novel's canonization of phallic potency reaches an alarmingly literal climax. Yet even *Dracula* is a novel of male sexual impotence; in the context of the bumbling brigade of men surrounding Mina and Lucy and failing to protect them from the predatory vampire, Lord Arthur's phallic assertion seems too little, too late.

In Trollope's *Small House at Allington*, Adolphus Crosbie jilts Lily Dale then marries unhappily and is divorced; Johnny Eames, ambitious, virile, and adoring Lily, is destined to spend his life a bachelor awaiting her attentions. Crosbie and Johnny alike channel their unsatisfied domestic energies into the pursuit of their professional careers as bureaucrats. Meantime, Mr. Rochester keeps his wife locked in the attic even as he guides an unwitting Jane to the altar, after hiring her in the first place as the governess to a child who may or may not be his illegitimate daughter. Rochester finally gets his happy ending and his legitimate son. But by that point he has been blinded and maimed, signifiers of a castration overdetermined in its symbolic, punitive effects. David Copperfield's world finally comes together once he finds a wife who can manage him effectively. And Emily Brontë's Heathcliff is tragically destined to wander the moors with the ghost of the woman he could never fully have in life. As this suggests, women offer a formidable, and frequently insurmountable, challenge to heterosexual male figures in Victorian fiction; just as Lily Dale thwarts the tortured passions of Johnny Eames, she appears parasitical – an Amelia Sedley figure – to Crosbie, who flees her grasp. Joe Gargery of *Great Expectations* vividly symbolizes the power relation that presents male characters as the meek chattel of strong women. Pip reports:

> She was not a good-looking woman, my sister; and I had a general impression that she must have made Joe Gargery marry her by hand. Joe was a fair man, with curls of flaxen hair on each side of his smooth face, and with eyes of such a very undecided blue that they seem to have somehow got mixed with their own whites. He was a mild, good-natured, sweet-tempered, easy-going, foolish, dear fellow – a sort of Hercules in strength, and also in weakness. (Ch. 2: 39–40)

Loving and sweet, passive and fair, manipulable, gentle, and weak, Joe Gargery makes a better Angel in the House than any of his female counterparts in *Great Expectations*.

As these examples begin to suggest, conventional masculinity in Victorian fiction slips the divide of sexual difference and converges toward a feminized ideal. This 'masculine femininity' is every bit as problematic for the novel's male characters as it is for its women, and indeed, it is a far cry from the hybrid, strong, masculinized women, the Marians, Minas, and even Dorotheas who challenge the sex/gender system more audaciously. Oscar Wilde's *The Picture of Dorian Gray* takes on the problem of masculine sexuality in ways that are both direct and elliptical. The novel opens as Lord Henry Wotton watches his friend, the artist Basil Hallward, finish the portrait of a beautiful young man. '"You seem to forget that I am married",' Lord Henry says to Basil, '"and the one charm of marriage is that it makes a life of deception absolutely necessary for both parties"' (Ch. 1: 8). Into this discussion walks Dorian Gray, the beautiful subject of Basil's painting; and from the convergence of artist, aristocrat, and beautiful boy emerges a doctrine of aestheticist beauty, linking masculine sexuality directly to the fair and the youthful. For Lord Henry, Dorian becomes the emblem of 'A New Hedonism' that celebrates joy, youth, and beauty (Ch. 2: 28), while for Basil Dorian stands for '"a motive in art . . . He is never more present in my work than when no image of him is there"' (Ch. 1: 15).

Following the Faustian pact he makes in order to stay beautiful, Dorian himself, in a mode reminiscent of Thackeray's Becky Sharp, seeks to live that New Hedonism, finding sensuous pleasures in the trade of flesh as well as goods. First, however, Dorian dallies with the marriage-plot convention, engaging himself to the actress Sybil Vane. To Sybil, Dorian is her 'Prince Charming'. Once she accepts his love, she reveals herself as a horrible failure as an actress. As Sybil steps out of art and onto the stage of reality, Dorian, in love with art for art's sake, ceases to be enchanted. Jilted, Sybil kills herself; thus from the ashes of Sybil Vane rises a hedonism that eventually destroys a number of young men as well. Years later, Basil Hallward asks Dorian:

> 'Why is your friendship so fatal to young men? There was that wretched boy in the Guards who committed suicide. You were his great friend. There was Sir Henry Ashton, who had to leave England, with a tarnished name. You and he were inseparable. What about Adrian Singleton, and his dreadful end? What about Lord Kent's only son, and his career? . . . What about the young Duke of Perth?' (Ch. 12: 165–6)

Dorian's beauty, his hedonism, his fatal influence on young men conspire to produce a portrait of what Oscar Wilde's lover Lord Alfred Douglas will later call 'the love that dare not speak its name': sexual desire between men. *The Picture of Dorian Gray* both is and is not 'about' male homosexuality; rather, homosexuality in this text is akin to what Foucault described as the 'secret' inhabiting all discourse, the unspoken desire hiding in plain view. D. A. Miller (1991) has written about the communicative power of unspoken desire. In an analysis of the Hitchcock film *Rope*, Miller argues that the film's representational strategy involves a strategic deflection from what is said – the denotative level of meaning – to the unsaid – the connotative. Following connotations requires a reader to seek the unsaid, to seek what is hinted or suggested rather than stated outright. Reading for connotation, suggest Miller and Eve Kosofsky Sedgwick, introduces a new tactic for understanding sexual representation, what Sedgwick (1990) describes as the 'epistemology of the closet'. Reading Victorian novels as well as Hitchcock, Shakespeare, and others, Miller and Sedgwick offer a strategy for reading between the lines, and thus for identifying erotic subtexts that emerge from significant silences.

In *Between Men: English Literature and Male Homosocial Desire* (1985), Sedgwick argues that to read for male homosocial bonds is to read for the innermost workings of patriarchy itself. Sedgwick suggests that patriarchy is by definition a form of male homosocial bonding. As

Foucault and Rubin have both argued, patriarchy, embedded in the marketplace of industrial capitalism, with its twinned desires for commodities and for power, is the shaping force behind erotic identity. The Victorian novel is rife with scenes of male bonding – scenes that demonstrate the profound links between male homosociality and material power. Dorian and his young men, the platoon of chivalrous vampire-fighters in Dracula, David Copperfield and his beloved Steerforth, the inextricable protagonists of Wilkie Collins's *Armadale*. Not only are these and other male homosocial bonds eroticized; they provide a means of forging and testing a unique form of patriarchal power. Individual men in Victorian fiction often seem wispy and angelic, more often than not ineffectual. In contrast, masculine power in Victorian fiction emerges as a collaborative phenomenon. Effective action and the achievement of desire require both other men and, sometimes, the aid of manly women like Marian.

Infantile Sexuality in Victorian Fiction

In July 1885, the journalist W. T. Stead published a series of articles titled 'The Maiden Tribute of Modern Babylon' in the *Pall Mall Gazette*. Presented as Stead's response to the slave trade in young, white, virginal British girls, the articles mapped Stead's sensational intervention in the problem. In order to illustrate the ease with which young girls might be purchased on the open market, Stead reported his own purchase of a 13-year-old Cockney girl, Lily, for the sum of five pounds, plus the costs of the examination required to certify her virginity, and of the chloroform to subdue her. Predictably, Stead's 'Maiden Tribute' created a terrific stir, and served its desired effect. In his 'warning' to readers on 4 July 1885, in advance of the first installment, Stead positioned his report as an attempt to 'open the eyes of the public' to an upcoming vote on the Criminal Law Amendment Act.

Not least because of the furor caused by Stead's report, the Criminal Law Amendment Act was ratified later that year. The Act intervened in the legislation of sexual activity in several contexts: it raised the age of consent for females from 13 to 16; strengthened regulations against prostitution in general and brothels in particular; and declared as criminal 'Any male person who in public or private commits, or is party to the commission of or procures or attempts to procure the commission by any male person of any act of gross indecency with another male person'. The Criminal Law Amendment Act linked issues of female consent, prostitution, and male homosexuality within a unified legal category, the criminal. Even as it helped to invent male homosexual identity by means of its criminalization, the Act also extended the age of innocence that marked off and protected virtuous girlhood.

In some sense such a desexualization of childhood reflects the many constructions of innocence found in Victorian novels. In the work of Dickens alone, ill-fated children such as the crossing-sweep Jo in *Bleak House*, ancient little Paul Dombey of *Dombey and Son*, and most vividly, perhaps, Little Nell of *The Old Curiosity Shop* demonstrate a purity of intention, and a clarity of vision, completely alien to the dynamics of secrecy and shame that subtend Victorian representations of sexuality. While these children are arguably quite eroticized figures – their deaths involve the most attenuated bedroom scenes in Victorian fiction, they are physically and psychologically compelling, and their bodies are rendered in terms evoking physical transcendence – their erotic qualities are purified, rendered virtuous, by their status as innocent babes. All three of the children die young. Their marriage beds are their deathbeds, and their small bodies model an ideal of virtue accessible only in martyrdom.

Although Jo, Paul, Little Nell, Oliver Twist, and their kind seem far afield from the culture that produced Stead's 'Maiden Tribute', it also seems worth noticing that Dickens and other Victorian novelists invest in these childish figures as preternaturally knowing. I would suggest that in their clear, albeit innocent, knowledge of the world, they embody a kind of access to sexuality reflected vividly in other Victorian renderings of childhood.

Consider, for example, young David Copperfield at school, gazing on the sleeping face of Steerforth: 'I thought of him very much after I went to bed, and raised myself, I recollect, to look at him where he lay in the moonlight, with his handsome face turned up, and his head reclining easily on his arm' (Ch. 6: 140). Had David had a sister, Steerforth reports, '"I should think she would have been a pretty, timid, little bright-eyed sort of girl. I should have liked to know her"' (Ch. 6: 140). Uriah Heep, his entire body crawling with unrestrained twitching and seeping with damp, suggests the private pleasures of the onanist; having shaken his hand, David writes, 'But oh, what a clammy hand his was! as ghostly to the touch as to the sight! I rubbed mine afterwards, to warm it, *and to rub his off* (Ch. 15: 281, emphasis in original). Dickens's Oliver Twist maintains his purity even in the secret den of Fagin, where the old man educates a platoon of young boys in the sexualized act of reaching into the pockets of men on the streets, stealing away their secret contents. Fagin hangs for his crimes. Consider, too, Lewis Carroll's Alice. Catherine Robson argues that Alice inverts the pyramid of power and elevates little girls over men such as Carroll himself:

> Although Alice has a series of encounters with figures whom one could try to force into the older male role (the White Rabbit, the Dodo, the Caterpillar, the Cheshire Cat, the March Hare, the Hatter, the King of Hearts, the Gryphon, and the Mock Turtle, to name the likeliest suspects), the balance of power is never weighted with any certainty or for any length of time in their favor. Alice's frequent comments about eating remind us that a little girl is just as likely to devour as to be devoured, while her equally frequent changes in size destroy the conventional arrangement in which an older male can be sure of being bigger than a younger female. (2000: 146)

Time and again Victorian novelists locate the origins of both power and sexuality in childhood innocence. Following her unwitting betrayal of Heathcliff, for example, the adolescent Catherine Earnshaw describes the primeval quality of her passion for this boy – only now verging on manhood – who has been her constant companion from earliest consciousness: '"My love for Heathcliff resembles the eternal rocks beneath – a source of little visible delight, but necessary. Nelly, I *am* Heathcliff – he's always, always in my mind – not as a pleasure, any more than I am always a pleasure to myself – but as my own being . . . "' (Ch. 9: 122, emphasis in original). Fused from earliest childhood, divided by the worldly world and reunited to walk the moors after death, Heathcliff and Catherine express a passion that suggests the bonds forged in childhood innocence are the only true bonds. In Catherine's heart, the infant self is the authentic self – and thus infantile desire is authentic desire, uncorrupted by worldly considerations. In that vein, Maggie Tulliver the child *is* Maggie Tulliver the woman, authentic to the last. The flood that takes the lives of Maggie and her brother Tom signifies the sexuality suffusing the sibling relation, as it did for Heathcliff and Catherine:

> 'It is coming, Maggie!' Tom said, in a deep hoarse voice, loosing the oars, and clasping her . . . The boat reappeared – but brother and sister had gone down in an embrace never to be parted – living through again in one supreme moment, the days when they had clasped their little hands in love, and roamed the daisy fields together. (Eliot 1880, Ch. 5: 655)

Taken cumulatively, these examples suggest that the function of childhood in Victorian fictional texts involves its identification as a source of sexuality and sexual knowledge. Childhood is no mere sexless phase, and adult sexuality does not abruptly commence at the wedding altar, on the last page of the novel. In 1905, just four years after the deaths of Queen Victoria and Oscar Wilde, Sigmund Freud 'discovered' childhood sexuality. 'So far as I know', writes Freud, 'not a single author has clearly recognized the regular existence of a sexual instinct in childhood' (1971: 173). What the psychologists of the day might not have recognized the novelists knew well: sexual complexities originate with the individual and never proceed straight and true. In those erotic intricacies dwells some of the fascinating power of Victorian fiction.

References and Further Reading

Adams, James Eli (1995) *Dandies and Desert Saints: Styles of Victorian Masculinity*. Ithaca: Cornell University Press.

Althusser, Louis (1971) Ideology and ideological state apparatuses: Notes towards an investigation. In Ben Brewster (Trans.) *Lenin and Philosophy and Other Essays*, pp. 121–73. London: New Left Books.

Anderson, Amanda (1995) *Tainted Souls and Painted Faces: The Rhetoric of Fallenness in Victorian Culture*. Ithaca: Cornell University Press.

Armstrong, Nancy (1987) *Desire and Domestic Fiction: A Political History of the Novel*. New York: Oxford University Press.

Auerbach, Nina (1982) *The Woman and the Demon*. Cambridge, MA: Harvard University Press.

Braddon, Mary Elizabeth (1861–2; 1987) *Lady Audley's Secret*. ed. David Skilton. New York: Oxford University Press.

Bristow, Joseph (1997) *Sexuality*. New York: Routledge.

Brontë, Charlotte (1847; 1985) *Jane Eyre*. ed. Q. D. Leavis. New York: Penguin.

Brontë, Emily (1847; 1985) *Wuthering Heights*. ed. David Daiches. New York: Penguin.

Boone, Joseph Allen (1998) *Libidinal Currents: Sexuality and the Shaping of Modernism*. Chicago: University of Chicago Press.

Brooks, Peter (1984) *Reading for the Plot: Design and Intention in Narrative*. New York: A. A. Knopf.

Carroll, Lewis (1865; 1998) *Alice's Adventures in Wonderland*. ed. Roger Lancelyn Green. New York: Oxford World's Classics.

Cohen, Ed (1993) *Talk on the Wilde Side: Towards a Genealogy of a Discourse of Male Sexualities*. New York: Routledge.

Cohen, William (1996) *Sex Scandal: The Private Parts of Victorian Fiction*. Durham, NC: Duke University Press.

Collins, Wilkie (1864–6; 1989) *Armadale*. ed. Catherine Peters. New York: Oxford University Press.

——(1860; 1999) *The Woman in White*. ed. Matthew Sweet. New York: Penguin.

Craft, Christopher (1994) *Another Kind of Love: Male Homosexual Desire in English Discourse, 1850–1920*. Berkeley: University of California Press.

Dever, Carolyn (1998) *Death and the Mother From Dickens to Freud: Victorian Fiction and the Anxiety of Origins*. Cambridge: Cambridge University Press.

Dickens, Charles (1852–3; 1985) *Bleak House*. ed. Norman Page. New York: Penguin.

——(1847–8; 1985a) *Dombey and Son*. ed. Peter Fairclough. New York: Penguin.

——(1849–50; 1985b). *David Copperfield*. ed. Trevor Blount. New York: Penguin.

——(1860–1; 1985c) *Great Expectations*. ed. Angus Calder. New York: Penguin.

——(1840–1; 1985d) *The Old Curiosity Shop*. ed. Angus Easson. New York: Penguin.

——(1837–8; 1985e) *Oliver Twist*. ed. Peter Fairclough. New York: Penguin.

Dowling, Linda (1994) *Hellenism and Homosexuality in Victorian Oxford*. Ithaca: Cornell University Press.

Eliot, George (1871–2; 1965) *Middlemarch*. ed. W. J. Harvey. New York: Penguin.

——(1880; 1985). *The Mill on the Floss*. ed. A. S. Byatt. New York: Penguin.

Foucault, Michel (1990) *The History of Sexuality: An Introduction*. Volume 1, trans. Robert Hurley. New York: Vintage Books.

Freud, Sigmund (1905; 1971) *Three Essays on the Theory of Sexuality*. In James Strachey (trans. and ed.), *The Standard Edition of the Complete Psychological Works of Sigmund Freud* (Vol. 7, pp. 125–245). London: The Hogarth Press and the Institute for Psycho-Analysis.

Gagnier, Regenia (2000) *The Insatiability of Human Wants: Economics and Aesthetics in Market Society*. Chicago: University of Chicago Press.

Gilbert, Sandra M. and Gubar, Susan (2000; 1979) *The Madwoman in the Attic: The Woman Writer and the Nineteenth-Century Literary Imagination*, second edition. New Haven: Yale University Press.

Hardy, Thomas (1891; 1978) *Tess of the D'Urbervilles: A Pure Woman*. ed. David Skilton. New York: Penguin.

Kincaid, James R. (1992) *Child-Loving: The Erotic Child and Victorian Culture*. New York: Routledge.

Kucich, John (1987) *Repression in Victorian Fiction: Charlotte Brontë, George Eliot, and Charles Dickens*. Berkeley: University of California Press.

Lane, Christopher (1999) *The Burdens of Intimacy: Psychoanalysis and Victorian Masculinity*. Chicago: University of Chicago Press.

Mangum, Teresa (1998) *Married, Middlebrow, and Militant: Sarah Grand and the New Woman Novel*. Ann Arbor: University of Michigan Press.

Marcus, Steven (1966) *The Other Victorians: A Study of Sexuality and Pornography in Mid-Nineteenth-Century England*. New York: Basic Books.

Mason, Michael (1994) *The Making of Victorian Sexuality*. New York: Oxford University Press.

Matus, Jill (1995) *Unstable Bodies: Victorian Representations of Sexuality and Maternity*. New York: Manchester University Press.

Mavor, Carol (1995) *Pleasures Taken: Performances of Sexuality and Loss in Victorian Photographs*. Durham, NC: Duke University Press.

Maynard, John (1993) *Victorian Discourses on Sexuality and Religion*. Cambridge: Cambridge University Press.

McClintock, Anne (1995) *Imperial Leather: Race, Gender and Sexuality in the Colonial Contest*. New York: Routledge.

Michie, Helena (1987) *The Flesh Made Word: Female Figures and Women's Bodies*. New York: Oxford University Press.

Miller, Andrew and Adams, James Eli (eds.) (1996) *Sexualities in Victorian Britain*. Bloomington: Indiana University Press.

Miller, D. A. (1991) Anal *Rope*. In Diana Fuss (ed.) *Inside/Out: Lesbian Theories, Gay Theories*, pp. 119–41. New York: Routledge.

Mort, Frank (2000) *Dangerous Sexualities: Medico-Moral Politics in England Since 1830*. New York: Routledge.

Nunokawa, Jeff (1994) *The Afterlife of Property: Domestic Security and the Victorian Novel*. Princeton: Princeton University Press.

Pearsall, Ronald (1969) *The Worm in the Bud: The World of Victorian Sexuality*. New York: Macmillan.

Poovey, Mary (1988) *Uneven Developments: The Ideological Work of Gender in Mid-Victorian England*. Chicago: University of Chicago Press.

Robson, Catherine (2001) *Men in Wonderland: The Lost Girlhood of the Victorian Gentleman*. Princeton: Princeton University Press.

Rubin, Gayle (1975) The traffic in women: Notes on the 'political economy' of Sex. In Rayna R. Reiter (ed). *Toward an Anthropology of Women*, pp. 157–210. New York: Monthly Review Press.

Sedgwick, Eve Kosofsky (1985) *Between Men: English Literature and Male Homosocial Desire*. New York: Columbia University Press.

——(1990) *Epistemology of the Closet*. Berkeley: University of California Press.

The Sins of the Cities of the Plain, or the Recollections of a Mary-Ann, with Short Essays on Sodomy and Tribadism (1881). In two volumes. London: Privately printed.

Stoker, Bram (1897; 1993) *Dracula*. ed. Maurice Hindle. New York: Penguin.

Sussman, Herbert (1995) *Victorian Masculinities: Manhood and Masculine Poetics in Early Victorian Literature and Art*. Cambridge: Cambridge University Press.

Thackeray, William (1847–8; 1968) *Vanity Fair*. ed. J. I. M Stewart. New York: Penguin.

Trollope, Anthony (1857; 1994) *Barchester Towers*. ed. Robin Gilmour. New York: Penguin.

——(1864; 1991) *The Small House at Allington*. ed. Julian Thompson. New York: Penguin.

Trudgill, Eric (1976) *Madonnas and Magdalens: The Origins and Development of Victorian Sexual Attitudes*. New York: Holmes and Meier.

Vicinus, Martha (1985) *Independent Women: Work and Community for Single Women, 1850–1920*. Chicago: University of Chicago Press.

Walkowitz, Judith (1992) *City of Dreadful Delight: Narratives of Sexual Danger in Late-Victorian London*. Chicago: University of Chicago Press.

——(1980) *Prostitution and Victorian Society: Women, Class, and the State*. Cambridge: Cambridge University Press.

Weeks, Jeffrey (1989) *Sex, Politics, and Society: The Regulation of Sexuality Since 1800*. Second edition. New York: Longman.

Wilde, Oscar (1891; 1985) *The Picture of Dorian Gray*. ed. Peter Ackroyd. New York: Penguin.

Chapter 9

'One of the larger lost Continents': Religion in the Victorian Novel

Michael Wheeler

Losing the Plot

During the 1980s and 1990s, a series of surveys monitored church attendance worldwide. Recent figures indicate that 44 percent of Americans attend church once a week, not counting funerals, christenings, and baptisms, compared with 27 percent of people in Great Britain, 21 percent of the French, 4 percent of Swedes, and 3 percent of Japanese (Anon 1997). Fifty-three percent of Americans say that religion is very important in their lives, compared with 16 percent, 14 percent, and 13 percent, respectively, of the British, French, and Germans. So marked is the decline of organized religion in northern Europe that Latin American countries are sending missionaries to save the souls of their former colonizers.

Even more significant for our generation, with respect to literary study, is the dramatic fall in recent years in the levels of biblical literacy and general knowledge of foundational Christian doctrines. Many young British adults know virtually nothing about Christianity. Yet in order to understand Victorian fiction it is essential to understand Victorian religion – perhaps the most passionately contested aspect of a culture, which seems increasingly remote from us, two centuries on.

Victorian Britain was Christian and largely Protestant. Copies of the Bible and of Bunyan's *Pilgrim's Progress* were to be found in the homes of the 'deserving poor'. Novel readers, rich and poor, but mainly middle class, knew their Bibles. Novelists could therefore make creative use of biblical allusions, not merely as decoration or to add a touch of pietism, but as important thematic and structural references to the richest intertext of them all – the Authorized Version, or King James Bible of 1611. Everyone was also familiar with the rhythms of the Book of Common Prayer, as even Dissenters were obliged to have the Burial Service read over their dead until late on in the nineteenth century. Some Victorian fiction can be categorized in the sub-genre of the 'religious novel'. All Victorian novels, however, use narrative techniques which owe something to scriptural and confessional forms of narrative, whether spiritual autobiographies or testimonies, tracts or sermons, histories or letters. The church or chapel affiliations of individual novelists had a profound effect upon their work.

In other words, the 'grand narrative' of the Judeo-Christian tradition – Milton's subject in *Paradise Lost* – still shaped the 'common culture' of the Victorian Age. Today, in a post-modern, multicultural, and multi-faith Britain, we are in the process of losing that particular plot and therefore losing informed access to a thousand years of English literature, or at least to a full understanding and appreciation of that literature. This new cultural situation has been met with two contrasting responses from modern scholars, which can be loosely categorized as deconstructive and reconstructive.

Those who espouse what has come to be known as the 'hermeneutics of suspicion' go to Victorian novels in order to explore their hidden agendas and to read their sub-texts. This has a leveling effect upon the canon of Victorian literature, as an obscure pot-boiler can be more truly reflective of the culture than a 'great novel', so defined precisely because it breaks or transcends the received conventions of the genre. When applied to religious texts, deconstructive moves are often associated with a declared or undeclared 'atheology' on the part of the critic, and an assumption that Christianity is history. In interrogating the Christian 'hegemony' of nineteenth-century Britain, some scholars have focused upon the cultures of small minority groups, such as Jews, Muslims, and secularists, and this has certainly broadened the agenda for those engaged in the study of literature and religion in the period. (For revaluations of Victorian Anglo-Jewish literary history, see Scheinberg 1999.)

The reconstructionists, on the other hand, address our current situation by seeking to provide the modern reader with ever more detailed and accurate maps of what our own secular culture now largely regards as *terra incognita*. Owen Chadwick's magisterial study on *The Victorian Church* (1966–70) covered a huge amount of terrain in two volumes. Since then, what Chadwick covered in each chapter has become the subject of whole books, as ecclesiastical and cultural historians have produced specialized studies on topics such as the Oxford Movement or 'muscular Christianity', and have discussed the significance of these subjects for Victorian culture in general and literature in particular.

This chapter will focus upon reconstruction, as I believe that, in the field of religion at any rate, it is of more immediate value to students of Victorian fiction and will prove to have more lasting significance for future scholars than deconstruction. In the sections that follow, I first discuss ways in which scholars have 'picked up the threads' of a tradition that is in danger of disappearing from view. I then give some examples of critical reading 'with the grain' of Victorian culture, before finally speculating on 'Victorian futures'.

Picking Up the Threads

In the preface to their invaluable *Oxford Companion to Christian Art and Architecture*, Peter and Linda Murray explain that they wrote the book in order to meet a crying need. One of them, standing in London's National Gallery in front of Piero della Francesca's *Baptism of Christ*, heard someone ask his companion, 'What's the pigeon for?' The other capped this with the assertion that she had heard an English couple, in front of Leonardo da Vinci's *Last Supper* in Milan say, 'I don't know what they are doing, but they seem to be having some sort of a meal' (Murray 1996: vii). The *Companion* includes not only short biographies of artists and architects, emperors and popes, patrons and artistic movements, but also entries on saints and martyrs, doctrines and sects, biblical characters and incidents – always citing the most important examples of their representation in art.

John Sutherland, author of one of the best companions to Victorian fiction, has different priorities. He wants to open up 'one of the larger lost continents' through 1,606 entries on novelists and novels, genres and modes, publishers and critics, who together made up the literary industry which generated somewhere around 60,000 works of adult and juvenile fiction published between 1837 and 1901 – that is, 20 percent of total book production in the period (Sutherland 1988: 1). So there is no space in his *Companion* for contextual material. While carefully identifying the religious orientation of Victorian novelists and offering a short entry on 'The Religious Novel', Sutherland leaves to other reference books, such as the *Oxford Companion to English Literature*, the task of explaining the many aspects of religion upon which the reader of Victorian fiction is likely to stub his or her toe.

And yet it could be argued that an understanding of religion is just as important for the student of Victorian fiction as it is for the student of Renaissance art. I addressed this issue in *The Art of Allusion in Victorian Fiction* (1979), where I showed that the use of biblical quotations and references was adopted as a recognized convention by many novelists, in the knowledge that the Bible was the central plank of what can be described as the 'common culture' of Victorian Britain. Elizabeth Gaskell's *Mary Barton* represents early Victorian Manchester as the city of Dives and Lazarus. *Hard Times* is more than a 'social-problem novel', in that Dickens's pointed biblical allusions broaden the novel's schema to that of an apocalypse in a mechanical age. And so on. (We will return to this theme later, in 'Reading with the grain'.)

By the time that my volume on *English Fiction of the Victorian Period, 1830–1890* (1985) was published, Victorian scholarship had firmly embraced interdisciplinarity as a way of living with literary theory. Those of us who in 1987 were involved in the founding of the journal *Literature and Theology* – Britain's answer to two thriving journals in the United Staes, *Religion and Literature* and *Christianity and Literature* – debated the balance that such a journal should strike between theoretical and critical articles. We were all agreed that truly interdisciplinary work had to press beyond the shared borders of different scholarly disciplines. Our editorial in the first number included this statement:

> For some time now theologians have recognized that they must pay more attention to narrative, figurative discourse and liturgy as the primary language of faith, and that the analysis and interpretation of texts is not a mere prologue to theology but is central to the whole theological task. Literary theory, which many would argue merely transfers hermeneutics to a new (secular) body of texts, has not only come to see how close are many of its questions concerning intentionality, canonicity and the criteria for interpretation to those raised by traditional biblical hermeneutics, but has also raised in a new form metaphysical issues concerning 'presence' which seem to demand either nihilistic or else distinctly theological resolutions. In this context we hope that *Literature and Theology*, far from dealing with matters which only overlap at the margin, will situate itself at the theoretical centre of both disciplines.

Both the journal and the international conferences of the Centre for the Study of Literature and Theology (then at Durham, now at Glasgow), organized by David Jasper and Terry Wright, provided much of the stimulus to their helpful introductory books on the methodologies available to students of literature and theology (Jasper 1989, Wright 1988).

Three kinds of critical study of Victorian fiction emerged from this revival of interest in relations between literature and religion, each of which was made possible by earlier, ground-clearing work. First, there were books that addressed particular kinds of Victorian religious fiction. A Harvard Professor of History, Robert Lee Wolff, published *Gains and Losses: Novels of Faith and Doubt in Victorian Fiction* in 1977 – the critical introduction to a large reprint series published by Garland, which made many a lost title available to a modern readership. The 121 novels in that series are divided up into sections which tell us much about Victorian sectarianism and which usefully outline the field of the religious novel. Part I is on 'The Church of Rome', with a chapter on 'The Catholics, and their Friends and Enemies' (including Newman, Grace Kennedy, and Frances Trollope). Part II is on 'The Church of England', and contains three chapters on 'The High Churchmen and some Opponents' (Charlotte Yonge, Margaret Oliphant, Joseph Henry Shorthouse, Walter Pater), 'The Low Churchmen (Evangelicals) and their Enemies' (F. W. Farrar, George Eliot, Emma Worboise, Sarah Smith ('Hesba Stretton'), Elizabeth Charles), and 'Broad Church' (Charles Kingsley, F. D. Maurice, William John Conybeare). Part III covers 'The Dissenting Churches', with a chapter on 'Dissent' (Margaret Oliphant, George MacDonald, William Hale White ('Mark Rutherford'), Edmund Gosse). Part IV, '"No Church:" Varieties of Doubt', has five chapters: '"Only infinite Jumble and Mess and Dislocation"' (William Hale White, Eliza Lynn Linton), '"Spiritual Agonizing Bellyaches"' (J. A. Froude, Geraldine Jewsbury, William Delafield Arnold), 'The Impact of Science' (Winwood Reade, Charlotte Yonge, Samuel Butler), 'Earnestness in the Third Generation: Mrs. Humphry Ward', and '"Souls Bereaved:" The Novels of W. H. Mallock'.

Gains and Losses is a useful supplement to Margaret Maison's splendidly titled *Search your Soul, Eustace: A Survey of the Religious Novel in the Victorian Age* (1961), but is limited critically and is prone to inaccuracy. Far more sophisticated are two focused studies by young Oxford scholars who homed in on religious fiction with specific sectarian affiliations. Valentine Cunningham's *Everywhere Spoken Against: Dissent in the Victorian Novel* (1975) discusses the Brontës, Elizabeth Gaskell, George

Eliot, Dickens, Margaret Oliphant, and William Hale White, and regards the sympathetic treatment of dissent as a touchstone of judgment. Elisabeth Jay's *The Religion of the Heart: Anglican Evangelicalism and the Nineteenth-Century Novel* (1979) offers a very thorough treatment of Evangelicalism – the most powerful religious revival of the century – before analyzing the novels of George Eliot, Emma Warboise, and Samuel Butler.

The second kind of critical study to emerge strongly from the late 1970s onwards took a theme or concept and traced its development in a wide variety of Victorian fiction, much of which would not be classified as specifically 'religious'. The American critic, Barry V. Qualls, for example, published *The Secular Pilgrims of Victorian Fiction: The Novel as Book of Life* in 1982. Here he identifies seventeenth-century religious writings and Romantic 'revisionings' as the context in which Thomas Carlyle, Charlotte Brontë, Dickens, and George Eliot worked. Both Norman Vance's *The Sinews of the Spirit: The Ideal of Christian Manliness in Victorian literature and Religious Thought* (1985) and my own *Death and the Future Life in Victorian Literature and Theology* (1990) drew upon fiction of the period, along with poetry and non-fictional prose.

The third kind of study (a close relation of the second) is by literary intellectual historians – the descendants of Basil Willey, Walter Houghton, and Jerome Buckley – who include fiction in their arguments. Gillian Beer's *Darwin's Plots: Evolutionary Narrative in Darwin, George Eliot and Nineteenth-Century Fiction* was published in 1983, and includes discussion of Thomas Hardy, who lost his religious faith in the 1860s, as we will see in a later section. In *Providence and Love: Studies in Wordsworth, Channing, Myers, George Eliot, and Ruskin* (1998), John Beer discusses the sense of Providence, the growing awareness of its loss in the nineteenth century, and the pressure on the ideal of Romantic love that came to be regarded as a substitute. George Eliot, the Victorian intellectual *par excellence*, is also an important presence in Alison Milbank's *Dante and the Victorians* (1998), a study on the intersections between history, nationalism, aesthetics, and gender.

As even such a breathless review suggests, research into Victorian fiction and religion has become increasingly ambitious in recent years. It has also been more highly regarded professionally, perhaps as a result of a growing awareness of the need to keep religion in the forefront of Victorian studies during a period in which the majority of scholars and students have no strong religious commitment. The organizers of a major international conference in London in 2001, marking the centenary of Queen Victoria's death and the 150th anniversary of the Great Exhibition, were surprised and delighted to see high attendances at the sessions devoted to religion. Scholars are increasingly aware both of the need for this kind of work and of its increasingly high standard.

Reading with the Grain

No interpretation, we are often reminded, is innocent of ideology. Consider, for example, Stephen Greenblatt's famous essay on Shakespeare's history plays, entitled 'Invisible Bullets', published in 1988 and frequently reprinted since. Commenting on Elizabethan hostility to atheism, he writes: 'The stance that seemed to come naturally to me as a green college freshman in mid-twentieth-century America seems to have been almost unthinkable to the most daring philosophical mind of late sixteenth-century England' (Barratt *et al.* 1995: 100). Greenblatt states in passing that atheism came to him 'naturally', when he first encountered serious ideas as a naïve first-year college student.

John D. Cox, writing on 'The turn to history' in a collection of essays entitled *The Discerning Reader: Christian Perspectives on Literature and Theory*, is troubled by Greenblatt's 'suave aside', and thinks that we should be, too (Barratt *et al.* 1995: 100–2). First, Greenblatt's 'easily assumed atheism makes him, on the face of it, an unsympathetic reader of texts from a traditional culture that was deeply religious'. Secondly, his comparison between the 'most daring philosophical mind of late sixteenth-century England' and himself as a freshman is 'breathtakingly arrogant'. Cox believes that Greenblatt's writing should be approached with 'both gratitude and wariness':

> It deserves gratitude for its wit, grace, insight, learning, and – yes – for its moral wisdom. But that wisdom is reduced by its debt to the materialist metanarrative – a story that is not the Christian story and is, in fact, antithetical in many respects to it. One way to tell Stephen Greenblatt's story might be to position his moral wisdom more accurately against his Jewish cultural background than against historical materialism – in other words, to show what his moral wisdom owes to the ongoing narrative of God's faithfulness to Israel, including God's faithfulness to Stephen Greenblatt. But this is not the place to attempt such an account. More important for Christian readers is to remember their own story and always to endeavour to assess other stories in light of it, rather than the other way round.

Unusually, Cox's essay, like some others in *The Discerning Reader*, argues that a 'Christian' reading of a text is as committed as, say, a Marxist reading. Christians, he believes, 'need to see things differently from the way they are seen by those who are not Christians; that is, Christians need to see their own story, not only in terms of their individual dialogue with God (as in Augustine's *Confessions*), but also in terms of their culture'.

In Cox's view, then, Marxists should acknowledge their Marxism in their criticism, Christians their Christianity, and Greenblatt his Jewishness: there is no such thing as on objective or neutral reading of literature. But is the Christian reader best placed to read 'Christian' literature? As English literature before the Second World War was informed by a broadly Christian culture, are we to assume that the best modern critics of historical English literature must be Christians? Cox does not say so, and indeed, it would be difficult to mount such an argument, not least because there is no obvious relationship between personal Christian commitment and such things as intellectual ability, range of reading, and critical acumen. I would argue, however, that, irrespective of creed or lack of creed, a 'discerning reader' of historical English literature in general, and of Victorian fiction in particular, needs to be sufficiently well read in the Christian culture that produced it to be able to offer a 'sympathetic' reading. I would further argue that this is particularly true of the 'reconstructionist' critic, whose aim is to explain the context in which any particular author wrote, in order to read the author's work 'with the grain' – admittedly a somewhat problematic metaphor, bearing in mind Victorian fiction's often critical stance towards nineteenth-century culture and society, but nevertheless a useful one.

I will now suggest some ways in which reading with the grain of the Victorian 'common culture' that I mentioned earlier – the Bible, Bunyan, and the Book of Common Prayer – can put the modern reader in closer touch with both the fiction and the context in which it was first published. Having briefly compared two 'classic' Victorian novels – Charlotte Brontë's *Jane Eyre* (1847) and Hardy's *Jude the Obscure* (1895) – in order to give a sense of change in the intellectual milieu during the Victorian Age, I will discuss the theme of confession in Brontë's *Jane Eyre* and *Villette* (1853), and an unknown novel by Emma Robinson, entitled *Westminster Abbey* (1854), in order to show how novels – both canonical and non-canonical – can be read as interventions in the hot religious debates of their day.

Jane Eyre is a rewriting (and revision) of the *Pilgrim's Progress* – itself a rewriting of the Bible. The novel, and Jane's spiritual journey, open at Gateshead Hall, which, like all the locations, is allegorically named. Brocklehurst, the Evangelical 'black pillar' of a clergyman, then tries to break her spirit at Lowood school, where Miss Temple relieves her of a 'grievous load' (Brontë 1987: ch. 4, 26; ch. 8, 65). The wedding fiasco takes place at Rochester's Thornfield, from which Jane escapes to Whitcross, her Valley of Humiliation: 'Want came to me, place and bare. . . . The burden must be carried . . . I set out' (Brontë 1987: ch. 28, 285–6). At Moor House, which is strongly reminiscent of Bunyan's Palace Beautiful, she is welcomed by the Rivers girls, Diana and Mary, and by St John Rivers, a more intelligent and thus potentially controlling Evangelical than Brocklehurst. As in the *Pilgrim's Progress*, in which the Interpreter plays a crucial role, interpretation is central to the schema of *Jane Eyre*, the climax of which is Jane's response to the uncanny cry of the distant Rochester: 'Jane! Jane! Jane!' (Brontë 1987: ch. 35, 369). She rejects both an orthodox Christian interpretation of the cry ('miracle') and a Gothic reading ('superstition'), relying instead upon her own instinct ('nature'). Reunited with a now tamed Rochester at Ferndean, she enters, not the Celestial City of Bunyan's Christian, but an earthly paradise: marriage and family life with her beloved master. Part One of the *Pilgrim's Progress* ends, not with Christian, but with Ignorance, who is sent directly from the gates of heaven to hell. In a further inversion, Charlotte Brontë parallels Bunyan by ending the novel, not with Jane and Rochester, but with Rivers, a missionary in India, whose life expectation is low, and who anticipates 'his sure reward, his incorruptible crown' in the heaven of Christian orthodoxy.

Whereas *Wuthering Heights* (1847) ends in a graveyard near a crumbling 'kirk' at the edge of the moors, *Jane Eyre* is less radical, remaining within a broadly Christian framework. Having heard Rochester's cry, Jane 'breaks away from St John', her own powers 'in play' (Brontë 1987: ch. 35, 370). But when she then rushes upstairs, falls on her knees, and prays in her 'own way', she seems to 'penetrate very near a Mighty Spirit', and her soul rushes out 'in gratitude at *His* feet' (my emphasis). Whereas *Wuthering Heights* puzzled contemporary readers and critics, *Jane Eyre* was a best seller, combining domesticated Gothic romance and recognizably Christian allegory in ways that made the more shocking aspects of the novel, such as Rochester's confession, acceptable to readers of the 1840s, when Evangelical pietism dominated early-Victorian culture. The last word in the novel is 'Jesus'.

Almost half a century later, Hardy's *Jude the Obscure* ends with the robust Arabella standing beside Jude's 'handsome corpse', and commenting upon Sue Brideshead's claim to Mrs Edlin that she has found peace: 'She may swear that on her knees to the holy cross upon her necklace till she's hoarse, but it won't be true! . . . She's never found peace since she left his arms, and never will again till she's as he is now!' (Hardy 1985: pt 6, ch. 11, 491). Early in their relationship, Sue gloried in reading skeptical writers such as Gibbon, Shelley, and Swinburne, while Jude was reverently reading his Greek New Testament. For Hardy, whose response to Darwin led to his giving up church-going in the 1860s, the negative response of Oxford (or 'Christminster') to Jude's intellectual and spiritual aspirations represents a stifling of potential which, unlike in the case of Jane Eyre, eventually leads to Jude's death, with the 'dog-eared Greek Testament on the neighbouring shelf' (Hardy 1985: pt 6, ch. 11, 490). The Church of England now seems simply irrelevant in the face of human tragedy. Shortly after Jude and Sue find the children hanged, 'because we are too menny', Jude overhears two clergymen of different views arguing outside about the eastward position of the celebrant at communion: 'Good God – the eastward position, and all creation groaning!' (Hardy 1985: pt 6, ch. 2, 410–11). Contemporary readers would have recognized not only the biblical allusion (Romans 8.11), but also the ironic reference to the kind of ecclesiastical debate that preoccupied the Ritualists – High Church descendants of the Oxford Movement – and their opponents in the Victorian church. In Hardy's malevolent universe, there is no loving 'Mighty Spirit' to whom Jude can pray. Jude's dying words are from the third chapter of Job: 'Wherefore is light given to him that is in misery, and life unto the bitter in soul?' (Hardy 1985: pt 6, ch. 11, 486).

Turning now to the theme of confession, it is worth reminding ourselves of a feature of *Jane Eyre* that is usually overlooked by critics: Rochester's confession. When he tells Jane the story of his marriage to Bertha Mason in the West Indies, he uses the kind of language that was familiar from Protestant spiritual autobiographies, such as Bunyan's *Grace Abounding to the Chief of Sinners*: 'Oh, I have no respect for myself when I think of that act! – an agony of inward contempt masters me' (Brontë 1987: ch. 27, 269–71). He speaks of 'sin', 'repentance', and 'vices', and of being rescued by 'Wisdom', 'Hope', and 'Regeneration'. Later, at Ferndean, he explains to Jane that his cry of desolation, which she somehow heard at Moor House, followed his own journey through the 'valley of the shadow of death': '*His* chastisements are mighty; and one smote me which has humbled me for ever' (Brontë 1987: ch. 37, 393).

Rochester's confession to Jane is couched in specifically Protestant terms: one contrite Christian addresses another, and speaks of a direct, personal relationship with God, which she shares with him. Six years later, in *Villette,* Charlotte Brontë takes the Protestant English reader into foreign terrain – the Roman Catholic tradition of auricular confession. Parched in the spiritual desert of the long vacation, Lucy Snowe is driven to attend a French Catholic priest in his confessional, although she is ignorant of the 'formula of confession' (Brontë 1904: ch. 15, 153). The priest, speaking kindly to this English stranger, comments that she has poured her heart out to him: 'a thing seldom done'. She is made for the Catholic faith, he argues: 'Protestantism is altogether too dry, cold, prosaic for you.' In recording her response, Lucy assumes that her reader is a Protestant:

> Did I, do you suppose, reader, contemplate venturing again within that worthy priest's reach? As soon should I have thought of walking into a Babylonish furnace. . . . Had I gone to him, he would have shown me all that was tender, and comforting, and gentle, in the honest Popish superstition. . . . I might just now, instead of writing this heretic narrative, be counting my beads in the cell of a certain Carmelite convent on the Boulevard of Crécy, in Villette.

In other words, she might now be 'buried' in a convent, like the nun whose ghost is said to walk in the school garden, containing a 'vault, imprisoning deep beneath that ground, on whose surface grass grew and flowers bloomed, the bones of a girl whom a monkish conclave of the drear middle ages had . . . buried alive for some sin against her vow' (Brontë 1904: ch. 12, 98–9).

Far from being simply another example of Brontë's domestication of the Gothic, these references to convent life and auricular confession had a particular topical resonance in 1853. Protestant commentators had been alarmed to find that in 1850 there were 50 convents in England, whereas in 1830 there had only been 10. In 1851, during a debate in the House of Commons, Henry Drummond had described convents as being 'either prisons or brothels'. The context for this anti-Catholic jibe was the so-called 'papal aggression' crisis, following Pope Pius IX's sudden announcement from Rome, on 29 September 1850, that the Catholic hierarchy of England was to be restored. On 21 November, the *Daily News* thundered: 'A Papal Bull, insulting to the nation, to its history, its noble struggles, and its as noble tolerance, is flung in the country's face.' In the words of a leading Roman Catholic, Bishop Ullathorne, the 'papal aggression' crisis put the whole country 'in a boil'.

During the crisis, comic-strip versions of English Reformation history featured in anti-Catholic sermons, speeches at public meetings, popular books and pamphlets, and newspapers and periodicals, most of which had specific sectarian affiliations. Several anti-Catholic manuals were adopted by the Reformation Society and the Scottish Protestant Association during the 1850s for use in their adult classes, which were taught using the catechistic method adopted in school textbooks, and satirized in the opening chapters of Dickens's *Hard Times* (1854). In one of them, the Revd Dr Blakeney deals with 'the reign of Mary, known as the Bloody Queen', by simply summarizing John Foxe's descriptions, in his still hugely popular *Book of Martyrs*, of the executions of the leading Protestant martyrs, and asking for their names in the 'Questions and Answers' section at the end of the chapter (Blakeney 1855: 118–23).

Apart from the doctrine of transubstantiation, nothing disturbed the sensibilities of what George Eliot called 'English Puritanism' more than auricular confession – penance being one of the seven sacraments of Catholicism. The dangers associated with the confessional seemed obvious to the Revd Dr Blakeney, who wrote in his *Manual of Romish Controversy* (1851):

> The priest, bound by the unnatural law of celibacy, is placed at the head of a parish or congregation. All ages, of both sexes, repair to him and kneel at his side. It is not at all unlikely, that an avowal of love is the frequent subject of such confession, especially when the confessor is young, handsome, and popular. We would not enlarge upon a topic such as this, but we cannot refrain from observing what an immense power such a system affords to a wicked man of carrying out his designs, without danger of detection. (Blakeney 1855: 87)

Mothers, daughters, and wives, he points out, tell the priest 'their most secret thoughts and sins', and eighteenth-century treatises by Liguori, Dens, and others, for the 'guidance of the confessional', are 'so polluted and filthy, that we do not use language too strong, when we say they are only fit for the abodes of hell'. The depth of revulsion from auricular confession during the 'papal aggression' crisis is reflected in the fact that, in December 1850, the Revd Dr M'Neile of Liverpool, a respected Canon of Manchester, got carried away during an extempore sermon, and called for all confessors to be executed.

Whereas Victorian clergymen were reported in the newspapers when they made such wild and irresponsible suggestions, popular writers of historical romance were free to play out their own fantasies, and those of their readers, by describing confessors actually being executed. Prior 'Sancgraal' Bigod, Emma Robinson's villain in her anonymous and now unknown *Westminster Abbey; or, The Days of the Reformation* (1854), is frequently described as the 'confessor', this being the pastoral role in which we see him most often in the novel, and which he most often abuses for his own dastardly ends. At the end of the novel, Henry VIII condemns him to be burnt at the stake for murder and sacrilege, back to back with the novel's hero, Raphael Roodspere, a Cambridge Doctor of Divinity who dies a confessed heretic, having become a Lutheran 'Reformer' within the church.

Robinson uses the love plot as the vehicle for her religious themes, worked out through two different kinds of confession, as hero and villain vie for the hearts and souls of two women – the angelic novice, Lily-Virgin, who is loved by and later married to the hero, but is finally driven mad by the villain, and the cross-dressing precentor in the Abbey, 'Dan Gloria', who is in love with the hero, but is seduced and finally murdered by the villain. Roodspere's falling in love with the Lily-Virgin is presented as natural and liberating, and his marriage implicitly parallels that of Martin Luther to a nun. In stark contrast, Cardinal Wolsey's violent attempt to seduce Lily-Virgin, under the pretext of 'shriving' her in his oratory, is used to establish the novel's link between auricular confession and carnality. 'Save me – save me from worse than death!', cries Lily-Virgin, in true melodramatic style, before fainting in Roodspere's arms that are 'extended passionately and lovingly as its nest receives the throbbing fugitive back again', her clothes 'disordered' by the Cardinal (Robinson 1859: 91–92, 97).

Four years after the ultramontane (or Rome-centered) Nicholas Wiseman became Cardinal Archbishop of Westminster, looking like 'some Japanese god' in his full canonicals, Robinson focused her readers' attention upon the 'otherness' of Cardinal Wolsey's oratory, where sexual abuse takes place behind its heavy, locked door:

> The chamber whence he had emerged rather resembled the cave of some eastern genie, blazing with a sunglow of jewels and gold, than the devote retirement of an ecclesiastic of the west. . . . an altar there visibly was

> within, covered with ornaments of beaten gold, surrounded by blazing tapers that burned daylight; censers were still smoking with rich perfumes on its steps; magnificently-bound mass-books and other necessaries for the ceremonial worship – which, at all events, Wolsey never neglected – were profusely scattered about.

Wolsey, magnificently dressed in the crimson of a cardinal, quails before Roodspere, his bastard son, an 'ill-clad, poverty-stricken student', whose beating against the door of the oratory hints at the impending dissolution of the monastery and the sweeping away of what the Reformers regarded as the idolatrous trappings of a corrupt, semi-pagan church, in which the mass and the taking of virginities are sacrilegiously conflated as 'sacrifices'.

Lily-Virgin, in Cromwell's eyes a 'snow-feathered pullet' among the Prioress of Clerkenwell's 'grey geese', is even more vulnerable when confessing to the scheming Sancgraal in the crypt of the convent chapel. Whereas Wolsey's wanton kisses were rebuffed, Sancgraal's 'kiss of peace' on Lily-Virgin's brow is received with 'meek and tremulous humility', as an indignant Roodspere arrives in the 'gloomy chamber', too late to prevent the 'profanation' (Robinson 1859: 76, 85, 123, 223). In the following chapter, entitled 'The Rival Confessors', Roodspere, who has officially replaced Sancgraal as her confessor, can make no progress in his attempt to persuade her that there is 'no salvation, no redemption, to be hoped from human works, or prayers, or sacrifice', as Sancgraal has skillfully turned her against him.

In a novel that looks back to the Gothic sublime of Ann Radcliffe and forward to the sensationalism of Wilkie Collins, Sancgraal hears confessions in marginal locations, separated from the busy life of monastery and court, at extremes of depth and height. Driven out of the gloomy convent crypt, he retires to the dizzying height of his own lair under the roof of the Cathedral, the 'Hermitage of St Wulfin' – a vast loft in which instruments of mortification are prominently displayed, and from which, Quasimodo-like, he spies on all that passes far below. Even Queen 'Katharine' (Catherine of Aragon) and the Duke of Norfolk are in Sancgraal's power as a confessor: 'The queen herself was said to have paid this lofty confessional a revential visit; and here, at the moment we proceed in our record, no less a personage than that great duke of Norfolk who won Flodden Field, was kneeling in abject superstition, in confession, at the prior's feet!' (Robinson 1859: 169, 184). It is through Norfolk's confession that Sancgraal learns of Wolsey's plot to obtain a royal divorce. In contrast,

Roodspere refuses to hear the confession of Dan Gloria, the precentor, on the grounds that 'Paternosters, Ave Marias, candles lighted to St. Thomas and St. Edward' are of no avail: 'The word of the Christ that pardoned, was not – go on a pilgrimage – whip yourself till the blood flows – give treasures to this shrine, or to that – but GO, AND SIN NO MORE!' (Robinson 1859: 178). The color drains from Dan Gloria's face, as Roodspere has discovered that she is in fact a woman. She was the wife of Marchant Hunne, who betrayed him to the monks and was seduced by Sancgraal, her confessor, with the promise of 'remission and pardon' for the 'sin passion sanctified'.

The turning point in the novel is Roodspere's extempore sermon in front of King Henry and his court. Whereas Sancgraal relishes officiating in the Cardinal's place at the service, and 'raising the gorgeous mass of plate from which he derived his name', Roodspere tears up his carefully prepared and self-protecting script, and chooses a startling text: 'Why seek ye the living among the dead?' (Luke 24.5). 'Nature' makes him eloquent, and he adopts 'a similitude of the decadence of the true Gospel Christianity to the betrayal, death, and burial of Christ himself, likening in every imaginable form the destruction effected in the practice and faith of the Church founded by that divine original – especially all that the monks had done to deprive it – to the death-swathings, spices, and massive stone used in the sepulchring of the crucified Saviour! He compares the new learning to the break of day over the tomb' (Robinson 1859: 235). He is now a marked man as a 'Reformer', and it is simply a matter of time before he becomes a martyr.

Sancgraal makes Roodspere's vivid analogy grotesquely literal when he drugs Dan Gloria and places her in the tomb of Edward the Confessor, the most sacred site in the cathedral, where she starves to death, having first gnawed away some of her own flesh. A 'dark ooze' later trickles from the middle recess of the tomb. In contrast, the 'break of day' of the Reformation is marked by Roodspere's renunciation of the confessional and Anne Boleyn's smiling agreement to 'confess to one another . . . after old Christian fashion' (Robinson 1859: 281). Roodspere's subsequent trial, in the presence of the king, turns upon different kinds of 'confession'. Roodspere's is the most authoritative voice at the trial, as he 'confesses' what the court regards as 'heresy': 'I have confessed, without blenching, what consigns men, in the least article thereof, to the flames'. He has thus both answered Wolsey's demand that he make full 'confession' of his 'errors and offences', in the legal sense, and has made a testimony of faith. His denunciation of Sancgraal – 'this man – this priest – this confessor – rather this devlish incubus!' – links the monk's crimes with the third meaning of 'confession': the corrupted practice associated with the sacrament of penance. He explains to the court that the Lily-Virgin, his wife, has been 'maddened' by the 'superstitions' of the confessor, Sancgraal, and of Dame Barbara at the convent. Her death, smiling, in her husband's arms, is presented as 'love triumphant over death!'.

Even in the final chapter, 'The Martyr', Robinson sustains her attack upon auricular confession (Robinson 1859: 437–41). When the hero and the villain are imprisoned together in the vertiginous Hermitage, the night before their execution, Roodspere manages to bring Sancgraal to repentance, and together they take the reformed sacrament 'of penance and conciliation by a spiritual instead of a physical oblation'. In a last desperate bid to avoid the horror of the flames that will soon 'drink' their 'living blood', however, Sancgraal appears to have a change of heart, and asks for confession and abolution from Father Giselbert, in a corner of the Hermitage. This is merely a ruse, however, to allow him to take poison, and it is thwarted. Struggling against his physical and spiritual extinction to the last, Sancgraal provides a ghastly contrast to the 'Reformer', as Roodspere is now called, who, in the style of Foxe's martyrs, refuses Cromwell's final invitation to recant before the faggots are lit: 'Nay, sir! for even now I behold the gates of paradise open to receive me, and one beckon me who I know will gladly welcome me! – I recommend my spirit to Him who gave it, and desire no further discourse with any in the flesh!' (Robinson 1859: 446). He is already with Christ in glory, as Sancgraal is already in eternal torment.

When it was announced that Wiseman, formerly Vicar Apostolic of the London district, was to be Archbishop of Westminster, shock waves were felt throughout the English establishment. To most English ears, this sounded like a contradiction in terms, as no such title existed and Westminster symbolized the nation itself. Parliament met in the Palace of Westminster. Westminster Abbey, a shrine to England's monarchs and fallen heroes, was drenched in national pride and a semi-mystical sense of antiquity. The Abbey had no bishop's throne, let alone an archbishop's, as it was a 'royal peculiar', with a Dean appointed by Queen Victoria, who was the Supreme Governor of the Church of England. Leading English commentators, including Macaulay, had formerly applied territorial metaphors to the revival of Catholicism across Europe. Now the pope seemed to be invading the very citadel of England and its constitution.

Today, the title of Emma Robinson's novel, *Westminster Abbey*, evokes a popular tourist site in London, famous for its Poets' Corner and the scene of H.M. the Queen Mother's funeral in 2002 and similar ceremonies. In 1854 its resonance was quite different and its significance much greater, being inextricably mixed with the religious cultural values of the day. The 'reconstructive' move of the religious cultural historian is towards reading Victorian fiction in its richly documented context.

Victorian Futures

Three areas of current research activity will, I believe, continue to develop, and may prove to be particularly relevant to the study of Victorian fiction in the early twenty-first century: the study of religious cultural history (discussed in the previous section); the study of narrative in theology and literature; and gender studies.

One of the most interesting examples of cross-fertilization between literary study (broadly defined) and theology is 'narrative theology', which considers that stories express the truth about life 'more convincingly if less confidently than doctrinal propositions, offering a description of life rather than a definition of reality' (Wright 1988: 83). Virtually all our basic convictions about the nature and meaning of our lives, it has been argued, 'find their ground and intelligibility in some form of overarching, paradigmatic story'. Narrative theologians can turn to the 'story' content of both the Old and New Testaments as authoritative texts to which generations of scholars have applied 'literary criticism' (in the sense familiar to biblical scholars). Their methods, however, are also suited to secular writing in a cultural environment in which Matthew Arnold's prediction has proved to be correct: for most people, literature has more and more replaced religion.

The work of two very different literary scholars focuses upon issues that are relevant to the study of Victorian fiction. The American critic, George P. Landow, published his book on *Victorian Types, Victorian Shadows: Biblical Typology in Victorian Literature, Art, and Thought* in 1980, at the height of the revival of interest in literature and theology in the anglophone world. Inspired by John Ruskin from the nineteenth century and Northrop Frye from the twentieth, Landow examines typological interpretation of the Bible in the Victorian period, which he then relates to typology as it functions in fiction and non-fiction, the visual arts, poetry, and politics. The fulfillment of a history-like event in the Old Testament in a history-like event in the New provides a powerful model for Victorian novelists in their handling of plot and symbolism, as Landow demonstrates in Charlotte Brontë and George Eliot. Landow's claims are sometimes somewhat exaggerated, however, as he is convinced of the total supremacy of typology. More work still needs to be done on the analogical tradition that came down to the Victorians from Bishop Butler, for example. Nevertheless, Landow's sweep through Victorian cultural forms was valuable, as it suggested ways of interpreting the age in ways that acknowledged the central importance of the Bible.

Most of Stephen Prickett's work over the past 30 years has focused upon the history of ideas in relation to eighteenth- and nineteenth-century religion and literature. *Origins of Narrative: The Romantic Appropriation of the Bible* concerns 'the way in which the Romantics read the Bible itself: how it was responsible not merely for much Romantic literary theory, but had, in the process, been so irrevocably altered by the new hermeneutic assumptions it had engendered that it became for the nineteenth century virtually a different book from that of a century before' (Prickett 1996: xi). Having devoted the central section of the book to 'The Romantic Bible', containing chapters on 'The Bible as Novel', 'The Bible and History: Appropriating the Revolution', and 'The Bible as Metatype: Jacob's Ladder', Prickett concludes with a chapter on 'Hermeneutic and Narrative: The Story of Self-consciousness', including a discussion of the 'erotics of intuition' in two Victorian 'religious' novels by seasoned antagonists – Charles Kingsley's *Hypatia* and John Henry Newman's *Callista*. Whereas Newman adhered to a Christian tradition which venerated chastity and celibacy, Kingsley had read Schleiermacher, whose religious eroticism was Romantic – 'instinctive, subliminal and unconfined' (Prickett 1996: 223). If there is a common source, Prickett argues, 'it lies not with German theology but with a common romantic heritage'.

Like Landow, though with different emphases, Prickett makes the student of literature aware of the origins of modern secular narratives in biblical myth, parable, and history, and how patterns of crisis and conversion in Victorian fiction, for example, relate to these origins. Again, so broad is Prickett's range of reference that there are plenty of opportunities for future research into individual Victorian novelists, and into different sub-genres of the fiction of the period, with reference to narratology in general and narrative theology in particular.

Gender studies represent the biggest growth area in the discipline of English literature throughout the world, and gendered readings of Victorian fiction in relation to religion have increased in number over the past 10 or 15 years. Elisabeth Jay offers wide-ranging reflections on feminist literary criticism and Christianity in an essay in *The Discerning Reader* (Barratt 1995). Christine L. Krueger, in her study on women preachers and writers in the nineteenth century, argues that 'evangelical hermeneutics and the practices which followed, by decentering exegetical authority, encouraged women to bring into public (i.e. male) view – and specifically, into social discourse – a significant facet of their activities as readers and writers'. Having examined the preachers in Part One, Krueger turns to the writings of Hannah More, Charlotte Elizabeth Tonna, Elizabeth Gaskell, and George Eliot in Part Two. From the 'women preachers of the eighteenth century to the Victorian novelists who were their heirs', she states, 'women's writings testify to their ability to recognize the ideological conflicts in scripture that were suppressed in the patriarchal feminine ideal, and to interpret scripture as offering divinely sanctioned challenges to masculine authority' (Krueger 1992: 8). Mention should also be made of a collection of essays entitled *Women of Faith in Victorian Culture: Reassessing the Angel in the House* (Hogan and Bradstock 1998).

The editors of *Women of Faith*, Anne Hogan and Andrew Bradstock, together with two other editors, went on to commission a companion volume entitled *Masculinity and Spirituality in Victorian Culture*, in which they acknowledge the 'extent to which the study of masculinity lags behind that of femininity', perhaps because, in John Tosh's formulation, 'men's presence within the historical record is both ubiquitous and invisible' (Bradstock 2000: 2). Anne Hogan argues that in *Villette*, Charlotte Brontë's characterizations of Paul Emanuel and Graham Bretton 'offer a shrewd critique of both men and aspects of Victorian masculinity' (Bradstock 2000: 58). Catherine Wells-Cole considers that Charlotte M. Yonge, albeit a conservative Christian writer, whose adored mentor was John Keble, creates heroes who are problematic: they 'strive towards a spiritually informed ideal, but rarely achieve it' (Bradstock 2000: 71). Neil McCaw examines George Eliot's *Daniel Deronda* as a 'novel in crisis', in which the 'conflicting vision of masculinity, expressed through the character of Daniel Deronda, blends a radical nationalism with a more conservative metaphysics of belonging': 'This is represented as distinctly positive, giving coherence to fragmented, previously impotent social forces, and providing the quasi-religious locus for fundamental political and social change' (Bradstock 2000: 149).

Gender studies, then, is contributing an increasingly large body of critical and theoretical work in the field of Victorian fiction in relation to religion. As the Victorian Age recedes further from view, and contemporary culture becomes less literate in Christian tradition, the need for further work in this and other critical areas will increase, if we are to understand the more nuanced aspects of the most important period in the history of fiction in English.

References and Further Reading

Anon (1997) *Study of Worldwide Rates of Religiosity, Church Attendance*. University of Michigan news release, 10 December 1997. www.umich.edu/~newsinfo/Releases/1997/Dec97/r121097a.html.

Barratt, David, Pooley, Roger, and Ryken, Leland (eds.) (1995) *The Discerning Reader: Christian Perspectives on Literature and Theory*. Grand Rapids, MI: Apollos.

Bebbington, David (1989) *Evangelicalism in Modern Britain: A History from the 1730s to the 1980s*. London: Unwin, Hyman.

Beer, Gillian (1983) *Darwin's Plots: Evolutionary Narrative in Darwin, George Eliot and Nineteenth-Century Fiction*. London: Routledge, Paul.

Beer, John (1998) *Providence and Love: Studies in Wordsworth, Channing, Myers, George Eliot, and Ruskin*. Oxford: Clarendon.

Blakeney, R[ichard] P[aul] (1855) *Popery in its Social Aspect; being a Complete Exposure of the Immorality and Intolerance of Romanism*. Sixth thousand. Edinburgh: Paton, Ritchie.

Bradstock, Andrew, Gill, Sean, Hogan, Anne, and Morgan, Sue (eds.) (2000) *Masculinity and Spirituality in Victorian Culture*. Basingstoke and London: Macmillan and New York: St Martin's Press.

Brontë, Charlotte (1904) *Villette*. New Edition. London: Smith, Elder.

——(1987) *Jane Eyre*. Norton Critical Edition, 2nd edn. Ed. Richard J. Dunn. New York and London: Norton.

Chadwick, Owen (1966–70) *The Victorian Church*. Ecclesiastical History of England, ed. J. C. Dickinson, vols VII–VIII. London: Black.

Cunningham, Valentine (1975) *Everywhere Spoken Against: Dissent in the Victorian* Novel. Oxford: Clarendon.

Foucault, Michel (1999) *Religion and Culture*. Manchester: Manchester University Press.

Hardy, Thomas (1985) *Jude the Obscure*. Penguin Classics. Ed. C. H. Sisson. London: Penguin.

Hogan, Anne and Bradstock, Andrew (eds.) (1998) *Women of Faith in Victorian Culture: Reassessing the Angel in the House*. London: Macmillan and New York: St Martin's.

Jasper, David (1989) *The Study of Literature and Religion: An Introduction*. Basingstoke: Macmillan.

Jay, Elisabeth (1979) *The Religion of the Heart: Anglican Evangelicalism and the Nineteenth-Century Novel*. Oxford: Clarendon.

Krueger, Christine L. (1992) *The Reader's Repentance: Women Preachers, Women Writers, and Nineteenth-Century Social Discourse*. Chicago and London: Chicago University Press.

Landow, George P. (1980) *Victorian Types, Victorian Shadows: Biblical Typology in Victorian Literature, Art, and Thought*. Boston: Routledge, Paul.

Maison, Margaret M. (1961) *Search Your Soul, Eustace: A Survey of the Religious Novel in the Victorian Age*. London: Sheed and Ward.

Milbank, Alison (1996) *Dante and the Victorians*. Manchester: Manchester University Press.

Murray, Peter and Linda (1996) *The Oxford Companion to Christian Art and Architecture*. Oxford and New York: Oxford University Press.

Neill, Stephen (1966) *The Interpretation of the New Testament, 1861–1961*. The Firth Lectures 1962. Oxford: Oxford University Press.

Norman, Edward (1984) *The English Catholic Church in the Nineteenth Century*. Oxford: Clarendon.

——(1987) *The Victorian Christian Socialists*. Cambridge: Cambridge University Press.

Prickett, Stephen (1996) *Origins of Narrative: The Romantic Appropriation of the Bible*. Cambridge: Cambridge University Press.

Qualls, Barry V. (1982) *The Secular Pilgrims of Victorian Fiction: The Novel as Book of Life*. Cambridge: Cambridge University Press.

Robinson, Emma (1859) *Westminster Abbey; or, The Days of the Reformation*. Routledge's Railway Library. London: Routledge.

Scheinberg, Cynthia (ed) (1999) Editors' topic: Anglo-Jewish writers in Victorian England. *Victorian Literature and Culture*, **27**(1), 115–248.

Sutherland, John (1988) *The Longman Companion to Victorian Fiction*. Harlow: Longman.

Thompson, David M. (ed.) (1972) *Nonconformity in the nineteenth century*. Birth of Modern Britain series, eds. A. E. Dyson and R. T. Shannon. London and Boston: Routledge.

Vance, Norman (1985) *The Sinews of the Spirit: The Ideal of Christian Manliness in Victorian Literature and Religious Thought*. Cambridge: Cambridge University Press.

Wheeler, Michael (1979) *The Art of Allusion in Victorian Fiction*. London and Basingstoke: Macmillan.

——(1985, 1994) *English Fiction of the Victorian Period, 1830–1890*. London and New York: Longman.

——(1990) *Death and the Future Life in Victorian Literature and Theology*. Cambridge: Cambridge University Press.

Wolff, Robert L. (1977) *Gains and Losses: Novels of Faith and Doubt in Victorian England*. London: Murray.

Wright, T. R. (1988) *Theology and Literature*. Signposts in Theology series. Oxford and New York: Blackwell.

Chapter 10

'The difference between human beings': Biology in the Victorian Novel

Angelique Richardson

In *The Victorian Age in Literature* (1913), G. K. Chesterton (1874–1936) remarked that the Victorian novel was 'a thing entirely Victorian' (p. 26). Its conscious circularity notwithstanding, the comment is an illuminating one; there is no expressive form more closely bound to the dominant social and political concerns of the period. Chesterton went on to define the novel as 'a fictitious narrative (almost invariably, but not necessarily in prose) of which the essential is that the story is not told for the sake of its naked pointedness as an anecdote, or for the sake of the irrelevant landscapes and vision that can be caught up in it, but for the sake of some study of the difference between human beings' (p. 26). In *Middlemarch* (1871–2), Dorothea's recognition of Casaubon's difference provides the Victorian novel with one of its great epiphanies. Casaubon may be a 'great bladder for dried peas to rattle in' (Eliot 1871, ch. 6: 82), but he still has subjectivity, 'an equivalent centre of self, whence the lights and shadows must always fall with a certain difference' (ch. 21: 243). Difference between human beings during the nineteenth century was subject to peculiar scrutiny and massively shifting perception. The complexities of mind and memory were explored by scientists and writers alike (Herbert Spencer, the sociologist and intellectual ally of George Eliot published 'The Comparative Psychology of Man' in 1876), and new journals were launched, devoted to the subject, for example *The Journal of Psycholog-*

ical Medicine and Mental Pathology and *Mind*. The uniqueness of the each individual was increasingly recognized, and in keeping with this the novel opened the way to new subjectivities.

Central to the life sciences lie questions of what make us live and develop as individuals and species; central to the novel are questions of how and why we develop as individuals and communities. 'Man – like infusoria in a drop of water under microscope' Thomas Hardy noted from Schopenhauer (1891: 39, in Björk II: 29), while George Eliot sets up her study of provincial life in Middlemarch as an experiment. As Thomas Kuhn demonstrated in *The Structure of Scientific Revolutions* (1962), scientific truth is a matter of consensus and choice of theory among the scientific community. And no science operates in a social, or value-free, vacuum. This is especially pertinent for biology. As ideas in biology shift, they have a direct impact on how we see ourselves. As Heschel noted in 1965 in *Who is Man*? 'A theory about the stars never becomes a part of the being of the stars [yet] we become what we think of ourselves' (1965: 7). The relationship between biology and the perception of self, other, and other nations, is a tightly reciprocal one which is closely informed by, and informs, ideas about class, race, sex or gender that are in vogue at any time. Biology was crucial to the politics and aesthetics of the Victorian novel (see Amigoni and Wallace 1995, Beer 1983, Ebbatson 1982, Greenslade 1994, Levine 1988, Morton 1984), and it is vital that we reinsert it into our reading of the Victorians.

'The survival of the fittest', perhaps the most frequently evoked of nineteenth-century phrases, repays close attention. It was coined not, as is the common assumption, by Darwin, but by Herbert Spencer (1864, ss. 164: 165) who did more than anyone to popularize the term 'evolution'. Spencer's ideas lent themselves to a biologization of racial and social hierarchies that would underpin late nineteenth-century 'social Darwinism' – the selective application of Darwinian ideas to society. The idea of the survival of the fittest is predicated on the idea of *difference*, which was becoming central to the Victorian world-picture. It raised the question, what was to be done about the unfit – at home and abroad? Were they biologically destined to become extinct, or at least subject to imperial rule for, among other things, their own good? This is a question which finds increasing expression in the novel. Are Hardy's supersensitive Jude and Sue unfit for late nineteenth-century life? Several New Woman writers argued that the unfit should be left to die out; Sarah Grand remarked 'Let the unfit who are with us live, and save them from suffering where you can, by all means; but take pains to prevent the appearance of any more of them. By the reproduction of the unfit, the strength, the beauty, the morality of the race is undermined, and with them its best chances of happiness' (1897: 442). Grand called publicly for a 'certificate of health' before a marriage could take place (Tooley 1896: 168), and in her controversial novel *Gallia*, Ménie Muriel Dowie, charting Gallia Hamesthwaite's choice of a eugenically fit partner in preference to a dysgenic partner, pronounced 'people will see the folly of curing all sorts of ailments that should not have been created, and then they will start at the right end, they will make better people' (Dowie 1895: 129).

Alternatively, could the unfit be restored to health through *environmental* change? Hardy, for one, copied into his notebooks from Leslie Stephen's 'An Attempted Philosophy of History' in the *Fortnightly Review* (1880): 'history depends upon the relation between the organism & the environment' (677: in Björk I. 132). Hardy was also struck by Comte on the relation between organism and environment: 'Biological Dependence . . . The nobler phenomena are everywhere subordinate to those which are grosser, but also simpler & more regular . . . Man is entirely subordinate to the World – each living being to its own environment' (Comte 15 in Björk I. 74). This was an expression of Hardy's socialist politics no less than his adherence to evolutionary ideas. Environment, or circumstance, rather than heredity or *breeding*, are fundamental to social progress, as Mona Caird insisted in her novels and contribution to the periodical press (see also Huxley and Kropotkin). But, some contended, the very notion of fitness, and its inevitable double, unfitness, was a pernicious ideological construction. Debates over precisely these questions raged in the closing decades. As the language of biology was shaping the debates on poverty and the role of women in society, so it underpinned new aesthetic discourses in the second half of the nineteenth century; symbols of the ugly ('diseased') and beautiful ('healthy') sustained social order through biological narratives (see Gilman 1995). In an article in the *Leader* in 1854, 'Personal Beauty', Spencer argued a *necessary* relationship 'between ugly features and inferiority of intellect and character', concluding 'the saying that beauty is but skin-deep is but a skin-deep saying' (pp. 356–7).

In his treatise of 1877, *Physiological Aesthetics* (dedicated to Herbert Spencer), the prolific writer and biologist Grant Allen (1848–99), author of the infamous and ultimately repressive hereditarian novel *The Woman Who Did*, set out his objective to 'exhibit the purely physical origin of the sense of beauty, and its relativity to our nervous organization' (p. 2). He added:

> The ugly for every kind, in its own eyes, must always be (in the main) the deformed, the aberrant, the weakly, the unnatural, the impotent. The beautiful for every kind must similarly be (in the main) the healthy, the normal, the strong, the perfect, and the parentally sound. Were it ever otherwise – did any race or kind ever habitually prefer the morbid to the sound, that race or kind must be on the highroad to extinction. (Allen 1879: 448, 449)

In 1876 Hardy copied into his notebooks a passage from Theodore Watts-Dunton: 'science tells us that, in the struggle for life, the surviving organism is not necessarily that which is absolutely best in an ideal sense, though it must be that which is most in harmony with the surrounding conditions' (1985, I: 40). And this, after all, was how Darwin had originally conceived the idea of fitness. Thomas Huxley, Darwin's 'bulldog', questioned the 'unfortunate ambiguity of the phrase "survival of the fittest,"' remarking: 'I sometimes wonder whether people, who talk so freely about extirpating the unfit, ever dispassionately consider their own history' (1894: 80). And Mona Caird delivered a sustained satirization of the idea through her fiction, arguing strongly from an environmental perspective. Her novels expose the bias of biology and reclaim the importance of environment and culture in shaping individuals (see Richardson 2000, 2001). She published her first novel *Whom Nature Leadeth* the year that Darwin's cousin Francis Galton coined the term eugenics (1883: 24–5); the title itself offers an ironic critique of the idea of nature having determining power, which the novel develops as Caird exposes the political assumptions and biases underpinning the notion of fitness. In a chapter entitled 'The Extinction of the Unfit', the luckless Crawford, convinced he is to become extinct, resorts to killing himself when nature fails to extinguish him. In *The Stones of Sacrifice*, written during the First World War, Caird declared the idea of the survival of the fittest to be no more than 'primitive savagery made into a cult' (p. 236). Such debates raged, and received wide-reaching exploration in the novel.

In the closing decades of the nineteenth century, Giles Winterbourne in *The Woodlanders* looks and smells like 'Autumn's very brother' (Hardy 1887, ch. 28: 261), and the pig in *Jude the Obscure*, Jude's 'fellow-mortal', recognizes at last 'the treachery of those who had seemed his only friends' as his blood stains the white snow (1895, part first ch. 10: 110). These are not the idealized images of Romantic nature, or travesties of them, but something else: expressions of a post-Darwinian world in which humans, whatever distinguishes them from other forms of life, are fully integrated into the animal and plant economy, and subject to the same unruly contingencies. Quoting Tolstoy, Hardy wrote in his notebooks 'the first condition of happiness, he (T.) tells us, is that the link between man & nature shall not be broken'; 'in the eyes of science man is not "higher" than the other animals'; 'Man – The very ground-thought of Science is to treat man as part of the natural order' (Ellis 1890: 205, in *Björk* II 16; Guenther 1906: 424, in *Björk* II 225). But, in *Tess*, Hardy focused on the unholiness of nature: 'Some people would like to know whence the poet whose philosophy is in these days deemed as profound and trustworthy as his song is breezy and pure, gets his authority for speaking of "Nature's holy plan"', remarks the narrator in *Tess of the D'Urbervilles* (ch. 4: 62), taking issue with Wordsworth (the quotation is from 'Lines Written in Early Spring' [1798] 1. 22).

In the late eighteenth and early nineteenth centuries, evolutionary thought endeavored to combine with, or even express, rather than contradict, belief in God. Even the idea that struggle lay at the heart of nature was not necessarily in tension with a concept of God. For example, Gilbert White observed the struggle among swifts in *The Natural History of Selborne* (1789):

> I am now confirmed in the opinion that we have every year the same number of pairs invariably; at least, the result of my enquiry has been exactly the same for a long time past. The number that I constantly find are eight pairs, about half of which nest in the church, and the rest in some of the lowest and meanest thatched cottages. Now, as these eight pairs – allowance being made for accidents, – breed yearly eight pairs more, what becomes annually of this increase? (Letter dated 13 May 1778, in White 1789: 193–4)

The image of swifts finding a home in the church enacts a reciprocal relation between nature and God. In the century that followed, evolution would come to overshadow the Church. By the time of *Jude the Obscure*, Nature seems to lament the loss of God – Paradise lost, again – but is soon resigned to its fall: 'a mournful wind blew through the trees, and sounded in the chimney like the pedal notes of an organ. Each ivy leaf overgrowing the wall of the churchless churchyard hard by, now abandoned, pecked its neighbour smartly' (Part second, ch. 7: 176).

Jude the Obscure struggles to resist this bleak view of existence through communitarian ideas which biology was capable of endorsing just as well as cooperation. In a letter to Secretary of the Humanitarian League (10 April 1910), Hardy, vice-president of the Animal Defence and Anti-Vivisection League from 1923, grounded possibilities for social harmony in natural law:

> few people seem to perceive fully as yet that the most far-reaching consequence of the establishment of the common origin of all species is ethical; that it logically involved a readjustment of altruistic morals by enlarging as a necessity of rightness the application of what has been called 'The Golden Rule' beyond the area of mere mankind to that of the whole animal kingdom. Possibly Darwin himself did not wholly perceive it, though he alluded to it. (*The Life* II: 141)

In the *Origin*, Darwin had indeed alluded to such a possibility: 'plants and animals, most remote in the scale of nature, are bound together by a web of complex relations' (p. 61). However, Darwin's vision tended, more generally, to the reverse. Darwin had emphasized that the struggle between beings that were close geographically, and in kind, was intense and illustrated competition through the image of a tree whose branches war with one another. *Jude the Obscure* tests the limits of sympathy in such a world. It offers an acute attack on class and race prejudice: 'what does it matter, when you come to think of it', ponders Jude:

> whether a child is yours by blood or not? All the little ones of our time are collectively the children of us adults of the time, and entitled to our general care. That excessive regard of parents for their own children, and their dislike of other people's, is, like class feeling, patriotism, save-your-own-soul-ism, and other virtues, a mean exclusiveness at bottom. (part fifth, ch. 3: 340–41)

Such sentiments prove difficult to live out in a brutal, Malthusian, economy. 'Be kind to animals and birds, and read all you can' is Phillotson's parting advice to the young Jude, but Jude soon receives a sharp slap from Farmer Troutham for attempting at least the first of these instructions (part first, ch. 1: 49; ch. 2: 54).

Darwin had found in the ideas of the Reverend Thomas Malthus his single greatest inspiration for the *Origin*. *An Essay on the Principle of Population* was saturated in the political and economic assumptions of its time, and evidences a clear social bias. From 1805 to his death in

1834, Malthus held the first Professorship of Political Economy in Britain. Unsurprisingly, the *Essay* influenced politicians at least as much as scientists; it was motivated largely by a distrust and fear of the poor, whom Malthus figured as dangerously fertile, referring to the 'natural tendency of the labouring classes of society to increase beyond the demand for their labour, or the means of their adequate support' (p. 270). Attacking the poor laws, he argued they encouraged those predisposed to live off others to do so, encouraging them to increase their numbers without increasing food for their support (p. 97). He argued 'if we could find out a mode of government by which the numbers in the extreme regions would be lessened and the numbers in the middle regions increased, it would be undoubtedly our duty to adopt it' (p. 207). In 1800, in response to Malthus, William Pitt the younger, Tory Prime Minister, withdrew a bill which would have provided allowances from the poor rates to supplement the wages of agricultural workers, based on the size of their families and the current price of bread. From 1834, the workhouse stopped those who asked for relief from increasing in number, to this end segregating the sexes within its confines. These ideas find satirical treatment in Dickens's *A Christmas Carol*. Surprised by the size of the Ghost's family (1,800 brothers) Scrooge observes 'a tremendous family to provide for!', remarking of the poor who would rather die than go to the workhouse that they had better do so 'and decrease the surplus population' (ch. 3: 40; ch. 1: 12 and ch. 3: 47).

Malthus introduced into popular circulation the idea that nature was excessive and wasteful, producing life forms in far greater quantity than the environment could sustain. That some forms of life would be deformed, superfluous, useless, closely informed Darwin's thinking about variation and found extreme expression in Jack London's novel of 1904, *The Sea-Wolf*. Coming to underpin theories of racial and social hierarchy, these ideas pervaded Victorian social thought, in looser, and more diffuse form. The young Jude must learn painfully through Troutham that there is not enough food for the birds, and his own son takes Malthusian ideas of population to heart with the earnestness of a child trying to help: 'done because we are too menny' (part sixth, ch. 2: 410). Sex and race can be seen to have lent themselves more readily to biological treatment, but the extent to which class, a social category, was biologized, offers striking evidence of the extent to which social agendas were hung onto apparently biological facts.

The difference between the social politics of the French zoologist Jean-Baptiste de Lamarck (1744–1829), author of *Philosophie*

Zoologique (1809), and the grotesque racialism that underpinned the ideas of the physical anthropologists of the 1860s, is startling. The use of the term 'biology' to refer to the new science of living bodies marked a new emphasis on organisms as living, interacting with each other and their environment. One of the first people to use the term was Lamarck. According to Lamarck (to whom Darwin's ideas are closer than is often held; see Bowler 1983 and Richardson 2003) an animal could transform itself into a higher being and pass on all gains or 'acquired characteristics'. Arguing for the transmutation of species, it posited that in learning to cope with environmental changes, organisms were constantly susceptible to structural and functional changes. In 1851 – the year of the Great Exhibition – Herbert Spencer published his pioneering work of sociology, *Social Statics or the Condition Essential to Human Happiness Specified*, sketching out a eugenic panacea for poverty and disease, and denouncing the effects of charity:

> A sad population of imbeciles would our schemers fill the world with, could their plans last . . . the average effect of the laws of nature is to 'purify' society from those who are, *in some respect or other*, essentially faulty. (p. 379)

Drawing a close analogy between social and biological processes, most strikingly in his article of 1860 'The Social Organism' which appeared in the *Westminster Review*, Spencer drew on the idea of adaptation for quite different social ends from Lamarck. Lamarck's theory empowered the powerless, emphasizing that under the influence of environmental factors, notably education, they might rise up the social scale; Spencer argued that the process of adaptation must occur without any charitable or state intervention, for only a competitive free-for-all would ensure the survival of the fittest.

Mutability – It is Like Confessing a Murder

In 1844 Darwin wrote to his friend the botanist Joseph Hooker, 'species are not (it is like confessing a murder) immutable' (Desmond and Moore 1992: xxix), though he did not publish his ideas for another 15 years. 'Once grant that species mutate', he wrote in his notebook, and 'the whole fabric totters and falls' (Darwin 1989: C76). Certainly, mutability sounded the death knell for the fixity of species, and thus for the story of creation as it had been known – and the idea of the mutability of species informed rising concerns over the possibility of social and racial contamination. Fear of the unbounded – of loss of differentiation – invariably led difference to be overstated and to an inflexible approach to differences of class, race, and gender, and to the belief that such differences were inevitable. Social roles were naturalized – or biologized: women were considered biologically destined to inhabit a separate sphere from men, poverty understood as a product of defective biology, and imperial rule regarded as the expression of 'the survival of the fittest'.

In the same year that Darwin confessed to Hooker the mutability of species, Robert Chambers, Edinburgh publisher and amateur naturalist, published the runaway bestseller *Vestiges of Creation*, an account of natural history which substituted for God active in the formation of new species, a 'law of development', at work among plants and animals (1844: 196). This moved the world to more complex forms of organization and left the individual without the protection of a benevolent creator:

> The individual, as far as the present sphere of being is concerned, is to the Author of Nature a consideration of inferior moment, Everywhere we see the arrangements for the species perfect; the individual is left, as it were, to take his chance amidst the *mêlée* of the various laws affecting him. If he be found inferiorly endowed, or ill befalls him, there was at least no partiality against him. The system has the fairness of a lottery, in which every one has the like chance of drawing the prize. (p. 377)

While *Vestiges* did little more than transcribe teleological Lamarckianism, its popularity paved the way for Darwin. Bearing the brunt of theological fire, *Vestiges* introduced ideas about evolutionary development and the idea of chance into wide circulation. The first four editions appeared in the first six months, and, as a mark of its inflammatory content, all editions before Chamber's death in 1871 were published anonymously. Adam Sedgwick, Professor of Geology at Cambridge, declared in a private and often-quoted letter:

> If the book be true, the labours of sober induction are in vain, religion is a lie, human law is a mass of folly, and a base injustice; morality is moonshine; our labours for the black people of Africa mere works of madmen; and man and woman are only better beasts. (Clarke and Hughes 1890: 84)

Benjamin Disraeli offered a belittling satire in his novel *Tancred; or The New Crusade* (1847). Lady Constance picks up *The Revelations of Chaos* ('a startling work just published') and advises Tancred:

> 'it is one of those books one must read. It explains everything, and is written in a very agreeable style: You know, all is development. The principle is perpetually going on. First there was nothing, then there was something; then I forget the next, I think there were shells, then fishes; then we came, let me see, did we come next? Never mind that; we came at last. And the next change there will be something very superior to us, something with wings. Ah! that's it: we were fishes, and I believe we shall be crows. But you must read it.' (bk II, ch. 9)

Tancred refuses to believe he was ever a fish, but Lady Constance is adamant:

> 'Oh! but it is all proved . . . We are a link in the chain, as inferior animals were that preceded us: we in turn shall be inferior; all that will remain of us will be some relics in a new red sandstone. This is development. We had fins; we may have wings.'

The fear of transformation that lies behind Tancred's bravado finds repeated expression in the Victorian novel, reaching its apotheosis in *Dracula*. This novel's treatment of race and biology has been well documented, but the social and scientific context for the novel cannot be overstated. Samuel Butler's autobiographical, eponymous character, in *Ernest Pontilex; Or, The Way of All Flesh: A Story of English Domestic Life* (completed in 1884, but not published until 1903) remarked that between 1844 and 1859 there had not been 'a single book published in England that caused serious commotion within the bosom of the Church' (ch. 47: 180). The suggestion is, that whatever the popular effects of *Vestiges*, it was the *Origin* that caused the havoc.

Satirical cartoons on 'the monkey theory' crowded into the periodical press, providing instances of bravado which were clear testimonies to self-doubt, and reluctant admissions of the decenterings that science was bringing in train. Darwin's open-ended story created new possibilities for human intervention in the course of human development. His text was – and is – often erroneously interpreted as a story of progress, though Darwin had made it clear in the *Origin* that progress was no inevitable rule. But an alternative narrative was emerging – a narrative of death and decay. Hardy copied into his notebooks the words of G. B. Shaw on Darwinism: 'As compared to the open-eyed wanting & trying of Lamarck, the Darwinian process may be described as a chapter of accidents' (Massingham 1926: 393, in Björk II. 237). Natural selection (the survival of those individuals who were best able to fit, or adapt to, their environment) worked toward adaptation, not progress; it was opportunistic and ungoverned. Here, the life history of barnacles played a key role; beginning life as free-swimming larvae they lose their freedom and become attached to rocks, demonstrating through a single life span the possibility that evolution can move backwards as indifferently as forwards: life is in flux. The idea that development might move in a direction that could be conceived as backward – that humans might reel back to their primordial ancestors – posed a terrifying threat to a Victorian concept of progress. Various nineteenth-century thinkers grappled with the implications of the undirected nature of biological development; in the process, biology, which exposed the essential chanciness of nature, the randomness of life, and offered the ultimate challenge to the Creationist narrative, was looked to as a new authority. It became overlaid with deterministic ideas.

Elizabeth Gaskell's last novel, *Wives and Daughters* (1864), is peppered with chance and coincidence – a plot device that Hardy is often taken to task for overusing; in a haphazard, post-Darwinian world, the path not taken, the letter left unopened is no flight of fancy. George Eliot's characters inhabit a deterministic world, and frequently come to rue the consequences of rash acts; Bulstrode is closely shadowed by his past misdeeds as he strides through *Middlemarch*. But then, in *Felix Holt,* one of Eliot's servant characters – the 'hard-headed godless little woman' Denner has a rather different, and profoundly Darwinian, view of the universe: 'Things don't happen because they're bad or good, else all eggs would be addled or none at all, and at the most it is but six to the dozen. There's good chances and bad chances, and nobody's luck is pulled only by one string' (ch. 1: 103).

Separation

The life sciences, which were coming into their own in the early decades of the century, were used to mark differences, to divide and separate sections of society into racial and class categories that, in biological terms, were more inflexible that those of a past age. Within the era of empire, these complex struggles for identity, power, and dominance formed part of the climate which saw a gradual shift from monogeny – the belief in the ultimate unity of humanity, going back to a single set of parents – to polygeny. For some, biological difference provided justification for the state to abdicate responsibility for poverty on the grounds that what is determined by nature – or biology – cannot be altered by charity. In the words of Karl Pearson, Britain's first appointed Professor of National Eugenics, science 'can on occasion adduce facts having far more *direct* bearing on social problems than any theory of the State propounded by the philosophers from the days of Plato to those of Hegel'. He insisted that heredity was a 'vital social question' to which the scientific classification of facts, biological or historical, would give answers (1900: 27).

For the best part of the nineteenth century internal division was considered to be of more use to British social order – providing it was peaceable – than national unity, and the discourse of biology or race was more likely to be used in Britain to *separate* than unite the classes. Such separation finds expression in Eliot's *Felix Holt*, and in her 'Address to Working Men' which appeared in the first number of *Blackwood's Magazine* for 1868. Written at the instigation of the editor, John Blackwood, in response to the Second Reform Bill (1867), Eliot reminded working-class men of the weight of their new responsibilities. She spoke through Felix Holt, a respectable member of the working class whose face bears the 'stamp of culture' (ch. 30: 398), and who expounds on different types of the poor: 'roughs are the ugly crop that has sprung up while the stewards have been sleeping; they are the multiplying brood begotten by parents who have been left without all teaching save that of a too craving body.' Identifying the absence of teaching as a factor in the growth of what Eliot referred to as 'the criminal class', she urged trade union members to send their children to school, 'so as not to go on recklessly breeding a moral pestilence among us' (1868: 618, 624). The target of the address were the 'roughs', whom she described as 'the hideous margin of society, at one edge drawing towards it the undesigning ignorant poor, at the other darkening into the lowest criminal class' (1868: 618–19). This distinction between the respectable or 'deserving' poor and the unrespectable was culturally widespread. Indeed, the tension between a developing recognition of and respect for individual difference, and a parallel homogenizing and 'othering' of large social and racial groups, inland and overseas, on new and spurious scientific grounds, might be described as a defining feature of the Victorian age.

Biology and Gender

In the *Descent of Man* Darwin naturalized gender difference, positing that 'with woman the powers of intuition, of rapid perception, and perhaps of imitation, are more strongly marked than in man', while man, by contrast, was 'more courageous, pugnacious, and energetic' with 'a more energetic genius' (II: 326–7). In spite of the emphasis in his work on change and mutability, Darwin did not challenge sexual stereotyping. In 1859 in the *Quarterly Review*, Spencer warned of the 'pale angular, flat-chested young ladies so abundant in London drawing rooms', emphasizing that by subjecting their daughters to a 'high-pressure system of education', parents frequently ruined their prospects in life; 'besides inflicting on them enfeebled health, with all its pains and disabilities and gloom, they not infrequently doom them to celibacy' (1859: 174, 176). This piece, along with several others by Spencer from 1859 from the transatlantic periodical press, was republished in *Education: Intellectual, Moral, and Physical* (1861); the book went through several editions, with a cheap edition appearing in 1880, and remained in print well into the twentieth century. The following year, in *The Mill on the Floss*, Maggie Tulliver chafes against the perceptions of gender that find their way into Darwin. She learns from her brother's tutor that girls:

> 'can pick up a little of everything, I daresay . . . they've a great deal of superficial cleverness: but they couldn't go far into anything. They're quick and shallow.' Tom, delighted with this verdict, telegraphed his triumph by wagging his head at Maggie behind Mr Stelling's chair. As for Maggie, she had hardly ever been so mortified: she had been so proud to be called 'quick' all her little life, and now it appeared that this quickness was the brand of inferiority. It would have been better to be slow, like Tom.

Resistances to gendered stereotyping recur repeatedly through the nineteenth-century novel, from Austen through Hardy to Sarah Grand. Silas Marner mothers a child, Sarah Grand's heavenly twins cross-dress in childhood in one of Grand's more radical passages (1893), and in *The Well-Beloved* (1897) Hardy's narrator points out that it is childbearing and rearing that hold women back: 'they move up and down the stream of intellectual development like flotsam in a tidal estuary. And this perhaps not by reason of their faults as individuals, but of their misfortune as child-rearers' (part third, ch. 4: 161). While

Darwin had certainly not challenged gender stereotyping, however, neither had he ruled out possibilities for change. Other scientific thinkers were more inflexible. In 1874 the Darwinian psychiatrist Henry Maudsley stated 'sex is fundamental, lies deeper than culture, cannot be ignored or defied with impunity' (p. 477). In 1890 in 'The Girl of the Future', Allen mocked any change which sought to undo 'nature': 'not all the Mona Cairds and Olive Schreiners that ever lisped Greek can fight against the force of natural selection. Survival of the fittest is stronger than Miss Buss, and Miss Pipe, and Miss Helen Gladstone, and the staff of the Girls' Public Day School Company, Limited, all put together' (p. 52). The eugenist Caleb William Saleeby remarked that 'a generation of the highest intelligence borne by unmaternal women would probably succeed in writing the blackest and maddest page in history' (1909: 153). With characteristic verve and intellectual rigor, Caird asks why, if this were the case, these critics were so hostile towards the new varieties of women which appeared to be cropping up: if modern women 'are really insurgents against evolutionary human nature, instead of being the indications of a new social development, then their fatal error will assuredly prove itself in a very short time' (1892: 169). For male scientists, the (uniqueness of the) maternal function was seen as both justification of and compensation for the perceived mental and physical inferiority, and evolutionary stasis, of women. The Italian doctor Cesare Lombroso (1835–1909) observed 'in figure, in size of brain, in strength, in intelligence, woman comes nearer to the animal and the child'; he balanced this remark with an elevation of her reproductive organs: 'on the other hand in the distribution of the hair, in the shape of the pelvis, she is certainly more highly developed than man' (1895: 48). Grant Allen had his own reasons for the elevation of woman: if her status was not redefined, then the 'girl of the future' would soon be 'as flat as a pancake' (1890: 57). By contrast, Galton's eugenic and unpublished treatise, 'Kantsaywhere', is peopled by buxom women. Grant Allen observed that healthy girls who embarked on higher education became unattractive and unsexed; if they married at all they were either sterile or 'physically inefficient mothers' (1889: 21).

Biology and Race

Biology of course, would prove vital to arguments about the relative worth of different races. In 1833, slavery was abolished in British colonies (for popular representation of continued agitation against the slave trade, see Figure 1). William Wilberforce's first bill to abolish the slave trade in 1791 was defeated in the House of Lords by 163 votes to 88. John Wesley wrote in a rallying letter:

> Unless God has raised you up for this very thing, you will be worn out by the opposition of men and devils. But if God be for you, who can be against you? Are all of them together stronger than God? O be not weary of well doing! Go on, in the name of God and in the power of his might, till even American slavery (the vilest that ever saw the sun) shall vanish away before it. (Balam, February 24, 1791)

In 1807 the bill was carried in the House of Lords by 41 votes to 20, and in the House of Commons by 114 to 15. In August 1833, a month after Wilberforce's death, Parliament passed the Slavery Abolition Act that granted slaves of the British Empire their freedom, but slavery continued to exercise the public imagination (see, for example, Figure 1). In the same year that the Abolition Act was passed, Charles Lyell was publishing his voluminous study, *The Principles of Geology*, which did more to affect the course of biology than its title might suggest. The discourse of biology – and its close relation physical anthropology – divided the races over the course of the century to an unprecedented extent.

The Victorian novel is preoccupied and absorbed by biologically informed issues of race well before Darwin published *The Origin*. Where is Heathcliff from? – his darkness is singled out, and Nelly invents a Chinese/Indian genealogy for him. In the 1840s, the Chinese empire was resisting British colonization and the allusion may have suggested ways in which the colonized might rise up and take revenge. Susan Meyer (1996) points out that Heathcliff's absence takes place between 1780 and 1783, the last three years of the American Revolutionary War – 'the archyteypal war of successful colonial rebellion' (p. 115). Gaskell seeks to heal splits between the classes through romantic relationships, but when it comes to race even she shows herself party to certain pervasive ideas on the racial superiority of the English. And Mrs. Tulliver, exercised by Maggie's general waywardness, seeks genealogical distance from her daughter, declaring that 'idiocy' 'niver run i' my family, thank God, no more nor a brown skin as makes her look like a mulatter', thereby linking dark skin with low intelligence. She wishes Maggie had '*our* family skin' (Eliot 1860: 493, emphasis in original). Skin color signals kinship, a metonymic

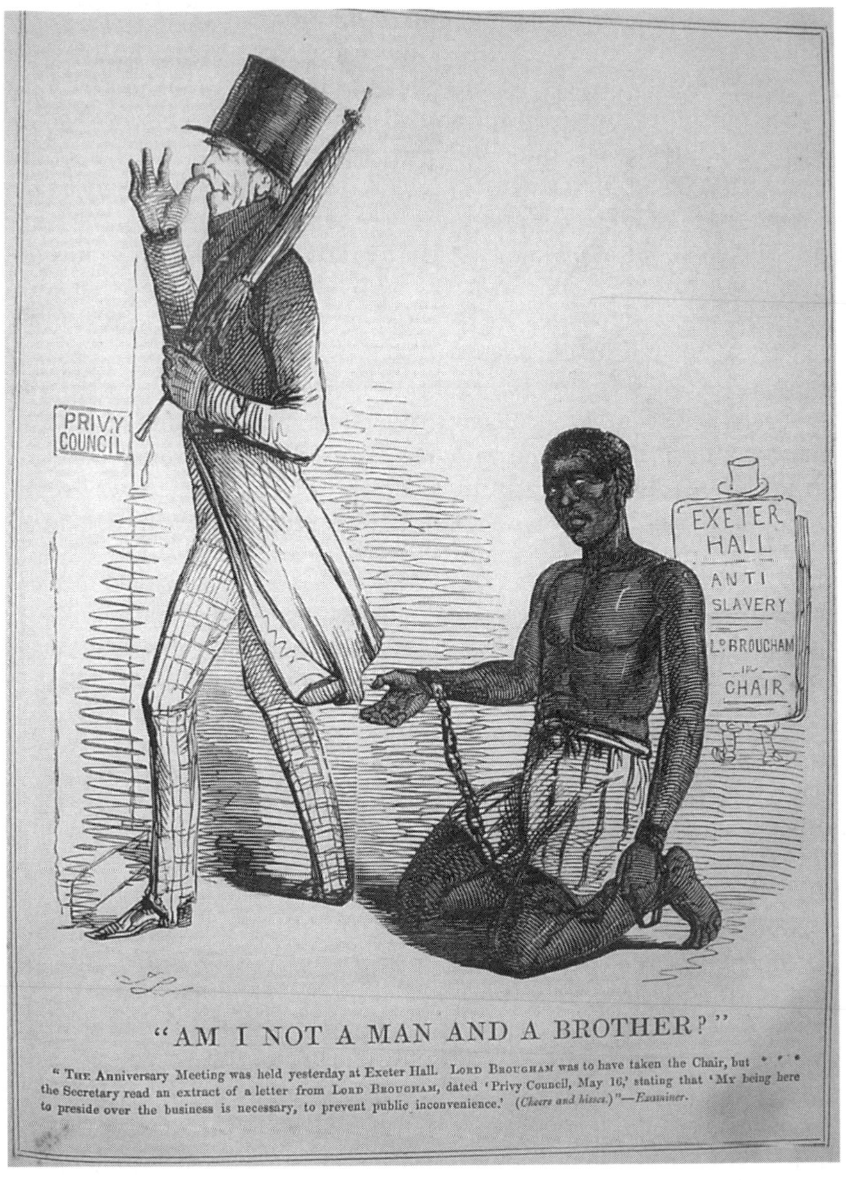

Figure 1 'Am I Not a Man and a Brother?' *Punch*, **6** (1844). The question is a reference to the emblem of the Britain's Society for the Abolition of Slavery, a kneeling, enchained African slave partly encircled by these words. In the early 1840s, London's Exeter Hall was the centre of the anti-slavery campaigns. Reproduced courtesy of Exeter University Library.

figuring of race. Pondering the difference between his offspring, Mr. Tulliver remarks: 'that's the worst on't wi' the crossing o' breeds: you can never justly calkilate what'll come on't' (Eliot 1860, ch. 2: 59).

But resistance to racialism, and to the encroachments of science, were certainly to be found. Charles Kingsley declared in a public lecture in 1871 at Sion College, London, 'The Natural Theology of the Future' that 'As for the Negro, I not only believe him to be of the same race as myself, but that – if Mr Darwin's theories are true – science has proved that he must be such' (1885: 322). Kingsley accepted that competition was everywhere, but stressed 'I believe not only in Nature, but in Grace'. In *Zuleika Dobson* (1911) Beerbohm offers a masterly satire on sexual selection. More seriously, Hardy in 1917 in a letter to the Secretary of the Royal Society of Literature, responded to a memorandum 'proposing certain basic principles of international education for promoting ethical ideals that shall conduce to a League of Peace'. He argued that he was 'in hearty agreement with the proposition' adding:

> I would say in considering a *modus operandi*: that nothing effectual will be accomplished in the cause of *Peace* till the sentiment of *Patriotism* be freed from the narrow meaning attaching to it in the past (still upheld by Junkers and Jingoists) and be extended to the whole globe. On the other hand, the sentiment of *Foreignness* – if the sense of a contrast be really rhetorically necessary – attach only to other planets and their inhabitants, if any. I may add that I have been writing in advocacy of these views for the last twenty years' (Hardy, 8 February 1917: *Life* II 174)

While Darwin unfixed species in the *Origin*, he sided with the monogenists, preferring to term human races 'sub-species'. By contrast, within anthropology (from which Darwin would borrow heavily in the *Descent*), the races were pushed apart, through the new polygenisism, while simultaneously seen as increasingly vulnerable to contamination. At the heart of the fears over racial mix, or miscegenation, lay the fear of loss of *separateness*, and hence of identity or self. As one anti-evolutionary protestor put it, 'As the races intermix | You can't be certain about the chicks' (Anon., *Dr Darwin. New Edition* in Ritvo 1997: 130).

In 1891, Karl Pearson wrote:

> it is a false view of human solidarity, a weak humanitarianism, not a true humanism, which regrets that a capable and stalwart race of white

> men should replace a darkskinned tribe which can neither utilize its land for the full benefit of mankind, nor contribute its quota to the common stock of human knowledge.

Pearson states at this point in a footnote:

> This sentence must not be taken to justify a brutalizing destruction of human life. The anti-social effects of such a mode of accelerating the survival of the fittest may go far to destroy the preponderating fitness of the survivor. At the same time, there is cause for human satisfaction in the replacement of the aborigines throughout America and Australia by white races of far higher civilization.

He continues: 'the struggle of civilized man against uncivilized man and against nature produces a certain partial "solidarity of humanity" which involves a prohibition against any individual community wasting the resources of mankind' (1900: 310).

The cluster of fears centering on miscegenation only increased as the century progressed. The powerful and derogatory idea of the 'half-breed' was establishing itself, so that, by 1913, the Eurasian in a novel of that name could be betrayed as a despicable and vulgar upstart. The author, Henry Bruce, a historical biographer, creates as his anti-hero Robert Slow, a lowly clerk. Slow marries an English servant-girl, Cherry, and is described as a 'man of streaks, all striped, like a barber's pole. He's not a whole man. Many mixtures are good, but not this one. The only certainty about a Eurasian is his uncertainty.' Slow 'degenerates' to his Hindu level. His daughter is described as puny and yellow: 'her little alien eyes . . . were pools of shadow' (Bruce 1913: 206).

Eugenics

In the *Descent,* drawing on ideas of 'artificial selection,' Darwin declared that man might:

> by selection, do something not only for the bodily constitution and frame of his offspring, but for their intellectual and moral qualities. Both sexes ought to refrain from marriage if in any marked degree inferior in body or mind; but such hopes are Utopian and will never be even partially realized until the laws of inheritance are thoroughly known. All do good service who aid towards this end. (II: 403)

However, he followed the most eugenic passage – 'excepting in the case of man himself, hardly anyone is so ignorant as to allow his worst animals to breed' – with an emphatic refutation of eugenic principles on the grounds that 'the noblest part of our nature' would be lost if 'we were intentionally to neglect the poor and helpless' (a strategy of negative eugenics) (1871: I, 168, 169). For Galton (and, later, eugenic feminists), the novel was the main way in which eugenic ideas might receive wider public circulation. He wrote in his notebook in 1888:

> No theme is more trite than that of the sexual instinct. It forms the principal subject of each of the many hundreds, four hundred, I believe, of novels, and of the still more numerous poems that are annually written in England alone, but one of its main peculiarities, has never, so far as I know, been even yet clearly set forth. It is the relation that exists between different degrees of contrast and different degrees of sexual attractiveness. (Galton Papers 138/3)

Galton set up a laboratory at the International Health Exhibition of 1884 at which volunteers were comprehensively measured and provided with a card recording their details which were also kept 'for statistical purposes' at the total cost of the three pence fee charged for admission (Galton Papers 57: 295–310 (see Figures 2 and 3)). Around 10,000 persons were measured at this laboratory, and 400 complete sets of data were published in the *Anthropological Institute Journal*, 1889 (Galton Papers: 296). When the exhibition closed the following year, Galton recorded: 'it seemed a pity that the laboratory should also come to an end, so I asked for and was given a room in the Science Galleries of the South Kensington Museum, where I maintained one during about 6 years' (301). The laboratory was even visited by Gladstone.

H. G. Wells' novel of 1905, *A Modern Utopia*, embraces eugenics with a conviction that is as unequivocal as it is disturbing. In a chapter headed 'Failure in a Modern Utopia' the narrator declares:

> It is our business to ask what Utopia will do with its congenital invalids, its idiots and madmen, its drunkards and men of vicious mind, its cruel and furtive souls, its stupid people too stupid to be of use to the community, its lumpish, unteachable and unimaginative people? And what will it do with the man who is 'poor' all round, the rather spiritless, rather incompetent low-grade man who on earth sits in the den of the sweater, tramps the streets under the banner of the unemployed, or trembles – in another man's cast-off clothing, and with an infinity of

Figure 2 Photograph of Galton's Anthropocentric Laboratory at the International Health Exhibition, South Kensington Museum (1884–5). Two years earlier, Galton had urged in the *Fortnightly Review* the importance of such national laboratories, to provide posterity with vital records on national health. Reproduced courtesy of University College London.

> hat-touching – on the verge of rural employment? These people will have to be in the descendant phase, the species must be engaged in eliminating them; there is no escape from that, and conversely the people of exceptional quality must be ascendant. (pp. 80–1)

In *Anticipations of the Reaction of Mechanical and Scientific Progress Upon Human Life and Thought* (1901) – the work he would refer to in his autobiography (1934) as 'the keystone to the main arch of my work' (Wells 1913: iii, xi) – Wells argued that the mentally and physically handicapped should not be allowed to be born, and that if they did manage to come into the world they should be 'removed': 'the men of the New Republic will not be squeamish, either, in facing or inflicting death, because they will have a fuller sense of the possibilities of life than we possess' (p. 169). He urged that 'the inferior races' should not be treated 'as races', but rather that 'efficiency will be the test' of 'world-citizenship'.

ANTHROPOMETRIC LABORATORY

For the measurement in various ways of Human Form and Faculty.

Entered from the Science Collection of the S. Kensington Museum.

This laboratory is established by Mr. Francis Galton for the following purposes:—

1. For the use of those who desire to be accurately measured in many ways, either to obtain timely warning of remediable faults in development, or to learn their powers.

2. For keeping a methodical register of the principal measurements of each person, of which he may at any future time obtain a copy under reasonable restrictions. His initials and date of birth will be entered in the register, but not his name. The names are indexed in a separate book.

3. For supplying information on the methods, practice, and uses of human measurement.

4. For anthropometric experiment and research, and for obtaining data for statistical discussion.

Charges for making the principal measurements:
THREEPENCE each, to those who are already on the Register.
FOURPENCE each, to those who are not:— one page of the Register will thenceforward be assigned to them, and a few extra measurements will be made, chiefly for future identification.

The Superintendent is charged with the control of the laboratory and with determining in each case, which, if any, of the extra measurements may be made, and under what conditions.

H. & W. Brown, Printers, 20 Fulham Road, S.W.

Figure 3 Advertisement calling for volunteers to be measured at Galton's National International Health Exhibition of 1884. 10,000 people were measured, including Gladstone. When the exhibition was over, Galton kept a room for these purposes for six more years in the Science Galleries of South Kensington Museum. Reproduced courtesy of University College London.

The fear of degeneration is central to Kinglsey's *The Water-Babies*, subtitled 'A Fairy Tale for a Land-Baby', published in 1863, and palpable amid the magic:

> 'Yes!' said the fairy, solemnly, half to herself, as she closed the wonderful book. 'Folks say now that I can make beasts into men, by circumstance, and selection, and competition, and so forth. Well, perhaps they are right; and perhaps, again, they are wrong. That is one of the seven things which I am forbidden to tell, till the coming of the Cocqcigrues; and, at all events, it is no concern of theirs. Whatever their ancestors were, men they are; and I advise them to behave as such, and act accordingly. But let them recollect this, that there are two sides to every question, and a downhill as well as an uphill road; and, if I can turn beasts into men, I can, by the same laws of circumstance, and selection, and competition, turn men into beasts. You were very near being turned into a beast once or twice, little Tom. (ch 6: 237–9)

Behind this apparently democratic idea is a deeply conservative social politics underpinned by the conflation of the social and the biological: the poor who are not willing to follow a moral code will degenerate. The water-baby in the following passage is quite clearly a child of the slums:

> efts are nothing else but the water-babies who are stupid and dirty, and will not learn their lessons and keep themselves clean; and, therefore (as comparative anatomists will tell you fifty years hence, though they are not learned enough to tell you now), their skulls grow flat, their jaws grow out, and their brains grow small, and their tails grow long, and they lose all their ribs (which I am sure you would not like to do), and their skins grow dirty and spotted, and they never get into the clear rivers, much less into the great wide sea, but hang about in dirty ponds, and live in the mud, and eat worms, as they deserve to do. (ch. 8 'Moral': 328)

Macmillan's 1885 edition of the book is richly illustrated by the *Punch* cartoonist Linley Sambourne (1844–1910); Figure 4, which accompanies the fairy's parable of degeneration 'the History of the great and famous nation of the Doasyoulikes, who came away from the country of Hardwork, because they wanted to play on the Jews' harp all day long', foregrounds a beautiful white woman, luxuriating, at civilization's zenith, beneath flapdoodle-trees, surrounded by degenerating humans and apes.

Figure 4 Illustration from the 1885 reprinting of Charles Kingsley, *The Water-Babies*: *A Fairy Tale for a Land-Baby*, with 100 illustrations by Linley Sambourne. Accompanying the fairy's warning to Tom and Ellie of the perils of a life of idle luxury, the illustration shows that even those at the zenith of civilization are not invulnerable to degeneration but, rather, precariously proximate to the life forms against which they define themselves and their civilization. Reproduced courtesy of Exeter University Library.

Biological readings of the social persist, visceral at times, in the novels of Gissing and Jack London, who for the most part stand back and present – rather than counter – an extreme application of Darwinian ideas. London, in the *People of the Abyss* (1903), offered a sympathetic treatment of the poor and 'in the heart of the greatest, wealthiest, and most powerful empire the world has ever seen' and flouted the idea that charity was unhelpful, but the same year he published *The Sea-Wolf*, in which Wolf Larsen is an inveterate social Darwinian. As he explains to the narrator, Humphrey Van Weyden:

> 'The big eat the little that they may continue to move, the strong eat the weak that they may retain their strength. The lucky eat the most and move the longest, that is all. What do you make of those things?' (ch. 5: 46)

For Hardy, Jude doesn't want to live – he is over-evolved, his mind over-developed. In *The Sea-Wolf*, we find the inverse, although both London and Hardy have a strong social conscience. 'Then why move at all, since moving is living?', Larsen remarks, going on to explain:

> 'Without moving and being part of the yeast there would be no hopelessness. But, – and there it is, – we want to live and move, though we have no reason to, because it happens that it is the nature of life to live and move, to want to live and move. If it were not for this, life would be dead. It is because of this life that is in you that you dream of your immortality. The life that is in you is alive and wants to go on being alive for ever.' (ch. 5: 47)

Are we to read this satirically? – after all, London's politics, at least for the early part of his life and writing career, were progressive. In *The Sea-Wolf* he gives us a world that is all matter and no spirit, a world straight out of Malthus. For Wolf Larson, humans are infinitely expendable – simply material expressions of the will to live. The man whose life he takes is an example of someone who has delusions of grandeur:

> He held on as if he were a precious thing, a treasure beyond diamonds or rubies. To you? No. To me? Not at all. To himself? Yes. But I do not accept his estimate . . . He alone rated himself beyond diamonds and rubies. Diamonds and rubies are gone, spread out on the deck to be washed away by a bucket of sea-water, and he does not even know that the diamonds and rubies are gone. (ch. 6: 63)

Larson draws attention here to the transience of the life of the individual, denying any possibility of consciousness beyond life, or of consciousness of death. The image of precious stones serves to highlight both the comparative worthlessness of human life, and the finite nature of existence. Bleak and without purpose, Larson's view of life and his pessimistic application of Victorian biology is shocking but unmemorable, failing to represent either the resistance to, or the complex negotiations with and reworkings of science which characterize the place of biology in the literary imagination. Much more representative of an age which heralded the triumph of science, far more memorable and emblematic of this era of clashing creeds, faltering faith, mystery and belief, are the works which struggle to find new meaning to life rather than delight in *meaningless*. The rubies and diamonds that have no value for Larson are celebrated in Hopkins's 'That Nature Is a Heraclitean Fire, and of the Comfort of the Resurrection' (1888):

> and
> This Jack, joke, poor potsherd, 'patch, matchwood, immortal diamond,
> Is immortal diamond. (ll.22–4)

Note

I am grateful to University College London for permission to quote from the Galton archive; to Exeter University Library and University College London for permission to reproduce the illustrations; and to John Plunkett for reproducing them. I would also like to thank my students Gillian Travis and Michael Cussen for talking to me about *The Water-Babies* and *The Sea-Wolf.*

References and Further Reading

Anon. (1851) Woman in her psychological relations. *Journal of Psychological Medicine and Mental Pathology*, **4**: 18–50.

Allen, Grant (1877) *Physiological Aesthetics*. London: King.

——(1879) Aesthetic evolution in man. *Mind*, **4**: 301–16.

——(1885) *Charles Darwin*. London: Longmans, Green.

——(1889) Plain words on the woman question. *Popular Science Monthly*, **46**: 170–81.

——(1890) The girl of the future. *Universal Review*, **7**: 49–64.

——(1895; 1995) *The Woman Who Did*. Oxford: Oxford University Press.

Amigoni, D. and Wallace, J. (eds.) (1995) *Charles Darwin's* The Origin of Species. Manchester: Manchester University Press.

Beer, G. (1983) *Darwin's Plots: Evolutionary Narrative in Darwin, George Eliot and Nineteenth-Century Fiction*. London: Routledge & Kegan Paul.

Beerbohm, Max (1911; 1998) *Zuleika Dobson*. New York: Random House Modern Library.

Biddis, Michael D. (ed.) (1979) *Images of Race*. Leicester: Leicester University Press.

Björk, Lennart A. (ed.) (1985) *The Literary Notebooks of Thomas Hardy*. London and Basingstoke: Macmillan.

Booth, William (1890) *In Darkest England and The Way Out*. London: Salvation Army.

Bourne Taylor, Jenny and Shuttleworth, Sally (eds.) (1998) *Embodied Selves: An Anthology of Psychological Texts, 1830–1890*. Oxford: Oxford University Press.

Bowler, Peter (1983) *Evolution: The History of an Idea*. Berkeley: University of California Press.

Bruce, Henry (1913) *The Eurasian*. London: Long.

Burdett, Carolyn (2001) *Olive Schreiner and the Progress of Feminism: Evolution, Gender and Empire*. Basingstoke: Palgrave.

Burrow, John (1966) *Evolution and Society: A Study in Victorian Social Theory*. Cambridge: Cambridge University Press.

Butler, Samuel (1903; 1965) *Ernest Pontilex, or The Way of All Flesh*, ed. Daniel F. Howard. London: Methuen.

Caird, Mona ('G. Noel Hatton') (1883) *Whom Nature Leadeth*. London: Longman.

——(1892; 1998) A defence of the so-called 'wild woman'. *Nineteenth Century*, **31**: 811_29. Reprinted in Ann Heilmann (ed.) *The Late Victorian Marriage Question: A Collection of Key New Woman Texts*, 5 vols. Vol. 1. London: Routledge/Thoemmes.

——(1915) *The Stones of Sacrifice*. London: Simpkin, Marshall, Hamilton, Kent.

Chambers, Robert (1844; 1969) *Vestiges of the Natural History of Creation*. Leicester: Leicester University Press.

Chesterton, G. K. (1913; 2001) *The Victorian Age in Literature*. London: Stratus.

——(1922) *Eugenics and other Evils: An Argument against the Scientifically Organized State*, ed. Michael W. Perry. Seattle: Inkling.

Clarke, Edward H. (1874) *Sex in Education: Or, A Fair Chance for Girls*. Boston, MA.

Clarke, J. W. and Hughes, T. M. (1890) *The Life and Letters of the Reverend Adam Sedgwick*. 2 vols. Cambridge: Cambridge University Press.

Craik, Dinah (1850; 1996) *Olive: A Young Girl's Triumph over Prejudice, and 'The Half-Caste'*. Oxford: Oxford University Press.

Darwin, Charles (1989) *Charles Darwin's Notebooks, 1836–1844: Geology, Transmutation of Species, Metaphysical Enquiries*, eds. Barrett et al. Ithaca: Cornell University Press.

——(1859; 1985). *The Origin of Species, or the Preservation of Favoured Races in the Struggle for Life*. Harmondsworth: Penguin.

——(1871; 1981) *The Descent of Man, and Selection in Relation to Sex*. Princeton: Princeton University Press.

Desmond, Adrian and Moore, James (1992) *Darwin*. Harmondsworth: Penguin.

Dickens, Charles (1843; 1994) *A Christmas Carol*. In *The Christmas Books*. Harmondsworth: Penguin.

Digby, Anne and Stewart, John (eds.) (1996) *Gender, Health and Welfare*. London: Routledge.

Disraeli, Benjamin (1847) *Tancred; or The New Crusade*. 3 vols. London: Colburn.

Dowie, Ménie Muriel (1895; 1995) *Gallia*. London: Dent.

Ebbatson, R. (1982) *The Evolutionary Self: Hardy, Forster, Lawrence*. Brighton: Harvester.

Eliot, George (1860; 1985) *The Mill on the Floss*. Harmondsworth: Penguin.

——(1866; 1988) *Felix Holt*. Harmondsworth: Penguin.

——(1868; 1988) Address to working men, *Blackwood's Magazine*, in *Felix Holt* (1866). Harmondsworth: Penguin.

——(1871–2; 1985) *Middlemarch*. Harmondsworth: Penguin.

——(1954–78). *George Eliot Letters*, 9 vols, ed. George S. Haight. New Haven: Yale University Press.

Ellis, Havelock (1890) Tolstoi. In *The New Spirit*. London: Bell.

Galton, Francis (1882) The anthropometric laboratory. *Fortnightly Review*, **37**: 332–3.

——(1883) *Inquiries into the Human Faculty and its Development*. London: Macmillan

Galton Papers, University College London. 138/6: 'The Eugenic College of Kantsaywhere', enclosed in a letter from Millicent Galton Lethbridge to Edward Galton Wheeler-Galton (c. 1911).

Gilman, Sander (1995) *Health and Illness: Images of Difference*. London: Reaktion.

Grand, S. (1893; 1992) *The Heavenly Twins*. Michigan: Ann Arbor.

——(1897; 1994) *The Beth Book, Being a Study from the Life of Elizabeth Caldwell Maclure, A Woman of Genius*. Bristol: Thoemmes.

Greenslade, W. (1994) *Degeneration, Culture and the Novel 1880–1940*. Cambridge: Cambridge University Press.

Guenther, Conrad (1906) *Darwinism and the Problems of Life*, trans. J. McCabe. London.

Hardy, Thomas (1887; 1986) *The Woodlanders*. Harmondsworth: Penguin.

——(1891; 1986) *Tess of the D'Urbervilles*. Harmondsworth: Penguin.

——et al. (1890) Candour in English fiction. *New Review*, **2**: 15–21.

——(1892; 1986) *The Well-Beloved*. Oxford: Oxford University Press.

——(1928–30; 1994) *The Life of Thomas Hardy*, 2 vols (published in Florence Hardy's name). London: Studio.

——(1967) *Thomas Hardy's Personal Writings*, ed. Harold Orel. London: Macmillan.

——(1978–88) *The Collected Letters of Thomas Hardy*, eds. Richard L. Purdy and Michael Millgate. Oxford: Clarendon.

——(1985) *The Literary Notebooks of Thomas Hardy*. 2 vols, ed. Lennart A. Björk. Basingstoke: Macmillan.

——(1990) *The Complete Poems of Thomas Hardy*, ed. James Gibson. Basingstoke: Macmillan.

Heschel, A. J. (1965) *Who is Man?* Stanford: Stanford University Press.

Himmelfarb, Gertrude (1985) *The Idea of Poverty: England in the Early Industrial Age*. New York: Vintage.

Hunt, James (1863–4) On the Negro's place in nature. *Memoirs read before the Anthropological Society of London*, **I**: 1–63.

Huxley, T. H. (1864; 1906) Darwin on the origin of species. In *Man's Place in Nature and Other Essays*. London: Dent.

——(1894; 1989). *Evolution and Ethics* (including 'Prolegomena'), eds. J. Paradis and G. C. Williams. Princeton: Princeton University Press.

Jones, Greta (1980) *Social Darwinism and English Thought: The Interaction between Biological and Social Theory*. Brighton: Harvester.

Keating, P. J. (1971) *The Working Classes in Victorian Fiction*. London: Routledge.

Kingsley, Charles (1863; 1895) *The Water-Babies: A Fairy Tale for a Land Baby*. London: Macmillan.

——(1871; 1885) The natural theology of the future. In *Scientific Lectures and Essays*. London: Macmillan.

Kropotkin, P. (1890) Mutual aid among animals. *Nineteenth Century*, **28**: 337–54; 699–719.

——(1902; 1998) *Mutual Aid: A Factor of Evolution*. London: Freedom.

Kuhn, T. (1962) *The Structure of Scientific Revolutions*. Chicago: University of Chicago Press.

Lamarck, Jean-Baptiste de (1809) *Philosophie Zoologique*. Paris.

Lankester, E. R. (1880) *Degeneration: A Chapter in Darwinism*. London: Macmillan.

Levine, G. (1988) *Darwin and the Novelists: Patterns of Science in Victorian Fiction*. Chicago: Chicago University Press, 1991.

Lombroso, Cesare (1895) Atavism and evolution. *Contemporary Review*, **63**: 42–9.

London, Jack (1904; 2000) *The Sea-Wolf*. Oxford. Oxford University Press.

Lyell, Charles (1830–3; 1997) *Principles of Geology*. Harmondsworth: Penguin.

Malchow, H. L. (1996) *Gothic Images of Race in Nineteenth-Century Britain*. Paolo Alto: Stanford University Press.

Malthus, T. R. (1798; 1988) *An Essay on the Principle of Population*. Harmondsworth: Penguin.

Mandler, Peter (2000) 'Race' and 'Nation' in mid-Victorian thought. In Stefan Collini, Richards Whatmore and Brian Young (eds.) *History, Religion and*

Culture, British Intellectual History 1750–1950. Cambridge: Cambridge University Press.

Massingham, H. J. (1926) *Downland Man.* London: Cape.

Maudsley, Henry (1874) Sex in mind and education. *Fortnightly Review,* **21**: 466–83.

McGrigor, Allan J. (1869) On the real differences in the minds of men and women. *Anthropological Review,* **7**: 195–216.

Mearns, Andrew (1883) *The Bitter Cry of Outcast London – An Inquiry into the Condition of the Abject Poor.* London: Clarke.

Meyer, Susan (1996) *Imperialism at Home: Race and Victorian Women's Fiction.* Ithaca: Cornell University Press.

Morton, P. (1984) *The Vital Science: Beyond the Literary Imagination 1860–1900.* London: Allen & Unwin.

Moscucci, Ornella (1990) *The Science of Woman, Gynaecology and Gender in England 1800–1929.* Cambridge: Cambridge University Press.

Nelson, Claudia and Holmes, Ann Sumner (eds.) (1998) *Maternal Instincts: Visions of Motherhood and Sexuality in Britain, 1875–1925.* Basingstoke: Macmillan.

Nordau, Max (1892; 1993) *Degeneration.* Lincoln: University of Nebraska Press.

Oldroyd, D. R. (1980; 1983) *Darwinian Impacts: An Introduction to the Darwinian Revolution.* Milton Keynes: Open University Press.

Pearson, Karl (1894) Woman and labour. *Fortnightly Review,* **61**: 561–77.

——(1900) *The Grammar of Science.* London: Black.

Pick, Daniel (1993) *Faces of Degeneration: A European Disorder, c.1848–c.1918.* Cambridge: Cambridge University Press.

Poovey, Mary (1989) *Uneven Developments: The Ideological Work of Gender in Mid-Victorian England.* London: Virago.

Postlethwaite, Diana (1984) *Making it Whole: A Victorian Circle and the Shape of their World.* Columbia: Ohio State University Press.

Prichard, James Cowles (1813; 1973) *Researches into the Physical History of Man,* ed. George W. Stocking, Jr. Chicago: University of Chicago Press.

Richardson, Angelique (2000) Biology and feminism. *Critical Quarterly,* **42**: 35–63.

——(2001) 'People talk a lot of nonsense about heredity': Mona Caird and anti-eugenic feminism. In Angelique Richardson and Chris Willis (eds.) *The New Woman in Fiction and in Fact:* Fin-de-Siècle *Feminisms,* pp. 183–211. Basingstoke: Palgrave.

——(2002) The life sciences: 'Everybody nowadays talks about evolution'. In David Bradshaw (ed.) *Modernism,* pp. 7–33. Oxford: Blackwell.

——(2003) *Love and Eugenics in the Late Nineteenth Century: Rational Reproduction and the New Woman.* Oxford: Oxford University Press.

Ritvo, Harriet (1997) *The Platypus and the Mermaid and Other Figments of the Classifying Imagination.* Cambridge, MA: Harvard University Press.

Rowold, Katharina (ed.) (1996) *Gender and Science: Nineteenth-Century Debates on the Female Mind and Body*. Bristol: Thoemmes.

Russett, Cynthia Eagle (1989) *Sexual Science: The Victorian Construction of Womanhood*. Cambridge, MA: Harvard University Press.

Saleeby, Caleb William (1909) *Parenthood and Race Culture: An Outline of Eugenics*. London: Cassell.

Schopenhauer, Arthur (1891) *Studies in Pessimism*, trans. T. Bailey Saunders. London: Sonnenschein.

Secord, James (2003) *Victorian Sensation: The Extraordinary Publication, Reception, and Secret Authorship of 'Vestiges of the Natural History of Creation'*. Chicago: University of Chicago Press.

Smith, Sheila M. (1980) *The Other Nation: The Poor in the English Novels of the 1840s and 1850s*. Oxford: Oxford University Press.

Soloway, Richard Allen (1982) *Birth Control and the Population Question in England, 1877–1930*. Chapel Hill: North Carolina University Press.

Spencer, Herbert (1851) *Social Statics or the Conditions Essential to Human Happiness Specified, and the First of Them Developed*. London: Chapman.

——(1854) Personal beauty. *Leader*, 15 April: 356–7.

——(1859; 1861) The aesthetic principle in females. *Quarterly Review*, reprinted in *Education: Intellectual, Moral, and Physical*. London: Williams & Norgate.

——(1860) The social organism. *Westminster Review*, **73**: 90–121.

——(1876) The comparative pyschology of man. *Mind*, **1**(i).

——(1864–7) *Principles of Biology*. London: Williams and Norgate.

Stepan, Nancy (1982) *The Idea of Race in Science: Great Britain 1800–1960*. London: Macmillan.

Stephen, L. (1880) An attempted philosophy of history. *Fortnightly Review*, **27**.

Tooley, S. A. (1896) The woman question: An interview with Madame Sarah Grand. *Humanitarian*, **8**: 161–9.

Warwick, Alexandra (1995) Vampires and the empire: Fears and fictions of the 1890s. In Sally Ledger and Scott McCracken (eds.) *Cultural Politics at the Fin De Siècle*, pp. 202–20. Cambridge: Cambridge University Press.

Wells, H. G. (1895; 1998) *A Modern Utopia*. London: Dent.

——(1901; 1999) *Anticipations of the Reaction of Mechanical and Scientific Progress Upon Human Life and Thought*. New York: Dover.

——(1913; 1997) *'The Country of the Blind' and Other Science-Fiction Stories*, ed. Martin Gardner. New York: Dover.

Wesley, John to William Wilberforce (February 24, 1791), Balam, England (ms in Drew University Methodist Library).

White, Arnold (1901) *Efficiency and Empire*. Brighton: Harvester.

White, Gilbert (1789; 1993) *The Natural History of Selborne*. Oxford: Oxford University Press.

Young, Robert (1995) *Colonial Desire: Hybridity in Theory, Culture and Race*. London: Routledge.

Chapter 11

'One great confederation?': Europe in the Victorian Novel

John Rignall

When Henry James conceives his American heroine Isabel Archer for *The Portrait of a Lady* (1881) and poses the question 'what will she do?', the answer is self-evident: 'Why, the first thing she will do will be to come to Europe; which, in fact, will form, and all inevitably, no small part of her principal adventure' (*The Portrait of a Lady*, preface, p. xvi). From James's American perspective Europe includes, of course, the British Isles, and his heroine's first and decisive experiences are set in an old English country house on the banks of the Thames. To see England and the British Isles in this way, as part of Europe, is not unique to Henry James nor confined to Americans, for Victorian intellectuals and writers in general were not inclined to make the distinction between Britain and Europe that is commonplace today (Seeber 1997: 22–3). At the beginning of the Victorian period a reviewer of Henry Hallam's *Introduction to the Literature of Europe* (1837) could maintain that 'the History of European Literature ought to be *one* work' and not divided into genres and nationalities (*Quarterly Review*, vol. 58, 30); and the 12-volume *Periods of European Literature* edited by George Saintsbury at the end of the century was predicated on the same assumption, taking as its motto a passage from Matthew Arnold's 1864 essay on 'The Function of Criticism at the Present Time': 'The criticism which alone can much help us for the future is a criticism which regards Europe as being, for intellectual and spiritual purposes, one great confederation, bound to a joint action and working to a common result' (Arnold 1962: 284). What Arnold proposed was already substantially in existence, for to read Victorian periodicals is, indeed, to get a sense of European intellectual culture as something like his 'one great confederation' to which the British intelligentsia felt itself to belong. The review pages of publications like the *Athenaeum*, the *Foreign Quarterly Review*, and the *Westminster Review* show how well informed the serious reading public was about the latest works of literature and history not only in France and Germany, but also in Italy, Spain, and the smaller countries of Europe. This was reciprocated by the knowledge of English fiction fostered on the Continent of Europe from 1841 onwards by the German publisher Tauchnitz's cheap one-volume reprints in English of Victorian novels, in addition to the many translations. But the sense of a common European culture co-existed, of course, with an awareness of important political and national differences, and the Victorian novel bears the imprint of both.

The co-existence of, and the tension between, a common European culture and the distinctive features of English national life, are dramatized in exemplary fashion in George Eliot's *Middlemarch* (1871–2). As the translator of Strauss, Feuerbach, and Spinoza, and with her ability to read seven languages besides English, George Eliot had a profound knowledge of European literature and culture; she uses it to provide the wider context of the lives of the English provincial community of Middlemarch – a context alluded to in the chapter epigraphs drawn from writers such as Cervantes, Dante, and Goethe as well as more familiar English sources, and experienced in Lydgate's medical training in Paris and Dorothea's unhappy honeymoon in Rome. Lydgate, following in the footsteps of Bichat, is inspired by the work that is 'already vibrating in many currents of the European mind' (book 2, ch. 15: 147), and although his 'foreign ideas' meet with resistance from conventional Middlemarch, his intellectual ambitions mark him out for approval as a member of an enlightened elite. That elite also includes the half-Polish and German-educated Ladislaw and all those who are open to the wider world of ideas beyond the limited horizons of provincial England. It is in such people that George Eliot's hopes for a better future are invested. The intellectual limitations of the gentleman scholar Casaubon are defined, as Ladislaw points out, by his ignorance of German, which cuts him off from a crucial dimension of that wider world, the most advanced scholarship in Europe in relation to his field of mythology. But against that admiring view of European intellectual culture are set less positive experiences. Lydgate's ominous and hopeless infatuation with the actress Laure in Paris associates the foreign setting with destructive sexual passion, and that metonymical association of Continental Europe with dangerous sexual experience is a recurrent one in the Victorian novel, as will be discussed later. Dorothea's experience in Rome also carries a charge of threatening eroticism and sexual frustration as, married to a desiccated pedant, she looks with incomprehension at the 'eager Titanic life gazing and struggling on walls and ceilings' while 'forms both pale and glowing took possession of her young sense, and fixed themselves in her memory' (book 2, ch. 20: 191). The sensuous richness and multiplicity of pagan and Catholic Rome, with its 'ruins and basilicas, palaces and colossi set in the midst of a sordid present', overwhelm the sensibility of 'a girl who had been brought up in English and Swiss Protestantism, fed on meager Protestant histories and on art chiefly of the handscreen sort' (book 2, ch. 20: 191). In her misery Dorothea presents a graphic image of, among other things, the discomfiture of the English mind in the presence of the foreign. George Eliot herself may feel at home in European culture, but she is also aware of how disturbing and challenging it may be to an English Protestant sensibility; and the reactions of her heroine to the foreignness of Rome may be more characteristic of Victorian writers in general than her own comfortable familiarity.

Like Dorothea's, then, the imagination of the majority of Victorian novelists tends to be ill at ease with abroad, although there is evidence, as I shall show, that the Victorian novel becomes more cosmopolitan in the last quarter of the nineteenth century. But one further qualification is necessary. Whereas Dorothea finds both the sordid present and the unintelligible weight of Rome's history to be a dispiriting burden, the novelistic imagination seems to be far more at home with European history than with the contemporary world of Continental Europe. When Victorian novelists turn to historical subjects, they range uninhibitedly over foreign countries and different periods as though, in historical terms, Europe was indeed that 'one great confederation' of which Arnold wrote. In his early works Bulwer-Lytton tackles *The Last Days of Pompeii* (1834) and then fifteenth-century Rome in *Rienzi* (1835); Wilkie Collins's first novel *Antonina* is an historical romance about the fall of Rome in the fifth century (1850); Anthony Trollope writes about the royalist uprising in France after the Revolution in *La Vendée* (1850); Charles Reade tells the story of Erasmus's parents in the low countries in the fifteenth century in *The Cloister and the Hearth* (1861); Dickens examines eighteenth-century England and revolutionary France in *The Tale of Two Cities* (1859); and George Eliot recreates *quattrocento* Florence in the days of Savonarola in *Romola* (1862–3). When, in the Proem to that novel, she describes 'the angel of the dawn' traveling 'with broad slow wing from the Levant to the Pillars of Hercules, and from the summits of the Caucasus across all the snowy Alpine ridges to the dark nakedness of the western isles' (*Romola,* Proem: 1), that flight of fancy nicely captures the sweep and freedom of the novelist's historical imagination in relation to the geographical and cultural diversity of Europe.

With some exceptions, Victorian novelists are less bold in their imaginative response to contemporary Continental Europe, which commonly features only on the margins of the main action as the location of a holiday interlude or a place of refuge from problems at home. Trollope's Palliser novels, for example, use Continental settings in this way. In *The Prime Minister* (1876) Italy is where Emily travels with Ferdinand Lopez on their honeymoon, though it remains a largely abstract setting for her realization of his pressing financial needs and demands. In *Phineas Finn* (1869) and *Phineas Redux* (1874) Lady Laura Kennedy seeks refuge from her miserable marriage in her father Lord Brentford's house and moves with him to exile in Dresden; and in *Can You Forgive Her?* (1864) Plantagenet Palliser rescues his marriage to Lady Glencora by refusing a Cabinet post and taking her off to Switzerland to escape the attractions of Burgo Fitzgerald. But none of these places is given any more than the kind of cursory general description afforded to Dresden: 'a clean cheerful city [. . .] in which men are gregarious, busy, full of merriment, and pre-eminently social' (*Phineas Redux,* vol. 1, ch. 11, 93). In *Can You Forgive Her?* Trollope's narrator draws attention to his refusal to describe the Swiss landscape where the Vavasors take their holiday, and offers a justification: 'I am not going to describe the Vavasors' Swiss tour. It would not be fair on my readers. [. . .] No living man or woman any longer wants to be told anything of the Grimsell or of the Gemmi. Ludgate Hill is now-a-days more interesting than the Jungfrau' (vol. 1, ch. 5: 78). The abundance of travel writing has, it seems, queered the novelist's pitch. Trollope's dismissive aside may also be taken as a passing rebuke to Ruskin's celebrations of the Swiss Alpine landscape, but the most significant aspect of this self-justification is the metropolitan bias that it reveals. The true business of the novelist lies at home; abroad is merely peripheral. Trollope did set two of his shorter works on the Continent of Europe, the fairytale-like *Nina Balatka* in Prague and *Linda Tressel* in

Nuremberg, but the fact that he published them anonymously indicates their marginal status.

Even when a novelist does succeed in bringing foreign scenes to vivid life, as Dickens does in *Little Dorrit* (1855–7), their vitality is subordinate to the more powerful pressures and concerns of the metropolitan center. Dickens, who, like George Eliot, spent considerable periods of time abroad and did some of his writing in European locations, responded openly and sympathetically to foreign cultures, and to France in particular (Schlicke 1999: 240–3). In *Little Dorrit* he caricatures the self-satisfied imperviousness to abroad that was more common among his countrymen in the bluff figure of Mr. Meagles, 'who never by any accident acquired any knowledge whatever of any country into which he travelled', and whose habit it was 'to address individuals of all nations in idiomatic English, with a perfect confidence that they were bound to understand it somehow' (book 1, ch. 2: 27). The Meagles family, whose foreign tour has consisted of 'staring at the Nile, and the Pyramids, and the Sphinx, and the Desert, and all the rest of it', is one of many testimonies in Victorian fiction to the truth of Thackeray's observation in 'The Kickleburys on the Rhine': 'Yes, we all flock the one after the other, we faithful English folks. [. . .] We carry our nation everywhere with us; and are in our island, wherever we go. *Toto divisos orbe* – always separated from the people in the midst of whom we are' (p. 158). Thackeray's insight informs his own presentation of the English and Irish abroad in *Vanity Fair* (1847–8), where the satirical drama of intrigue and ambition around Becky Sharp is played out with the same cast of characters in Belgium, Paris, and Pumpernickel as in England, with only incidental variations occasioned by the local culture. In *Little Dorrit* Dickens develops that notion of separateness in the experience of the Dorrit family on the Continent after their release from the debtors' prison, giving it a particular psychological significance and a personal pathos in the figure of Amy Dorrit. As the Dorrits travel through Italy, she finds all the beauty and squalor, misery and magnificence of the country simply dreamlike and unreal; and, sitting alone on her balcony in the 'crowning unreality' of Venice, she keeps casting her mind back to the Marshalsea prison and its inmates, 'all lasting realities that had never changed' (book 2, ch. 3: 474–5).

Dickens's sympathetic interest in France in particular, and his openness to foreign cultures in general, are not much in evidence in his fiction. His great set-piece descriptions of Marseilles and Southern France at the beginning of the first book of *Little Dorrit* and of the Great

Saint Bernard Pass at the beginning of the second, are brilliant evocations of alien landscapes whose otherness is registered as a threat to the beholder. Under the burning sun of Marseilles 'strangers were stared out of countenance by staring white houses, staring white walls, staring white streets, staring tracts of arid road, staring hills from which verdure was burnt away' (book 1, ch. 1: 5). The Alpine pass is similarly hostile to human life in its desolation: 'No trees were to be seen, nor any vegetable growth, save a poor brown scrubby moss, freezing in the chinks of rock. Blackened skeleton arms of wood by the wayside pointed upward to the convent, as if the ghosts of former travellers overwhelmed by the snow haunted the scene of their distress' (book 2, ch. 1: 440). By contrast London, however dark and oppressive, is busy with restless life (Showalter 1979: 26–7). It is a world of teeming activity, of hidden secrets and startling transformations; the variegated world of 'sunshine and shade' which surrounds Amy Dorrit and Arthur Clennam in its eager clamor at the novel's close. Against the crowded, particularized life of London, even the *chiaroscuro* of Italy with its juxtaposition of beauty and poverty is only a generalized and distanced survey, and it is marked in places by a distinctly Meaglesish impatience with, and recoil from, the foreign. When 'whole towns of palaces' are described as being populated by nothing but 'swarms of soldiers', 'swarms of priests', and 'swarms of spies' (book 2, ch. 3: 474), the description sounds the note of an English and Protestant sensibility aware of its own political freedoms and affronted by the spectacle of a priest-ridden Continental autocracy and its infamous spy system.

That reaction is not peculiar to Dickens. The same suspicion of a culture dominated by priests and spies can be found in Charlotte Brontë's response to Belgium in *Villette* (1853) and *The Professor* (1857). Lucy Snowe has to resist the kindly Père Silas's subtle attempt to lure her from her sturdy Protestantism into embracing 'popish superstition' (*Villette*, vol. 1, ch. 15: 235), while Crimsworth can only account for the flirtatiousness of the girls he teaches in Brussels by recourse to Protestant prejudice, suspecting that 'the root of this precocious impurity, so obvious, so general, in popish Countries, is to be found in the discipline, if not the doctrines of the Church of Rome' (*The Professor*, ch. 12: 89). And Madame Beck's school in Villette is a model in miniature of the continental spy system: '"Surveillance", "espionage," – these were her watch-words'; and she runs her establishment by 'plotting and counter-plotting, spying and receiving the reports of spies all day' (vol. 1, ch. 8: 135). But Charlotte Brontë's achievement in these novels amounts to more than simply bearing English prejudices abroad in the persons of her protagonists. Her fictional response to Europe is both fuller and more ambivalent than Dickens's in *Little Dorrit,* since the European perspective allows her to transcend and at the same time to criticize her native culture. Belgium, and Continental Europe in general, serve as a means of escape from the narrow views and values of home. England and what it represents are tested and challenged by foreign experience. As Lucy Snowe sails to Labassecour, her journey stimulates a romantic dream:

> In my reverie, methought I saw the continent of Europe, like a wide dream-land far away. Sunshine lay on it, making the long coast one line of gold; tiniest tracery of clustered town and snow-gleaming tower, of woods deep-massed, of heights serrated, of smooth pasturage and veiny stream, embossed the metal-bright prospect. For background, spread a sky, solemn and dark-blue, and – grand with imperial promse, soft with tints of enchantment – strode from North to South a God-bent bow, an arch of hope. (vol. 1, ch. 6: 117)

The origins of this vision are historical and artistic, suggesting Gothic painting or illuminated medieval manuscripts rather than any representation of the contemporary world; but even though it is immediately dismissed as a day-dream and overtaken by the anxiety and alienation of midnight arrival in a land whose language is incomprehensible, this visionary landscape bears a promise of hope that is later to be fulfilled when Europe eventually becomes for Lucy the realm of self-realization and requited love. The same is true for Crimsworth in *The Professor*. He has no romantic dreams on his journey abroad but the flat Flemish landscape on the road to Brussels – 'a grey, dead sky, wet roads, wet fields, wet house-tops' – is transfigured by the freedom he is enjoying for the first time and the hope he has for the future: 'not a beautiful, scarcely a picturesque object met my eye along the whole route, yet to me, all was beautiful, all was more than picturesque' (ch. 7: 50).

What Belgium affords is contact with cosmopolitan life and a vantage point from which some of the limitations of English society can be seen. In response to the teasing taunts of the Napoleonic Paul Emmanuel, Lucy Snowe may mount a stoutly patriotic defense of her country and nationality, denouncing France as the land of fiction and fops (vol. 3, ch. 29: 429), but she comes to appreciate the good sense of the people of Villette in comparison with the English in that they are 'infinitely less worried about appearance, and less emulous of display' (vol. 3, ch. 31: 450). This is one of the uses of Europe in Victorian fiction: to provide a critical perspective on matters at home. Dickens does this in passing in *Little Dorrit*, when Daniel Doyce, whose invention has been rejected by the Circumlocution Office, is recruited by a 'certain barbaric Power with valuable possessions on the map of the world' which wants to get things done and is not hampered by British red tape (book 2, ch. 22: 683). That Power is not explicitly European, but the description fits Russia, then in the public mind on account of the Crimean War. In the same decade Trollope introduces a subversively European element into the essentially English setting of the cathedral town in *Barchester Towers* (1857) in the form of the Stanhope family, whose 12 years of idleness in Italy have left them entirely impervious to conventional English proprieties and the strenuous demands of the Protestant work ethic. Like the inhabitants of Charlote Brontë's Labassecour, the Italianate Stanhopes are both the objects and the agents of criticism. They may be censured for their heartlessness, but they help to expose the human and institutional frailties of the cathedral culture. It is the dangerously attractive and cunningly manipulative Madeline Stanhope, the self-styled Signora Vesey Neroni, who brings about the morally desirable comic resolution by luring the oily ambitious Mr. Slope into a fatal flirtation and ruining his hopes both of marrying the wealthy widow Mrs. Bold and of securing the position of Dean. With their experience of life on the Continent and their foreign tastes (they read French novels and distribute them as gifts), the Stanhopes are outsiders who intrude upon the English provincial world but only in the end to bring about the restoration of a proper social order.

In *The Professor* Charlotte Brontë goes further in articulating a critique of Englishness from a wider European perspective which anticipates both Arnold's sense of 'one great confederation' and the wider horizons of novels like George Eliot's *Daniel Deronda* (1876) later in the century. The radical English manufacturer Hunsden becomes the spokesman for a cosmopolitan point of view that challenges patriotic loyalty with provocative insults. Teasing the Anglophile Frances Henri, he denounces his own country as 'a little corrupt, venal, lord-and-king-cursed nation, full of mucky pride [. . .] and helpless pauperism; rotten with abuses, worm-eaten with prejudices!' (ch. 24: 218). He claims to speak here as 'a universal patriot' whose 'country is the world' (ch. 24: 222), and his politics are, indeed, those of a European liberal in the period leading up to the revolutions of 1848. At his home in England he consorts with English businessmen interested chiefly in free trade and European intellectuals with wider horizons: 'The foreign visitors too are politicians, they take a wider theme – European progress – the spread of liberal sentiments over the continent; on their mental tablets, the names of Russia, Austria and the Pope are inscribed in red ink' (ch. 25: 238). Foreign in his appearance, unpredictable in his movements, and mysterious in his motives, Hunsden is an overtly Mephistophelean figure whose role is to energize others with his provocative spirit of negation. His literary antecedents are European – Goethe's Mephistopheles in *Faust* not least – and his participation in the political and intellectual life of Continental Europe is an essential component in his elusive otherness.

The revolutions of 1848, along with the unification of Italy and the Franco–Prussian War with its immediate aftermath of the Paris Commune, were the political events in Europe that had the greatest impact in Victorian Britain. Writing in the *Athenaeun* on 16 September 1848 T. A. Trollope, Anthony Trollope's elder brother, remarked on one aspect of that impact. Escaping from the late summer heat of Italy, where he was living, to the mountains of Switzerland, he found that country empty of its customary contingent of British holidaymakers, the 'rich flood of English' that once a year spread its wealth abroad like the fertilizing waters of the Nile but which this year had stayed at home because of the political upheavals on the continent. This was evidence to him of the close-knit nature of modern civilized life, of 'the exceeding close connexion [. . .] between all the portions of Europe', which was like a lake rippled across all its surface by a stone thrown into the water (*Athenaeum*, no. 1090: 934). The February Revolution in Paris in 1848 caused the greatest stir among British novelists, whose reactions ranged from the radical enthusiasm of Dickens and the future George Eliot to the skepticism and fears of violence expressed by Charlotte Brontë and Thackeray. But the only major literary work to engage directly with the revolutionary events that began in 1848 was A. H. Clough's poem, or epistolary novel in verse, *Amours de Voyage* (1858), which focuses on the experiences of a hesitant Englishman caught up in the fall of Mazzini's short-lived Roman Republic in 1849.

The struggle for Italy's freedom was also near to the heart of George Meredith, who had yet to begin his literary career. Having spent two formative years from 1842 to 1844 in the liberal atmosphere of the Moravian school at Neuwied on the Rhine, he was in close sympathy with the ideals and aspirations of the men of 1848 and held to those principles for the rest of his life. More than half a century later he looked back from old age to that period:

> the first and greatest enthusiasm of my youth, when Italy's young heroes appeared at times to be falling hopelessly, and Mazzini, while his heart bled for them, never wavered in the faith he had that their sacrifice would lead to the Risorgimento. In that we have the main historical fact of the 19th century. (Cline 1970: 1436)

It was only after the Risorgimento had become a historical fact that he turned to the earlier events in Italy as a subject for fiction. *Vittoria* (1866), whose heroine gives the signal for the rising against the Austrians in Milan by singing a patriotic song from the stage of La Scala, traces the course of the 1848 revolution in Northern Italy; and although the failure of that revolution is enacted in the suffering and death of individuals, political failure and personal tragedy are framed by the knowledge that they are the prelude to eventual success, so that, with its idealized portrait of Mazzini, this uneven, involved and often melodramatic novel is a belated act of homage to the 'first and greatest enthusiasm' of the novelist's youth.

The Franco–Prussian War, by contrast, was not an event that aroused enthusiasm, but it had the effect of changing the Victorians' image of Germany; and fiction played an important part in that development. Writing *Vanity Fair* in the late 1840s Thackeray could portray Germany with a combination of affection and condescending irony. The narrator warmly recalls the landscape of the Rhine as a pastoral idyll:

> To lay down the pen, and even to think of that beautiful Rhineland makes one happy. At this time of summer evening, the cows are trooping down from the hills, lowing and with their bells tinkling, to the old town, with its old moats and gates, and spires, and chestnut-trees, with long blue shadows stretching over the grass; the sky and the river below flame in crimson and gold; and the moon is already out, looking pale towards the sunset. (*Vanity Fair*, vol. 2, ch. 62: 718)

It is the same Rhine landscape that impresses George Eliot's narrator in *The Mill on the Floss* (1860) with its mellow harmony, while its picturesque ruined castles inspire a 'sense of poetry' and a sense of the 'grand historic life of humanity' (book 4, ch. 1: 271). Thackeray's tiny duchy of Pumpernickel, on the other hand, is mildly mocked for its petty provincialism and grandiose pretensions; but in neither case does Germany present anything to disturb the sense of superior power, wealth, and political freedom enjoyed by the British visitor. However, Prussia's military victory over France in 1870 and the declaration of the Second German Empire at Versailles in 1871 marked a dramatic break with that Germany of petty principalities, picturesque old towns, and backward provincial life. The sense of a new power and a new threat to British supremacy was dramatically captured by Colonel G. T. Chesney's invasion-scare story 'The Battle of Dorking', first published in the immediate aftermath of the war in *Blackwood's Magazine* in May 1871. The narrator of the story looks back from 50 years in the future to recall a German invasion which routed the ill-prepared British defenders at Dorking and brought about the end of British imperial power. Chesney's tale caused a sensation, selling 80,000 copies when it was published in a sixpenny edition in June 1871 (Sutherland 1988: 51), and it is the first in a line of futuristic fictions of invasion which include William Le Queux's *The Great War in England in 1897* (1892) and H. G. Wells's *The War of the Worlds* (1898), and which proliferated around the turn of the century as Germany's economic, industrial, and military power became an inescapable fact of European political life.

The Paris Commune, which followed the Prussian victory, and its bloody suppression reaffirmed France's association in the Victorian mind with revolutionary violence, what Tennyson called 'the red fool-fury of the Seine' (*In Memoriam*, CXXVII). In *A Tale of Two Cities* (1859) Dickens brilliantly dramatizes that fury in the mob scenes of the first French Revolution. His imagination seems both compelled and repelled by the spectacle of violence, entering with grim relish into the antics of the blood-stained crowd around the grindstone or dancing the ferocious Carmagnole, but then taking flight from the Terror with Lorry, the Manettes and the rescued Darnay as their coach escapes from Paris and the narration assumes the urgency and immediacy of the first person plural and the present tense: 'Houses in twos and threes pass by us, solitary farms, ruinous buildings, dye-works, tanneries, and the like [. . .]. Look back, look back, and see if we are pursued!' (book 3, ch. 13: 386). Duality governs this novel from its title onwards, and the mesh of links and parallels between the two cities and the countries of which they are capitals, between their different forms of oppression and violence, ensures that 'the red fool-fury' is not presented as an exclusively French phenomenon. Rather, what occurs on the banks of the Seine illustrates what is latent in any society and can serve as a warning to Dickens's readers in Britain. When a lesser novelist, Eliza Lynn Linton, makes fictional use of the Paris Commune in *The True History of Joshua Davidson, Christian and Communist* (1872), she too employs the events in France to criticize her own society, mounting both an impassioned defense of the Commune and a powerful attack on the hypocrisy of professing Christians at home who acquiesce in a system that perpetuates injustice and inequality. But although this polemical work – more a socio-political pamphlet in the guise of a novel than a successful work of fiction – urges a radical transformation of society, it does so in a very English way. By making her protagonist a saintly and pacific Christian, Linton implicitly rejects the revolutionary violence historically associated with France as the agent of social change.

France's other prominent association in Victorian fiction is with sexual license. When, in *Jane Eyre* (1847), Rochester's marriage to Jane is aborted, it is to France that he tries to persuade her to accompany him as his wife in name but not in law: 'You shall be Mrs Rochester [. . .]. You shall go to a place I have in the south of France: a white-washed villa on the shores of the Mediterranean' (ch. 27: 301). It is to France, too, that Steerforth initially takes Little Em'ly when he elopes with her in *David Copperfield* (1849–50), and in France that George Eliot's Lydgate conceives his wild passion for an actress who is married and who then murders her husband on stage. In *The Professor* Crimsworth the narrator characterizes his rival Pelet as a typical Frenchman in his lax moral behavior: 'Pelet's bachelor life had been passed in proper French style with due disregard for moral restraint [. . .]. He often boasted to me what a terror he had been to certain husbands of his acquaintance [. . .]' (ch. 20: 172). But as this novel illustrates, the national stereotyping extends to French fiction, which was, after all, the likely source of most Victorian assumptions about French sexual behavior and morality. When Pelet announces that he is to marry Zoraïde Reuter, the self-regarding Crimsworth is convinced that she is still so powerfully attracted to him that if he were to stay at the school 'the probability was that in three months' time, a practical Modern French Novel would be in full process of concoction under the roof of the unsuspecting Pelet' (ch. 20: 173–4). Illicit affairs, or 'interesting and romantic domestic treachery' as he decorously puts it, are assumed to be the province of contemporary French fiction, and he works himself up into a lather of moral indignation at the thought: 'No golden halo of fiction was about this example, I saw it bare and real and it was very loathsome' (ch. 20: 174). This association of the

French novel with sexual immorality and attitudes offensive to a British sense of propriety is a recurrent motif in the Victorian novel. When Trollope's Lizzie Eustace in *The Eustace Diamonds* is preparing to receive the pious Lady Fawn, she is shown putting away her French novels and replacing them with the Bible (vol. 1, ch. 9: 121). In M. E. Braddon's *Lady Audley's Secret* (1862) Robert Audley's idle existence as a briefless barrister is defined, and morally placed, by the fact that he spends his time 'smoking his German pipe, and reading French novels' (vol. 1, ch. 4: 32). And when he finds himself attracted to his uncle's new young wife, it is to French fiction that he flippantly alludes to illustrate his predicament: 'I feel like the hero of a French novel: I am falling in love with my aunt' (vol. 1, ch. 7: 56). Reference to the French novel serves to indicate a realm of moral complexities and problematic sexual relations, 'a surreptitious fingering of forbidden zones of sexuality' as it has been nicely described (*Lady Audley's Secret*, introduction, p. xiv). Such territory may be suggested but cannot be too openly explored within the bounds of an English novel. Braddon was well read in French fiction, but when she attempted her own version of Flaubert's *Madame Bovary* in *The Doctor's Wife* (1864), the result is an anodyne bowdlerization that bears only the most superficial thematic resemblance to the French novel that inspired it. It took a much greater novelist, Thomas Hardy, to produce a novel about a provincial woman that could match Flaubert's in its tragic power, but even then Hardy's late addition of the provocative subtitle 'A Pure Woman' to *Tess of the d'Urbervilles* (1891) shows a concern for the moral implications of his heroine's experience that clearly distinguishes him from his French predecessor.

The impropriety of French fiction was a critical commonplace in the Victorian period. In the year before Victoria came to the throne a polemical article on 'French Novels' in the Tory *Quarterly Review* of April 1836 mounted an intemperate attack on their seditious effect:

> Such publications pervert not only private but public morals – they deprave not only individuals but nations, and are alternately the cause and the consequence of a spirit which threatens the whole fabric of European society. (vol. 56: 66)

And at the other end of her reign, in 1889, Henry Vizetelly would be charged with obscene libel for publishing his own translations of Zola and sent to prison for three months. The 'French novel' in Victorian usage is a term which covers a wide range of disparate fiction, from the popular, perhaps even pornographic works Robert Audley is doubtless reading, through Balzac's masterpieces of social realism to Zola's grimly determinist naturalism; but the common element is a capacity to offend Victorian notions of propriety. But of course there were readers who were far from offended, and there was a persistent counter-current of critical opinion which defended French fiction for its truthfulness and honesty in comparison with its English counterpart. G. W. M. Reynolds was moved to combat what he saw to be the disgraceful assault on French literature in the *Quarterly* article, and the typical narrow-mindedness of his fellow-countrymen in relation to France which it expressed, by writing *The Modern Literature of France* (1839). Arguing for the liberating effect of the Revolution of 1830, he maintained that French writers now painted the truth in all its reality and that, by contrast, 'in any English book which professes to be a history of man or of the world, the narrative is but half told' (Reynolds 1839: xviii). In 1846 Robert Browning, writing to Elizabeth Barrett, agreed with her estimation of French and English 'Romance-writing' and claimed that he 'bade the completest adieu to the latter on my first introduction to Balzac' (Kintner 1969: 658). And in Gissing's *New Grub Street* (1891) Amy Reardon asks why people don't write about the really important things of life. She answers her own question:

> Some of the French novelists do; several of Balzac's, for instance. I have just been reading his 'Cousin Pons', a terrible book, but I enjoyed it ever so much because it was nothing like a love story. (ch. 26: 396)

This combination of recoil and admiration was not unusual. George Eliot found Balzac's *Le Père Goriot* a 'hateful book' (Harris and Johnston 1998: 81) and claimed that in many novels he 'drags one by his magic force through scene after scene of unmitigated vice, till the effect of walking among this human carrion is a moral nausea' (Pinney 1963: 146); and yet she could still praise him as 'perhaps the most wonderful writer of fiction the world has even known' (Pinney 1963: 146). These ambivalent responses testify to the power of the French novel, and it is a power that disturbs by breaking with the conventions of so much English fiction in the Victorian period.

George Eliot's observations on Balzac are made in the discussion of another European novelist, Goethe, in her essay on 'The Morality of *Wilhelm Meister*' published in the *Westminster Review* in 1855. Goethe's novel, too, she claims, is supposed by many in Britain to be disturbing in its almost complete lack of moral bias and in its presentation of scenes and incidents that are offensive to 'the refined moral taste of these days' (Pinney 1963: 145). But in this case she is unambivalent in her defense of the foreign novel against such narrowly moralizing criticism. Unlike Balzac, Goethe never oversteps the legitimate limits of art, and she finds his calm and unmelodramatic treatment of 'mixed and erring' humanity to be essentially moral in its influence and praises his 'large tolerance' as the true mark of moral superiority (Pinney 1963: 146–7). The qualities she admires in Goethe are ones she is to display in her own novels, and her familiarity with his work informs her own (Rignall 2000: 139–43). As the archetypal *Bildungsroman*, or novel of education, *Wilhelm Meister's Apprenticeship* is of particular importance not only in her own work but also in Victorian fiction in general. Its presence can be felt behind novels as different as her own *Daniel Deronda* (1876) and Meredith's *The Ordeal of Richard Feverel* (1859), although Goethe's novel is more abstract, playfully ironic and self-conscious than most Victorian novels with their commitment to the presentation of a rich and complex social world. Goethe, however, is an exception among German novelists in his influence on the Victorian novel. Until the appearance of Theodor Fontane toward the end of the nineteenth century, the finest achievements of German fiction were in the shorter form of the Novelle, and the German novel remained an undistinguished backwater of European literature. In an article on modern German fiction in the *Westminster Review* in 1858 G. H. Lewes, who wrote the first biography of Goethe and was familiar with the German language and culture, forcefully defines and explains its lowly reputation. Reflecting on how the 'novels of Germany are singularly inferior to those of France or England' (Lewes 1858: 491), he proceeds to dismiss them with a flourish: 'If German novels are, for the most part, dreary inflictions, it is because they have so little realism that they resemble nothing on earth or under it' (Lewes 1858: 518).

French novels may be disturbing to Victorian readers but they can never be so scornfully dismissed. Indeed, the French novel takes on the role of the Victorian novel's significant other. Attempts to define the distinctive qualities of English fiction commonly have recourse to comparisons across the Channel. When Henry James comes to reflect on the achievement of Anthony Trollope in a memorial article of 1883, he repeatedly draws contrasts between this most English of novelists and his French counterparts. Trollope's realism may be as instinctive as theirs, but his novels have 'a spacious, geographical quality' which is very different from the 'limited world-outlook' of 'the brilliant writers of fiction who practise the art of realistic fiction on the other side of the Channel' (Smalley 1969: 539). Claiming that Trollope's 'perception of character was naturally more just and liberal than that of the naturalists', James then proceeds to reflect in general terms on the differences between English and French novelists:

> This has been from the beginning the good fortune of our English providers of fiction, as compared with the French. They are inferior in audacity, in neatness, in acuteness, in intellectual vivacity, in the arrangement of material, in the art of characterizing visible things. But they have been more at home in the moral world; as people say today they know their way about the conscience. (Smalley 1969: 540)

It is that same moral dimension that is later singled out by F. R. Leavis when, looking back from the middle of the twentieth century, he defines his 'great tradition' of the English novel by arguing that his chosen novelists – Jane Austen, George Eliot, Henry James, Conrad, and D. H. Lawrence – are 'all distinguished by a vital capacity for experience, a kind of reverent openness before life, and a marked moral intensity' (Leavis 1962: 17). Once again a French novelist, this time Flaubert, is conscripted as the symbolic antithesis of this English tradition, since his perversely heroic preoccupation with form excludes precisely the moral vision that, for Leavis, characterizes his English counterparts. In criticizing Flaubert's aestheticism Leavis cites D. H. Lawrence's view that, far from being open to life, Flaubert 'stood away from life as from a leprosy' (Leavis 1962: 16); but he could equally well have cited an influential Victorian critical voice, that of Matthew Arnold. In an article on Tolstoy in the *Fortnightly Review* in December 1887, Arnold took Flaubert to task in similar terms, maintaining *Madame Bovary* to be 'a work of *petrified feeling*: over it hangs an atmosphere of bitterness, irony, impotence: not a personage in the book to rejoice or console us' (Knowles 1978: 359). There is an irony in the fact that Arnold, who elsewhere championed a closer connection between England and Continental Europe and was the spokesman for a wider European perspective, here takes the narrow view; but he was clearly speaking for his culture at large. The need for forms and figures of consolation was obviously felt by many Victorian readers, and the English novel's readiness to provide them was one of the less strenuous aspects of its moral vision.

The context of Arnold's strictures on *Madame Bovary* is a revealing one, for the contrast he is drawing is not with an English novel but with Tolstoy's *Anna Karenina*, which he had read in French translation.

Although conceding rather primly that 'an English mind will be startled by Anna's suffering herself to be so overwhelmed and irretrievably carried away by her passion' (p. 357), he finds in Tolstoy nothing like Flaubert's power to offend the English moral sensibility: much is painful and unpleasant in *Anna Karenina*, 'but nothing is of a nature to trouble the senses, or to please those who wish their senses troubled' (p. 359). More radical than English fiction in its dramatic rendering of passionate sexual love, Tolstoy's novel, unlike Flaubert's, nevertheless places that adulterous desire in a reassuring moral framework and is rich in characters to 'rejoice or console' the reader who requires such consolation. Arnold was writing as Tolstoy was bursting on the Victorian literary world and the timing is significant. Unknown in England in 1885, by 1889 all his work had been translated into English (Orel 1977: 4). This explosion of interest coincided with the controversial popularity of French naturalist fiction, chiefly Zola's, which sold well but provoked strong criticism and the moral outrage that led to the imprisonment of Vizetelly. In Tolstoy, and the Russian novel in general, English critics of Zola and naturalism found a form of fiction that could be praised for its realism and at the same time distinguished from French insistence on the ugly and shameful side of human nature (Orel 1977: 3–4). As the *Saturday Review* put it in January 1887, Tolstoy's realism, unlike that of contemporary French novelists, was the higher realism of mental and spiritual truth (Decker 1937: 543). One European novelist was thus recruited to counter the supposedly subversive effect of another European form of fiction at a time when some judged even the English novel to have succumbed to decadence.

Although curiosity about Russia had been aroused in the mid-1850s by the Crimean War, during which the first English translations of Turgenev's *Sportsman's Sketches* had been published, British interest in the Russian novel is a late-Victorian phenomenon; and it is not only the reading public but the English novel itself that engages more fully with Continental Europe in this period. European novels have a new power of influence. Where Trollope seems to have been innocent of the fact that Balzac had pioneered the device of having the same characters recur in different novels which he employed himself, George Moore is clearly indebted to Zola in novels like *A Mummer's Wife* (1885) and *Esther Waters* (1894) and then comes under the influence of Turgenev in his later work. Oscar Wilde's *The Picture of Dorian Gray* (1891) shows the importance of his reading of the French novelist Joris-Karl Huysmans's *À Rebours* (1884). European philosophy also has an impact, with Schopenhauer's pessimism striking a particular chord with Gissing and Comte's Positivism with Hardy. Robert Louis Stevenson may not have been influenced by his reading of European fiction but in 1886 he declared that Dostoyevsky's *Crime and Punishment* was the greatest novel he had read in 10 years (Orel 1977: 5).

In the last quarter of the nineteenth century, then, the English novel shows a new openness to Europe and it also engages more adventurously with the contemporary European world. Meredith, for instance, bases *The Tragic Comedians* (1880) on the unhappy love story of the German socialist Ferdinand Lassalle who met his death in a duel in 1864; and in her last novel, *Daniel Deronda* (1876), George Eliot turns away from the provincial English world of her earlier fiction to focus on cosmopolitan society in the 1860s. The opening scene of *Deronda* around the gaming tables of a German spa presents that society in an unflattering light. The assembled company may show 'very distant varieties of European type: Livonian and Spanish, Græco-Italian and miscellaneous German, English aristocratic and English plebeian'; but this variety is reduced to an ironic 'human equality' by the leveling effect of the monotonous pursuit of money, so that 'while every player differed markedly from every other, there was a certain uniform negativeness of expression that had the effect of a mask' (*Daniel Deronda*, book 1, ch. 1: 7–8). Resistance to the uniformity of this cosmopolitan materialist culture is embodied in the morally superior figure of Deronda himself, whose cosmopolitanism is of a different kind. Born a European Jew but raised as an English gentleman in ignorance of his origins, he represents a positive form of hybridity that crosses cultural boundaries. In her sympathetic portrayal of Judaism, of an ethnically Jewish hero and of Jewish artists and performers as the standard-bearers of European high culture, George Eliot is not only seeking to widen English vision in this novel, but is clearly countering a tendency of some Victorian novelists to see both Europe and Jewishness as threatening sources of contagion. Trollope's disreputable Jews are European in origin: Emilius in *The Eustace Diamonds* and *Phineas Redux* comes from Prague, and Lopez in *The Prime Minister* from Portugal. The swindling financier Melmotte in *The Way We Live Now* (1875) is not explicitly Jewish, though he has a Jewish wife, but the whole of Continental Europe is the stage for his shady dealing: he has apparently made his money in France, and is reputed to have built a railway across Russia and supplied Austria with arms. Like Dickens's villainous Blandois-Rigaud before him, he could claim to be 'a cosmopolitan gentleman' who 'own[s] no particular country [. . .] a citizen of the world' (*Little Dorrit*, book 1, ch. 1: 14). It is against such sinister figures that Daniel Deronda should be read. Where they circulate malignly, his movement between cultures and countries is in the service not only of his race but also of humanity at large. In this the most European of her novels about nineteenth-century life, George Eliot presents a critique both of English society and of a shallow materialist cosmopolitanism by creating an idealized hero who transcends boundaries of race and class and finally those of Europe itself.

References and Further Reading

Argyle, Gisela (1979) *German Elements in the Fiction of George Eliot, Gissing, and Meredith*. Frankfurt am Main: Peter Lang.

Arnold, Matthew (1962) *Lectures and Essays in Criticism*. Ann Arbor: University of Michigan Press.

Ashton, Rosemary (1980) *The German Idea: Four English Writers and the Reception of German Thought 1800–1860*. Cambridge: Cambridge University Press.

Braddon. M. E. (1987) *Lady Audley's Secret*, ed. David Skilton. Oxford: World's Classics.

Brontë, Charlotte (1953) *Jane Eyre*. Harmondsworth: Penguin.

——(1979) *Villette*, ed. Mark Lilly. Harmondsworth: Penguin.

——(1991) *The Professor*, eds. Margaret Smith and Herbert Rosengarten. Oxford: World's Classics.

Buzard, James (1993) *The Beaten Track: European Tourism, Literature, and the Ways to 'Culture'*. Oxford: Oxford University Press.

——(1999) 'There on the shores of the wide world': the Victorian nation and its other. In Herbert F. Tucker (ed.) *A Companion to Victorian Literature and Culture*, pp. 438–55. Oxford: Blackwell.

Cheyette, Brian (1993) *Constructions of 'The Jew' in English Literature and Society: Racial Representations 1875–1945*. Cambridge: Cambridge University Press.

Cline, C. L. (ed.) (1970) *The Letters of George Meredith*. 3 vols. Oxford: Clarendon.

Couch, John Philip (1967) *George Eliot in France*. Chapel Hill: University of North Carolina Press.

Davie, Donald (1990) Mr Tolsoy I presume? The Russian novel through Victorian spectacles. In *Slavic Excursions: Essays in Russian and Polish Literature*. Manchester: Carcanet.

Decker, Clarence (1937) Victorian comment on Russian realism. *PMLA*, **52**: 542–9.

Dickens, Charles (1970) *A Tale of Two Cities*, ed. George Woodcock. Harmondsworth: Penguin.

——(1999) *Little Dorrit*, ed. Angus Easson. London: Everyman.
Duthie, Enid L. (1975) *The Foreign Vision of Charlotte Brontë*. London and Basingstoke: Macmillan.
Eliot, George (1996) *The Mill on the Floss*, ed. Gordon S. Haight. Oxford: World's Classics.
——(1996) *Romola*, ed. Dorothea Barrett. Harmondsworth: Penguin.
——(1997) *Middlemarch*, ed. David Carroll. Oxford: World's Classics.
——(1999) *Daniel Deronda*, ed. John Rignall. London: Everyman.
Gissing, George (1968) *New Grub Street*, ed. Bernard Bergonzi. Harmondsworth: Penguin.
Hardy, Barbara (1993) Rome in *Middlemarch*: A need for foreignness. *George Eliot–George Henry Lewes Studies*, **24–5**: 1–16.
Harris, Margaret and Johnston, Judith (eds.) (1998) *The Journals of George Eliot*. Cambridge: Cambridge University Press.
James, Henry (1963) *The Portrait of a Lady*. Harmondsworth: Penguin.
Kendrick, Walter M. (1976) Balzac and British realism: Mid-Victorian theories of the novel. *Victorian Studies*, **20**: 5–24.
Kintner, Elvan (ed.) (1969) *The Letters of Robert Browning and Elizabeth Barett 1845–1846*. Cambridge, MA: Harvard University Press.
Knowles, A. V. (ed.) (1978) *Tolstoy: the Critical Heritage*. London: Routledge.
Leavis, F. R. (1962) *The Great Tradition*. Harmondsworth: Penguin.
Lewes, G. H. (1858) Realism in art: modern German fiction. *Westminster Review*, **70**: 491–518.
Michie, Helena (2001) Victorian honeymoons: Sexual reorientations and the 'sights' of Europe. *Victorian Studies*, **43**: 229–51.
Monod, Sylvère (ed.) (1979) *Dickens et la France*. Lille: Presses Universitaires de Lille.
Orel, Harold (1977) The Victorian view of Russian literature. *Victorian Newsletter*, **51**: 1–5.
Phelps, Gilbert (1956) *The Russian Novel in English Fiction*. London: Hutchinson.
Pinney, Thomas (ed.) (1963) *Essays of George Eliot*. London: Routledge.
Reynolds, George W. M. (1839) *The Modern Literature of France*. London: Henderson.
Rignall, John (ed.) (1997) *George Eliot and Europe*. Aldershot: Scolar.
Rignall, John (ed.) (2000) *The Oxford Reader's Companion to George Eliot*. Oxford: Oxford University Press.
Seeber, Hans Ulrich (1997) Cultural synthesis in George Eliot's *Middlemarch*. In John Rignall (ed.) *George Eliot and Europe*, pp. 17–32. Aldershot: Scolar.
Schlicke, Paul (ed.) (1999) *The Oxford Reader's Companion to Dickens*. Oxford: Oxford University Press.
Showalter, Elaine (1979) Guilt, authority, and the shadows of *Little Dorrit*. *Nineteenth-Century Fiction*, **34**: 20–40.
Smalley, David (ed.) (1969) *Anthony Trollope: The Critical Heritage*. London: Routledge.

Stark, Susanne (ed.) (2000) *The Novel in Anglo-German Context: Cultural Cross-Currents and Affinities*. Amsterdam: Rodopi.

Sutherland, John (1988) *The Longman's Companion to Victorian Fiction*. London: Longman.

Thackeray, William Makepeace (1895) The Kickleburys on the Rhine. In *The Works of William Makepeace Thackeray*. Vol. 12. London: Smith, Elder.

——(1968) *Vanity Fair*, ed. J. I. M. Stewart. Harmondsworth: Penguin.

Thompson, Andrew (1998) *George Eliot and Italy*. Basingstoke: Macmillan.

Thomson, Patricia (1977) *George Sand and the Victorians*. London and Basingstoke: Macmillan.

Trollope, Anthony (1972) *Can You Forgive Her?* ed. Stephen Wall. Harmondsworth: Penguin.

——(1969) *The Eustace Diamonds*, eds. Stephen Gill and John Sutherland. Harmondsworth: Penguin.

——(1983) *Phineas Redux*, ed. John C. Whale. Oxford: World's Classics.

Turton, Glyn (1992) *Turgenev and the Context of English Literature 1850–1900*. London and New York: Routledge.

Chapter 12

'A long deep sob of that mysterious wondrous happiness that is one with pain': Emotion in the Victorian Novel

Francis O'Gorman

Victorian fiction aims to move its readers – but we are too often suspicious of its power. Familiarized with the self-conscious practices of post-modernity, readers of the nineteenth-century novel's scenes of high feeling may find them insufficiently self-aware. Three decades of important theoretical debates have made the present moment wary of fiction's power to shape consciousness, to smuggle ideology into feeling, and Philip Davis – one of the few contemporary critics to consider the place of emotion in Victorian fiction – is right to remark that today's readers are more likely to say that they have been 'manipulated' than 'moved' (Davis 1999: 13). The shift from universalism in Anglo-American literary criticism has deepened suspicion of Victorian fiction's scenes of feeling – the sacrifice of Sydney Carton in Dickens's *A Tale of Two Cities* (1859), the drowning of Maggie and Tom in Eliot's *The Mill on the Floss* (1860), the fate of Michael Henchard in Hardy's *The Mayor of Casterbridge* (1886) – because they have been judged as predicated on a naïve assumption of commonality between human beings across time and cultures. To be unselfconsciously affected by a Victorian novel now, from this perspective, is to risk being accused of accepting a simplistic concept of 'universal human nature'; a notion exposed in modern theoretical debate as contaminated by the power politics of the privileged. The admission that one has *felt* the climactic scenes of Victorian fiction, the scenes of death, loss, realization, and calamitous failure, is almost outlawed from current critical discussion because, at its worst, it seems to mark the reader as unprofessional, unrigorous, and unintellectual.

The price paid is a misunderstanding of a distinctive quality of the Victorian novel, and an impoverishment of the reading experience. Victorian fiction considered in this chapter asks its readers to be moved but it does so neither gratuitously nor unsophisticatedly. Ideas are clothed with emotion and readers are asked to feel their force in writing that is subtle and, as this chapter is at pains to point out, variously self-aware. After considering the eighteenth-century inheritance of Dickens's scenes of high feeling, this essay reflects on the moral purposes of George Eliot's literary emotion and on her cautioning against readers who feel excessively. *The Mill on the Floss* provides an instantiation both of her ethical investment in sympathy and an example of a distinctive feature of Victorian fictional affectivity more generally – the narrative that presents a series of 'what if' questions or possibilities that would secure comic resolution (in the formal sense of the term) to plot lines rather than tragic. This element, I suggest, encourages a form of readerly speculation on narrative outcomes, an equation between the reader and the gambler that is the subject of fictional reflection. Considering both *The Mill* and Hardy's *The Return of the Native* (1878), I argue for recognition of the complex ways in which, through figures of financial speculation and gaming, prominent examples of Victorian fiction are self-conscious of the workings of their scenes of high emotion.

Beginning with the death of Little Nell in *The Old Curiosity Shop* (1841), Dickens's art became associated with climactic instances of literary emotion from early in his career. Often involving the death of children, such tableaux – Little Nell, Paul Dombey in *Dombey and Son* (1847–8), Jo the crossing sweeper in *Bleak House* (1852–3) – were high pitched in their emotional ambition but regarded uneasily. Dickens's 'sentimentality' was not universally admired in his own time – it seemed too obviously calculated to please a popular market – and was in due course to be the victim of Oscar Wilde's wit at the end of the century. Famously remarking that a man would have to have a heart of stone to read the death of Little Nell without laughing, Wilde was exploiting his familiar *fin de siècle* skepticism about any discourse that was not self-consciously ironizing. He was also admitting that the intentions of Dickens's death scenes seemed too obvious, their aims to move too palpable, so that they were amusingly self-defeating. Yet the seriousness of Dickens's intentions, in his great scenes of grief as in his use of the conventions of melodrama, is easy to overlook (on Dickens and melodrama, see John 2001). At the heart of his assumptions about feeling and fiction, and governing the intentions of the deathbed episodes, was an optimistic conviction about the redeemability of human nature.

Little Nell expires after a life of hardship leading her grandfather away from the clutches of the evil dwarf Quilp and from his own addiction to gambling. Her death gains poignancy from the fact that, while she has at last obtained security and contentment in the cottage under the shadow of the old church, it has come too late. Dimunition and fragility are the guiding terms of her end; the purity and grace of her personality survive beyond her body in Dickens's chaste but oddly erotic meditation:

> They who were left behind, drew close together, and after a few whispered words – not unbroken by emotion, or easily uttered – followed him. They moved so gently, that their footsteps made no noise; but there were sobs from among the group, and sounds of grief and mourning.
>
> For she was dead. There, upon her little bed, she lay at rest. The solemn stillness was no marvel now.
>
> She was dead. No sleep so beautiful and calm, so free from trace of pain, so fair to look upon. She seemed a creature fresh from the hand of God, and waiting for the breath of life; not one who had lived and suffered death.
>
> Her couch was dressed with here and there some winter berries and green leaves, gathered in a spot she had been used to favour. 'When I die, put near me something that has loved the light, and had the sky above it always.' Those were her words.
>
> She was dead. Dear, gentle, patient, noble Nell was dead. Her little bird – a poor slight thing the pressure of a finger would have crushed – was stirring nimbly in its cage; and the strong heart of its child mistress was mute and motionless for ever. (Ch. 71, 652–3)

Victorian fiction would become richer and more demanding in its scenes of high feeling. But in aspiring to move his readers with this iterative tableau of loss, Dickens was testing them, setting a moral challenge of self-knowledge that aimed to defy the arresting power of social decay. An ability to suffer sorrow at Nell's death was implicitly to be reminded that modernity had failed to crush entirely the natural sympathies still surviving in human nature.

The eighteenth-century Scottish Enlightenment philosopher David Hume had argued in *Enquiries Concerning the Principles of Morals* (1751) against a Classical notion of reason as the central guide of a good life. Reason, for Hume, was insufficient to encourage men and women to moral action for it was only with the addition of '*sentiment*', a 'feeling for the happiness of mankind, and a resentment of their misery' (286, italic original), that an ethical sense could be said to exist as a motivating power. One might intellectually know something to be right but only feeling would lead to action. The association had been conspicuous in the eighteenth-century novels of sensibility: in Henry Mackenzie's *The Man of Feeling* (1771), Harley, the delicate hero, is typically moved to tears. The novel, to which Walter Scott would return for inspiration for his hero in *Waverley* (1814), is an incomplete and broken narrative; its series of supposedly accidental interruptions – pages of the manuscript have been used as wadding for a gun – mimics Harley's own history, broken by his recurrent floods of tears that cut short his speaking. Aposiopesis characterizes his way of being – 'he could not speak, had it been to beg a diadem' (ch. 28: 66) – as it is echoed in the novel's. And the capacity to feel acts as a spur for philanthropic intervention – most obviously Harley's benevolence to the prostitute he meets in Chapter 26 – enacting the link on which Hume had insisted in the *Principles of Morals*.

Dickens reinterpreted this eighteenth-century inheritance for the new industrial age. Preserving the notion that there remained a necessary association between the expression of feeling and the possession of virtue, he conceived the *reader's* feeling as confirmation of surviving goodness. To be moved at the death of Little Nell – innocent, undeserving of misfortune – was to show that one's heart had not, despite the benighted condition of the contemporary world, become wholly atrophied. *The Old Curiosity Shop* implicitly reminded its readers, in its broadly Christian framework, of the natural goodness of human nature. Oscar Wilde, in Dickens's terms, failed the test of the death scene and, by remaining unmoved, confessed his own moral dilapidation. A later scene from Dickens's fiction would be explicit in its confrontation of the conditions of modernity that threatened the innocence of the heart. The death of Jo in *Bleak House* is bitterer than Little Nell's, its grief metamorphosing into a denunciation of the metropolis and the machinery of English government that could do nothing to save him: 'Dead, your Majesty. Dead, my lords and gentlemen. Dead, right reverends and wrong reverends of every order. Dead, men and women, born with heavenly compassion in your hearts. And dying thus around us every day' (ch. 47: 705). Testing the quality of that 'heavenly compassion', Dickens's descriptions of virtuous death undertook moral labor in their resistance to forces that would obliterate pity.

Dickens's sense of the moral task of the novel was not peculiar to him. Indeed, one of the significant differences between the contemporary expectation of the form and the early and mid-Victorian is to do with its functioning as a moral agent. Fiction did not simply contribute neutrally to intellectual debate about values but for some played active roles in the ethical life of the nation. The Swedish novelist and feminist Frederika Bremer (1801–65) wrote to Elizabeth Gaskell on 29 September 1854 to describe the ethical power of Gaskell's early fiction, concluding that the novel 'had never a larger and nobler sphere of action than now a days' (Gaskell papers, 2.10). Others shared Bremer's association between the form and actual moral practice: for George Eliot the subject of the moral possibilities of literary emotion was an important element of her continual reflections on the role of fiction in the modern world. Not only did good, moral fiction draw an emotional response in Eliot's conception, it taught men and women to feel, it revealed to them the nature of sympathy of the sort that underpinned successful human societies. Eliot satirized writing in October 1856 that had little contact with ordinary life, detesting the 'frothy, the prosy, the pious, or the pedantic' as contemporary absurdities in 'silly novels by Lady Novelists' (Eliot 1856b: 301). She hoped instead that better texts – in effect, she was producing an outline for her own future purposes beginning with *Scenes of Clerical Life* (1857) – would educate the heart, encouraging men and women to see and sympathize with that which was beyond the scope of their own lives. To sympathize with a character in a literary representation was to begin to learn how to understand real men and women whose lives were sharply different from one's own. Eliot's conception of her realist project would have such purposes at its core: far too many books, she declared in July 1856, 'profess to represent people as they are', but are inept. She could only condemn 'the unreality of their representations' that were too often the result as 'a grave evil' which compromised the ethical work a good novel undertook. 'The greatest benefit we owe to the artist', she continued:

> whether painter, poet, or novelist, is the extension of our sympathies. Appeals founded on generalizations and statistics require a sympathy ready-made, a moral sentiment already in activity; but a picture of

> human life such as a great artist can give, surprises even the trivial and the selfish into that attention to what is apart from themselves, which may be called the raw material of moral sentiment (Eliot 1856a: 270).

To be moved by fictional characters accurately and sympathetically represented by the realist artist is, in this quietly class-conscious formulation, part of an education in which 'moral sentiment' – the term continues to recognize its inheritance from Hume and the eighteenth-century tradition – becomes that which is prepared for and fortified by the novel.

Yet Eliot was also wary of readers who felt too much. Reading was properly a process that took one outside oneself – but it could be dangerously solipsistic. For Matthew Arnold, feeling excessively as a reader was a sign of narrowness. The 'provincial spirit', he said in his Oxford lecture of 1864 published as 'The Literary Influence of the Academies', 'weeps hysterical tears, and its disapprobation foams at the mouth'. Judicious readers immersed in a wider culture, in contact with broader horizons of thought and art, were not inclined to such effusion. Maggie Tulliver in Eliot's *The Mill on the Floss* has little access to any such culture, denied the Classical education that her brother Tom disdains and remote from any center of intellectual discussion. But she also has burning private needs, products of her nature as well as her circumstances, that help determine her response when at last she finds a text that moves her, Thomas à Kempis's fifteenth-century meditation *The Imitation of Christ*:

> She read on and on in the old book, devouring eagerly the dialogues with the invisible Teacher, the pattern of sorrow, the source of all strength; returning to it after she had been called away, and reading till the sun went down behind the willows. With all the hurry of an imagination that could never rest in the present, she sat in the deepening twilight forming plans of self-humiliation and entire devotedness; and, in the ardour of first discovery, renunciation seemed to her the entrance into that satisfaction which she had so long been craving in vain. She had not perceived – how could she until she had lived longer? – the inmost truth of the old monk's outpourings, that renunciation remains sorrow, though a sorrow borne willingly. Maggie was still panting for happiness, and was in ecstasy because she had found the key to it. She knew nothing of doctrines and systems – of mysticism or quietism; but this voice out of the far-off middle ages was the direct communication of a human soul's belief and experience, and came to Maggie as an unquestioned message. (Book 4, ch. 3: 384)

Maggie is enthralled. But her own imperatives determine her reading experience, her 'ardour' impedes her understanding of the wisdom of the text so that she mistakenly finds only an eagerly devoured form of the intense happiness for which she is too strongly 'panting'. The cautioning voice of the narrator sympathetically acknowledges her error, her misprision of the 'old monk's outpourings', and the scene acts pointedly as a revelation of Maggie's naivetée. But it also serves as a broader reflection on wise and unwise reading, in which an excess of personal feeling distracts, and the meaning and fullness of a text is lost because seized too ardently.

Victorian fiction of the sort I am considering belongs loosely in a Western tradition of the literary representation of human calamity that stretches back to antiquity. Ancient Greek drama offered spectacles of tragedy which invited, for aesthetic theorists, a question about why audiences enjoy the artistic representation of events that, in real life, would distress or appall: the question, as A. D. Nuttall put it in his disarmingly straightforward title, of 'Why does tragedy give pleasure?'. Aristotle's quasi-medical theory of *catharsis* – the spectacle of tragedy purges potentially disruptive emotions – offered one answer of authority in the ancient world. The overarching theoretical structure for George Eliot's dealings with scenes of grief and loss was not Aristotle's but a belief in the moral value of literary sympathy as social agent; rather than purging emotion, these incidents cultivated it. But the conundrum of the *pleasure* that literary pain involved still remained. *The Mill on the Floss* reflected on the curious mixed nature of tragic emotion, secretly disclosing an acceptance that the reader's feelings in the scene of Maggie and Tom's death comprise satisfaction, enjoyment, and emotional fulfillment as well as anguish. Maggie reaches Tom in her boat during the final flood and her brother is amazed at her presence, unable to find words. 'But at last', Eliot writes, 'a mist gathered over [his] blue-grey eyes, and the lips found a word they could – utter: the old childish – "Magsie!" Maggie could make no answer but a long deep sob of that mysterious wondrous happiness that is one with pain' (Book 7, ch. 5: 654–5). The final sentence – the final sob – clinches Maggie's complicated family history in which fraternal love has never been free from anxiety, but it also reflects back to the reader his or her own mixed condition where experience of this fictional representation of misfortune is a species of emotional distress and triumph, a release of feeling that is both contentment and pain, a compound of pleasure and suffering. Such pleasurable pain is alluring, but, like all Eliotian literary emotion, the reader is silently challenged to discern its broader moral function and allow it to fulfil its social purpose. Maggie's solipsistic encounter with Kempis remains silently in the background as an admonishing episode, reminding that reader, even in the midst of the intense feelings of the conclusion, not mistakenly to appropriate *The Mill*'s high literary affectivity as an answer only to the emotional demands of a needy self.

Eliot's novel also reflects on the reader's experience by constructing a model of his or her affective responses in the fabric of its narrative by drawing silent parallels between the business of reading tragic fiction and, however improbably it might seem, the practice of financial speculation. If one of the objections to the Victorian novel's handling of scenes of high emotion is the unselfconsciousness of its affective purposes, then Eliot's *The Mill on the Floss* offers, like a number of other major Victorian novels, a counter instance where awareness of readerly experience is subtly but significantly present in its plot. The association between the emotions of the text and the behavior of the gambler provides a suggestion of how significant expectation and anticipation, disappointed hopes for satisfaction and content, are in the affective identity of Victorian fiction. While *The Mill on the Floss* plans for its conclusion, even from its first sentence's prescient description of the 'loving tide' meeting the Floss in an 'impetuous embrace' (Book 1, ch. 1: 53), it is also a text in which other narrative outcomes, alternative potential trajectories, are frequently present. In allowing the reader to infer tantalizingly alternative and more reassuring histories, the novel increases the emotional torsion of its final outcome. If Wakem had lost his law suit and Mr. Tulliver won; if Tulliver had not lost his temper and beaten Wakem; if Stephen and Maggie's boat had not drifted so far as to be irretrievable; if Maggie's meetings with Philip at the Red Deep had remained secret; if the Floss had carried Maggie beyond the mouth of the Ripple; if Tom and Maggie had escaped the machinery that engulfed them as Maggie avoided it as she turned her boat towards the Mill; if Tom, perhaps most of all, had understood the damage his principles were doing to Maggie's happiness. . . Eliot controls the direction of the fiction, yet she presses her reader to imagine it as different, to think of the novel not as a contrived scheme that forbids the lure of 'what if' but a malleable one that encourages it, which tempts and frustrates the reader by suggesting but then not allowing replacements for its own narratives.

Eliot's preoccupation with the deterministic force of events, the ways in which the past controls the terms of the future, is well recognized. But her determinism makes its patterns from the precarious and contingent. *The Mill* readily suggests how things might easily have been different. The narrative of Book 6, chapter 10, gains its force from its proximity to another one, from its implicit suggestion of how close Maggie's story is to an alternative. Philip and Maggie are speaking together. Maggie, much troubled by her conflicted feelings for her brother and her lover, announces that she is going away, freeing herself from temptation. Philip replies that, therefore, their future together is a 'book' that is now to be 'quite closed':

> 'That book never will be closed, Philip,' she said, with grave sadness; 'I desire no future that will break the ties of the past. But the tie to my brother is one of the strongest. I can do nothing willingly that will divide me always from him.'
>
> 'Is that the only reason that would keep us apart for ever, Maggie?' said Philip, with a desperate determination to have a definite answer.
>
> 'The only reason,' said Maggie, with calm decision. And she believed it. At that moment she felt as if the enchanted cup had been dashed to the ground. The reactionary excitement that gave her a proud self-mastery had not subsided, and she looked at the future with a sense of calm choice.
>
> They sat hand-in-hand without looking at each other or speaking for a few minutes: in Maggie's mind the first scenes of love and parting were more present than the actual moment, and she was looking at Philip in the Red Deeps. (Book 6, ch. 10: 564)

The open book is an apt metaphor for the narratives that contend here. Between Maggie and union with Philip stands but *one reason*. It is substantial, of course, and the novel will prove it defining. But the episode, in dwelling on the solitary nature of the obstacle to Maggie's union, insists how close Philip Wakem is to content – even he realizes that he ought to have 'been thoroughly happy' in Maggie's calmly decisive words (Book 6, ch. 10: 564). The narrative is seemingly on the verge of securing Philip's happiness – and the reader's hope is to be disappointed all the more painfully for having been so close to satisfaction.

The felt presence of lost paths that might lead to contentment feature distinctively in the affective identity of the mid-period novel that makes of cauterized possibilities compelling scenes of literary emotion. Charles Darwin's evolutionary theory emphasized from 1859 onwards – the year of the publication of *The Origin of Species* – how minute variations in species biology, food availability, climate, and environment broadly defined had major consequences on the life of plants and animals; in doing so it suggested both the strength of a biological determinism and paradoxically how easily, with only the smallest of changes further back in history, the nature of the present moment could have been radically different. The presence of possibilities, the proximity of markedly different narrative outcomes in any narrative instance, was intriguing novelists well before *The Origin of Species* gave scientific shape to patterns of experience already prominent in literary culture. The missed possibilities of ordinary lives engaged Elizabeth Gaskell in her domestic fiction and *Cranford* (1852–3) explored the affective potential of the lost opportunity, the suggested but not followed narrative path, with poignancy. Miss Matty's 'Love Affair of Long Ago' probes the emotional bereavements that linger behind the everyday. Thomas Holbrook proposed to Miss Matty many years previously. Class divisions prevent the union, and the two lovers do not see each other again, as it turns out, for 30 or 40 years. They have lived separate lives, their marriage formed only of a memory of what might have been. At the end of the chapter is the narrator's account of their unexpected re-encounter in the village milliner's shop. Mr. Holbrook catches Matty's name spoken by the shopman:

> 'Matty – Miss Matilda – Miss Jenkyns! God bless my soul! I should not have known you. How are you? how are you?' He kept shaking her hand in a way which proved the warmth of his friendship; but he repeated so often, as if to himself, 'I should not have known you!' that any sentimental romance which I might be inclined to build was quite done away with by his manner.
>
> However, he kept talking to us all the time we were in the shop; and then waving the shopman with the unpurchased gloves on one side, with 'Another time, sir! another time!' he walked home with us. I am happy to say my client, Miss Matilda, also left the shop in an equally bewildered state, not having purchased either green or red silk. Mr Holbrook was evidently full with honest loud-spoken joy at meeting his old love again; he touched on the changes that had taken place; he even spoke of Miss Jenkyns as 'Your poor sister! Well, well! we have all our faults'; and bade us good-bye with many a hope that he should soon see Miss Matty again. She went straight to her room, and never came back till our early tea-time, when I thought she looked as if she had been crying (ch. 3: 70).

The narrator takes the lead in what he calls 'castle-building' (ch. 3: 70), constructing an imaginative outcome to this long-ago fractured narrative of love that is, as he realizes from Holbrook's repeated 'I should not have known you', finally revealed irreparable in the drama of ordinary events. Understated throughout – Gaskell certainly does not allow us to see Miss Matty's tears – the emotional pressure of the passage is concentrated, as it is in Tom's word 'Magsie!', in its finest textures. Holbrook's valedictory address to the shopman – 'Another time, sir!' – poignantly reminds the reader that, for the impeded romance, there can be no airy optimism about returns because there is no more time. The commonplace utterance over the shop counter insists both on the possibilities of buying gloves some other day, and on the singleness of an individual human life that permits no second chance.

Gaskell's drama of missed marriage involves a narrator undertaking the work of the reader in imagining happier outcomes than that secured by the events he witnesses. He figures as narrator and as reader; in *The Mill on the Floss*, Eliot offers the more extensive comparison between the reader of her novel and another textual figure, the financial speculator, marking a structural correspondence between the former's choked desires for comic resolution – again, in the strict sense of the term – and speculation of a literally disastrous kind. The intensity of the reader's response to the calamity that befalls Maggie and Tom is partly consequent on the number of potential narratives that Eliot's text has implied: the reader is variously and painfully enticed into hoping for the better, only to know bitter but perversely pleasurable disappointment. Aspiring and failing is the condition of Mr. Tulliver and his financially devastating lawsuit against Wakem over rights to the waters of the Floss, which, in its collapse, sets in motion the events that will lead to the estrangement between Maggie and Tom. Tulliver doggedly believes he will succeed – has little doubt that he will defeat the lawyers who represent Mr. Privart and his aspirations for legitimate access to the river. 'It's plain enough what's the rights and the wrongs of water, if you look at it straight-forrard' (Book 2, ch. 2: 226), he says. But things are not 'straight-forrard'. Tulliver is ignorantly gambling against Wakem's brains with only the power of iteration – repeating his point not arguing for it – to support him. And iteration, Eliot's narrator sharply remarks, 'like friction, is likely to generate heat instead of progress' (Book 2, ch. 2: 230). The failure of Tulliver's belief in his own judgment costs dear – 'the mill and the land and everything' (Book 2, ch. 7: 266), Maggie says with pathetic vagueness and stark precision – and, in losing his money, Tulliver commits Tom to a lifetime of work to redeem the family's dignity. The tragic emotional pressure of *The Mill,* with its dreadful sense of possibilities lost, mirrors, just as much as it is partly caused by, an unwise hope in financial prosperity.

With a single word – 'Magsie!' – Eliot had signified that the union between Tom and his sister was renewed. With another word, which the novel has made even more meaningful, she suggests the circuitry that links the death scene and all its tragic power back to the dismal matter of money lost and clinches the correspondence between the reader's gamble with the outcome of the novel and Mr. Tulliver's gamble with the outcome of his lawsuit. Layers of reference accumulate on 'golden', and each appearance draws the novel back to earlier scenes that root the calamity in mistaken financial optimism. Eliot's title for Chapter 7 of Book 2 is 'The Golden Gates are Passed', words transparent in their allusion to Eden and the Fall. Chapter 7 contains the account of Tulliver's loss – Maggie's journey to Tom, Tom's initial half-comprehending 'My father will have to pay a good deal of money, then?' (Book 2, ch. 7: 266), and the final horrible revelation of the extent of his financial failure and physical paralysis – so that, at the end, Tom and Maggie set out on a journey home in a world radically changed. With Miltonic gravity, Eliot invokes the words of her title in a plot that will find its redemption not in divine intervention but only in a moment's human affection before the obliterating waters. 'They had entered the thorny wilderness,' the narrator says of the children walking home in grief, 'and the golden gates of their childhood had forever closed behind them' (Book 2, ch. 7: 270). 'Golden': it raises to consciousness the riches that are now the opposite of the Tullivers' condition. The auction of the Tullivers' possessions, the first material consequence of Tulliver's loss, occurs with deepening irony in the Golden Lion, where Mrs. Tulliver endures the 'hateful publicity' (Book 3, ch. 6: 321) of public shame: 'Such things bring lines in well-rounded faces,' the narrator comments on this event that secures, of course, no real gold for the impoverished family, 'and broaden the streaks of white among the hairs that once looked as if they had been dipped in pure sunshine' (Book 3, ch. 6: 321–2). The textual economy of this poignant moment refuses to balance the dismal events of the Golden Lion with the sadly remembered golden hair of Elizabeth Dodson's youth, her tranquillity irrecoverably lost to the financial misjudgment that has taken away all the sunlight.

Suggestive of the very substance that lies at the heart of the Tullivers' collapse, of the fall that has brought Tom and Maggie's childhood to an end, and of the scene of their public humiliation, 'golden' bears the weight of the novel's history. It would perform a similarly complex but more explicit role as material and metaphor later in Eliot's *Silas Marner* (1861). But at the tragic peak of *The Mill on the Floss* the word returns, taking the narrative momentarily back to the events of the past, insisting at its climax on the recollection of lost childhood, lost possessions, and lost peace, and of the vanished wealth that darkened lives and embittered human relationships. Maggie and Tom's boat is capsized by the machinery, and their death, their drowning in the turbulent waters, is figured only by the apparently innocent words: 'But soon the keel of the boat reappeared, a black speck on the golden water' (Book 7, ch. 5: 655). Yet 'Golden' is no innocent word. The aurelian water has darkened their lives though it has momentarily provided them with access to the imagined affections of their childhood, a time before the golden gates were passed, and before the Golden Lion witnessed the conversion of their property into debtors' dues. 'Golden' tugs the climax back to its origins – a trajectory of persistent lure in Eliot's plotting throughout her fiction – and subtly implies the complex relations between the tragic sense in *The Mill* and the material world of financial risk. Eliot's narrative suggests a host of possible outcomes for the story of Maggie and Tom, and, like the optimistic speculator, the reader hopes for the best. But the final scene closes down the possibility of happiness other than in death and the reunion of the last embrace. In the painfully pleasurable sorrow of this finale, the reader finds that her speculation in a happy outcome has failed just as, within the texture of the narrative itself, Tulliver's iterative optimism in financial success yielded catastrophe.

Gillian Beer remarks that dramatizations of gambling in the nineteenth- and twentieth-century novel act out aspects of the reader's experience of fictional prose, the 'wager' we take when picking up any novel, in anticipating the turns of its plot, in laying out hopes for its conclusions (Beer 1990). The suggestion is helpful. But the correspondence between gambling and the emotional economy of Victorian fiction of the sort I am considering is more exact. *The Mill on the Floss* connects a kind of financial gamble with the patterns of its readers' feelings, but the climax of this form of association, this quality of the novel's self-consciousness in its dealings with emotion, is Thomas Hardy's tragic novel of mistaken judgment and lost emotional speculation, *The Return of the Native*. Mapping the reader's feelings against the practice of gambling, Hardy's text is exceptionally self-aware about the affective workings of realism – but without any of the constructive social purposes Eliot found in literary emotion. Eliot softly compares the reader to the disappointed speculator but nonetheless hopes that he or she will gain in moral stature from the sympathies tested in the fiction; Hardy compares the reader to the man or woman at the gaming table also, but what strikes him primarily in the comparison is the searing experience of loss.

The shiftiness of *The Return*, the repeated scenes of chance, the tempting possibilities of success and content with which it flirts, and the strong sense of prospects just beyond paradoxically co-exist with the firmly tragic nature of the novel's inevitable movement toward grief made clear by the narrator's periodic remarks about calamities to come. Eliot's plot combines determinism with teasing suggestions of how things might be different; Hardy's offers a sternly ineluctable movement toward sorrow with the continual recognition of how it could be averted with the smallest assistance from chance or prior knowledge. 'If I had only known – if I had only known!' (Book 2, ch.7: 146), Eustacia remarks, and her words echo in the novel. She feels their force with peculiar strength when Clym, her husband, fails to provide her with the Parisian life for which she had hoped. The speculation of her marriage – the most significant of her emotional gambles – is that he will return to high society but it is a speculation on a human being's choice of life that does not pay off. Wildeve comments on Clym's apparent reluctance to go to France:

> 'I was quite surprised to hear that he had taken a cottage. I thought, in common with other people, that he would have taken you off to a home in Paris immediately after you had married him. "What a gay, bright future she has before her!" I thought. He will, I suppose, return there with you, if his sight gets strong again?'
>
> Observing that she did not reply he regarded her more closely. She was almost weeping. Images of a future never to be enjoyed, the revived sense of her bitter disappointment, the picture of the neighbour's suspended ridicule which was raised by Wildeve's words, had been too much for proud Eustacia's equanimity (Book 4, ch. 3: 258)

This 'image of a future never to be enjoyed' perturbs Eustacia – it will eventually help drive her to her death – because it is a gamble that has not succeeded. Eustacia's loss is her own. But her predicament subtly figures that of the reader who is tempted across the whole seductive terrain of the novel to hope that things will work out for the better. The reader sees that only the smallest change in the events would secure some form of comic resolution, yet *The Return of the Native* pays back such broken hopes only in the dark coin of tragedy, the strangely pleasurable pain of literary emotion.

The most celebrated scene of resolution so nearly achieved and so catastrophically missed is Mrs. Yeobright's visit to her son Clym. The journey, across the sun-baked heath, is intended to be reconciliatory but Clym, when his mother knocks at last at the door, is fast asleep on the floor. Eustacia, meanwhile, is secretly meeting Wildeve in another room and does not, for the obvious reason, want to be discovered. Disastrously – this is the kind of event that seems to imply the workings of a malevolent force deep in the feral heart of Hardy's imagination – she mistakenly thinks that Clym has woken and answered the door because she has heard what proves later to have been mutterings in sleep. Mrs. Yeobright, receiving no answer, concludes that Eustacia and Clym have refused her entry and spurned her gesture of goodwill. Stung by betrayal she turns away only, in a grim parody of her emotional condition, to be stung by an adder. She dies wretchedly on Egdon Heath, alone, believing she is a 'broken-hearted woman cast off by her son' (Book 4, ch. 6: 281). The reader is goaded to realize that there are multiple ways in which this ghastly scene could have been avoided. If Clym had woken, if Eustacia had not mistaken his unconscious sounds, if Mrs. Yeobright had persisted in her call, if the weather had been cooler, if the snake had not crossed her path. Hardy allows his reader the torturing pleasure of fantasizing with possibilities just as he reminds her that her only power over the direction of fiction is imaginative rebellion against its course. Desperate speculation, uncomfortably earnest hoping for a reverse of fortune and a successful outcome: these are the terms of the reader of *The Return of the Native*. They are also the terms of the gambler. It is an association Hardy makes unavoidable by staging at the heart of the novel a ghostly scene of a game at dice that neatly dramatizes the reader's predicament and figures the mechanisms of the text's affectivity.

Mrs. Yeobright, with a grave lapse of judgment, entrusts Christian Cantle – a Shakespearean lowlife peasant – with money to be divided between Eustacia and Thomasin. But he is waylaid on his journey by Wildeve – Thomasin's husband – who tempts his integrity with stories of enrichment over the gambling table – the Italian who played all night starting with merely a *louis* and left with ten thousand pounds; Rumbold, a waiter whose gambling made him so wealthy he became Governor of Madras; the American who lost everything over a game and then won it all back. Cantle is entranced, and sits down to play

Wildeve using money not his own with dice thrown on a 'large flat stone' (Book 3, ch. 7: 223), lit only by a lantern, in the midst of the darkened Heath. Inevitably, the tales that enticed Christian into this absurdly vulnerable position prove from a different realm: his own miserable losses that follow are a gruesome distortion of any story of a poor man's fortune transformed. Almost 'with a shriek' (Book 3, ch. 7: 224), he lays down his last coin, and loses it. The novel now is poised on the verge of a calamity as the gambling scene has opened up a narrative possibility of grave consequence – Wildeve possesses money that rightly belongs to Clym and Eustacia and which would utterly change their financial position. Now enters a figure of salvation who proves – perversely – the agent of an even greater disaster: Diggory Venn, the reddleman. With the gambling stone lit by the eerie light of glow worms (the lantern has been extinguished by an ominous death's-head moth), and periodically regarded by the spectral forms of the heath ponies, Venn and Wildeve play out another dreadful game with the same coins. Wildeve, reversing the patterns of enrichment that his own tales to Christian had enshrined, loses all the money he had won. The possibility of resolution, the restoration of rightful property, the avoidance of gross hardship now seems within the novel's reach and the reader is sorely tempted to hope for the best, to gamble with her own feelings and believe that, through the chancy play of the gaming table, all will work out. But the story has within it its own warning against such speculation – for this is what Christian had done, and lost. The monstrous difficulty now, the chapter suddenly reveals, is that Venn is unaware that only half the money belongs to Wildeve's wife. It was 'an error', Hardy records with grim relish, 'which afterwards helped to cause more misfortune than treble the loss in money value could have done' (Book 3, ch. 8: 232).

Hardy remarks in the midst of this fevered scene of readerly optimism and bruising disappointment that the 'incongruity between the men's deeds and their environment was striking' (Book 3, ch. 8: 229). But there is no incongruity in the scene's relation to the broader environment of the novel or its reading. It is a mirror and a lamp; a reflection of and a commentary on the consumption of the fiction itself and the workings of its affectivity; it acts out for the reader her own role, forming a meta-commentary on the sorrowful/alluring business of reading figured as a process of speculating, hoping, and losing. My concatenation of present participles – speculating, hoping, losing – describes the reader's emotional experience with *The Return of the Native* as it exactly captures the gambler's, clinching a correspondence between the affective achievement of the novel – the way in which our strangely pleasurable anguish is heightened by recognition of how nearly it could have been avoided – and the fraught business of gaming for money or speculating with cash about the turns the future will take. As such *The Return* provides a particularly vivid example not only of the power of Victorian literary emotion as it is found in scenes of cauterized possibility and lost speculation, but of a novel's self-consciousness about the nature and workings of its affectivity. *The Return of the Native* engages its readers' feelings, but, with a level of exceptional sophistication, it also offers them a subtle model of how their emotional response works, suggesting how self-aware Victorian literary emotion could be without losing its remarkable power to compel.

References and Further Reading

Beer, Gillian (1990) The reader's wager: Lots, sorts, and futures. *Essays in Criticism*, **40**: 99–123.

——(2000) *Darwin's Plots: Evolutionary Narrative in Darwin, George Eliot and Nineteenth-Century Fiction*, 2nd edn. Cambridge: Cambridge University Press.

Brantlinger, Patrick (1996) *Fictions of State: Culture and Credit in Britain, 1694–1994*. Ithaca and London: Cornell University Press.

Colby, Christina (1999) 'Financial'. In H. F. Tucker (ed.), *A Companion to Victorian Literature and Culture*. Oxford: Blackwell, pp. 225–43.

Davis, Philip (1999) Victorian realist prose and sentimentality. In A. Jenkins and J. John (eds.) *Rethinking Victorian Culture*. Basingstoke: Macmillan, pp. 13–28.

——(2002) *Oxford English Literary History: 1830–1880, The Victorians*. Oxford: Oxford University Press.

Dickens, Charles (1841) *The Old Curiosity Shop*. Harmondsworth: Penguin, 1972.

——(1853) *Bleak House*. Harmondsworth: Penguin, 1971.

——(1859) *A Tale of Two Cities*. Harmondsworth: Penguin, 1970.

Eliot, George (1856a). The natural history of German life. In T. Pinney (ed.) *Essays of George Eliot*. New York: Columbia University Press and London: Routledge and Kegan Paul, 1963, pp. 266–99.

——(1856b) 'Silly novels by Lady Novelists'. In Thomas Pinney (ed.), *Essays of George Eliot*. New York: Columbia University Press and London: Routledge and Kegan Paul, 1963, pp. 300–24.

——(1857) *Silas Marner*. Harmondsworth: Penguin, 1994.

——(1860) *The Mill on the Floss*. Harmondsworth: Penguin, 1979.

Franklin, J. Jeffrey (1999) *Serious Play: The Cultural Form of the Nineteenth-Century Realist Novel*. Philadelphia: University of Pennsylvania Press.

Gaskell, Elizabeth (1851–3) *Cranford/Cousin Phillis*. Harmondsworth: Penguin, 1986.

Gaskell papers, Special Collections, Brotherton Library, University of Leeds (and as microfilmed by Adam Matthew Publications, 2003).

Hardy, Barbara (1970) Dickens and the passions. *Nineteenth-Century Literature*, **24**: 449–66.

Hardy, Thomas (1878) *The Return of the Native*. Harmondsworth: Penguin, 1999.

—— (1886) *The Mayor of Casterbridge*. Oxford: Oxford University Press, 1987.

Hume, David (1751) *Enquiries concerning Human Understanding and concerning the Principles of Morals*, reprinted from the 1777 edition, 3rd edition (Oxford: Clarendon, 1975).

John, Juliet (2001) *Dickens' Villains: Melodrama, Character, Popular Culture*. Oxford: Oxford University Press.

Kaplan, Fred (1987) *Sacred Tears: Sentimentality in Victorian Literature*. Princeton: Princeton University Press.

King, Jeannette (1978) *Tragedy in the Victorian Novel: Theory and Practice in the Novels of George Eliot, Thomas Hardy and Henry James*. Cambridge: Cambridge University Press.

Mackenzie, Henry (1771) *The Man of Feeling*. Oxford: Oxford University Press, 1987.

Nuttall, A. D. (1996) *Why does Tragedy give Pleasure?* Oxford: Clarendon.

Reed, John (1984) A friend to Mammon: Speculation in Victorian literature. *Victorian Studies*, **27**: 179–202.

Skinner, Gillian (1998) *Sensibility and Economics in the Novel, 1740–1800: The Price of a Tear*. Basingstoke: Macmillan.

Weiss, Barbara (1986) *The Hell of the English: Bankruptcy and the Victorian Novel*. Bucknell University Press; London: Associated University Presses.

Zemka, Sue (1993) From the Punchmen to Pugin's Gothics: The broad road to a sentimental death in *The Old Curiosity Shop*. *Nineteenth-Century Literature*, **48**: 291–309.

Index

Abercrombie, John 95
actresses in Victorian fiction 66
Adam, Barbara 132
Adams, James Eli 157
Adorno, Theodore
  Minima Moralia 43
aesthetic
  as a set of contexts for Victorian fiction 2
  legal debates about the aesthetic 79–90
  Victorian authorship and supposed aesthetic autonomy 134–55
  Victorian fiction criticism returns to the aesthetic 76–7
Allen, Grant 204–5, 215
Althusser, Louis 162
Altick, Richard 36
Armstrong, Isobel 77
Armstrong, Nancy 28
Arnold, Dr Thomas 56
Arnold, Matthew 232–3, 247–8
artists, female, in Victorian fiction 66
associationism (psychological theory) 94–7
authorship in the Victorian period 134–55

Bakhtin, Mikhail 7–8
Bain, Alexander 98, 99, 109–10
Balzac, Honoré de
  Le Père Goriot 245
bankruptcy 59
Barthes, Roland 40
Beer, Gillian 265
Beerbohm, Max
  Zuleika Dobson 218
Beetham, Margaret 131
Behn, Aphra 113
  Oroonoko 7, 11
Besant, Walter 145, 151
  All Sorts and Conditions of Men 64–5
Bhabba, Homi 17
Biblical criticism 2–3
Bildungsroman 137–8, 159, 246
biology
  and eugenics 219–26
  and gender 214–15
  and race 18–20, 215–19
  and separation of classes and races 212–13
  the Victorian novel 202–31

Booth, Charles 64
Braddon, M. E.
  Lady Audley's Secret 32, 57, 109, 244
Brake, Laurel 124–5
Bremer, Frederika 257
Brontë, Anne
  The Tenant of Wildfell Hall 34
Brontë, Charlotte 102
  Jane Eyre 33, 52–3, 54, 170, 188–90
  Shirley 103
  The Professor 98, 237–8, 239, 243–4
  Villette 32–3, 34, 190–1, 237–9
Brontë, Emily
  Wuthering Heights 175, 188–9, 216
Browne, Hablôt K. ('Phiz') 116
Bulwer-Lytton, E. 137–8, 144–5, 234
Burton, J. H. 86
Butler, Samuel
  The Way of All Flesh 211

Carlyle, Thomas 48–9, 134–6
  'The Hero as Man of Letters' 134, 137–55
'cerebral reflex' 108–9
Chambers, Robert
  Vestiges of Creation 210–11
chartism 63
Chesney, G. T.
  'The Battle of Dorking' 242
Christianity 2–3
class
  and the fallen woman 65–6
  and male aggression 65–6
  and representation of speech 60–1
  in the Victorian novel 47–70
  middle–class emphasis 52–3, 65–6
  tripartite division in Victorian society 50
  uncertain boundaries in Victorian society 50–2
Cohn, Bernard 11
Collins, Wilkie
  Antonina 234
  Armadale 173
  Man and Wife 84
  The Law and the Lady 84–88
  The Moonstone 18–19
  The Woman in White 15, 47–8, 109, 164–6
Combe, George 98, 99
confession in Victorian fiction 190–6
Conrad, Joseph
  Heart of Darkness 11–13
  Nostromo 13–14
consumerism, Victorian novel as part of modern 29–30
copyright and Victorian fiction 77–90
  Talfourd's Copyright Bill 77–8
  Copyright Act of 1842 80
    compared to Patent Act of 1852 80
Cornhill, The 120–1, 127–30
  title page illustrations 129–30
Craik, Dinah
  John Halifax, Gentleman 57
Crary, Jonathan 27–8
  and 'visuality'/'visibility' distinction 27–8
credit 58
  as faith in appearance 58
Criminal Law Amendment Act 173–4
Cross, Wilbur 91–2

daguerreotypes and Victorian fiction 36–7
Dallas, E. S. 99, 106
Darwin, Charles 18–19
  and evolutionary theory 18–19, 202–31, 261–2
Davis, Philip 253
death of children
  in Dickens's fiction 254–7
Defoe, Daniel 113
  Robinson Crusoe 7, 11

Dickens, Charles
  and his illustrators 30
  and journalism 140
  and liberal idea of property 81
  and 'The Guild of Literature and Art' 145–6
  and visuality 26
  Works
  A Christmas Carol 208
  A Tale of Two Cities 55, 62, 131, 235, 242–3, 253
  Barnaby Rudge 62, 120
  Bleak House 54, 55, 59, 65, 81–2, 83, 85, 120, 174, 254, 256–7
  David Copperfield 94, 120, 138–55, 174–5, 243
  Dombey and Son 4–6, 20–1, 59, 167, 174, 254
  Great Expectations 35, 48, 49–50, 52, 60, 61, 81, 82, 86, 171
  Hard Times 55, 57, 183
  Little Dorrit 33, 57, 82–3, 85, 236–7, 238, 250
  Master Humphrey's Clock 120
  Nicholas Nickleby 55
  Oliver Twist 30, 64, 66, 107, 140, 174
  Our Mutual Friend 31, 55, 56, 57
  The Old Curiosity Shop 30, 120, 174, 254–5
  The Pickwick Papers 64, 67, 80–1, 83, 115–17, 119–20
'Dignity of Literature' debate 141–55
Disraeli, Benjamin
  Tancred 211
  'Young England' Trilogy 55
distribution practices of fiction 79
Dixon, Ella Hepworth
  The Story of a Modern Woman 33–4
Dolin, Kieran 73–6
Doppelgänger 42, 166
Dostoyevsky, Fyodor
  Crime and Punishment 249
doubles in Victorian fiction 165
Dowie, Ménie Muriel
  Gallia 204
Durkheim, Emile 125
Du Maurier, George
  Trilby 66

Eagleton, Terry 136
East End, condition of 64–5
Eliot, George 102
  and reading badly 258–9
  reviewing Kingsley's *Westward Ho!* 91
  and sympathy 257–8
  and 'true seeing' 37
  and visuality 26–7
  as translator 233
  Works
  Adam Bede 37, 66
  Daniel Deronda 19–20, 55, 66, 239–40, 246, 249, 250
  Felix Holt 32, 55, 82, 213
  Middlemarch 19, 37, 47, 52, 53–4, 55, 60, 67, 82, 105, 170, 202–3, 233–4
  'Natural History of German Life' review 36–7
  Romola 235
  Scenes of Clerical Life 257
  Silas Marner 59
  The Mill on the Floss 58, 175–6, 214, 216, 241, 253, 258–9, 260–1, 263–5
emotion in Victorian fiction 253–70
  and moral purpose 254–60
  and speculation/gambling 260–70
  self-consciousness in emotion 260–70
Empire 4–24
  and adventure fiction 14–15
  and Anglo–Indian words 17–18
  and binary oppositions of power 8
  and British expansionism 9
  and Charles Dickens 4–6, 20–1
  and commerce 21

Empire *cont.*
and forms of documentary knowledge 11
and George Eliot 19–20
and Ian Watt's *The Rise of the Novel* 7
and Joseph Conrad 11–14
and novel form 6–8
and the scramble for Africa 9
and the Victorian novel 4–24
environments in fiction, related to mesmerism 107
eugenics 219–26
Europe in the Victorian novel 232–52

faculties of mind, as innate 95–6
faculty psychology 95–7, 110
female sexuality in the Victorian novel 163–70
Flaubert, Gustave 244, 247
Fleming, Sandford 123
Foucault, Michel
and sexuality in Victorian Britain 159–60
Discipline and Punish 74
Foucaultian readings of Victorian fiction 74–5, 87
Post-Foucaultian readings 75
France
association with revolution 242–3
association with sexual licence 243–4
French naturalism 65
Freud, Sigmund 157, 176
Freudian psychoanalytical theory 92–3

Gall, F. J. 101
Galton, Francis 220–6
Gambling and emotion in Victorian fiction 260–70
Gaskell, Elizabeth 92
Cousin Phillis 128–9
Cranford 262–3
Mary Barton 60, 63, 107, 136–7, 183
Ruth 66
The Life of Charlotte Brontë 146–7
Wives and Daughters 56, 212
'gentlemanliness' 56–7
ghosts 40–1
Gissing, George 50, 65
New Grub Street 137, 151–4, 245
Goethe, J. W. 138, 240, 245–6
governesses in Victorian fiction 58–9
Grand, Sarah 203
Green-Lewis, Jennifer 36
Grossmith, George and Weedon 60

Habermas, Jürgen 84
Haggard, H. Rider
King Solomon's Mines 14
She 14–15, 16, 31
Hall, Catherine 8, 9–10
Hallam, Henry 232
Hamilton, Sir William 97, 98
Hardy, Thomas 110
A Laodicean 40
'An Imaginative Woman' 41
A Pair of Blue Eyes 37–8
Desperate Remedies 25–6, 40
Jude the Obscure 57, 189, 206–7
Tess of the D'Urbervilles 61, 67, 244
The Hand of Ethelberta 66
The Mayor of Casterbridge 38, 39–40, 253
The Return of the Native 254, 265–70
The Well-Beloved 82, 214
The Woodlanders 39, 205–6
Harrison, Frederic 72
Henty, G. A.
The Treasure of the Incas 14
hidden self 105–10
historical difference 1–2
Hobsbawm, Eric 66
homosexuality 158–9
Hopkins, Gerard M. 226
Hume, David 256

illustrations in Victorian fiction 29–31
industrial novel 63–4
infant sexuality in the Victorian novel 173–6
inner temple, relationship with fiction 71–2
Iser, Wolfgang 131

James, Henry 29, 39, 118, 246–7
'The Art of Fiction' 151
The Awkward Age 27
The Portrait of a Lady 50, 55
'The Turn of the Screw' 41
Jay, Elisabeth 185, 198
Jewishness 19–20
Jewsbury, Geraldine *The Half-Sisters* 31
journalism, as precursor to the Victorian novel 140

Keating, Peter 63–4
Kingsley, Charles
and race 218
as author of 'psychological novels' 91
The Water-Babies 223–4
Kipling, Rudyard
'At the End of the Passage' 41
Kim 16
Krasner, James 28–9
Kucich, John 157

Lamarck, Jean-Baptiste de 208–9
Landow, George 196–7
Lavater, J. C. 101
law and Victorian fiction 71–90
and aesthetics 76–90
and public/private 84–90
Prisoners' Counsel Act 76
intellectual property law 78–90
law schools, use of fiction in 73–4
Levine, George 37
Levy, Amy
The Romance of a Shop 34–5
Lewes, G. H. 26, 72, 99, 108, 109–10, 202–3
Linton, Eliza Lynn 243
Locke, John 94
London, Jack
People of the Abyss 225
The Sea-Wolf 208, 225–6
lower middle classes 59–60

Mackenzie, Henry
The Man of Feeling 256
Magazine Day 125–6
Maison, Margaret 184–5
male sexuality in Victorian fiction 170–3
Malthus, Thomas 207–8
Marx, Karl 49
masturbation 174–5
material culture of Victorian fiction 79, 113–33
Mayhew, Henry 64, 65
McClintock, Anne 12, 161–2
Meisel, Martin 26
memory crisis in the nineteenth century 126–7
Meredith, George 92, 240–1
Diana of the Crossways 66
The Ordeal of Richard Feverel 246
The Tragic Comedians 249
Vittoria 241
mesmerism 97, 107–8
Mew, Charlotte
'Mark Stafford's Wife' 41–2
Mill, James 95
Mill, J. S. 106
Miller, Andrew 157
Miller, D. A. 172
Moore, George 248
moral purpose of fiction 254–9
Morrison, Arthur
A Child of the Jago 65
Mudie's Select Library 114
Mukherjee, Upamanyu Pablo 75
mutability of species and Victorian fiction 209–12

'Newgate' novel 64
New Hedonism 172
New Journalism 124
Nietzsche, Fredrich
  On the Genealogy of Morals 6–7
Nuttall, A. D. 259

'Occidentalism' 10
Oliphant, Margaret 147–8
originality in Victorian fiction 82–3, 87–8
'Orientalism' 10

Parry, Benita 13
Pater, Walter
  The Renaissance 39
Patten, Robert 116
Pearson, Karl 218–19
photography and fiction 28, 34–41
  photography and ghosts 40–1
phrenology 97, 98, 101–5
physiognomy 97
Poovey, Mary 141, 162–3
'popular' publishing
  shift to 'mass' publishing 119
Porter, Bernard 8
Posner, Richard 73
Pratt, Mary Louise 17
'presentism' 1
Prickett, Stephen 197
profession of letters 72, 141–55
professional labor and fiction writing 141–55
psychology
  and associationism 94–7
  and the Victorian novel 91–112
  diversity in the Victorian period 93–4
publishers
  modern packaging of Victorian fiction 113–14
  Victorian methods of fiction publishing 113–33

Reade, Charles
  The Cloister and the Hearth 234–5
Reform crisis 62
  Second Reform Bill 213
Reid, Thomas 95–6
religion and the Victorian novel 180–201
revolution 62
Ribot, Théodule 94–5
Rigby, Cathy
  review of *Jane Eyre* 62
Robbins, Bruce 86–7
Robinson, Emma
  Westminster Abbey 187, 191–96
Robson, Catherine 175
Ross, Trevor 84
Rubin, Gayle 160–1
Ruskin, John 39, 43, 196
Russell, Percy 150
Rylance, Rick 97

Said, Edward *Orientalism* 10
Sambourne, Linley 223–4
Schramm, Jan-Melissa 75–6
Scott, Walter 136, 256
Second Reform Bill 213
Sedgwick, Adam 210
Sedgwick, Eve Kosofsky 172–3
sensation fiction
  and the unconscious 109
serial publishing of fiction 115–33
  and the media 122–26
  and seasonality 117
'Separate spheres' ideology 162–3
sexuality and the Victorian novel 156–79
  female sexuality in the Victorian novel 163–70
    and the subversion of binary oppositions 165–70
  infant sexuality in the Victorian novel 173–6
  male sexuality in Victorian fiction 170–3
  theories of sexuality in Victorian Britain 158–63
Shuttleworth, Sally 104
slavery 215–16

Smith, Adam
  Wealth of Nations 50
Smith, W. H. 114
Society of Authors 145
speculation and emotion in Victorian fiction 260–70
Spencer, Herbert 110, 203, 209, 214
Stead, W. T. 173–4
Stevenson, R. L. 249
  The Strange Case of Dr Jekyll and Mr Hyde 17
  Treasure Island 14
Stewart, Dugald 95
Stoker, Bram *Dracula* 168–9, 170
Sunday reading 126
surfacing of character 104–5

Terdiman, Richard 126–7
Thackeray, William Makepeace
  Barry Lyndon 140
  Catherine: A Story 140
  Lovel the Widower 120
  Pendennis 30, 71, 138–55
  Vanity Fair 30, 56, 59, 140, 169–70, 241
time
  and Victorian serial fiction 122–33
  not standardized in the Victorian period 122–3
Tolstoy, Leo *Anna Karenina* 247–8
tragedy 259–60
Trollope, Anthony 29–30, 148–51
  writing methods 118
  works
  An Autobiography 118, 148–51
  Barchester Towers 127–8, 167
  Barsetshire novels 127
  Can You Forgive Her? 235
  Framley Parsonage 119, 120, 127
  La Vendée 234
  Palliser novels 54–5, 235
  The Eustace Diamonds 52, 167, 244, 249
  The Prime Minister 100–1, 235, 249
  The Small House at Allington 127, 156–7, 167, 170
  The Warden 127
  The Way We Live Now 59, 65, 249
Trollope, T. A. 240
typography 30–31

unconscious, Victorian ideas of 106–10

'Victorianism' 53–4
visuality and Victorian fiction 25–46
  defamiliarization 29–46
  integrity/reliability of vision 29–46

Ward, Ian 73–4, 75
Watt, Ian 7, 73
Wells, H. G.
  A Modern Utopia 220–1
  Anticipations of the Reaction of Mechanical and Scientific Progress Upon Human Life and Thought 221
Wheeler, Michael 183–4
White, Gilbert
  The Natural History of Selbourne 206
White, James Boyd 73
Wilde, Oscar 254
  The Picture of Dorian Gray 42, 55, 171–2, 248
Wolff, Robert Lee 184
Wood, Ellen
  East Lynne 109
working classes 60

Young, Robert J. C. 16–17
Yule, Henry 17–18

Zola, Emile 244–5, 248–9